The Essential Guide to Processing for Flash Developers

Ira J. Greenberg

friendsof

DESIGNER TO DESIGNER™

an Apress® company

THE ESSENTIAL GUIDE TO PROCESSING FOR FLASH DEVELOPERS

ISBN-13 (pbk): 978-1-4302-1979-8

ISBN-13 (electronic): 978-1-4302-1980-4

Printed and bound in the United States of America 9 8 7 6 5 4 3 2 1

Trademarked names may appear in this book. Rather than use a trademark symbol with every occurrence of a trademarked name, we use the names only in an editorial fashion and to the benefit of the trademark owner, with no intention of infringement of the trademark.

Distributed to the book trade worldwide by Springer-Verlag New York, Inc., 233 Spring Street, 6th Floor, New York, NY 10013. Phone 1-800-SPRINGER, fax 201-348-4505, e-mail orders-ny@springer-sbm.com, or visit http://www.springeronline.com.

For information on translations, please e-mail info@apress.com, or visit http://www.apress.com.

Apress and friends of ED books may be purchased in bulk for academic, corporate, or promotional use. eBook versions and licenses are also available for most titles. For more information, reference our Special Bulk Sales–eBook Licensing web page at http://www.apress.com/info/bulksales.

The information in this book is distributed on an "as is" basis, without warranty. Although every precaution has been taken in the preparation of this work, neither the author(s) nor Apress shall have any liability to any person or entity with respect to any loss or damage caused or alleged to be caused directly or indirectly by the information contained in this work.

Credits

President and Publisher:
Paul Manning

Lead Editor:
Ben Renow-Clarke

Technical Reviewer:
Ian Piper

Editorial Board:
Clay Andres, Steve Anglin, Mark Beckner, Ewan Buckingham, Gary Cornell, Jonathan Gennick, Jonathan Hassell, Michelle Lowman, Matthew Moodie, Duncan Parkes, Jeffrey Pepper, Frank Pohlmann, Douglas Pundick, Ben Renow-Clarke, Dominic Shakeshaft, Matt Wade, Tom Welsh

Coordinating Editor:
Fran Parnell

Copy Editor:
Mary Ann Fugate

Compositor:
Mary Sudul

Indexer:
BIM Indexing & Proofreading Services

Cover Image Designer:
Corné van Dooren

Cover Designer:
Kurt Krames

To Robin, Ian, and Sophie

Contents at a Glance

Contents

Foreword

When I first heard from Ira about his next book, *The Essential Guide to Processing for Flash Developers*, I was immediately excited. Processing, for me, has always been just the most wonderful thing ever. It's given me a mission and a passion, to bring computation to everyone: artists, designers, musicians, biologists, doctors, dancers, animators, bankers, photographers, librarians, fashion designers, architects, psychologists, journalists, and writers, just to name a few. Writing code can be scary, something many mistakenly think is reserved for computer scientists and engineers. Processing has helped eliminate that fear, making programming accessible to a wider audience, particularly artists. And if you look at the three first books about Processing, *Processing: Creative Coding and Computational Art* (by Ira), *Processing: A Programming Handbook for Visual Designers and Artists* (by Casey Reas and Ben Fry) and *Learning Processing: A Beginner's Guide to Programming Images, Animation, and Interaction* (by me), you'll notice this trend—Hey, you never thought you could program? Guess what? You can! And we're going to make it easy, creative, and fun!

But there's an audience we missed. Sure, Processing is just about as perfect as anything can be for taking your first steps into computational work. But what about for those people who already know how to program? Processing, it just so happens, is great for those people, too. It's free. It's open source. It's Java. It has a vibrant and active community of users extending it through libraries and tools. And its core library of 2D and 3D drawing functions is fantastic.

There are probably countless groups of programming experts out there who should know about Processing. I'm sure we could come up with a bunch of book ideas: The Essential Guide to Processing for Web Developers, The Essential Guide to Processing for LISP Aficionados, The Essential Guide to Processing for OPENGL Masters, The Essential Guide to Processing for Fortran Fanatics. Ira has made a very smart choice as to where to start: the Flash community. Flash has its upsides, but if you want to be a good citizen of the digital world, it's important to break out of being dependent on a single company and their proprietary software for your computational needs. Processing, along with all of its features and resources, is just that—freedom.

Though having corresponded online for some time, Ira and I first met in person when he set up the Oxford Project in 2008, a series of mini-development conferences to push Processing towards 1.0 status. I'll always be grateful to Ira for including me in these meetings. Not only did I learn a ton just through mere osmosis—I was able to be a part of continued development of Processing and give back to something that has given me so much, which is an opportunity I'll always cherish.

Ira is a true champion of Processing and I'm glad to see he is continuing to blaze new paths towards getting people excited and involved. I hope to follow in his "take over the world" footsteps, and continue to bring computation with Processing to beginners and experts alike.

Daniel Shiffman
Assistant Arts Professor, ITP, Tisch School of the Arts, NYU

About the Author

Ira Greenberg currently directs the Center of Creative Computation and is Associate Professor at Southern Methodist University, with a joint appointment in the Meadows School of the Arts and Lyle School of Engineering. Prior to SMU, Ira taught at Miami University (Ohio), University of Cincinnati, Lafayette College and Seton Hall University. He holds a BFA from Cornell University and an MFA from the University of Pennsylvania. Ira is the author of *Processing: Creative Coding and Computational Art* (friends of ED, 2007).

When not spending time with his family, or staring at one of his many screens, Ira can be found playing hockey at one of the local ice rinks around North Dallas.

Photo by Robin McLennan.

About the Technical Reviewer

David Wicks is a developer and maker. He worked as a Flash developer for Domani Studios in New York and The Barbarian Group in San Francisco before starting his MFA in Design|Media Arts at UCLA. David's latest activities can be found at `http://sansumbrella.com`.

Acknowledgments

It's been a long strange journey, and there are so many who helped along the way.

Thank you to Miami University (Oxford, OH) and Southern Methodist University (Dallas, TX) for allowing me the time and space to write this book. Most especially thank you to Dr. Glenn Platt (Miami) and Dean José Bowen and Dr. Marty Sweidel (SMU).

Once again, it was an absolute pleasure to work with friends of ED/Apress. Though the team names changed from my first book, the professionalism, support, compassion, and, yes, abundant tolerance for my deadline sliding, allowed me to pull this off (eventually)! Thank you to Molly Sharp, Mary Ann Fugate, and Tom Welsh for their constant encouragement and attention to detail, amidst the chaos. Especially thank you to coordinating editor/email therapist Fran Parnell for her "in the trenches" role—it was a real pleasure, even the more "persuasive" late-night emails. Most of all, I need to thank Ben Renow-Clarke for green-lighting this project and offering very sage advice from concept development through completion. Simply stated, this book would not have happened without his guidance and support, and I'm most grateful.

As with the first book, I need to thank the remarkable David Wicks. His technical reviewing was immensely helpful. As David was a past student of mine, it is both humbling and inspiring to be able to learn from him now!

Thank you to my fellow Processors, especially language originators Ben Fry and Casey Reas and Processing author/educator Dan Shiffman. It has been an honor and a joy getting to know each of them better, and I look forward to continuing the journey for years to come.

Thank you to: Hilary, Jerry, Eric, Ellen, Sarah, Danny, Ethan, Jack, Ron, Noreen, David, Cindy, Travis, Ed, Adriana, Ehren, Bill, and Rae Ann—my inner circle support team.

And of course, the people who deserve the most thanks (really much, much more than that) are my wonderful family, Robin, Ian, and Sophie.

Introduction

Back in 2004 I sent an unsolicited query letter to friends of ED ("foED") about writing a book on creative coding with ActionScript. In my note I also suggested some alternative book ideas, including one on the, then mostly underground, Proce55ing language (the "55" was eventually replaced with "ss"). As an unproven author, I didn't hold out much hope that I'd get a response, no less a favorable one. To my surprise, an editor promptly wrote back expressing interest in the Processing idea and wanting to know more. This was both exhilarating and terrifying, as, truth be told, I hardly used Processing back then, working almost exclusively in ActionScript and Java. I had downloaded some of the numerous alpha versions of the software, and I knew basically how it worked, but I had never taken the time to figure out how to integrate Processing in my work or teaching. I was also concerned about the moving target that Processing was at the time, still under extensive development—with, of course, no comprehensive language reference book yet written to refer to.

In 2007, *Processing: Creative Coding and Computational Art* was published. It was a grueling and exciting two years of researching, writing, and coding, and during this time I grew quite smitten with Processing. In addition to getting deeply involved with the software, I became more involved with the Processing online community and eventually met language originators Casey Reas and Ben Fry and, soon after, Processing author/educator Dan Shiffman. I also began teaching Processing, rightalongside ActionScript. It was exciting to teach the two environments side-by-side and illuminating to see how my students responded to each.

By 2008 there were three major introductory reference books published on Processing, as well as numerous others that covered it. Processing was receiving lots of buzz and many universities were beginning to teach it. Yet, in spite of all this interest and attention, Processing was still beta software, with lots of debugging occurring, tweaks to the API and new version releases coming every few weeks (or even more frequently). Processing was still a moving target, though a more stable and slower-moving one.

After the release of my first book, I wanted to stay connected to the Processing community and also contribute further to the "movement," if you will. I remembered a conversation I had with Casey Reas at one of our first meetings about how he and Ben worked on Processing from across the country (and beyond), and on the occasions when they were able to get together, usually in a hotel lobby or airport during a conference, a major version release of the software soon followed.

I approached Glenn Platt, the director of the Interactive Media Studies Program (now the Armstrong Institute of Interactive Media Studies), at Miami University, where I was teaching, about sponsoring a series of Processing events on campus. I didn't have much of a plan—just trying to get a group of people together to talk, think, and work on Processing. I also hoped that Casey and Ben might be interested in this crazy scheme, especially the part about leaving Los Angeles and Boston to come to a small cornfield community in southwest Ohio. Glenn somehow convinced the university to convert a visiting professorship to a Processing slush fund for a year's worth of events. (I still can't imagine how he sold this at the time—things like this just don't happen in academia.)

Now with funding in place, I still had the small problem of getting people to come. I was actually pretty worried about this, as I suspected Casey and Ben were getting plenty of offers to come to more exotic locations than Oxford, Ohio. And here's where fate intervened: It turned out that both Casey and Ben had connections to the area and even the university, having grown up in the mid-west, not that far away. They both agreed to come. Buoyed by these successes, I decided to go for broke and try to get Dan Shiffman, of NYU's Interactive Telecommunication Program and the remaining Processing author, on-board; Dan also signed on. At our second Processing summit in Oxford, Processing 1.0 was finally released. It was also at this time that I began thinking about writing another Processing book.

In similar fashion to my query in 2004, I approached foED with a book idea that got redirected. I'm going to refrain from discussing my initial idea, as I still hope to get to this book at some point. Editor Ben Renow-Clarke deserves credit for the final concept, introducing Flash developers to Processing, which I think was an inspired idea on his part and a strange sort of homecoming for me. Aside from bringing together Processing and ActionScript for me personally, I was excited that the project could also help bring the two communities closer together. In spite of the fact that both Flash and Processing are primarily designed for creative folks, and do many similar things, it's been surprising over the years how separate the two communities are. It is my hope that this book serves as a bridge to cross this divide.

In addition to the Flash community, I also designed this book for the wider Processing community, as well as developers in any language who want to learn more about Processing. The first part of the book is a fast-paced primer on the language and development environment, geared toward experienced coders. This section is followed by a series of projects, organized by chapter, that are more complex than the examples included in any of the three introductory Processing books. The projects are all object-oriented, and I include information on the relevant OOP theory. The final chapter introduces Processing's Java mode, which provides a gentle introduction to Java and is a nice jumping-off point for a more extensive investigation into Processing's "host" language, including Processing library and tool development.

Finally, I hope readers enjoy the creative approach taken in the book and have fun with the examples. I realize that writing a creative coding stylebook for the Flash community is like preaching to the choir. However, there is a grass-roots experience to using Processing that reminds me of the early days of Flash, when many of us were more concerned (really consumed) about the subtlety of an animated transition than, say, structural issues of a database. Perhaps more simply stated, working with Processing is fun, and I wish you many hours of happy coding.

Chapter 1

Flash vs. Processing: Let the Death Match Begin!

I thought I'd begin the book with a chapter title that generated some good old intrigue, controversy, and impassioned fist pumping. Well, sorry to disappoint you so soon, but the death match has been postponed, *indefinitely*! In fact, this chapter, rather than pitting Flash against Processing, is really about *finding the love*—the love for two of the most amazing *things* ever formed out of bits.

The main reason it seems completely and utterly fruitless to me to compare Flash and Processing in any "which is supreme" context is that doing so ultimately limits *your* creative potential. There are times I work in Flash and times I work in Processing, and other times I work with a 3D modeler, imaging software, video editor, or vector drawing tool, not to mention a myriad of different programming languages (even a pencil and paper sometimes). Each has its own creative potential and usefulness, and, much more importantly, each allows me to more fully explore and actualize my own creative potential (and ultimately usefulness). In addition, it's just simply too much fun to not learn something just because it lost some silly, erroneous comparison.

And your timing couldn't be better to be finding the love! During the preparation of this book, Adobe released Creative Suite 4 (CS4). This major release impacts the entire Adobe Creative Suite product line, most notably Flash, with some very exciting new features and capabilities enhancing both the authoring and programming environments. In addition, Processing 1.0 was released, which has been a *looong* time coming. I was very privileged to have participated in this release as part of a small team of developers, including Processing founders Ben Fry and Casey Reas and Processing guru Dan Shiffman.

Yet, in spite of Flash and Processing's mutual amazingness, there are obviously some major differences between the two environments, and ultimately how and why they are used. This chapter will discuss these differences—in the context of *the love*, of course.

What You Should Know (*Well, Sort of*)

This book assumes you are familiar with the Flash environment. In the late 1990s, I could have made some pretty good guesses as to what that meant in terms of your Flash skill-set, technical background, and aspirations with Flash. Today, however, that is much more difficult: Your Flash experience may be concentrated on the timeline-driven authoring environment; it might also include some familiarity with the Actions window (the internal editor for writing frame scripts); or perhaps your experience includes creating classes in the external Actionscript editor. You may have even moved completely outside of the Flash environment altogether and are generating Flash content using Adobe's Flex Builder, or even in a terminal application down at the command line. That's a very broad and complex range of experience, all housed under the title *Flash Developer*. In addition to the way you work with Flash, you also have specialized professional expertise—you may be a *pure* designer, who uses a smattering of ActionScript; or a *hybrid* type, who designs and writes code in equal proportions; or a *computer science* type, who sees the design component of a project as, *well*, someone else's concern.

Because you represent such a wide swath of interests, talents, and experiences, I'll make only a few sweeping assumptions about what you know about Flash, design, and development. Instead, as I introduce Processing concepts, I'll point to related concepts and structures in Flash to help bring some context to the discussion. That being said, I do make certain basic assumptions about what you do know, or, rather, should know to get the most out of this book:

I assume you have basic coding literacy. By literacy, I mean you understand core concepts in programming that extend across most programming languages (obviously including ActionScript). My main assumptions in regard to this literacy are

- You know what a variable is—and how to declare it of a type and assign it a value.
- You've used a while loop and/or a for loop.
- You've written conditional logic.
- You've worked with arrays.
- You've written a function.
- You've used classes/objects.

In addition, I assume you've worked with some integrated development environment (IDE) and/or a scripting editor; you've compiled and executed code; you know what a package is and how to import its contents into a project; and, finally, you understand (to some degree) the concept of inheritance. If, however, you don't have all that stuff quite under your belt, don't panic yet. Although I won't be spelling out in explicit detail what each of the bulleted items listed above is, I'll begin with simple examples that should help fill in any gaps. I'd at least stick it out through the end of this chapter before dumping the book back on the reshelve cart. If none of the bulleted concepts look familiar, or you feel like you could use a refresher, I recommend checking out my first book, *Processing: Creative Coding and Computational Art*, which you can read more about at http://www.friendsofed.com/book.html?isbn=159059617X. In that book I provide highly detailed and comprehensive information about basic programming concepts (as well as a number of more advanced concepts).

The Complexity of Simplicity

In 2004, the MIT Media Lab formed a research group to examine the concept of simplicity and its relationship to the design of technology. Co-directing this effort at the time was John Maeda, the inspirational father of Processing and the head of the Aesthetics + Computation Group, where Ben Fry and Casey Reas had been students. On the MIT simplicity site, at http://simplicity.media.mit.edu/ mambo/index.php?option=com_content&task=view&id=5&Itemid=37 (May 25, 2009, 10:02am EST), is a vision statement that describes the group's purpose. Here's an excerpt from it that I think best sums it up:

> "... To make something simpler, often means to make something less powerful. How do you make something powerful, but simple to operate at the same time? This is the challenge."

Most of us have had the frustrating experience of dealing with poorly designed technology. In fact, it doesn't take too much effort to make even the simplest process overly complex. Take my long-distance service for instance. I am fortunate to live near where I teach and can get my long-distance service through my university, at a discounted rate. To do so, though, I need to type a few extra numbers to activate this service. (I've changed the numbers for obvious reasons, but the number of digits presented is accurate). Here are the steps:

1. Dial 11.
2. Wait about 5 seconds.
3. Dial 012 3456.
4. Wait for the beep.
5. Dial 22.
6. Dial the long-distance number.

Clearly, the user experience did not factor high in the design decisions behind this technology. Of course, it's great that I get the discount, but the benefit barely outweighs the hassle, and, really, with a better design there would be no need for such a trade-off.

This is precisely the type of thinking that drove John Maeda and the Aesthetics + Computation group to explore new approaches in designing effective and powerful software tools (and processes) that also are simple (*and even pleasurable*) to use. I think you'll soon agree that with Processing, Ben and Casey not only met the challenge outlined in the Simplicity vision statement, but also exceeded it (which is all the more impressive considering their conception of Processing predates it)!

Simplicity is currently a major point of difference between Processing and Flash, especially as it pertains to the two development environments—*with an interesting history described next.*

Out-Yahoo'd

I remember *waaay* back, at the turn of the millennium, the first time I visited google.com; it really wasn't much to look at (*it still isn't*). At the time, Flash was all the rage, and I, and most designers I knew, were seeing how far we could push it—fighting with our employers and clients to let us build 100% Flash sites. If you're curious to get a glimpse of what the *Flashed-out* web looked like back then, check out the clip ("The Golden Age of Flash") Keith Peters put together on his blog, posted August 31, 2008 (`http://www.bit-101.com/blog/?p=1453`).

Google's stark minimalism at the time was, *well*, somewhat shocking. I had thought, up until that point, that Yahoo was the be-all and end-all of pure utilitarian search design, but Google took it to a whole new level—at a time when *more* really seemed like it WAS *more*! I remember commenting to a friend that Google had *out-Yahoo'd* Yahoo. There is a similar argument to be made today that Processing has *out-Flashed* Flash, creating an even simpler, more intuitive environment for exploring computational art/aesthetics. I do realize that this sort of statement seems a bit at odds with my earlier *finding the love* sentiment, but teaching Flash (really ActionScript) and Processing side-by-side for a number of years now has really drilled home this point.

In 2002, when I first began teaching semester-long classes on ActionScript, it was fairly easy to get my art students quickly up and running writing code. We'd create simple frame loops, drag some MovieClip instances to the stage and away we'd go. Soon after, they'd be attaching MovieClip instances dynamically out of the library and building fairly complex programmatic animations. Of course, they did have to memorize the syntax of some pretty strange-looking structures (e.g., `this["mc"+i]._x`), but other than that things felt pretty intuitive to them. Fast-forward to my current ActionScript 3.0 class; it's been two weeks into the semester and my students are completely stressed out over exactly what the heck all these object things are. And I *know* I'm not the only ActionScript instructor out there struggling with this issue. Of course, one pragmatic solution, built into Flash CS4, is to begin teaching the class using ActionScript 2.0 syntax and then transition into ActionScript 3.0 syntax. Well, this approach feels a bit hack-ish to me and doesn't really simplify things for my students (and I'm not willing to just skip ActionScript 3.0 altogether, for obvious reasons—*like their potential employment options*).

The other approach is to start them off in an ActionScript 2.0/ActionScript 3.0 hybrid manner, using frame scripts and the `MainTimeline` class. The benefit of this approach is that I can conceal most of the OOP stuff (but not all of it), and then when the students realize they need a little more structure in their code, I can slip in the document class, external ActionScript editor, import statements, inheritance, etc. Although this bait-and-switch tactic does offer an initially less-steep learning curve for the new coder, it also forces them to learn two very different ways of working, and I've always felt there was something inherently confusing about the relationship between the timeline and ActionScript.

In comparison, two weeks into my Processing class, students are beginning to move ball-like objects around the screen with simple physics—quite enjoying themselves! They're working with variables, functions, arrays, and conditionals and still haven't (consciously) instantiated a single object. Of course, this would be the case using any procedural language (and the way it used to go in my ActionScript 2.0 classes). However, as the students' Processing projects grow in complexity, and they, too, sense they need more organization in their program, I can introduce OOP concepts, which they can begin to integrate directly within the same environment—adding multiple classes into the current editor window, right next to their existing code.

K.I.S.S.—The Processing IDE

My dad worked out of a small, cramped office in our home his whole career. He used to joke that his morning commute was about 20 feet each day. In spite of his modest professional space, he was quite successful in his field and had numerous opportunities to "upgrade" his venue, but he always refused. Dad often referred to the K.I.S.S. principle—*Keep It Simple, Stupid*. He knew that bigger, glitzier surroundings wouldn't allow him to do his job better and would only bring increased overhead and ultimately loss of freedom. His daily carpeted commute allowed him to get to the dinner table every night on time, live well within his means (both from a time and monetary standpoint) and retire in his early 50s. The Processing founders practiced Dad's K.I.S.S. principle when they designed Processing (maybe one of the reasons I climbed aboard the bandwagon). Pictured in Figure 1-1 is the Processing IDE. *Yes*, that's all of it. Compared to the Flash IDE, it's pretty darn minimal (think Google minimal). In spite of the simple design, the Processing IDE is an efficient and effective development environment.

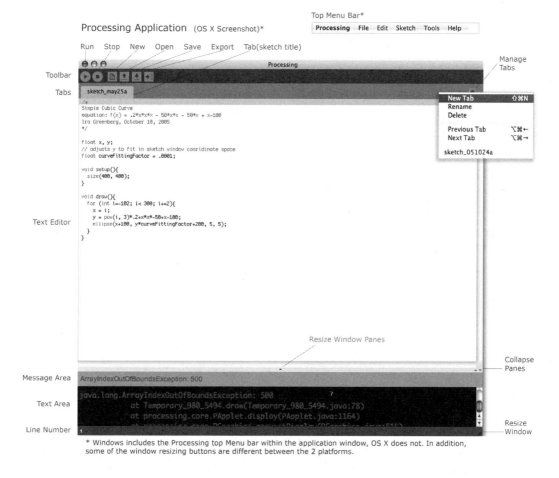

* Windows includes the Processing top Menu bar within the application window, OS X does not. In addition, some of the window resizing buttons are different between the 2 platforms.

Figure 1-1. Processing IDE

In *Processing: Creative Coding and Computational Art*, I provide a detailed description of the different parts of the Processing development environment, including each of the commands in the top menus. Since you presumably have some development experience, I'll just provide detailed information on the functions and features that aren't self-explanatory. The environment itself, as shown in Figure 1-1, is quite self-explanatory; that being said, next are descriptions of the different components making up the environment.

`Toolbar` includes icons for quick functionality. The six commands Run, Stop, New, Open, Save, and Export can also be executed from the top File and Sketch menus. I'll discuss these commands (at least the less than totally obvious ones) when I go through the top menus.

`Tabs/Manage Tabs` help you organize your code. Both functions and Processing classes (`.pde`'s) can be written in their own tabs. In addition, Java files (`.java's`) can be written in tabs. But once Java files are introduced into the environment, things get a bit more complicated, which I'll describe in detail in Chapter 8.

`Text Editor` is where code is typed. It includes **Cut**, **Copy**, **Paste**, **Find** and **Find/Replace with** text functionality.

`Message Area` displays simple, concise messages during saving and exporting and when errors occur.

`Text Area` displays full error messages and output by print(string) and println(string) function calls. println(string) is equivalent to ActionScript's trace(string); it outputs the string argument passed in the call and adds a line return. print(string) works similarly, without adding a line return after the call.

`Line Number` shows you the line number(s) currently highlighted in the Text Area. You can click and drag across multiple lines to highlight a text block.

You'll also notice in Figure 1-1 numerous window adjustment features for resizing, collapsing, and expanding sections. These functions are designed for ergonomics and have no effect on your code (though they may bring you a greater sense of peace when coding). Next, I'll discuss Processing's top menus. Figure 1-2 shows a composite view of all of the menus.

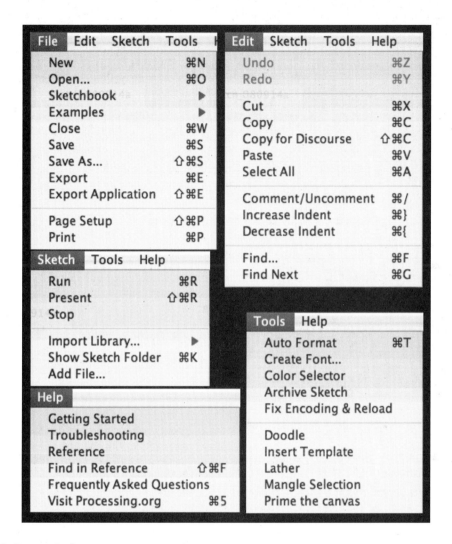

Figure 1-2. Processing's top menu commands

File

The **Sketchbook** menu item includes its own nested drop-down menu, shown in Figure 1-3. Sketchbook provides quick access to your saved Processing programs, referred to as *sketches* in Processing speak.

> *In keeping with Processing's speedy concept-to-code approach, the founders chose to use the term "sketch" to refer to Processing programs. Since the initial audience for Processing was designers and artists, this term was familiar and even friendly. To sketch implies a process of discovery and ideation, two areas Processing really excels at.*

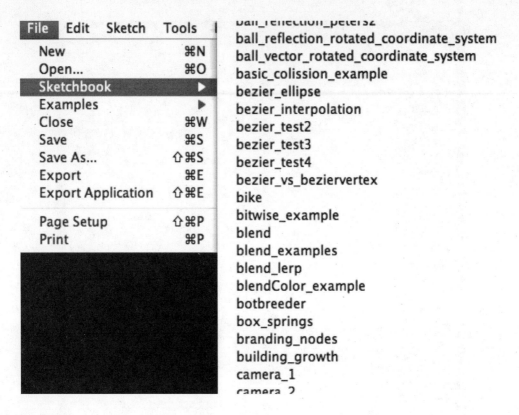

Figure 1-3. Processing exploded Sketchbook menu

By default your Processing sketches are saved to "My Documents/Processing" on Windows and "Documents/Processing" on OS X. To change this default location, select the preferences window in the Processing menu, shown in Figure 1-4, or edit the **per-user preferences.txt** file directly. The location of the per-user **preferences.txt** file is listed at the bottom of the preferences window (see Figure 1-4). It is also possible to save individual sketches to other locations by using the **Save** and **Save As**... dialog window options.

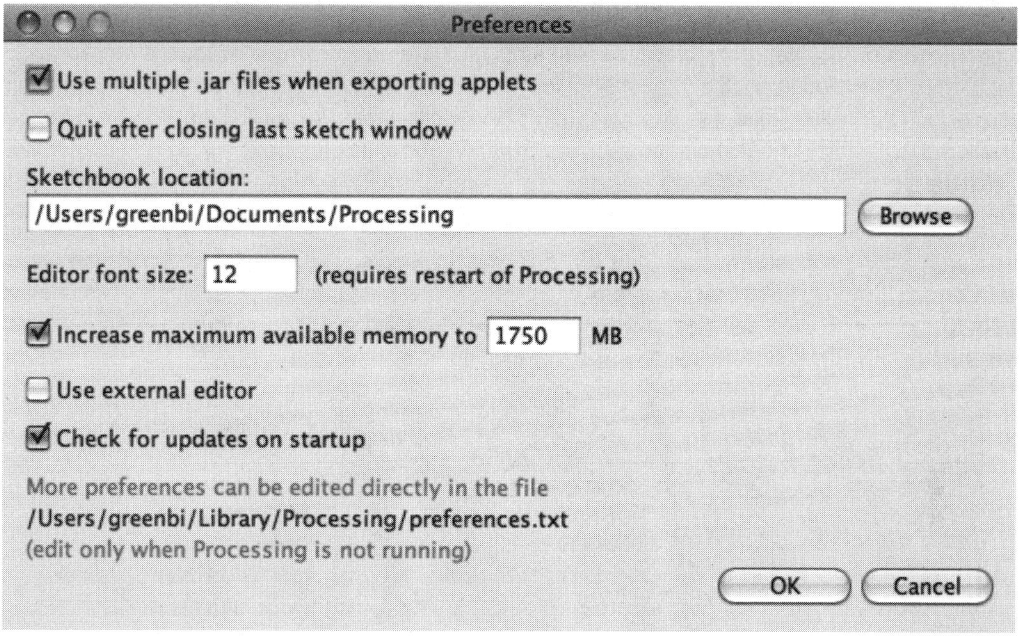

Figure 1-4. Processing's preferences window

The `Examples` menu item includes many Processing sketch examples, divided by categories, shown in Figure 1-5.

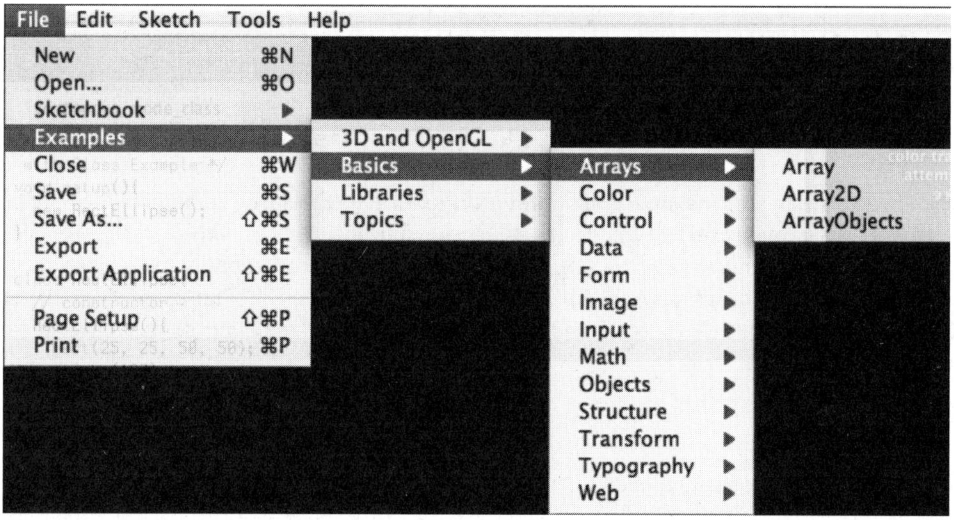

Figure 1-5. Processing's exploded Examples menu

The examples come pre-bundled within the Processing application download and are provided to both help new coders quickly get up to speed, as well as to give examples of more advanced functionality. The examples were developed by the Processing founders, as well as members of the user community—myself included. You can find the examples directory within your Processing application directory (or application bundle in OS X). It is also possible to expand your examples directory, simply by adding your own sketches to it.

The **Export and Export Application** menu items allow you to automatically generate a Java applet or Java application, respectively, based on your Processing sketch. The applet and application are saved in the current sketch directory. As an example, I took one of my Example sketches titled "**WaveGradient.pde**" and selected **Export** and **Export Application**. Figure 1-6 shows a screen shot of the WaveGradient sketch directory after my exports.

Figure 1-6. Screen shot of the WaveGradient sketch directory after exports

The applet directory contains the Java applet (**WaveGradient.jar**) as well as an html page that displays it. This functionality works similarly to Flash's **Publish** function, with regard to the **.swf** file and its enclosing **.html** page. When I selected **Export Application**, three separate directories containing a Windows, Mac, and Linux Java application, respectively, were created. Unlike applets, which run in the browser environment, applications are stand-alone and executable, requiring some native code for the different operating systems.

Edit

Copy for Discourse copies the code from the active tab in the open sketch into clipboard memory and adds style formatting for Processing's discourse board (http://processing.org/discourse). After the code is copied into memory, you can paste it using your standard OS specific paste function. Processing's discourse board is built using YaBB, an open source bulletin board system. YaBB utilizes its own HTML-like tag system for style formatting (called YaBBC). **Copy for Discourse** styles your sketch code to make it appear on the discourse board similarly to how it appears within the Processing environment. Figure 1-7 shows a snippet of sketch code, with the YaBBC style tags, after **Copy for Discourse**. To learn more about YaBB/YaBBC, visit www.yabbforum.com/community/YaBB.pl?action=help.

```
[quote]
[color=#777755]// Hybrid springy dude[/color]
[color=#777755]// "a polygon with attitude"[/color]
[color=#777755]// center point[/color]
[color=#996600]float[/color] centerX = 0, centerY = 0;
[color=#996600]float[/color] radius = 60, rotAngle = -90;
[color=#996600]float[/color] accelX, accelY;
[color=#996600]float[/color] springing = .0085, damping = .98;

[color=#777755]//corner nodes[/color]
[color=#996600]int[/color] nodes = 30;
[color=#996600]float[/color] nodeStartX[] = [color=#CC6600]new[/color]
[color=#996600]float[/color][nodes];
[color=#996600]float[/color] nodeStartY[] = [color=#CC6600]new[/color]
[color=#996600]float[/color][nodes];
[color=#996600]float[/color][]nodeX = [color=#CC6600]new[/color]
[color=#996600]float[/color][nodes];
[color=#996600]float[/color][]nodeY = [color=#CC6600]new[/color]
[color=#996600]float[/color][nodes];
[color=#996600]float[/color][]angle = [color=#CC6600]new[/color]
[color=#996600]float[/color][nodes];
[color=#996600]float[/color][]frequency = [color=#CC6600]new[/color]
[color=#996600]float[/color][nodes];
[color=#777755]// soft-body dynamics[/color]
[color=#996600]float[/color] organicConstant = 1;
```

Figure 1-7. Snippet of sketch code with YABB style tags added

> *At the risk of sounding cultish, Processing is much more than simply a clever, creatively-oriented coding environment—it's a very active and supportive development community. The Processing community comes together at Processing.org and most fully on the discourse board, which, up until the first Processing books were written, was one of the only places to learn about Processing.*

Comment/Uncomment adds or deletes comments to any highlighted text (including multiple lines) using the single line comment style //, the same one you're familiar with from ActionScript. The command is smart enough to know to add or remove the comment tags, based on the selection. Processing uses the following three comment styles:

- single line (//)

  // This line will be commented out.

- block (/* */)

  /* These lines will

  be commented out. */

- doc (/** */, Example shown in Figure 1-8)

  /** These lines will be commented out and also appear

  beneath the sketch window when exported to an applet. */

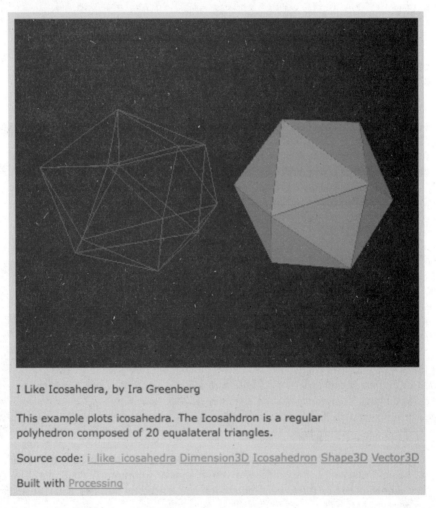

I Like Icosahedra, by Ira Greenberg

This example plots icosahedra. The Icosahdron is a regular
polyhedron composed of 20 equalateral triangles.

Source code: i_like_icosahedra Dimension3D Icosahedron Shape3D Vector3D

Built with Processing

Figure 1-8. Doc comment becomes sketch description in applet.

Find Next is a shortcut for quickly finding the last item searched for with the **Find** command. It allows you to step through your code, searching for a specific item, without the need for the **Find** window to remain open.

Sketch

Run converts your sketch code to Java and then compiles it into Java class files (bytecode), much as ActionScript is compiled to the **.swf** format; it then executes the Java bytecode. **Run** will fail if there are errors in your code, and those errors will be printed to the Processing Text Area (the black area at the bottom of the Processing application). Also, unlike ActionScript, which writes a **.swf to the hard drive**, no **.class** files are written to the sketch directory when you select **Run**.

Present attempts to execute your sketch at full screen. Other than full-screen functionality, **Present** operates like the **Run** command.

Import Library... adds import statements for Processing's core and user-generated libraries (shown in Figure 1-9) to your sketch. Libraries are packaged code that extend Processing's capabilities.

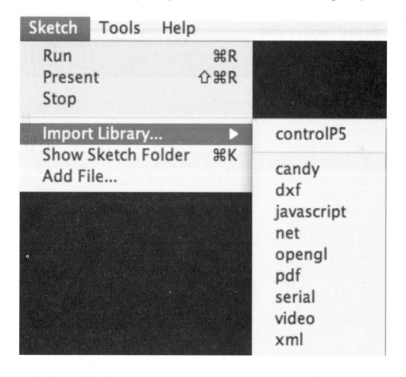

Figure 1-9. Processing's core libraries

The core libraries, shown below the horizontal line in Figure 1-9, are supported directly by the Processing development team. In addition, there are many user-contributed libraries, such as `ControlP5`, shown above the line in Figure 1-9, which you can read more about at http://processing.org/reference/libraries/.

Add File... opens a dialog window allowing you to import external resources into your current sketch folder. Resources can include images, fonts, and other media files, which get placed in a "**data**" directory. The **data** directory will be created automatically if one doesn't already exist. Code files (`.pde` and `.java`) may also be added, but will be placed in the main sketch directory, outside of any subdirectories. In addition, when code files are added, a new tab is automatically generated in the Processing editor containing the added code.

Tools

Auto Format attempts to format your code for increased readability only—no actual code is changed. Whitespace is preserved, and formatting primarily affects blocks. Similar to the **Auto format** command in Flash, errors in your code will cause this command to fail with error messages output to the Processing Message Area. Next is a simple example showing executable but poorly formatted code before and after **Auto Format**:

Before **Auto Format**

```
void draw(){background(75);drawClock();}
```

After **Auto Format**

```
void draw(){
  background(75);
  drawClock();
}
```

Create Font... opens a dialog window, shown in Figure 1-10, allowing you to select a font installed on your computer for conversion to Processing's `.vlw` format. This format creates a bitmap version of the selected font, ensuring that it will render properly on computers without the selected font installed. Options include specifying the **Size** of the bitmap, **Smooth** rendering (anti-aliasing), and converting **All Characters** in the font (including non-English characters, such as ü and Å). Larger values for **Size** as well as selecting **Smooth** and **All Characters** will increase the size of the `.vlw` file generated (sometimes dramatically). The font generated will be placed in the existing data directory of the current sketch. If no data directory exists, one is created automatically.

Figure 1-10. Processing's Create Font dialog window

`Color Selector`, shown in Figure 1-11, currently opens a dialog window allowing you to select a color and see its component values (HSB or RGB) as well as hexadecimal value.

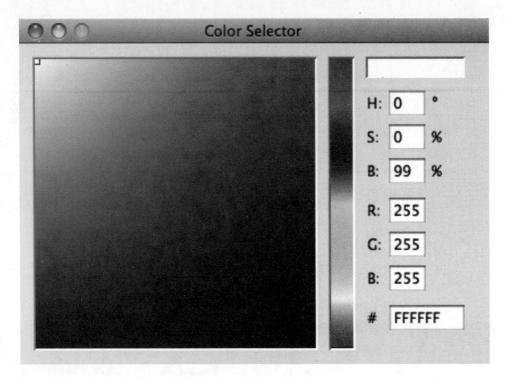

Figure 1-11. Processing's Color Selector dialog window

Archive Sketch generates a `.zip` archive of the current sketch directory and prompts you where to save it.

Fix Encoding & Reload corrects older sketches that used non-ASCII characters. Here's the official statement in the Processing web reference on the matter:

> "Sketches that contain non-ASCII characters and were saved with Processing 0140 and earlier may look strange when opened. Garbled text and odd characters may appear where umlauts, cedillas, and Japanese formerly lived. If this happens, use the "Fix Encoding & Reload" option under the Tools menu. This will reload your sketch using the same method as previous versions of Processing, at which point you can re-save it which will write a proper UTF-8 version."

User Contributed Tools is not listed as a menu item. The Tools menu includes two sections. The top of the menu displays Processing's core tools, developed and maintained by the Processing developers. User-contributed tools appear in the bottom of the Tools menu and are developed and maintained by individual users. Figure 1-12 shows a screen-shot of my **Tools** menu as proof.

Tools	Help
Auto Format	⌘T
Create Font...	
Color Selector	
Archive Sketch	
Fix Encoding & Reload	
Doodle	
Insert Template	
Lather	
Mangle Selection	
Prime the canvas	

Figure 1-12. Processing's Tools menu

Tools, like the libraries, extend Processing's functionality. The libraries expand the Processing language API. **Tools**, on the other hand, introduce the possibility of adding both GUI type controls and other environment functions into Processing. For example, I am developing a new lathing tool, which will enable users to create 3D objects for import into Processing. Figure 1-13 shows the current tool interface. Once users create a shape using the GUI controls, they can import the code and/or object 3D coordinates into Processing to generate the shape.

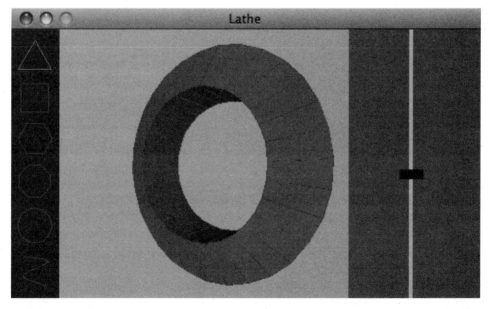

Figure 1-13. Lathe tool interface

Help

The menu items under `Help` are self-explanatory, except perhaps `Find in Reference`, which allows you to highlight a keyword in your sketch and jump to its description in the language reference. This works similarly to pressing the question mark icon in the top right corner of Flash's Actions window and external ActionScript editor. The Processing `Help` menu provides links to resources to help you along the way as you explore Processing. I also strongly encourage you to check out Processing's discourse board at `http://processing.org/discourse`, and don't be shy to post your questions (assuming you do a search of your question in the discourse board archive first).

Processing API from 30,000 Feet

I began my career as a painter (of the gallery variety). One of the things a painter needs to consider is the selection of a color palette—not the physical surface itself, but what colors to include on it. This choice may not seem like a big deal (especially if you haven't done much painting), but ultimately the palette you select controls the range of colors you're able to create. Teaching painting, I found it fairly common to come across a frustrated student who had been trying endlessly to mix a certain color. One glance at their palette and I could see the problem; they lacked the fundamental pigments to be able to mix it—no matter how much mixing and remixing they did. I've also experienced the other extreme, the student who has purchased every color in the art store and has mixed up an (expensive) pile of mud. It actually doesn't take many colors to be able to generate a full range of values across the color spectrum—it takes the right ones.

A language API is a palette of sorts, and it, too, needs the right amount of language elements. Too few can limit a programmer's expressive potential, while too many can create bloat, inefficiency, and even chaos. The Processing core API was purposely designed with this balance in mind, providing a lean yet comprehensive set of commands geared toward high-level, graphics programming. By **high-level** I mean that most of the gnarly math and computational processes (e.g., calculating anti-aliasing, communicating with the native windowing system, memory management, etc.) are handled internally, underneath the hood. By **graphics programming**, I mean commands especially designed for things like drawing, image/media processing, and interactivity. Some of these high-level functions are handled by Processing's host, Java, and others by Processing itself; though, to the user, it's a seamless process. In addition to graphics calls, the Processing API also includes a full set of structural elements common to most languages, including ActionScript—things like commas, curly braces, parentheses, and math constants.

Procedural Elegance

Processing greatly simplifies the act of writing code, *especially* graphically-oriented code, which is one of the most complex domains of programming. It achieves this by laying a super-high-level procedural language on top of object-oriented Java. A procedural programming language utilizes functions (as opposed to objects) for basic structure. ActionScript also includes some global functions, such as `trace()`, `int()`, or `Boolean()`, but these are few and far between. In Processing, functions make up nearly all the commands within the language. In all, the Processing core API contains around 300 unique elements (*including* keywords for constants, loops, curly braces, brackets, parentheses, etc). About 220 of these elements are function calls. As a point of comparison, ActionScript 3.0 includes around 330 classes alone, each with its own collection of member elements (properties and methods). But don't let the economy of the Processing core API concern you—Processing also has access to many libraries (with more being developed all the time), and, of course, Processing can utilize all of Java, which brings the actual number of language elements available to around a *bazillion*! This book will focus primarily on the Processing core API, but I'll also sneak in some Java at the end of the book as well.

Peeking Is Encouraged

As an experienced developer, you probably don't need me to tell you this, but DON'T worry about memorizing the Processing API. I still haven't, and I've written well over 1,000 pages on Processing (but I also play a lot of ice hockey, so there may be other factors at work). The API has an excellent web-based reference, located both locally in the **reference** subdirectory of your Processing application directory and also at http://processing.org/reference. Similar to ActionScript, the Processing API reference contains examples for most of the language elements, which you can copy and paste directly into the Processing Text Editor. In the examples to follow throughout the book, I'll cover the majority of the API in the context of tutorials. If you would like more in-depth information on the API, beyond the online reference, please refer to Processing: Creative Coding and Computational Art, or one of the other introductory books available on the language. I also, again, recommend the Processing.org discourse board.

Prototyping and Beyond

Processing is built for speed—both runtime performance and rapid development. Its zippy performance comes from being built on the back of Java. Back in ActionScript 2 days, I did a lot of my prototyping in Flash and then my more hard-core building in Java, especially when I needed robust performance. I found it difficult to quickly bang out graphics code in Java; it requires esoteric concepts and structures that impede rapid prototyping. (Ironically, this is the same issue, albeit to a lesser degree, that my present ActionScript students are struggling with.) Flash was great for hacking out some quick ideas, but lagged considerably behind Java in performance, and sometimes I just wanted to build something that *wasn't* for the web. Processing is, in a sense, a response to these two extremes. It facilitates quick prototyping, but also has the depth and performance to support more ambitious development, both on and off the web.

> Processing owes a debt to a little programming environment and language that most people have never heard of, called Design By Numbers, or DBN for short. DBN was developed at the MIT Media Lab by John Maeda and his A+C group, including Casey Reas and Ben Fry. Although primarily a teaching language for art and design students, and far more limited than Processing, DBN pioneered a new paradigm of creative coding and was the proof of concept for Processing. To learn more about DBN, check out: http://dbn.media.mit.edu/

One of the factors contributing to Processing's *concept-to-code* speed is its flexibility. Thus far I haven't really emphasized the distinction between Processing, *the programming environment,* and Processing, *the language*. Yet, these two parts of Processing are quite discrete, so much so that you can use Processing, the language, outside of Processing, the environment, just as you can use ActionScript outside of Flash. However, it is the integration of the Processing language within the Processing environment that really contributes to Processing's speed and flexibility and enables one of its most unique features—the ability to function as a multi-path programming (and learning) environment. By multi-path, I mean that you can write code in Processing in different ways, usually dictated by your experience level. This is a different type of multi-path approach than the one originally implemented in Flash (and even more infamously in Macromedia Director), where code could be put (more like hidden) in and on different structures within the development environment. Thankfully, this "where's Waldo" approach to embedding code seems to be going the way of the dodo.

Processing's multi-path approach is simpler (and less confusing). The different paths can be categorized as

- Basic Mode
- Continuous Mode
- Java Mode
- External ("pure") Java Mode

In **Basic Mode**, a newbie coder can write unstructured lines of code that execute sequentially (top to bottom). Next is a Processing sketch written in Basic Mode; the output is pictured in Figure 1-14. If you'd like to try to run the sketch, enter the code into Processing's Text Editor window and either press the **Run** button or, better yet, use the keystroke combination: **(Cmd+R on OS X; Ctrl+R on Windows)**.

```
// Processing Basic Mode Example
smooth();
rect(25, 25, 50, 50);
stroke(127);
fill(0);
ellipse(50, 50, 30, 30);
```

Figure 1-14. Processing Basic Mode example

Processing's Basic Mode removes many of the obstacles to programming, allowing new coders to see a nearly one-to-one correspondence between what they write and what they get. Notice in the Basic Mode example that I didn't need to explicitly set an initial stroke or fill style state before the rect(25, 25, 50, 50); call, as Processing has a default painting state (fill = white and stroke = black). My subsequent calls stroke(127); and fill(0); update this painting state for the final ellipse(50, 50, 30, 30); call. I also didn't need to use any curly braces, dot syntax, or explicit objects or add anything to a display list. I did, though, choose to use the optional smooth() call, which tells Processing to draw using anti-aliasing. As a comparison, here's the same simple program translated to ActionScript, using a frame script:

```
// ActionScript Frame Script Example
graphics.lineStyle(1, 0);
graphics.beginFill(0xFFFFFF);
graphics.drawRect(25, 25, 50, 50);
graphics.endFill();
graphics.lineStyle(1, 0x888888);
graphics.beginFill(0);
graphics.drawCircle(50, 50, 15);
graphics.endFill();
```

The ActionScript version is pretty simple as well. But it still requires explicit inclusion of the graphics object with dot syntax in the calls, as well as initial stroke and fill style calls, since there is no default painting style state.

Although Processing's Basic Mode is a great way to introduce beginners to programming, it's not terribly useful as a *real* development mode—especially for more experienced coders. Next, I've reformatted the sketch using Processing's **Continuous Mode**:

```
// Processing Continuous Mode Example
void setup(){
  smooth();
  drawShapes(25, 25, 50, 50);
}

void drawShapes(float x1, float y1, float x2, float y2){
  rect(x1, y1, 50, 50);
  stroke(127);
  fill(0);
```

```
  ellipse(x2, y2, 30, 30);
}
```

The bulk of Processing code is written using Continuous Mode. You probably recognize the inclusion of function blocks, which is the difference between Continuous Mode and Basic Mode. However, it is slightly more complicated than that. To include any custom functions, such as drawShapes(), you must also include Processing's built-in setup() function. setup() takes no arguments and is invoked automatically just once, making it a good place to initialize values in your sketch.

ActionScript, of course, also includes functions (which sometimes masquerade as methods). For comparison, here's the last sketch converted to ActionScript:

```
/* ActionScript Frame Script Example
with Function Block */
drawShapes(25, 25, 50, 50);

function drawShapes(x1:int, y1:int, x2:int, y2:int):void {
  graphics.lineStyle(1, 0);
  graphics.beginFill(0xFFFFFF);
  graphics.drawRect(x1, y1, 50, 50);
  graphics.endFill();
  graphics.lineStyle(1, 0x888888);
  graphics.beginFill(0);
  graphics.drawCircle(x2, y2, 15);
  graphics.endFill();
}
```

Functions operate pretty much the same in Processing as they do in ActionScript. But you'll notice Processing doesn't use the function keyword, and type specification precedes the identifier, with just whitespace separating them (no colons required). Scope also works similarly: variables declared outside of blocks are global, and variables defined within blocks, including parameters within function/method signatures, are local to the block.

Using continuous mode, in addition to functions, you can also include classes, right alongside your existing procedural code. Here's an example, shown in Figure 1-15:

```
/* Processing Continuous Mode
 with Class Example */
void setup(){
  // change default size of sketch window
  size(200, 100);
  smooth();
  // procedural approach to draw the shapes
  drawShapes(25, 25, 50, 50);

  // OOP approach to draw the shapes
  RectEllipse shapes = new RectEllipse(50, 50, 30, 30);
  // move shape over
  shapes.setLoc(150, 50);
  shapes.create();
}

// function to draw shapes
void drawShapes(float x1, float y1, float x2, float y2){
  rect(x1, y1, 50, 50);
  stroke(127);
  fill(0);
  ellipse(x2, y2, 30, 30);
}

class RectEllipse{
  // properties
  float x, y;  // group position
  float w1, h1, w2, h2; // dimensions

  // constructor
  RectEllipse(float w1, float  h1, float  w2, float  h2){
    this.w1 = w1;
    this.h1 = h1;
    this.w2 = w2;
```

```
    this.h2 = h2;
  }


  // methods
  void setLoc(float x, float y) {
    this.x = x;
    this.y = y;
  }


  void create(){
    // draw rectangle from center point
    rectMode(CENTER);
    // make sure default paint styles reset
    stroke(0);
    fill(255);
    rect(x, y, w1, h1);
    stroke(127);
    fill(0);
    ellipse(x, y, w2, h2);
  }
}
```

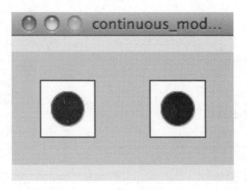

Figure 1-15. Processing Continuous Mode with Class Example

Obviously, the last example is a bit silly, as I have a function and a class that essentially do the same thing, but I wanted to emphasize the flexibility of the language and of course show how a class looks in Processing. If you look through the code carefully, you'll notice I snuck in two new commands, `size(200, 100);` in `setup()` and `rectMode(CENTER);` in the `RectEllipse create()` method. `size()` sets the dimensions of the sketch window. By default it's 100 px by 100 px. `rectMode()` allows you to control how the rectangle is drawn. The `CENTER` argument sets the drawing to occur from the rectangle's center point. By default, rectangles are drawn from the top-left corner and ellipses are drawn from the center point, but you can override these defaults. We'll look more at these commands and, of course, how OOP is implemented in Processing, in upcoming chapters. Here I just wanted to give you a taste of some Processing code and demonstrate the different modes of coding.

I'm not going to provide examples here of **Java mode**, as this mode adds a fair amount of complexity. In the last chapter in the book, I'll address this mode in detail.

Once we get to classes (and especially Java mode), the similarities between Processing and ActionScript begin to diverge. I'm not going to recode the last Processing class example in ActionScript, but I will enumerate some of the differences between how Processing and ActionScript (version 3.0) handle OOP constructs in general.

1. Processing allows you to declare as many classes as you'd like in the same file, without any required package blocks. ActionScript public classes are declared within a package block in their own external file and only one class may exist within the package block. (But it is possible to include additional classes outside of the package block.)

2. The convention in ActionScript is to use access modifiers, such as private and public. In Processing the convention is to not include them, and all class members (properties and methods) are assumed public. (In Java mode, access modifiers do come back into play.)

3. Processing allows overloading of methods (including constructors), ActionScript does not. If you're not familiar with overloading, it is the ability to use multiple methods by the same name, but with different signatures (number and type of parameters), in the same class.

4. Processing doesn't permit dynamic classes (as implemented in ActionScript), where instance properties can be dynamically added to individual objects.

5. Processing, like ActionScript, permits overriding of inherited methods, but doesn't use the "override" keyword.

Summary

This chapter provided a general overview of Processing and highlighted some of its similarities and differences with ActionScript, which I'll discuss in more detail throughout the book. As an experienced developer, you'll find learning Processing to be a smooth and fun journey. Many aspects of the Processing language will feel quite familiar, especially the block structures and coding conventions. I think you'll be very excited by the speed of Processing and its ability to handle complex drawing, allowing you to easily create things such as complex particle systems and other dynamic animations. I also know you'll come to appreciate the elegant simplicity of the Processing environment, allowing you to rapidly put your ideas into code. *And*, as you develop your Processing skills, you'll be able to integrate Java into your projects, blowing open the door for endless development and creative possibilities. In the next chapter, you'll dive into the Processing API and begin building cool programmatic images and animations.

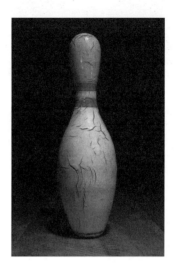

Chapter 2

Processing Primer I: *Just the Basics*

In the next two chapters you'll take a tour of the main graphics functions in the Processing API, with lots of examples and less of me waxing poetic. Many of the functions I'll introduce will be reused in later chapters in more developed projects. My main goal with the two primer chapters is to lay out a smorgasbord of possibilities and to demonstrate some cool examples. Now, I suggest you fire up Processing, get a good free-trade cup-o-joe and open the Processing reference.

Graphic Primitives

Most graphics programming libraries include commands for generating primitives—things like points, lines, rectangles, ellipses, etc. These are geometric building blocks for creating larger structures. Processing's core primitives commands include

- 2D Primitives
    - triangle(x1, y1, x2, y2, x3, y3)
    - line(x1, y1, x2, y2)
    - arc(x, y, width, height, start angle in radians, stop angle in radians)
    - point(x, y)
    - quad(x1, y1, x2, y2, x3, y3, x4, y4)
    - ellipse(x, y, width, height)
    - rect(x, y, width, height)

- 3D Primitives

    - point(x, y, z)
    - line(x1, y1, z1, x2, y2, z2)
    - box(size) or box(width, height, depth)
    - sphere(radius)

Notice that all the commands are function calls, which are invoked without any explicit object preceding the call. As an example, to draw two lines dividing the sketch window into four quadrants, you could use two **line()** calls:

```
line(0, height/2, width, height/2);

line(width/2, 0, width/2, height);
```

All the primitives (and the great majority of Processing's commands) work similarly. The API reference index page http://processing.org/reference/index_ext.html lists all the function calls without their required parameters. To see the parameters click on an individual command. As I mentioned in Chapter 1, the reference for each command usually includes example code, which you can cut and paste into the text editor. As an example, Figure 2-1 shows a screenshot of the reference page for the **arc()** command.

Name	**arc()**

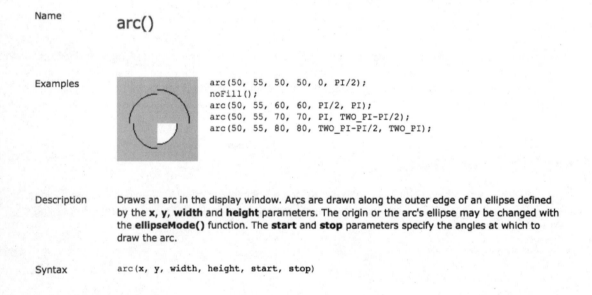

Examples	`arc(50, 55, 50, 50, 0, PI/2);`
	`noFill();`
	`arc(50, 55, 60, 60, PI/2, PI);`
	`arc(50, 55, 70, 70, PI, TWO_PI-PI/2);`
	`arc(50, 55, 80, 80, TWO_PI-PI/2, TWO_PI);`

Description	Draws an arc in the display window. Arcs are drawn along the outer edge of an ellipse defined by the **x, y, width** and **height** parameters. The origin or the arc's ellipse may be changed with the **ellipseMode()** function. The **start** and **stop** parameters specify the angles at which to draw the arc.
Syntax	`arc(x, y, width, height, start, stop)`

Figure 2-1. `Arc()` command API reference page

ActionScript, of course, also includes primitives, accessible through methods of the Graphics class. You don't instantiate the Graphics class directly, but instead target a built-in graphics object reference in the Shape or Sprite class, for example:

- mySprite.graphics.drawRect()
- mySprite.graphics.drawElllipse()
- mySprite.graphics.drawCircle()

In general, graphics primitives are a great place to begin when learning and creating, but not a place to stop. They are especially useful for prototyping forms—as a stepping-off point for further exploration or construction. One of the arguments against primitives (speaking as a teacher here) is that people can rely too heavily on them, trading specificity for ease of use. This especially became an issue when I taught 3D modeling/animation and my students would try to build everything out of cubes and spheres or use simple built-in transform functions (e.g., extrusion, lathing, etc.). Sometimes, you just have to get your hands dirty and start pushing around individual points (technically referred to as vertices).

In addition to primitives, graphics libraries usually include drawing methods, such as ActionScript's moveTo(), lineTo(), and curveTo() methods. These methods allow you to create your own higher order primitives in a sense. For example, Processing doesn't include a polygon primitive command, but using the drawing methods you can easily create your own, which I'll demonstrate a little later in the chapter.

In addition to the construction of the graphics primitives, they also need to be drawn, or rendered, to the screen. ActionScript and Processing differ significantly in the programmatic approaches they employ to handle this, which I'll elaborate on next.

Rendering

The primitives and drawing methods handle much of the internal processes (math and algorithms) to construct lines, curves, and shapes out of vertices, but this data also needs to be output somewhere. ActionScript uses a display list approach to manage the process of drawing stuff to the screen. The display list model encapsulates a shape's vertices and some graphics attributes (e.g., stroke and fill styles), as well as the overall stacking order—the order in which overlapping shapes are drawn. This all works in conjunction with ActionScript's painting system, coordinating screen updates.

The benefit of such a high-level approach is that it conceals a lot of the internal workings of keeping track of and managing graphical screen elements. The downside to this approach is that it is programmatically complex—substituting dense, object-oriented code for more low-level math and algorithms. For example, to transform the individual components (r, g, b) of a color in ActionScript, you might do something such as the following (this example is coded as a frame script):

```
// ActionScript 3.0 color transform example
var col1:uint = 0xCC34BB;
var s1:Sprite = new Sprite();
var s2:Sprite = new Sprite();
// add sprites to display list
this.addChild(s1);
this.addChild(s2);
```

```
s1.graphics.beginFill(col1);
s1.graphics.drawRect(50, 50, 100, 100);
s1.graphics.endFill();
// transform individual color components
var red:Number = s1.transform.colorTransform.redOffset - 75;
var green:Number = s1.transform.colorTransform.greenOffset + 130;
var blue:Number = s1.transform.colorTransform.blueOffset - 90;
s2.transform.colorTransform = new ColorTransform(1, 1, 1, 1, red, green, blue, 0);
s2.graphics.beginFill(col1);
s2.graphics.drawRect(150, 50, 100, 100);
s2.graphics.endFill();
```

If you're not a seasoned ActionScript coder, what's happening in the example is that each sprite object (s1 and s2) is instantiated and then added to Flash's display list, by way of the addChild method. Again, one of the benefits of using the display list is that once the sprites are added to it, Flash takes care of drawing any graphics associated with the sprites to the screen. As for the color transform operations, they aren't applied to the color itself, but to the transform object nested within the sprite. You can think of the transform object as an instruction set of rendering rules that tells the sprite how to paint itself with a specified color. I do realize that this may sound overly complex if it's new to you (probably because it is actually complex). Fortunately, though, you don't need to know most of this to work with graphics in Processing.

Processing uses a very different, and simpler, approach to rendering that can be described as a state change. Rather than encapsulating things like transform and graphics objects within a sprite object, you simply (and very directly) set the painting state using Processing's fill(color) and/or stroke(color) calls. These values will remain the painting state (for any graphics drawn) until the state is explicitly set again. Here's the last ActionScript example recoded in Processing:

```
/**
 * Processing color transform
 * using color component functions
 */
size(300, 200);
color col1 = #CC34BB;
fill(col1);
rect(50, 50, 100, 100);
float r = red(col1) - 75;
float g = green(col1) + 130;
float b = blue(col1) - 90;
```

```
col1 = color(r, g, b);
fill(col1);
rect(150, 50, 100, 100);
```

> *Looking at the Processing and ActionScript color transform examples, notice the different syntax used for type declaration of variables. ActionScript uses a post colon syntax, with strongly recommended typing, but not required by the compiler. In ActionScript I can write: var myName:String = "Ira". or var myName = "Ira". By contrast, Processing uses* **strict typing**, *enforced by the compiler, and type declarations precede the keyword with just a space separating the type and keyword. For example: String myName = "Ira".*

I used Processing's `color` data type in the last example. `color` is a Processing defined primitive data type for storing color values. Most of the other primitive data types in Processing (`int`, `float`, `Boolean`, etc) are borrowed directly from Java. In truth, `color` is really a 32-bit integer. The 32 bits are arranged (or packed) in four 8-bit groupings, one group for each color component: alpha, red, green, and blue. For example, here's how the `color` data type internally stores a color:

AAAAAAAARRRRRRRRGGGGGGGGBBBBBBBB

The A stands for the alpha component of the color, R is for red, G is for green, and B is for blue. The 32-bit color data type is a binary value, so each of the component letters would be replaced with either a 0 or a 1. For example, this is what pure red with 100% alpha would look like (Please note that I added a space after each component to make it easier to read):

11111111 11111111 00000000 00000000

The color value can also be represented in hexadecimal notation (base 16) as `0xAARRGGBB`, where each component letter would be replaced with a value 0–F (providing 16 unique values). The `0x` tells Processing to calculate the number as a hexadecimal (rather than decimal) value, which works similarly in ActionScript. Next is the same pure red with 100% alpha color in hexadecimal form:

0xFFFF0000

Also notice that the color's alpha value takes up the first 8-bit group in the 32-bit color data type; this can be confusing because when passing arguments to a color function, the alpha value is usually the last value.

In the color transform example, the assignment statement `color col1 = #CC34BB;` shows one way to create a color in Processing. There are actually a number of other ways (maybe too many), shown next:

```
// hexadecimal notation, in the form 0xAARRGGBB
color col = 0xFFCC34BB;
// hexadecimal notation, in the form 0xAARRGGBB, as color() argument
```

```
color col = color(0xFFCC34BB);
// web hexadecimal notation, in the form #RRGGBB, as color() argument
color col = color(#CC34BB);
// grayscale
color col = color(50);
// grayscale, alpha
color col = color(50, 200);
// R,G,B
color col = color(50, 200, 100);
// R,G,B,A
color col = color(50, 200, 100, 85);
// H,S,B mode (Hue, Saturation and Brightness) with single value
colorMode(HSB, 255);
color col = color(50, 200, 100);
// H,S,B mode with multiple values
colorMode(HSB, 360, 100, 100);
color col = color(140, 78, 75);
```

> One potentially confusing issue, and a point of difference between Processing and
> ActionScript, is that the color hexadecimal notation in Processing requires explicit alpha
> values (0xAARRGGBB), or it will default to 0 for the alpha component (0% opacity). By
> contrast, when using the ActionScript hexadecimal form 0xRRGGBB (without the explicit
> alpha values), alpha will default to 255 (100% opacity).

Processing's function color(color values) returns a color value, which I assigned to a color variable using the statement color col = color(color values);. This syntax may be a bit confusing, since the primitive data type and the function call share the same color keyword. To experienced object-oriented coders, it may also seem that the statements are missing the new keyword (and the color keyword should be capitalized). One way to help remember the syntax is to think of the statement as **type casting** the color value arguments to type color, which, again, is really just a packed integer. (Honestly, I think Processing's color syntax is awkward.)

> If you're not familiar with **type casting**, it means converting a value from one type to
> another. There are very specific rules about what types are allowed to be cast to other
> types, enforced by the compiler. In general, when a type is a narrower version of another
> type, it will be implicitly converted to the wider type. For example, since integers are a
> subset of floating values, you can safely assign an int value to a variable of type float.
> The float data type is Processing's default primitive type for values that include a
> decimal point, similar to ActionScript's Number type. The following is legal in Processing:

```
int num = 5;

float newNum = num;
```

newNum is now equal to 5.0 because of the implicit conversion from int to float. However, implicit conversion doesn't work in the other direction—from float to int (a wider to a narrower conversion). For example, the following is illegal in Processing and will generate a compiler error:

```
int num = 5.0;
```

This is where explicit casting comes in. Explicit casting allows you to override the compiler's type rules and force the conversion. For example, the following is legal using explicit type casting—from float to int:

```
int num = int(5.0);
```

The int(5.0) part of the expression is Processing's syntax for explicit type conversion, which converted (and truncated) the float value from 5.0 to 5, and to type int. Of course, had the float value had any meaningful digits after the decimal point, such as 5.3627, these digits would have been lost when the value was truncated. Because of Processing's relationship to Java, type casting rules are much more rigid in Processing than in ActionScript. To learn more about the rules governing type conversion in Java and Processing, check out: http://java.sun.com/docs/books/jls/second_ edition/html/conversions.doc.html

The Processing color transform example also included these statements:

```
float r = red(col1) - 75;
float g = green(col1) + 130;
float b = blue(col1) - 90;
```

These are very handy functions that parse out the individual color component values. There is also a similar function, not shown, for alpha, alpha(color). In spite of the convenience of these color component extraction functions, they come with some processing overhead. There is another more efficient way to get at the individual component values, which works similarly in ActionScript and Processing, called bitwise operations, shown next:

```
/**
* Fast color transform
* using bitwise color operations
* By Ira Greenberg <br />
* The Essential Guide to Processing for Flash Developers
* Friends of ED, 2009
*/
```

```
size(275, 150);
color col1 = color(200, 100, 40);
fill(col1);
noStroke();
rect(25, 25, 100, 100);
// get component values
int a = col1 >> 24 & 0xFF;
int r = col1 >> 16 & 0xFF;
int g = col1 >> 8 & 0xFF;
int b = col1 & 0xFF;
// transform individual components
r-=150;
g+=50;
b+=100;
// put color back together
col1 = (a << 24) | (r << 16) | (g << 8) | b;
fill(col1);
rect(150, 25, 100, 100);
```

The bitwise operations work by shifting through the 32-bit packed integer and separating out the specific bits relating to the component value. The shifting part is handled by the right shift >> and left shift << operators. To isolate the individual components, bits are shifted to the right the number of places necessary to get at the relevant bits using the right shift >>. Then, to reassemble the individual components, the left shift operator << is used. The separating-out part is done using the operators |, &, and ^, which work according to the following rules:

| evaluates to 1 if **either** bit is a 1.

& evaluates to 1 if **both** bits are 1.

^ evaluates to 1 if both bits are **different**.

Here are some examples:

```
     01101010
|    01100110
---------------
     01101110


     01101010
&    01100110
---------------
     01100010


     01101010
^    01100110
---------------
     00001100
```

To learn more about the inner workings of bits, packed integers, and the operations performed on them, check out the math reference in Appendix B, in *Processing: Creative Coding and Computational Art*.

A Primitive Sampler

Next, I'll review some of the concepts covered so far in the chapter and also showcase the set of Processing's 2D and 3D primitives with a primitive sampler sketch. The example also includes a number of new concepts, which I'll discuss as well.

To begin the sampler, I'll code a table structure in which to place the primitives. I find my students often struggle with the basic algorithm to generate a table structure, so I'll discuss that first and then add the primitive calls. Feel free to skip ahead if coding tables is old hat to you.

Coding a Table

The trick to building the table is using a nested loop structure, which is what usually confuses my less experienced coding students. I'll specify variables for the number of rows and columns, which I'll then use to control the loops. I'll size the table based on the sketch window, specifying a margin to give a little breathing room around the table and the window. The table will be pretty simple, with no cell padding or spacing, which could, of course, be added and would make an excellent future exercise. Here's the program to generate a table, shown in Figure 2-2:

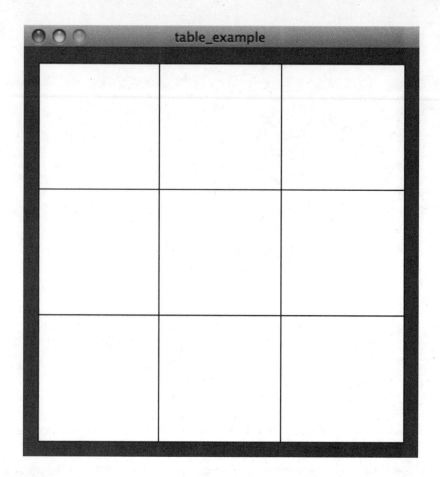

Figure 2-2. Table Example

Here are some examples:

```
/**
 * Table Example,
 * By Ira Greenberg <br />
 * The Essential Guide to Processing for Flash Developers
 * Friends of ED, 2009
 */


// table config global variables
float cellW, cellH;
```

```
int rows = 3;
int cols = 3;
float margin = 15;

void setup(){
  size(400, 400);
  background(75);
  buildTable();
}

void buildTable(){
  // initiatlize local variables x, y
  float x = margin;
  float y  = margin;

  cellW = (width - margin*2)/cols;
  cellH = (height- margin*2)/rows;

  for (int i=0; i<rows; i++){
    for (int j=0; j<cols; j++){
      // ensure default color values are reset
      fill(255);
      stroke(0);
      rect(x+cellW*(j), y+cellH*(i), cellW, cellH);
    }
  }
}
```

To experienced coders, this sketch should be pretty straightforward. However, for those of you still coming up to speed, I'll do an analysis of the code and table creation algorithm.

I begin the example using Processing's doc style block comment (/**   */). You'll remember that this comment style has the benefit of automatically adding the comment as a sketch caption when the sketch is output to an applet, shown in Figure 2-3.

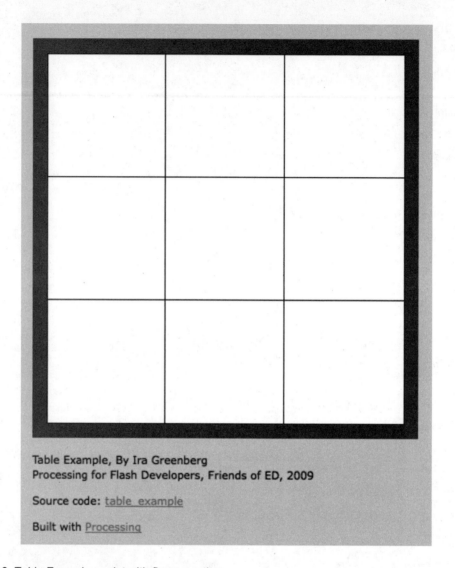

Table Example, By Ira Greenberg
Processing for Flash Developers, Friends of ED, 2009

Source code: table_example

Built with Processing

Figure 2-3. Table Example applet with figure caption

Next, I declare global variables at the top of the sketch. In general, I try to use local variables, unless

1. values need to be accessible in multiple blocks (functions) throughout the program
2. I want to give users the ability to set initial values at the top of the program

Below the global variables is Processing's setup() function. As I discussed in Chapter 1, this function is required if you want to add your own custom functions. Setup() runs once and is generally where you'll want to initialize program variables and set any initial state conditions (e.g., stroke or fill color). From setup() I invoke my custom buildTable() function.

The buildTable() function declares two local x, y variables, as these will only be used within the function. The cellW and cellH variables are initialized using Processing's built-in variables, width and height. These global variables contain the sketch window dimensions and are equivalent to ActionScript's stage.stageWidth and stage.stageHeight properties, except that width and height are global in scope from any Processing class (.pde).

The actual table-drawing algorithm uses Processing's rect() function. I added the fill(255) and stroke(0) commands within the nested for loops, which will be necessary to reset the default fill and stroke color values when I add the primitives creation function next. The first two arguments in the rect(x+cellW*(j), y+cellH*(i), cellW, cellH); call are what take care of actually drawing the table; if the call doesn't initially make sense, read it over a couple of times, and consider how nested for loops execute (which is identical in ActionScript and Processing):

> In a nested for loop the outer loop runs once, and then the inner loop runs all of its iterations, then the outer loop runs once again, and the inner loop runs all of its iterations; this pattern continues until the outer loop reaches its limit.

I recommend you take the time to fully understand the code in the last example before continuing. You can also try changing the values of rows and cols to see how the new values affect the table. Next, I'll discuss the primitives creation function, which adds some (interesting) complexity to the sketch.

Filling the Table

I'll create another function to fill the table with Processing's primitives, which will be invoked from within the nested for loops just discussed. The basic program flow will be to first create a table cell, then fill it with a primitive. This approach allows the for loops to do double duty, both building the table and filling it. The challenge will be identifying which primitive should be drawn during each loop iteration. I decided to handle this by using a switch statement, passing an integer value to identify which primitive to draw. It will be easiest to understand the program if you look at it in steps. Rather than drawing all of Processing's primitives, I'll begin by just drawing some points in the first table cell, shown in Figure 2-4. Here's the drawPrim() function, with just one case defined. Obviously, this code cannot be run in isolation—we'll get to that shortly.

```
void drawPrim(int index, float x, float y){
  switch(index){
  case 0:
    // draw 500 random points
    stroke(0);
    for (int i=0; i<500; i++){
      point(random(x-cellW/2, x+cellW/2), random(y-cellH/2, y+cellH/2));
    }
    break;
  }
}
```

The switch statement probably looks familiar, as it uses the same syntax as the switch statement in ActionScript. (If your memory is hazy about switch statements, see the Processing reference: http://processing.org/reference/switch_.html). Rather than draw a single point, I thought it would be somewhat more interesting to draw 500 random points, constrained within the table cell. Processing has two forms for its random() function:

```
random(max value)
```

```
random(min value, max value)
```

This function may bring some of you back to Flash 4 days, before ActionScript's static method Math.random took over. Processing's random() functions generate a float value, between 0 (or the min value argument specified) and the max (not including the max).

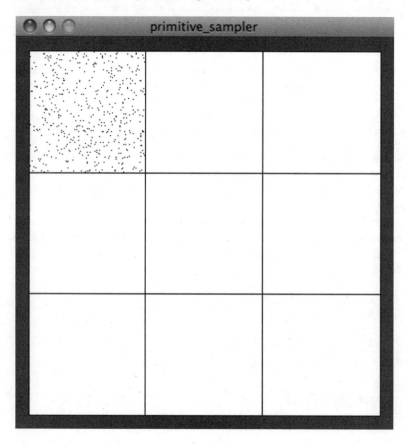

Figure 2-4. Primitive sampler with points

Next, we'll add the rest of the 2D primitives to the switch statement, as well as the setup()() and buildTable() functions, enabling you to run this sketch, shown in Figure 2-5.

```
/**
 * Primitve Sampler,
 * By Ira Greenberg <br />
 *  The Essential Guide to Processing for Flash Developers
 * Friends of ED, 2009
 */
// table config
float cellW, cellH;
int rows = 3;
int cols = 3;
float margin = 15;

void setup(){
  size(400, 400);
  background(75);
  buildTable();
}

void buildTable(){
  // initiatlize local variables x, y
  float x = margin;
  float y  = x;
  cellW = (width - margin*2)/cols;
  cellH = (height- margin*2)/rows;
  for (int i=0; i<rows; i++){
    for (int j=0; j<cols; j++){
      fill(255);
      stroke(0);
      rect(x+cellW*(j), y+cellH*(i), cellW, cellH);
      drawPrim(i*cols+j, x+cellW*(j)+cellW/2, y+cellH*(i)+cellH/2);
    }
  }
```

```
}

void drawPrim(int index, float x, float y){
  switch(index){
  case 0:
    // draw 500 random points
    stroke(0);
    for (int i=0; i<500; i++){
      point(random(x-cellW/2, x+cellW/2), random(y-cellH/2, y+cellH/2));
    }
    break;
  case 1:
    // draw 50 random lines
    stroke(0);
    for (int i=0; i<50; i++){
      line(random(x-cellW/2, x+cellW/2), random(y-cellH/2, y+cellH/2), ↵
          random(x-cellW/2, x+cellW/2), random(y-cellH/2, y+cellH/2));
    }
    break;
  case 2:
    // draw 50 random rectangles
    fill(255);
    stroke(0);
    for (int i=0; i<50; i++){
      float rectW = random(5, 30);
      float rectH = random(5, 30);
      rect(random(x-cellW/2, x+cellW/2-rectW), ↵
          random(y-cellH/2, y+cellH/2-rectH),rectW, rectH);
    }
    break;
  case 3:
    // draw 50 random triangles
    fill(255);
    stroke(0);
```

```
for (int i=0; i<50; i++){
  float radius = random(4, 20);
  float theta = random(TWO_PI);
  float tempX = random(x-cellW/2+radius, x+cellW/2-radius);
  float tempY = random(y-cellH/2+radius, y+cellH/2-radius);
  triangle(tempX+cos(theta)*radius, tempY+sin(theta)*radius, ↵
      tempX+cos(theta+PI/1.5)*radius, tempY+sin(theta+PI/1.5)*radius, ↵
      tempX+cos(theta+PI/1.5*2)*radius, tempY+sin(theta+PI/1.5*2)*radius);
}
break;
case 4:
  // draw 50 arcs
  noFill();
  stroke(0);
  for (int i=0; i<50; i++){
    float start = random(PI/4);
    float end = random(start, TWO_PI);
    float rectW = random(5, 60);
    float rectH = random(5, 60);
    arc(random(x-cellW/2+rectW/2, x+cellW/2-rectW/2), ↵
        random(y-cellH/2+rectH/2, y+cellH/2-rectH/2), rectW, rectH, start, end);
  }
  break;
case 5:
  // draw 50 quads
  fill(255);
  stroke(0);
  for (int i=0; i<50; i++){
    float radius = random(4, 20);
    float theta = random(TWO_PI);
    float jitterX = random(-8, 8);
    float jitterY = random(-8, 8);
    float tempX = random(x-cellW/2+radius+4, x+cellW/2-radius-4);
    float tempY = random(y-cellH/2+radius+4, y+cellH/2-radius-4);
```

```
        quad(tempX+cos(theta)*(radius+jitterX), tempY+sin(theta)*(radius+jitterY),⏎
            tempX+cos(theta+PI/2)*(radius+jitterX),⏎
            tempY+sin(theta+PI/2)*(radius+jitterY),
            tempX+cos(theta+PI)*(radius+jitterX),⏎
            tempY+sin(theta+PI)*(radius+jitterY), ⏎
            tempX+cos(theta+PI*1.5)*(radius+jitterX),⏎
            tempY+sin(theta+PI*1.5)*(radius+jitterY));
      }
    break;
  case 6:
    // draw 30 ellipses
    fill(255);
    stroke(0);
    for (int i=0; i<30; i++){
      float rectW = random(3, 40);
      float rectH = random(3, 40);
      ellipse(random(x-cellW/2+rectW/2, x+cellW/2-rectW/2), ⏎
          random(y-cellH/2+rectH/2, y+cellH/2-rectH/2),rectW, rectH);
    }
    break;
  }
}
```

Figure 2-5. Primitive sampler with 2D primitives

As with the points, I continued to use random values to plot the different primitives in their respective table cells. The only new Processing specific code I snuck in are the trigonometry functions sin(radians), cos(radians), which work just like the same-named static methods in ActionScript's Math class. The trig functions are very handy for generating things like rotations, waves, and other types of organic forms and motion, and I'll use them throughout the book. If trig was something you tried desperately to forget after school (or never remembered in the first place), please check out my trig tutorial at Processing.org (http://processing.org/learning/tutorials/trig).

One very handy use for trig is to easily find the coordinate location of any point around a circle. The two lines of code you should try to commit to memory are

```
x = cos(angle of rotation) * radius
y = sin(angle of rotation) * radius
```

So if you wanted to plot any regular polygon, a polygon with equal (congruent) angles and sides of the same length, you would increment the angle of rotation evenly around the circle based on the number of sides of the polygon. Later in the chapter, I'll provide a polygon example using the trig functions.

> *The trig functions use angles expressed in radians, as opposed to degrees. To convert between degrees and radians, you can use these equations: radians = angle in degrees*Pi/180 and degrees = angle in radians*180/Pi. Better yet, use Processing's very handy radians(ang in degrees) or degrees(ang in radians) functions.*

The final modification I'll make to the Primitive sampler example is adding the 3D primitives. In setup, add the third argument P3D to the existing size(400, 400); call. It should look like this now:

```
size(400, 400, P3D);
```

The size() call takes an optional third argument, specifying a renderer. When not explicitly set, Processing uses the JAVA2D renderer, a high quality, 2D renderer based on the Java 2D API. You can read more about the Java 2D API at: http://java.sun.com/products/java-media/2D. Besides JAVA2D, Processing includes three other renderers:

- P3D: a fast, web-enabled, software-based 3D renderer
- OPENGL: a hardware-accelerated 3D renderer, implemented through JOGL (a Java OpenGL implementation)

    - To learn more about OpenGL: http://www.opengl.org
    - To learn more about JOGL: https://jogl.dev.java.net

- P2D: a 2D renderer that is faster, but less accurate, than JAVA2D

Finally, in the switch statement add the following two cases, right beneath break; under case 6

```
case 7:
  // draw 30 random boxes
  fill(230);
  noStroke();
  lights();
  for (int i=0; i<30; i++){
    float rectW = random(2, 25);
    float rectH = random(2, 25);
    float rectD = random(2, 25);
    pushMatrix();
    translate(random(x-cellW/2.75+rectW/2, x+cellW/2.75-rectW/2), ↵
    random(y-cellH/2.75+rectH/2, y+cellH/2.75-rectH/2), 5);
    rotateX(random(TWO_PI));
```

```
      rotateY(random(TWO_PI));
      rotateZ(random(TWO_PI));
      box(rectW, rectH, rectD);
      popMatrix();
    }
    break;
  case 8:
    // draw 30 random spheres
    fill(110);
    noStroke();
    lights();
    for (int i=0; i<30; i++){
      float radius = random(2, 13);
      pushMatrix();
      translate(random(x-cellW/2.5+radius, x+cellW/2.5-radius), ↵
      random(y-cellH/2.5+radius, y+cellH/2.5-radius), 10);
      rotateX(random(TWO_PI));
      rotateY(random(TWO_PI));
      rotateZ(random(TWO_PI));
      sphere(radius);
      popMatrix();
    }
    break;
```

Cases 7 and 8 introduce a bunch of new commands and concepts, including P3D, lights(), pushMatrix()/popMatrix(), translate(), rotateX()/rotateY()/rotateZ(), box(), and sphere(). I'll discuss some of these in the next section on transformations. Here, I'll address rotateX()/rotateY()/rotateZ(), box(), and sphere. The three rotation commands control rotation around the individual axes (x, y, and z). Processing also includes a plain 2D rotate command. All four of the rotate commands take radian argument values. I'll be using these commands throughout the chapter (and the entire book), so you'll get lots of practice with them. The box() and sphere() commands draw 3D primitives. What might be unfamiliar about these commands is that they don't take any coordinate values for positioning, just values controlling their size. box() and sphere() draw 3D primitives around the origin (0, 0, 0). To move the primitives, you use transformations, which I'll discuss next. However, before reading on, I strongly recommend running the completed Primitive Sampler example, shown in Figure 2-6, and playing with the values in the sketch.

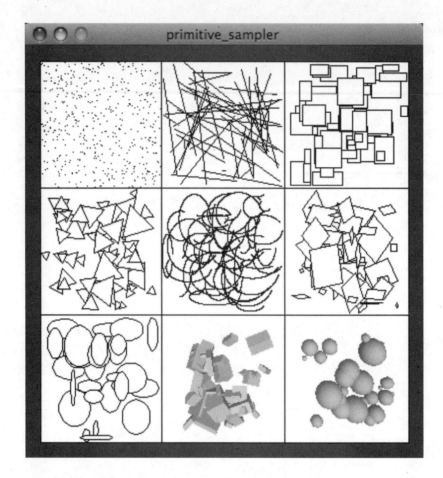

Figure 2-6. Finished Primitive Sampler

Transformations

Transformations, as they relate to computer graphics, is a general term used to describe, in the aggregate, procedures such as translating (moving), rotating, scaling, or skewing geometry (composed of vertices). Internally, these sorts of calculations can get fairly complex, relying on mathematical structures such as vectors and matrices; this is especially the case when working in 3D. You may be familiar with ActionScript's `Transform` class, which includes both `matrix` and `matrix3D` object properties. In this chapter, we'll take a glance at 3D concepts, which I'll explore in much greater detail in Chapter 8.

In the last modification to the Primitive Sampler example, as mentioned earlier, I added the following new Processing elements: `P3D`, `lights()`, `pushMatrix()`, `translate()`, and `popMatrix`. I'll discuss each next.

`P3D`, as discussed earlier, switches Processing's renderer from its default `JAVA2D` to `P3D`. In `JAVA2D`, the coordinate space is defined by the *x* and *y* axes, with the top left corner of the screen being point (0, 0), the *x* axis increasing to the right, and the *y* axis increasing downward. The P3D renderer adds a *z* axis to the mix, with *z* axis values increasing from the computer screen to the viewer. In computer graphics, the term *translate* is often used to describe moving geometry (or at least moving the view of geometry) along an axis. Next is an example that displays *z* axis translation, shown in Figure 2-7, using Processing's translate function.

```
/**
 * Translation along the Z-axis,
 * By Ira Greenberg <br />
 *   The Essential Guide to Processing for Flash Developers
 * Friends of ED, 2009
 */

void setup(){
  size(400, 200, P3D);
  background(175);
  noStroke();
  fill(255);
  lights();

  // sphere 1
  translate(100, height/2, 0);
  sphere(50);

  // sphere 2
  translate(150, 0, 50);
  sphere(50);
}
```

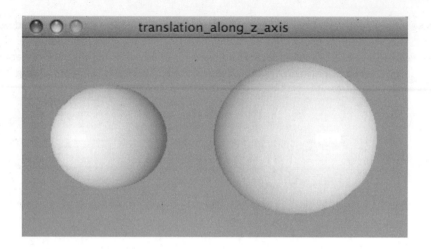

Figure 2-7. Translation along the z axis

When the sphere on the right is translated 50 pixels along the z axis, it appears to come toward you. You might also notice some slight perspective distortion of the sphere. P3D, like many other 3D renderers, uses a virtual camera for calculating this illusion of moving in and out of space. In addition, through some fancy math, other 3D perceptual dynamics can be calculated such as lighting, depth of field, fog, etc. Processing includes a number of commands for controlling these sorts of 3D properties, including the lights() command, which I called in the last two sketches. lights() is a very convenient function that sets up basic lighting in a 3D scene. Without including the lights() command, you'd need to use a bunch of other commands to control individual light properties (e.g., ambient, specularity, emissive color, shininess, etc.). I'll discuss lighting, as well as other 3D rendering effects, in Chapter 8. For now, just take a look at the last sketch without any lighting effects, shown in Figure 2-8.

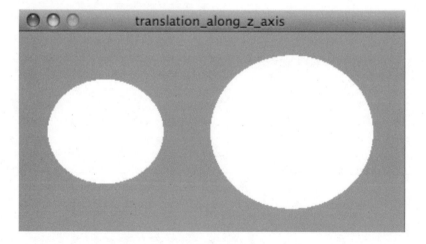

Figure 2-8. The effect of no lights in 3D

> It's easy to take for granted how we see three-dimensionally in the real world, especially once we get old enough to take it for granted. When I taught drawing, my biggest challenge was to convince the students that if they really wanted to learn to draw, they needed to make an effort (sometimes an emotionally fraught one) to see the world in 2D—as visual data is actually perceived on the flat surface of the retina. It's the brain (our own personal computer) that takes the incoming 2D data, collected from both eyes, and builds the 3D visual field we perceive. All of this is only possible because of light, which provides the critical visual cues to depth and spatial perception. To learn more about the science behind how we see, check out: http://www.webmd.com/eye-health/amazing-human-eye.

The commands pushMatrix(), translate(), and popMatrix() work together as a team and are used with all of Processing's 2D and 3D renderers. The translate() command, mentioned earlier, is the easiest of the three to understand, as it takes x, y, z arguments (x, y in 2D) and simply offsets geometry (really the virtual camera's view) the distance specified by the arguments (along the respective axis). However, the situation is not quite as simple as that (of course not). Next is a simple example, shown in Figure 2-9, that uses multiple translations, revealing the source of (some of) the complexity.

```
/**
 * Multiple Translations,
 * By Ira Greenberg <br />
 *   The Essential Guide to Processing for Flash Developers
 * Friends of ED, 2009
 */

void setup(){
  size(125, 125);
  background(255);
  noStroke();
  fill(127);

  // rect 1
  translate(25, 25);
  rect(0, 0, 25, 25);

  // rect 2
  translate(25, 25);
```

```
  rect(0, 0, 25, 25);

  // rect 3
  translate(25, 25);
  rect(0, 0, 25, 25);
}
```

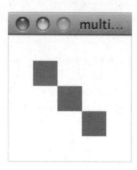

Figure 2-9. Multiple translations

Notice in the last example that each rect(0, 0, 25, 25); call drew the rectangle from point (0, 0), the origin. If it wasn't obvious, it's the multiple translations that caused the rectangle to shift. Similar to the fill()() and stroke() commands, you can think of the translate() command as creating a translate state. If you translate by 50 along the x axis, then everything else you draw (until you translate again) will be offset on the x by 50 pixels. However, unlike fill() and stroke(), translations are cumulative. The situation can get complicated when you combine multiple translations, as well as other types of transformations, which get combined mathematically.

> *Internally, the transformation state is stored in a matrix, which you can think of as a table of values. One of the really handy things about matrices (plural of matrix) is that you can combine different types of transformations into a single matrix. The way this works mathematically can get a bit complex. Processing includes a* printMatrix() *function, which prints to the screen the current transformation state, in matrix form. Figure 2-10 shows output using* printMatrix() *to incrementally reveal how individual transformations get stored in Processing's internal transformation matrix.*

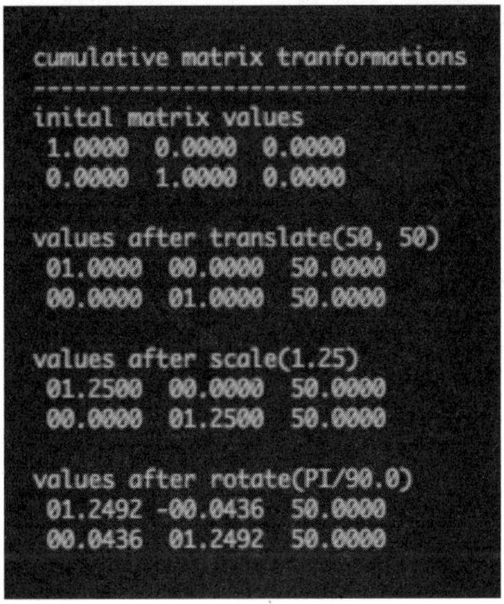

```
cumulative matrix tranformations
--------------------------------
inital matrix values
 1.0000  0.0000  0.0000
 0.0000  1.0000  0.0000

values after translate(50, 50)
 01.0000  00.0000  50.0000
 00.0000  01.0000  50.0000

values after scale(1.25)
 01.2500  00.0000  50.0000
 00.0000  01.2500  50.0000

values after rotate(PI/90.0)
 01.2492 -00.0436  50.0000
 00.0436  01.2492  50.0000
```

Figure 2-10. `printMatrix()` output

One approach to managing multiple transformations, which, remember, are cumulative, is to (for lack of a better term) un-transform your previous transformations, to bring the transformation state back to where it was initially. As you'll learn shortly, this is not an efficient approach, but implementing it does reveal an important aspect of transformations. Figure 2-11 shows a multiple transformation example using my manual un-transform approach.

```
/**
 * Multiple Transformations,
 * using manual un-transforms
 * By Ira Greenberg <br />
 * The Essential Guide to Processing for Flash Developers
 * Friends of ED, 2009
 */

void setup(){
  size(300, 300);
  background(127);
  smooth();
  noStroke();
  int arms = 72;
  float shades = 255.0/arms;
```

```
translate(width*0.66, height*0.625);

for (int i=0; i<arms; i++){
  fill((i+1)*shades);
  // set transformations
  translate(-i*2.7, -i*2.5);
  scale(1.0-(1.0/arms)*(i*.8));
  rotate(TWO_PI/arms*i);
  rect(0, 0, 100, 100);
  /* reset transformations
   in opposite order */
  rotate(-TWO_PI/arms*i);
  scale(1/(1.0-(1.0/arms)*(i*.8)));
  translate(i*2.7, i*2.5);
  }
}
```

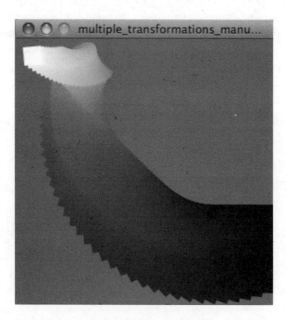

Figure 2-11. Multiple transformations using manual un-transforms

Although this last sketch did properly translate, rotate, and scale the geometry, the second scale(), rotate(), and translate() (un-transform) calls in the for loop are inefficient and an ugly hack. Processing includes a much better and far more efficient way to do this. Before I show you that, though, I want to discuss two details of the last example: the rotate(angle) command and the overall order of transformations.

Processing's rotate(angle) command works a little differently than the rotation property in ActionScript, as it expects an angle argument in radians, as opposed to degrees. If you've used trig functions in ActionScript, you're probably familiar with radians. If you're not, or you really hate them, you can still work in degrees in Processing by converting values using the function radians(angle in degrees). But once you get used to radians, it really is simpler to just work directly with them; the trick is to remember that 360 degrees is equal to Pi*2 (or 180 degrees is equal to Pi). Processing has constants for both of these: TWO_PI and PI, as well as HALF_PI.

Look at the order of the transformations in the last example:

```
translate(-i*2.7, -i*2.5);
scale(1.0-(1.0/arms)*(i*.8));
rotate(TWO_PI/arms*i);
```

Then look at the order of un-transforms:

```
rotate(-TWO_PI/arms*i);
scale(1/(1.0-(1.0/arms)*(i*.8)));
translate(i*2.7, i*2.5);
```

In addition to resetting the argument values, I needed to call the second group of un-transforms in the reverse order of the initial transforms. (If I changed the order, I could get different results.) Again, this is not an efficient way to handle multiple transforms. A much better way is to use Processing's cool sounding functions pushMatrix() and popMatrix()().

Here's an improved version of the last sketch:

```
/**
 * Multiple Transformations,
 * using pushMatrix()/popMatrix()
 * By Ira Greenberg <br />
 * The Essential Guide to Processing for Flash Developers
 * Friends of ED, 2009
 */


void setup(){
  size(300, 300);
```

```
background(127);
smooth();
noStroke();
int arms = 72;
float shades = 255.0/arms;
translate(width*0.66, height*0.625);
for (int i=0; i<arms; i++){
  fill((i+1)*shades);
  // set transformations
  pushMatrix();
  translate(-i*2.7, -i*2.5);
  scale(1.0-(1.0/arms)*(i*.8));
  rotate(TWO_PI/arms*i);
  rect(0, 0, 100, 100);
  popMatrix();
}
}
```

pushMatrix() and popMatrix() work their magic using a stack, technically a matrix stack. A stack is an abstract data type used ubiquitously in computing. If you're not familiar with them, don't worry as they are based on a pretty simple concept. Think of a stack of pancakes. If you add a pancake to the top of the stack, it will then be the first one that you can take (or eat) off the stack. This is different than, say, a line (or queue) at the movies, where the first person in line is the first one into the movie. Two acronyms commonly used to help remember these structures are LIFO and FIFO. Stacks are LIFO, or *Last In First Out* structures, and queues are FIFO, or *First In First Out* structures.

> *An abstract data type is a structure with a defined interface that is independent of any specific implementation. For example, if I create an abstract Quiche class (a class being a data type), I wouldn't want people to be too limited in how they used my class to create their own tasty quiche. However, there are some methods to creating quiches that are common to all: createDough(), combineIngredients(), season(), cook(), etc. These method names would be defined in the abstract class, but what happens within each method (its implementation) would not. In Chapter 4, I'll discuss classes and OOP in much more detail.*

pushMatrix() and popMatrix() work by copying (or pushing) the current transformation state (stored as a matrix of values) to an internal stack when pushMatrix() is called; then any subsequent transformation calls are executed, until popMatrix() is called, whereby the stored original transformation state is popped off the stack, returning the transformation state to the original values, prior to the transformations. This sounds more complex than it really is. Here's another example, shown in Figure 2-12. The sketch output on the left in the figure is without the pushMatrix()/popMatrix() calls and the sketch on the right is with them:

```
/**
 * Asterisks with
 * pushMatrix()/popMatrix()
 * By Ira Greenberg <br />
 * The Essential Guide to Processing for Flash Developers
 * Friends of ED, 2009
 */

float scl = 1.0;
void setup(){
  size(400, 400);
  background(0);
  stroke(255);
  smooth();
  translate(width/2, height/2);
  float theta = 0;
  float radius = 340;
  float strkWt = 6;
  while (radius>6){
    strokeWeight(strkWt*=.80);
    radius *= .705;
    theta += PI/4;
    for (int j=0; j<4; j++){
      line(cos(theta)*radius, sin(theta)*radius, cos(theta+PI/2)*radius,↵
      sin(theta+PI/2)*radius);
      asterisk(cos(theta)*radius, sin(theta)*radius, 20, 20);
      theta+=PI/2;
    }
  }
}

void asterisk(float x, float y, int sides, float rad){
```

```
pushMatrix();
translate(x, y);
scale(scl*=.96);
for (int i=0; i<sides; i++){
  rotate(TWO_PI/sides);
  line(0, 0, rad, rad);
}
popMatrix();
}
```

Figure 2-12. Asterisk example without and with pushMatrix()/popMatrix()

The pushMatrix() and popMatrix() calls in the asterisk() function ensure that the multiple transformations don't accumulate. Notice in setup() that I initially called translate(width/2, height/2); without nesting it between pushMatrix() and popMatrix(); that was because this initial translate() call moved the origin (0, 0) to the center of the sketch window and left it there. It's fairly standard in computer graphics to draw objects around their origin and then translate them into position. This issue becomes more critical when you begin adding rotations, since they occur relative to the origin. In Chapter 3 I'll discuss animation and revisit this concept.

The pushMatrix() and popMatrix() calls can be nested between other pushMatrix() and popMatrix() calls, allowing you to do more complex transformations. The nesting does add a level of complexity, though, which takes some practice to get the hang of. The next example demonstrates nesting pushMatrix() and popMatrix(), shown in Figure 2-13.

```
/**
 * Nested pushMatrix()-popMatrix()
 * By Ira Greenberg <br />
 * The Essential Guide to Processing for Flash Developers
 * Friends of ED, 2009
 */

void setup(){
  // set up environment
  size(400, 400);
  background(255);
  smooth();
  rectMode(CENTER);
  // declare some variables
  int cols = 6;
  int rows = 6;
  int margin = 50;
  float cellW = (width-margin*2)/cols;
  float cellH = (height-margin*2)/rows;

  for (int i=0; i<=cols; i++){
    for (int j=0; j<=rows; j++){
      //outer push-pop for table positioning
      pushMatrix();
      translate(margin+cellW*i,  margin+cellH*j);
      int rots = (int)random(12, 24);
      float len = random(10, 20);
      fill(0);
      noStroke();
      // inner push-pop for rotations
      pushMatrix();
      for (int k=0; k<rots; k++){
```

```
        rotate(TWO_PI/rots);
        rect(0, 0, random(.5, 1), random(15, cellH));

        /*inner, inner push-pops for
         translating along rotations*/
        pushMatrix();
        translate(0, 10);
        rect(0, 0, random(1, 3), random(1, 3));
        popMatrix();

        pushMatrix();
        translate(0, len);
        rect(0, 0, random(2, 4), random(2, 4));
        popMatrix();
      }
      popMatrix();
      // draw table cell outlines
      noFill();
      stroke(200);
      rect(0, 0, cellW, cellH);
      popMatrix();
    }
  }
}
```

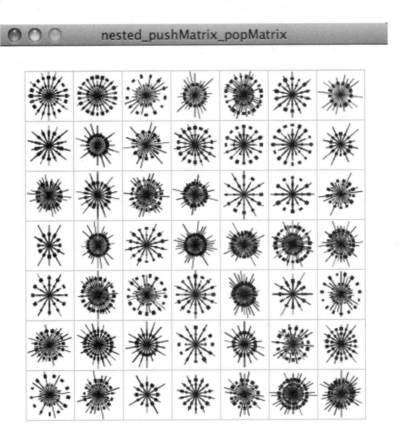

Figure 2-13. Nesting pushMatrix()/popMatrix()

This example uses another table structure to position dynamically generated images. The images are formed with simple rectangles and a series of transformations. The nested pushMatrix()/popMatrix() calls work similarly to other nested code structures, where the outside calls set the base state for the inner calls. Just remember that each popMatrix() call resets the transformation state to what it was prior to its paired pushMatrix() call. The best way to get a handle on this is to practice (as with most things). I suggest playing with this sketch a bit and commenting out some of the pushMatrix()/popMatrix() calls to see the impact.

Drawing

You can accomplish a lot using Processing's primitives and transformations (and a little creative elbow grease), but as you progress you'll want to be able to create more custom shapes. Processing includes functions for custom drawing, similar to the Graphics class methods moveTo(), lineTo(), and curveTo in

ActionScript. But the system works differently in Processing (which is actually simpler). In the next sketch example, you'll build a polygon function, shown in Figure 2-14.

```
/**
 * Polygon function drawing example
 * By Ira Greenberg <br />
 * The Essential Guide to Processing for Flash Developers
 * Friends of ED, 2009
 */

void setup(){
  // set up environment
  size(400, 400);
  background(0);
  stroke(255, 100);
  smooth();
  float scl = 1.0;
  float sclChange = .02;
  float radius = 500;

// drawing
  translate(width/2, height/2);
  while(scl > 0){
    fill(random(255), random(255), random(255), 100);
    pushMatrix();
    scl-=sclChange;
    scale(scl);

    createPoly(int(random(5, 12)), radius, 0);
    popMatrix();
  }
}

// calculate polygon
void createPoly(int sides, float radius, float startAng){
```

```
float px, py;
float theta = startAng;
beginShape();
for (int i=0; i<sides; i++){
  px = cos(theta)*radius;
  py = sin(theta)*radius;
  vertex(px, py);
  theta += TWO_PI/sides;
}
endShape(CLOSE);
}
```

Figure 2-14. Polygon function drawing example

The drawing part of the last example is the block:

```
beginShape();
  for (int i=0; i<sides; i++){
    px = cos(theta)*radius;
    py = sin(theta)*radius;
    vertex(px, py);
    theta += TWO_PI/sides;
  }
endShape(CLOSE);
```

The outer beginShape() and endShape() commands work as record and stop recording functions for any vertex() calls made between them. Once beginShape()() is called, subsequent calls to vertex()() record the vertex positions. When endShape()() is then called, the recording is stopped and the recorded vertices are all drawn to the screen.

> *Processing's default JAVA2D renderer uses only one stroke and one fill value to color all the geometry drawn between the beginShape() and endShape() calls. If more than one stroke() or fill() call is made between the calls, only the last calls affect the rendered color. However, Processing's other renderers (P2D, P3D and OPENGL) associate color values with individual vertices, enabling multiple fill()/stroke() commands to be called between beginShape()/endShape(), creating beautiful blends between the vertices. We'll look at this feature in Chapter 8.*

How the vertices are connected into geometry is controlled by a set of arguments passed to the beginShape() and endShape() commands. The potential arguments passed to beginShape() include

- POINTS
- LINES
- TRIANGLES
- TRIANGLE_FAN
- TRIANGLE_STRIP
- QUADS
- QUAD_STRIP

The endShape() command can only be passed an optional CLOSE argument, which closes the drawn path. (Please be aware that unclosed shapes will still be filled; to turn this off, use the noFill() command.) You'll notice the arguments are all caps, as they are constants, which evaluate to an integer value. For example, the command println(TRIANGLES) outputs 9.

Functions in Processing can optionally be put in their own tabs, to help you organize your code. Other than the organizational benefits (which are not insignificant), these functions perform identically to when they are all in the main tab. In fact, during compiling all the function code within any tabs are combined into the main .java file. Figure 2-15 shows a screen-shot of the last Polygon function drawing example organized in two tabs. In Chapter 4, I'll utilize the tabs feature extensively, when I introduce classes in Processing.

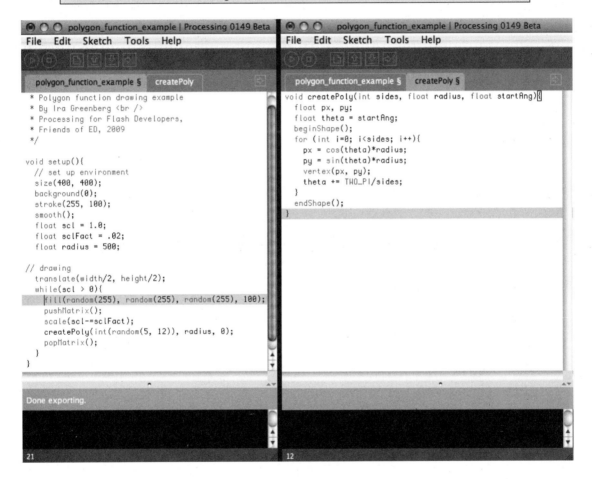

Figure 2-15. Tabs example

Next, I'll modify the createPoly() function to create a simple drawing mode sampler showcasing the results of the different arguments, shown in Figure 2-16.

```
/**
 * Drawing mode sampler
 * By Ira Greenberg <br />
 * The Essential Guide to Processing for Flash Developers
 * Friends of ED, 2009
 */

void setup(){
  // set up environment
  size(400, 400);
  background(0);
  stroke(255);
  noFill();
  smooth();
  float radius = 140;
  float theta = 0;
  int[] modes = {
    POINTS, LINES, TRIANGLES, TRIANGLE_FAN, TRIANGLE_STRIP, QUADS, QUAD_STRIP  };

// drawing
  translate(width/2, height/2);
  for (int i=0; i<modes.length; i++){
    pushMatrix();
    translate(cos(theta)*radius, sin(theta)*radius);
    createPoly(15, 45, 0, modes[i]);
    popMatrix();
    theta += TWO_PI/modes.length;
  }
}

// calculate polygon
void createPoly(int sides, float radius, float startAng, int mode){
  float px, py;
  float theta = startAng;
```

```
beginShape(mode);
for (int i=0; i<sides; i++){
  px = cos(theta)*radius;
  py = sin(theta)*radius;
  vertex(px, py);
  theta += TWO_PI/sides;

}
endShape();
}
```

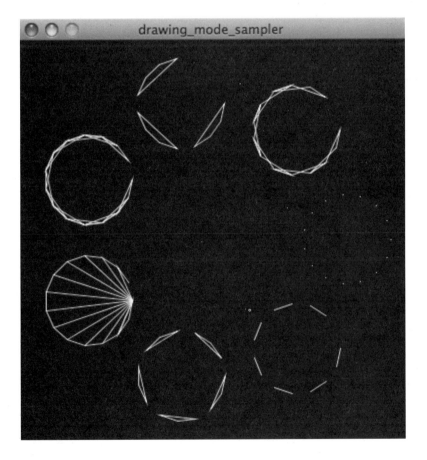

Figure 2-16. Drawing mode sampler

Some of the drawing modes are more useful in 3D, such as the fan and strip modes, which are used to subdivide geometry. Although Processing includes stand-alone drawing commands such as point(), line(), etc., it is generally more efficient to use the vertex() command (nested between beginShape()/endShape()).

Arrays

The last thing I want to discuss in this chapter is arrays, which you may have noticed I slipped into the previous example. As an experienced Flash developer, you already know what arrays are and the very important role they play in programming. If you're not familiar at all with arrays, I cover them extensively in my earlier book (as will any beginning programming book). What I do want to discuss is how Processing arrays differ from ActionScript arrays. Please note that this comparison is based on the ActionScript Array class and not the recently introduced Vector class. To learn more about the Vector class, see: http://help.adobe.com/en_US/AS3LCR/Flash_10.0/Vector.html (6/3/09, 6:34PM EST).

Here are some ways Processing and ActionScript arrays are similar:

- They both are 0-indexed (first position in the array is [0]).
- They both have length properties.
- They both can be passed as object reference arguments.

However, there are also numerous syntactic and functional differences. Next are the different ways to declare and instantiate arrays in both languages:

ActionScript

```
// just declare reference variable
var myArray:Array;
// declare and explicitly instantiate with no length
var myArray:Array = new Array();
// declare and explicitly instantiate with length
var myArray:Array = new Array(5);
// declare and explicitly instantiate with content (OOP form)
var myArray:Array = new Array("Sophie", "Ian", "Robin", "Ira", "Heidi", "Moonshadow");
// declare and implicitly instantiate with content (array literal form)
var myArray:Array = ["Sophie", "Ian", "Robin", "Ira", "Heidi", "Moonshadow"];
// declare and explicitly  instantiate with multiple content types
var myArray:Array = new Array("sophie", 4, true, ["painting", "reading", "skating"]);
```

Processing

```
// just declare reference variable
String[] myArray;
// declare and explicitly instantiate with length
String[] myArray = new String[5];
// declare and implicitly instantiate with content
String[] myArray = {"Sophie", "Ian", "Robin", "Ira", "Heidi", "Moonshadow"};
```

If it isn't obvious, Processing utilizes a much more minimalist (and rigid) approach to arrays than ActionScript. Processing arrays need to be declared of a specific type, instead of the more abstract Array type in ActionScript, and a Processing array can only contain data of its declared type. ActionScript arrays can hold multiple types, as demonstrated in the final ActionScript code array example. Processing does include some other structures for storing multiple data types, such as the ArrayList (http://processing.org/reference/ArrayList.html), which I'll demonstrate in the projects section of the book. In addition to differences in syntax, there are also some major differences in functionality between Processing and ActionScript arrays.

The following is perfectly legal in ActionScript:

```
var myArray:Array = new Array();
myArray[1] = "I like playing hockey";
myArray[78] = "code creatively!";
trace("length = " + myArray.length);
// outputs: length = 79
```

This won't work in Processing (you'll get an **arrayIndexOutOfBoundsException** if you try it). ActionScript arrays automatically resize themselves when data is added to an index position that doesn't exist. In Processing, you need to initialize your arrays, when first created, at the size they will ultimately be; you can't add a value to a position outside of the initially declared length. However, that being said, both ActionScript and Processing include numerous methods for operating on arrays, which will allow you to do things such as resize arrays. Next is an example that uses Processing's expand() function:

```
String[] myArray = {
  "Sophie", "Ian", "Robin", "Ira", "Heidi", "Moonshadow"  };
// increase array length by 2
println("initial array:");
println(myArray);
myArray = expand(myArray, 8);
myArray[6] = "Pearl";
```

```
myArray[7] = "Roo";
println("\nexpanded array:");
println(myArray);
```

This sketch outputs

```
initial array:
[0] "Sophie"
[1] "Ian"
[2] "Robin"
[3] "Ira"
[4] "Heidi"
[5] "Moonshadow"

expanded array:
[0] "Sophie"
[1] "Ian"
[2] "Robin"
[3] "Ira"
[4] "Heidi"
[5] "Moonshadow"
[6] "Pearl"
[7] "Roo"
```

The statement myArray = expand(myArray, 8); is obviously what expands the array. The function expects an array argument and the new size of the array; if no new size argument is specified, the array length is doubled. Trying to access the value of an unassigned array position returns a default value, based on the data type of the array. For example, if you use the expand() function, without a new length argument, on an array that initially has a length of 3, the new array will now have a length of 6. If you try to access index positions 3, 4, or 5, you'll get back a default value, per data type (e.g., int[] returns 0, float[] returns 0.0, boolean[] returns false, String[], or any object, returns null, etc.). This is different from ActionScript, where the value undefined is always returned for any unassigned array index position. Before moving on, I want to make sure you noticed the four println() statements in the previous code. (Please note I removed some code originally between the two sets of println() statements.)

```
println("initial array:");
println(myArray);
// removed code
println("\nexpanded array:");
println(myArray);
```

You may not be familiar with the characters "\n", called an *escape sequence*, which forces a new line. Escape sequences override default behavior, allowing you to do such things as outputting actual quotes, slashes, or other programming specific characters. The newline escape sequence "\n" works similarly in ActionScript and Processing. For a list of escape sequences check out http://java.sun.com/docs/books/tutorial/java/data/characters.html.

The astute reader may also have wondered why I didn't condense the previous four `println` statements down to two:

```
println("initial array: " + myArray);
println("\nexpanded array: " + myArray);
```

The + sign works similarly in Processing and ActionScript, as a concatenation operator in both `trace()` and `print()`/`println()` and an addition operator in mathematical expressions. When included in the `println()` statements the + operator changes how the function outputs the array. Instead of outputting the actual values in the array, it outputs the memory address that the array reference variable points to. For example, updating the previous code in the last example with the condensed form of the `println()` expressions (using the concatenation operator '+') outputs

```
initial array: [Z@df48c4
expanded array: [Z@54f9f1
```

I'll say a bit more about memory addresses next chapter. To learn more about each of Processing's array manipulation functions, look under **Array Functions,** in the Processing reference.

Summary

This chapter and the next are intended as a primer on Processing's main graphics capabilities. In each of the topics that I covered in this chapter—primitives, rendering, transformations, drawing, and arrays—I provided an overview of Processing's basic methodology and included examples to suggest creative possibilities. I discussed Processing graphics primitives as well as a more general drawing methodology for creating complex shapes. We looked at how rendering is handled in Processing, as compared to ActionScript, including how color is implemented as a painting state. We also created some sample programs that showcased Processing's graphics primitives and drawing methods, including how to transform geometry. Finally, I discussed how arrays are implemented in Processing and compared them to the Array class in ActionScript. In Chapter 3 I'll build upon what I covered this chapter and discuss variables, curves, motion, imaging, events, and typography in Processing. The primer section is also intended to function as a quick reference—to return to from time to time as you delve deeper into the language and more complex examples, which will begin in the projects section of the book, beginning in Chapter 4.

Chapter 3

Processing Primer II: *Beyond the Basics*

This chapter builds upon the last with a look at some more advanced language features and graphics functions in the Processing API. Some of the topics introduced in this chapter, such as curves, motion, and imaging, are complex and will be explored in greater depth in the later *Projects* section of the book. As with the last chapter, my goal here is to introduce topics through examples, and create a framework (and, I hope, excitement) for future exploration.

Primitive vs. Reference Variables

There are two main categories of variables in Processing, primitive and reference types. Primitive variables refer to a single value, such as `int`, `float`, and `boolean`. Reference variables are used for more complex structures, such as arrays and objects. The variable declaration `float x = 3.2;` is a primitive declaration, where the variable is directly connected to the assigned value in memory. With arrays, and objects in general, variables don't link directly to a specific assigned value; rather, they point to the place in memory (memory address) where the array/object data is stored. This subtle difference in how the variables are mapped to data has some major implications, demonstrated in the next sketch.

```
String[] menu = {
  "chicken parmigiana", "gnocchi", "spinach"};
String[] newMenu;
newMenu = menu;
```

```
newMenu[0] = "lasagna";
println("menu =");
println(menu);
println("\nnewMenu =");
println(newMenu);
output:
menu =
[0] "lasagna"
[1] "gnocchi"
[2] "spinach"

newMenu =
[0] "lasagna"
[1] "gnocchi"
[2] "spinach"
```

If you're not very experienced with arrays and object-oriented programming, the output of this last sketch may have been surprising. I assigned the menu array to the newMenu array. Then I assigned the string "lasagna" to the first index position in the newMenu array, replacing "chicken parmigiana". The strange part is that by changing the newMenu array, I also changed the menu array; this does not happen when working with primitive values. For example, here's an example using primitive variables:

```
String entree1 = "chicken parmigiana";
String entree2 = entree1;
entree2 = "lasagna";
println("entree1 = " + entree1);
println("entree2 = " + entree2);
output:
entree1 = chicken parmigiana
entree2 = lasagna
```

When one is working with primitive variables, assignment operations only affect the operands directly involved in the expression. With reference variables, assigning one array to another makes both arrays point to the same memory location. This situation works the same way when passing arrays as arguments, as shown in the next example:

```
String[] menu = {
  "chicken parmigiana", "gnocchi", "spinach"};

void setup(){
  setMenu(menu);
  println("\nmenu =");
  println(menu);
}
void setMenu(String[] menu){
  String[] newMenu = menu;
  newMenu[0] = "lasagna";
  println("newMenu =");
  println(newMenu);
}
```

output:

newMenu =

[0] "lasagna"

[1] "gnocchi"

[2] "spinach"

menu =

[0] "lasagna"

[1] "gnocchi"

[2] "spinach"

There are times when you want to create a copy of an array and not simply have two reference variables pointing to the same memory address. Processing includes the arraycopy() function, which efficiently handles this. arraycopy() works similarly to ActionScript's Array.slice method. (Please note that you could also theoretically use a loop to copy individual index values from one array to another, but arraycopy() is the most efficient—and easiest—way to handle this.) Here's the last example implemented using arrayCopy().

```
String[] menu = {
  "chicken parmigiana", "gnocchi", "spinach"};

void setup(){
```

```
    setMenu(menu);
    println("\nmenu =");
    println(menu);


}
void setMenu(String[] menu){
    String[] newMenu = new String[menu.length];
    arraycopy(menu, newMenu);
    newMenu[0] = "lasagna";
    println("newMenu =");
    println(newMenu);
}
output:
newMenu =
[0] "lasagna"
[1] "gnocchi"
[2] "spinach"


menu =
[0] "chicken parmigiana"
[1] "gnocchi"
[2] "spinach"
```

> In addition to arrays, both ActionScript and Processing can utilize complex data structures that allow you to refer to stored values by name (or key), instead of by index value. These types of structures are sometimes referred to as associative arrays, dictionaries, hash maps, or hash tables, depending upon the language implementation. In ActionScript, associative arrays are built using the `Object` or `Dictionary` class. Processing includes a `HashMap` class (`http://processing.org/ reference/HashMap.html`).

Curves

From my perspective, one of the most enjoyable things to do with code is to simulate natural phenomena. Simulation is an area that Processing excels at and what got many of us ActionScript types interested in it in the first place. One of the factors that contributes to good simulation is organic realism—the fuzzy, squishy, curvy, craggy, dirty irregularity of life. Although it is possible to use straight lines to approximate organic realism, it is very helpful to have curve algorithms in your arsenal as well. Most modern graphics libraries have some basic curve implementations—for example, the ubiquitous Bézier curve.

In *Processing: Creative Coding and Computational Art*, I cover theory about curves extensively, including going beneath the Processing API and providing custom mathematical implementations of curves. Here, I'll concentrate on demonstrating the curve functions in Processing and focus more on examples. If you do want to look beneath the hood, you can find the Processing internal curve implementations at `http://dev.processing.org/source/index.cgi/trunk/processing/core/src/processing/core/PGraphics .java?view=markup`.

> *For more experienced developers, who either have some knowledge of Java or would like to gain some, you can get a more behind-the-scenes view of Processing at http://dev.processing.org. Here you can view a full API reference of the entire language, as well as view the Processing source code. In fact, for the most experienced developers, you can download the Processing source code, edit it and compile your own custom version of Processing. Instructions on how to do this are here: http://dev.processing.org/build/.*

Processing has four functions for drawing curves:

- `bezier()(`
- `bezierVertex()(`
- `curve()(`
- `curve()(`

`bezier()` and `curve()` are really just (somewhat) simplified versions of `bezierVertex()` and `curveVertex()`, respectively. For example, here's a simple Bézier curve sketch, shown in Figure 3-1, using `bezier()` and then `bezierVertex()`. Don't worry about trying to understand all the code in the example yet; just run it to see how `bezier()` and `bezierVertex()` can be used to generate the same output.

```
/**
 * bezier() | bezierVertex(),
 * By Ira Greenberg <br />
 * The Essential Guide to Processing for Flash Developers
 * Friends of ED, 2009
 */
void setup(){
  size(600, 300);
  background(255);
  smooth();

  /*I used Processing PVector class
```

```
 for holding x,y coords*/
//for bezier()
PVector vec1 = new PVector(100, 250);
PVector vec2 = new PVector(50, 50);
PVector vec3 = new PVector(250, 50);
PVector vec4 = new PVector(200, 250);

//for bezierVertex()
PVector vec5 = new PVector(400, 250);
PVector vec6 = new PVector(350, 50);
PVector vec7 = new PVector(550, 50);
PVector vec8 = new PVector(500, 250);

//plot curve using bezier()
stroke(0);
strokeWeight(3);
bezier(vec1.x, vec1.y, vec2.x, vec2.y, vec3.x, vec3.y, vec4.x, vec4.y);
//draw control PVectors connected to anchor PVectors
stroke(150);
strokeWeight(1);
line(vec1.x, vec1.y, vec2.x, vec2.y);
line(vec3.x, vec3.y, vec4.x, vec4.y);
//control PVectors
ellipse(vec2.x, vec2.y, 10, 10);
ellipse(vec3.x, vec3.y, 10, 10);
//anchor PVectors
rectMode(CENTER);
rect(vec1.x, vec1.y, 10, 10);
rect(vec4.x, vec4.y, 10, 10);

//plot curve using bezierVertex()
stroke(0);
strokeWeight(3);
beginShape();
vertex(vec5.x, vec5.y);
bezierVertex(vec6.x, vec6.y, vec7.x, vec7.y, vec8.x, vec8.y);
```

```
  endShape();
  //draw control PVectors connected to anchor PVectors
  stroke(150);
  strokeWeight(1);
  line(vec5.x, vec5.y, vec6.x, vec6.y);
  line(vec7.x, vec7.y, vec8.x, vec8.y);
  //control PVectors
  ellipse(vec6.x, vec6.y, 10, 10);
  ellipse(vec7.x, vec7.y, 10, 10);
  //anchor PVectors
  rectMode(CENTER);
  rect(vec5.x, vec5.y, 10, 10);
  rect(vec8.x, vec8.y, 10, 10);
}
```

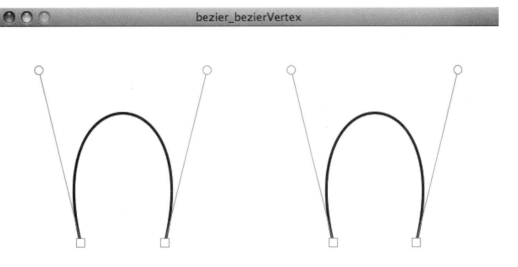

Figure 3-1. `bezier() | bezierVertex()`

I suspect you've used Bézier curves in some form. They work by defining anchor points and control points (the squares and circles, respectively, in Figure 3-1). The 2D `bezier()` call, shown next, takes eight arguments (there's also a 3D version that takes 12 arguments):

`bezier(anchor1_X, anchor1_Y, control1_X, control1_Y, control2_X, control2_Y, anchor2_X, anchor2_Y)`

The anchor points define where the terminal points of the curve lie, and the control points control how the curve bends between the points. If you look through the code in the last example, you'll notice that the main difference between bezier() and bezierVertex() is that the latter takes one less anchor point argument, and the calls are required to be between beginShape() and endShape(), which we looked at in Chapter 2. bezierVertex() is most useful when stringing together a bunch of curves. Before providing an example of that, I just want to give a shout-out to Processing's PVector class. This class is useful for storing 2D and 3D coordinate data. For this example, you can think of the PVector vec objects as simple points. However, the PVector class was designed to be able to work with a vector quantity (hence its name), which accounts for both direction and magnitude. I'll say more about vectors in Chapter 5.

The next example, shown on the right in Figure 3-2, creates a circle using bezierVertex().

```
/**
 * bezierVertex() circle
 * By Ira Greenberg <br />
 * The Essential Guide to Processing for Flash Developers,
 * Friends of ED, 2009
 */


int detail = 4;
PVector[] anchors = new PVector[detail];
PVector[] controlsRt = new PVector[detail];
PVector[] controlsLft = new PVector[detail];


void setup(){
  size(400, 400);
  background(200);
  translate(width/2, height/2);
  smooth();
  noFill();
  strokeWeight(3);
  rectMode(CENTER);
  calcCircle(150);
  drawCircle();
  showControls();
}
```

```
void calcCircle(float radius){
  /* cubic curve internal implementation
   only requires 4 anchor PVectors for circle*/

  // spacing of anchor PVectors
  float anchorTheta = 0;
  // spacing of control PVectors
  float controlTheta = TWO_PI/detail/3;
  // distance of control PVectors
  float controlRadius = radius/cos(controlTheta);
  // for anchors
  float px = 0;
  float py = 0;
  //for controls
  float cx1 = 0;
  float cy1 = 0;
  float cx2 = 0;
  float cy2 = 0;
  for (int i=0; i<detail; i++){
    // anchor PVectors
    px = cos(anchorTheta)*radius;
    py = sin(anchorTheta)*radius;
    anchors[i] = new PVector(px, py);

    // control PVectors
    cx1 = cos(anchorTheta+controlTheta)*controlRadius;
    cy1 = sin(anchorTheta+controlTheta)*controlRadius;
    controlsLft[i] = new PVector(cx1, cy1);
    cx2 = cos(anchorTheta+controlTheta*2)*controlRadius;
    cy2 = sin(anchorTheta+controlTheta*2)*controlRadius;
    controlsRt[i] = new PVector(cx2, cy2);
    // increment theta
    anchorTheta += TWO_PI/detail;
  }
```

```
}

void drawCircle(){
  beginShape();
  vertex(anchors[0].x, anchors[0].y);
  for (int i=0; i<detail; i++){
    if (i<detail-1){
      bezierVertex(controlsLft[i].x, controlsLft[i].y, controlsRt[i].x, ↵
      controlsRt[i].y, anchors[i+1].x, anchors[i+1].y);
    }
    else {
      // close circle
      bezierVertex(controlsLft[i].x, controlsLft[i].y, controlsRt[i].x, ↵
      controlsRt[i].y, anchors[0].x, anchors[0].y);
    }
  }
  endShape();
}

void showControls(){
  strokeWeight(1);
  fill(255);
  for (int i=0; i<detail; i++){
    line(controlsLft[i].x, controlsLft[i].y, anchors[i].x, anchors[i].y);
    if (i<detail-1){
      line(controlsRt[i].x, controlsRt[i].y, anchors[i+1].x, anchors[i+1].y);
    }
    else if (i==detail-1){
      line(controlsRt[i].x, controlsRt[i].y, anchors[0].x, anchors[0].y);
    }
  }
  // ensure lines stay underneath anchors/controls
  for (int i=0; i<detail; i++){
```

```
    // anchor PVectors and control handles
    ellipse(controlsLft[i].x, controlsLft[i].y, 8, 8);
    ellipse(controlsRt[i].x, controlsRt[i].y, 8, 8);
    rect(anchors[i].x, anchors[i].y, 8, 8);
  }
}
```

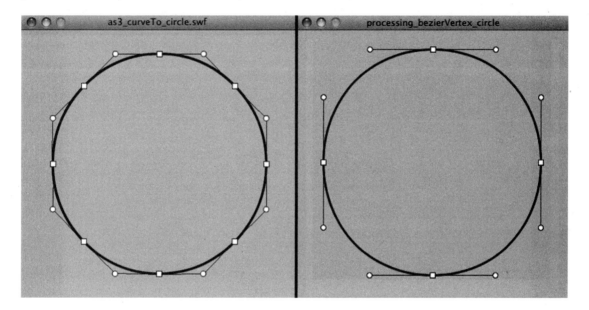

Figure 3-2. Quadratic vs. cubic Bézier curve

You can explore the Bézier curve algorithm a little by changing the detail variable in the last example. Initially I set it to four, which is the minimal number of vertices required to draw a circle-like shape using bezierVertex(). This is different from ActionScript's curveTo() method, which requires eight vertices to generate a circle, shown on the left in Figure 3-2. The reason for this is due to the underlying math behind the curves.

> In generating curves, ActionScript's curveTo() method is based on a quadratic polynomial, while Processing curves utilize cubic polynomials. In case your algebra is a bit rusty, these are equations in the form $f(x) = ax2+bx+c$ (quadratic) and $f(x) = ax3+bx2+cx+d$ (cubic), where a, b, c, and d represent real numbers. You can replace $f(x)$ with y to actually plot them. One of the implications of the different underlying equations used to generate the curves has to do with the number of required control points. Quadratic curves require one control point, while cubic curves require two.

If you're really math-averse, you don't need to deal with the underlying curve algorithms, which are safely encapsulated behind the API. However, with just a little tweaking beneath the hood, interesting possibilities suggest themselves, as I'll demonstrate in a bit.

To generate a circle using `bezierVertex()`, I needed to precisely calculate where to place the two control handles. By contrast, ActionScript's `curveTo()` method uses only one control handle. With `bezierVertex()`, I needed to space the two control points evenly around the arc between any two anchor points. The only part of the problem that required any math was the distance to offset the control points from the center of the circle, which I referred to as `controlRadius` in the code. If you are interested, Figure 3-3 shows how to solve the math.

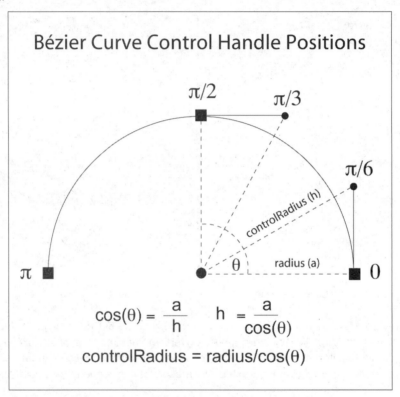

Figure 3-3. Calculating Bézier curve control handle positions

The rest of the code in the last example should be pretty self-explanatory, although the drawing algorithms are a bit dense. I recommend playing with this sketch before moving on, especially trying to break it a bit, which is one of the best ways to understand something. To learn more about Bézier curves check out Wikipedia's entry: http://en.wikipedia.org/wiki/Bezier_curves.

Processing includes a second curve implementation, poetically referred to as curve(), which also has a useful curveVertex() implementation. These two functions have a relationship similar to the one between bezier() and bezierVertex(). curve() and curveVertex() also draw cubic curves, but utilize a Catmull-Rom spline implementation, instead of the Bézier approach. You can learn more about Catmull-Rom splines at http://www.mvps.org/directx/articles/catmull/. The main difference between the Bézier and spline implementations is that the control points of the spline curve lie directly on the curve and are not offset as on the Bézier curve.

Next is a curve() circle example, shown in Figure 3-4. As in the earlier Bézier circle example, an approximate circle can be generated with four points, using curve()/curveVertex().

```
/**
 * curve() circle
 * By Ira Greenberg <br />
 * The Essential Guide to Processing for Flash Developers
 * Friends of ED, 2009
 */


float x, y;
PVector[] vecs = new PVector[4];


void setup(){
  size(300, 300);
  smooth();
  noFill();
  strokeWeight(4);
  // controls survature of spline
  curveTightness(-.7);
  translate(150, height/2);
  calcCircle(125);
  drawCircle();
  drawVecs();
}


void calcCircle(float radius){
  float px=0, py=0, theta=0;
  for (int i=0; i<4; i++){
    px = cos(theta)*radius;
    py = sin(theta)*radius;
```

```
    vecs[i] = new PVector(px, py);
    theta+=TWO_PI/4;
  }
}


void drawCircle(){
  // the loooong hand way
  curve(vecs[3].x, vecs[3].y, vecs[0].x, vecs[0].y, vecs[1].x, vecs[1].y, vecs[2].x,↵
      vecs[2].y);
  curve(vecs[0].x, vecs[0].y, vecs[1].x, vecs[1].y, vecs[2].x, vecs[2].y, vecs[3].x,↵
      vecs[3].y);
  curve(vecs[1].x, vecs[1].y, vecs[2].x, vecs[2].y, vecs[3].x, vecs[3].y, vecs[0].x,↵
      vecs[0].y);
  curve(vecs[2].x, vecs[2].y, vecs[3].x, vecs[3].y, vecs[0].x, vecs[0].y, vecs[1].x,↵
      vecs[1].y);
}


void drawVecs(){
  fill(255);
  strokeWeight(1);
  for (int i=0; i<4; i++){
    ellipse(vecs[i].x, vecs[i].y, 8, 8);
  }
}
```

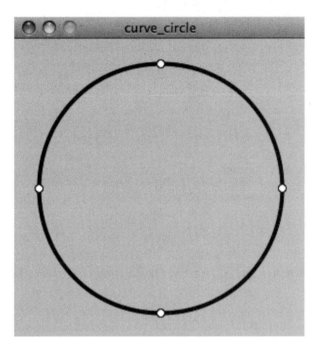

Figure 3-4. curve() circle

What might be initially confusing about this example is that there do not appear to be any additional control points, just the four anchor points. Since the control points can lie directly on the curve, the anchor points serve double duty as control points—remember, it's all *really* just a bunch of coordinate values. There are two aspects of the last sketch I'd like to clarify, the function call curveTightness(-.7) and the point order in the curve() calls. The curveTightness() function controls how the spline curve algorithm is calculated between anchor points. Try changing this argument value and rerunning the sketch—the effect can be dramatic. Figure 3-5 shows the last sketch using settings -5 (left image) and 5. There are some fun things you can do with curveTightness() such as simulating organic motion. To see an example of this, check out: http://processing.org/learning/topics/softbody.html.

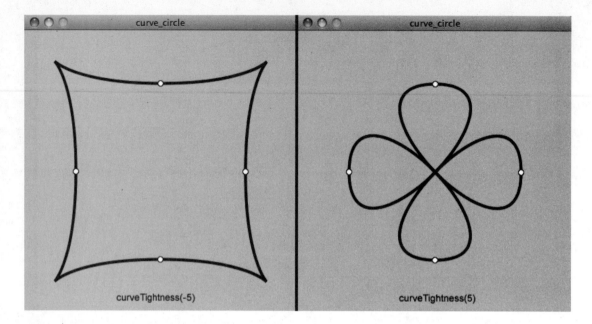

Figure 3-5. curveTightness extremes

One of the challenges of working with spline curves in Processing is specifying the order of points to use with them. Using Processing's `curve()` function, the first and last point arguments in the call can be considered control points for the two inner points. Next is a generalized point ordering approach for using this function, for both open and closed curves. (Please note that I specified four points (pt0, pt1, pt2, pt3) in the example, but any number of points can be used and will follow the same order.)

Generally, for an open curve between (and including) two terminal vertices, the first two point arguments (at the first vertex) will be the same, as will the last two (at the second vertex), shown next.

```
curve(pt0.x, pt0.y, pt0.x, pt0.y, pt1.x, pt1.y, pt2.x, pt2.y);
curve(pt0.x, pt0.y, pt1.x, pt1.y, pt2.x, pt2.y, pt3.x, pt3.y);
curve(pt1.x, pt1.y, pt2.x, pt2.y, pt3.x, pt3.y, pt3.x, pt3.y);
```

For a closed curve, the first point argument will be the last point (in this case pt3), while the last point argument in the closed curve will be the second point (pt1), as follows:

```
curve(pt3.x, pt3.y, pt0.x, pt0.y, pt1.x, pt1.y, pt2.x, pt2.y);
curve(pt0.x, pt0.y, pt1.x, pt1.y, pt2.x, pt2.y, pt3.x, pt3.y);
curve(pt1.x, pt1.y, pt2.x, pt2.y, pt3.x, pt3.y, pt0.x , pt0.y);
curve(pt2.x, pt2.y, pt3x, pt3.y, pt0.x , pt0.y, pt1.x, pt1.y);
```

The curveVertex() command is simpler to use than curve(), as you mostly just need to deal with the terminal points. For example, next are the last two curve() curve snippets implemented using curveVertex(). (Please note that for convenience I've structured these using a vecs[] array, for the curve coordinates.)

For an open curve

```
beginShape();
curveVertex(vecs[0].x, vecs [0].y);
for (int i=0; i<vecs.length; i++){
  curveVertex(vecs[i].x, vecs[i].y);
}
curveVertex(vecs[vecs.length-1].x, vecs[vecs.length-1].y);
endShape();
```

For a closed curve

```
beginShape();
curveVertex(vecs[vecs.length-1].x, vecs[vecs.length-1].y);
for (int i=0; i<vecs.length; i++){
  curveVertex(vecs[i].x, vecs[i].y);
}
curveVertex(vecs[0].x, vecs[0].y);
curveVertex(vecs[1].x, vecs[1].y);
endShape();
```

In the next example, shown in Figure 3-6, I'll create a spiral using curveVertex(); a description follows the code.

```
/**
 * curveVertex() spiral
 * By Ira Greenberg <br />
 * The Essential Guide to Processing for Flash Developers
 * Friends of ED, 2009
 */

int ptCount = 4;
int spiralRots = 32;
float spiralTightness = .979;
```

```
PVector[] vecs = new PVector[ptCount*spiralRots];

void setup(){
  size(400, 400);
  smooth();
  noFill();
  strokeWeight(2);
  curveTightness(-.7);
  translate(width/2, height/2);
  calcCurve(200);
  drawCurve();
  drawVecs();
}

void calcCurve(float radius){
  float px=0, py=0, theta=0;
  for (int i=0; i<vecs.length; i++){
    px = cos(theta)*radius;
    py = sin(theta)*radius;
    vecs[i] = new PVector(px, py);
    theta+=TWO_PI/ptCount;
    // slowly shrink radius to create spiral
    radius *= spiralTightness;
  }
}

void drawCurve(){
  beginShape();
  for (int i=0; i<vecs.length; i++){
    curveVertex(vecs[i].x, vecs[i].y);
  }
  endShape();
}
```

```
void drawVecs(){
  fill(255);
  strokeWeight(1);
  for (int i=1; i<vecs.length; i++){
    ellipse(vecs[i].x, vecs[i].y, 4, 4);
  }
}
```

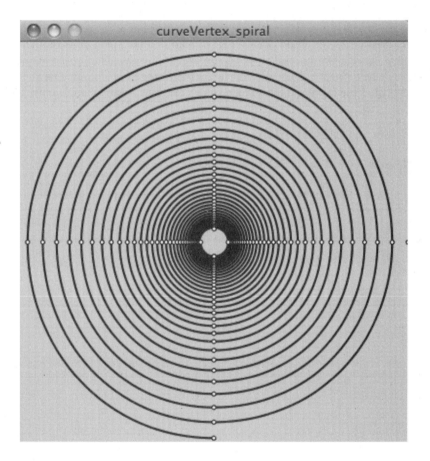

Figure 3-6. curveVertex() spiral

To calculate the spiral, I used the trig functions to generate the rotational positions and then simply decremented the radius value over time. The actual curveVertex() code that draws the spiral is

```
void drawCurve(){
  beginShape();
  for (int i=0; i<vecs.length; i++){
    curveVertex(vecs[i].x, vecs[i].y);
  }
  endShape();
}
```

I'm sure you'll agree that the two-argument curveVertex() function is far more elegant than the eight-argument curve() alternative discussed earlier. Please note that the spiral doesn't actually begin at the first vertex or end at the last vertex specified in the curveVertex() calls; this, you'll remember, would have required doubling up the calls for the first and last vertices arguments, which would have also distorted the beginning and ending curves of the spiral. I suggest, as an exercise, adding these vertex calls in to see the effect on the curve.

Next I'll show you how to animate the spiral.

Adding Motion

In ActionScript, to perform the simplest programmatic animation you might do something like this (within a frame script):

```
// AS 3 frame script animation example
addEventListener(Event.ENTER_FRAME, handleEnterFrame);

function handleEnterFrame(e:Event){
    // stuff to animate here
}
```

In Processing, animation is created simply by including the draw() function in your sketch.

```
void draw(){
  // stuff to animate here
}
```

Behind the scenes, of course, it's a bit more complicated. Processing uses a Java thread (technically "thread of execution") to create animation. Threads allow programs to do more than one thing at a time, such as listen for mouse and keyboard events while still performing standard program functions. In terms of animation, threads control the rate at which the sketch window is updated; by default in Processing this is 60 times per second. In Java you need to explicitly create threads and turn them on, but in Processing this is taken care of for you, behind the scenes—just include draw() and you're good to go. The next example spins the spiral from the previous sketch; to see it, make the following two modifications to the previous spiral sketch:

1. Replace the existing setup() function with this revised one.

```
void setup(){
    size(400, 400);
    smooth();
    strokeWeight(2);
    curveTightness(-.7);
}
```

2. Add this draw() function, beneath the setup() function.

```
void draw(){
    background(200);
    noFill();
    translate(width/2, height/2);
    rotate(-frameCount*PI/180);
    calcCurve(200);
    drawCurve();
    drawVecs();
}
```

That's it. Now your spiral should spin, and as it does, "you are getting sleepy…"

Notice that I moved translate(width/2, height/2); into the draw() function. I needed to do this because with each frame cycle in draw() the transformation state (the internal transformation matrix) is reset. Thus, if I only call translate() in setup, it's reset to the default state in draw() and the spiral rotates around the origin (0,0). (If you don't believe me, try moving the translate() call from draw() to setup() and rerunning the sketch.)

> By default, Processing tries to update the sketch 60 frames per second (fps). Of course, there is some variation in this rate, which, as with Flash, can slow down considerably when the system is heavily taxed. You can change the frame rate with the command frameRate(fps). You can also get the frame rate with the Processing system variable frameRate. If you want to change the frame rate, it should be set in setup().

Besides relocating the translate(width/2, height/2); call, I added the line rotate(-frameCount*PI/180);. Like translate(), rotate() updates the transformation matrix, which gets reset each frame cycle in draw(). So to continuously spin something, you need to keep updating the argument value passed to rotate(). rotate() spins the entire contents of the sketch window in relation to the origin, regardless of where it has been translated. In the example, I translate the origin to the center of the sketch window, so the spiral appears to rotate around the center of the window, even though it's technically still spinning around (0,0). The order of the transformations matters, so if you reverse the order of the rotate() and translate() calls, you'll get a very different result. I strongly encourage you to try this.

Spinning the spiral is nice, but there are a lot more interesting aesthetic modifications we can make to the sketch, such as drawing the spiral over time and adding varying stroke weight and line value. Here's a more interesting spinning spiral example, shown in Figure 3-7:

```
/**
 * spiral spin enhanced
 * By Ira Greenberg <br />
 * The Essential Guide to Processing for Flash Developers
 * Friends of ED, 2009
 */


// points per rotation
int ptCount = 12;
// number of rotations
int spiralRots = 6;
// controls spiral coiling
float spiralTightness = .955;

PVector[] vecs = new PVector[ptCount*spiralRots];
float[] strokeCols = new float[ptCount*spiralRots];
float[] strokeWts = new float[ptCount*spiralRots];
// inital stroke weight of line
float startWt = 40.0;
// used to draw spiral over time
float drawRate = 0.0;
// actual speed to draw spiral (.1 - 2)
float drawSpeed = .75;

void setup(){
  size(400, 400);
```

```
  smooth();
  strokeWeight(startWt);
  // controls curvature of individual segments
  curveTightness(-.1);
  // generate sprial geometry.
  calcCurve(320);
}

void draw(){
  noStroke();
  fill(250, 30);
  rect(-1, -1, width, height);
  translate(width/2, height/2);
  rotate(frameCount*PI/150);
  drawCurve(drawSpeed);
  // drawVecs();
}

void calcCurve(float radius){
  float px=0, py=0, theta=0;
  // for colors and weights
  float colRatio = 255.0/(strokeCols.length-10);
  float wtRatio = startWt/(strokeWts.length-25);
  for (int i=0; i<vecs.length; i++){
    // draw spiral
    px = cos(theta)*radius;
    py = sin(theta)*radius;
    vecs[i] = new PVector(px, py);
    theta+=TWO_PI/ptCount;
    // slowly shrink radius to create spiral
    radius *= spiralTightness;
    // fill color and weight arrays
```

```
    strokeCols[i] = colRatio*i;
    strokeWts[i] = startWt-wtRatio*i;
  }
}


void drawCurve(float rate){
  for (int i=0; i<drawRate; i++){
    stroke(max(0,strokeCols[i]));
    strokeWeight(max(0,strokeWts[i]));
    curve(vecs[i].x, vecs[i].y, vecs[i+1].x, vecs[i+1].y, vecs[i+2].x, vecs[i+2].y, ⏎
          vecs[i+3].x, vecs[i+3].y);
  }
  // draw spiral over time
  if (drawRate<vecs.length-4){
    drawRate+=min(2, rate);
  }
}


void drawVecs(){
  fill(255);
  strokeWeight(1);
  for (int i=1; i<vecs.length; i++){
    ellipse(vecs[i].x, vecs[i].y, 4, 4);
  }
}
```

Figure 3-7. Spiral spin enhanced

In this example, I used curve() instead of curveVertex(). I did this because I wanted to set different rendering styles for each curve segment (stroke weights and stroke colors). Since the curveVertex() calls are nested between beginShape()/endShape() and I'm using the default JAVA2D renderer, the points are all recorded after beginShape(), and then drawn to the screen after endShape() is called—with the last style calls setting the rendering state. In other words, putting stroke(strokeCols[i]) in a for loop will not allow you to draw different color curve segments each iteration of the loop—the last stroke color specified in the loop will be what's used, after the endShape() call, for all the curve segments.

Notice also in the last example that I left calcCurve(320) in setup(), since it needs to run only once, while I put drawCurve(drawSpeed) into draw(), which will run (approx) 60 fps. In the drawCurve(float rate) function,

```
void drawCurve(float rate){
  for (int i=0; i<drawRate; i++){
    stroke(max(0,strokeCols[i]));
```

```
    strokeWeight(max(0,strokeWts[i]));
    curve(vecs[i].x, vecs[i].y, vecs[i+1].x, vecs[i+1].y, vecs[i+2].x, vecs[i+2].y, ⏎
        vecs[i+3].x, vecs[i+3].y);
  }
  // draw spiral over time
  if (drawRate<vecs.length-4){
    drawRate+=min(2, rate);
  }
}
```

I used an if statement to control the sentinel value (i<drawRate) in the for loop. This allowed the spiral to be drawn progressively. Screen updates don't happen during a for loop, only after it terminates. By slowly incrementing the sentinel limit in the loop, I allowed the spiral growth to be displayed incrementally. Also notice the max(0, strokeCols[i]) and min(2, rate) calls in the function. These math functions return the max value and min values, respectively, between the two arguments; they work similarly to ActionScript's static methods by the same name. Processing's min() and max(),(), along with constrain(), ensure program values stay within safe ranges.

There is obviously a LOT more to be said about motion, which I'll discuss throughout the rest of the book. Yet, as demonstrated, Processing makes it incredibly simple to include motion in your sketches, which I'm sure you'll agree is wonderful!

Imaging

In addition to drawing functions, Processing has great imaging capabilities. This is a rich part of the API, with a bunch of cool features. Here, I'll demonstrate the basic loading and saving of images and how to access and manipulate image pixel data.

> *Images must be within the **data** directory of your current sketch to be accessed by Processing. You can add images to the data directory through the "**Add File…**" command under the **Sketch** menu or by simply copying images directly to the **data** directory of your current sketch. If no **data** directory exists you can create one as you would any directory on your system. If you use **Add File…** and no data directory exists, one will be created automatically for you.*

Loading Images

External image data can be loaded into Processing in a very high-level way. ActionScript exposes a bit more of the loading process, while also making use of loading events to manage issues such as latency. Latency is a delay that can occur while the program is busy doing something. For example, loading an image takes time, and trying to access information about the image data (such as the image width) before

```
// ActionScript image loading example (using a frame script)
function loadImg(url:String):void {
  var imgLoader:Loader = new Loader();
  imgLoader.contentLoaderInfo.addEventListener(ProgressEvent.PROGRESS, handleProgress );
  imgLoader.contentLoaderInfo.addEventListener(Event.COMPLETE, handleLoad );
  imgLoader.load(new URLRequest(url));
}


// start load image
loadImg("image1.jpg");


// image loading events
function handleLoad(e:Event):void {
  // Display Image
  e.target.removeEventListener( Event.COMPLETE, handleLoad);
  e.target.removeEventListener( ProgressEvent.PROGRESS, handleProgress );
  var img:DisplayObject = LoaderInfo(e.target).loader.content as DisplayObject;
  addChild(img);
}


function handleProgress(e:ProgressEvent):void {
  // get info about loading image
  trace(e.bytesLoaded);
}
```

ActionScript's eventListeners allow you to do things such as track the actual memory of the data as it loads (handleProgress() function) and know when all the data has fully loaded (handleLoad() function).

Processing includes two functions (really more like approaches) for loading images. The loadImage() function loads images using the sketch's main thread (synchronously), while the requestImage() function loads images using its own thread (asynchronously). The benefits of using loadImage() are that it's a little simpler, and (more importantly) it internally ensures the image is fully loaded in memory before it can be drawn to the screen; the negative is that it can temporarily freeze the running sketch (especially with large and/or multiple images). Next is a very simple loadImage() example that loads an image into Processing and then draws it to the sketch window, shown in Figure 3-8.

```
/**
 * Image loading using  loadImage()
 * drawing handled by background()
 * Requires: trinity.jpg image
 * in data directory.
 * By Ira Greenberg <br />
 * The Essential Guide to Processing for Flash Developers
 * Friends of ED, 2009
 */
size(600, 450);
PImage img = loadImage("trinity.jpg");
background(img);
```

Figure 3-8. Simple image loading

The line PImage img = loadImage("trinity.jpg"); loads the image and assigns it to the img variable, of type PImage. PImage is a Processing class for working with images/pixel data. The line background(img); handles the actual drawing of the image to the screen. One of the limitations of drawing the image using background() is that the image and sketch must be the same exact size. Try changing the arguments in the size(600, 450) call in the sketch and rerunning it; you should get an error. A more flexible way to draw the image to the screen is to use Processing's image() function, shown next:

```
/**
 * Image loading using  loadImage()
 * drawing handled by image()
 * Requires: trinity.jpg image
 * in data directory.
 * By Ira Greenberg <br />
 * The Essential Guide to Processing for Flash Developers
 * Friends of ED, 2009
 */
size(600, 450);
PImage img = loadImage("trinity.jpg");
image(img, 0, 0);
```

Processing includes two versions of the image() function:

```
image(img, x, y)
image(img, x, y, width, height)
```

Using the second version, you can do some visually interesting things. In the next sketch I'll create an image fan, shown in Figure 3-9, using the translate() and rotate() functions discussed earlier in the chapter. Remember, the **trinity.jpg** image needs to be in the sketch's data directory:

```
/**
 * Image fan()
 * Requires: trinity.jpg image
 * in data directory.
 * By Ira Greenberg <br />
 * The Essential Guide to Processing for Flash Developers
 * Friends of ED, 2009
 */
```

```
PImage img;

void setup(){
  size(600, 450);
  background(50);
  img = loadImage("trinity.jpg");
  translate(width/2, height/2);
  for (int i=1; i<500; i++){
    rotate(PI/180*i);
    image(img, 0, 0, width/(i*.15), height/(i*.15));
  }
}
```

Figure 3-9. Image fan

As I mentioned earlier, loading images using loadImage() ensures that images are properly loaded in memory before they can be drawn to the screen. The downside of this approach is performance, which I'll demonstrate in the next sketch.

The Processing API reference states

> *"In most cases, load all images in setup() to preload them at the start of the program. Loading images inside draw() will reduce the speed of a program."*

That being said, to help illustrate the performance differences between using loadImage() vs. requestImage(), I am going to both load and draw an image in the draw() function, while simultaneously checking the frameRate of the sketch. (Please note, you'll likely get different output values than I do, but the overall performance pattern should be similar.)

Here's the first sketch to run:

```
/**
 * loadImage() vs. requestImage()
 * Requires: trinity.jpg image
 * in data directory.
 * By Ira Greenberg <br />
 * The Essential Guide to Processing for Flash Developers
 * Friends of ED, 2009
 */


PImage img;

void setup(){
  size(600, 450);
  background(50);
}


void draw(){
  img = loadImage("trinity.jpg");
  println(frameRate);
}
```

The sketch continuously outputs the frame rate of the sketch. Here are lines 20–30 output by the println() statement:

12.624021

12.745854

12.881965

12.983391

13.0666485

13.169605

13.232297

13.321097

13.36403

13.425154

13.211523

Next, I changed the line

img = loadImage("trinity.jpg");

to

img = **requestImage**("trinity.jpg");

and reran the sketch. Lines 20–30 now output

52.222046

53.260796

52.369698

54.416576

55.076572

55.403557

55.94001

56.181335

56.8324

55.231792

57.83209

Because requestImage() runs in its own thread, it doesn't impact the performance of the running sketch nearly as much as loadImage(). When loading only one image, though, there is no advantage to using requestImage(). In fact, there is a disadvantage, as you need to perform your own check to ensure all the image data is loaded before you can begin drawing the image. For example, the following sketch should generate an error, since the draw() function (using the main thread) will attempt to draw the image before it is completely loaded, by its own thread.

```
// generates an error
PImage img;

void setup(){
  size(600, 450);
// requires trinity.jpg in data directory
  img = requestImage("trinity.jpg");
}

void draw(){
  image(img, 0, 0);
}
```

The error generated is: **IllegalArgumentException: Width (0) and height (0) cannot be <= 0.** To fix this, you need to check for the loaded image's dimension in the draw function, to ensure the data is fully loaded. Here's a corrected version of the last sketch:

```
/**
 * requestImage() example
 * Requires: trinity.jpg
 * in the data directory.
 * By Ira Greenberg <br />
 * The Essential Guide to Processing for Flash Developers
 * Friends of ED, 2009
 */

PImage img;

void setup(){
  size(600, 450);
```

```
  img = requestImage("trinity.jpg");
}


void draw(){
  if (img.width > 0){
    image(img, 0, 0);
  }
}
```

Notice the conditional check in draw(). The PImage class includes a number of public properties, including width and height. The if statement checks if the width is greater than 0, meaning the image has fully loaded and can be safely drawn. (Please note that it is possible for the width property to also return a -1, which means there was a problem loading the image.) Where requestImage() becomes really useful is when you need to load a bunch of images and you don't want your sketch to freeze up, waiting for the loading to finish. The next example, shown in Figure 3-10, loads ten large images, while a simple preloader animation runs. (I assume you are familiar with preloaders, made famous by Flash developers.)

```
/**
 * requestImage() with preloader animation
 * Requires: 10 images named dublin0.jpg...
 * dublin9.jpg in the sketch data directory.
 * By Ira Greenberg <br />
 * The Essential Guide to Processing for Flash Developers
 * Friends of ED, 2009
 */


int imgCount = 10;
PImage[] imgs = new PImage[imgCount];
float imgW;


// for loading animation
float loaderX, loaderY, theta;


void setup(){
  size(800, 60);
  smooth();
```

```
  imgW = width/imgCount;

  // load images asynchronously
  for (int i=0; i<imgCount; i++){
    imgs[i] = requestImage("dublin"+i+".jpg");
  }
}

void draw(){
  background(0);

  // when all images are loaded draw them to the screen
  if (checkLoadStates()){
    drawImages();
  }
  else {
    // only run the preloader if images aren't loaded
    runLoaderAni();
  }
}

void drawImages(){
  for (int i=0; i<imgs.length; i++){
    image(imgs[i], width/10*i, 0, imgW, height);
  }
}

// loading animation
void runLoaderAni(){
  // only run when images are loading
  if (!checkLoadStates()){
    ellipse(loaderX, loaderY, 10, 10);
    loaderX += 2;
    loaderY= height/2+sin(theta)*(height/2.5);
```

```
    theta += PI/22;
    // reposition ellipse if it goes off the screen
    if (loaderX>width+5){
      loaderX = -5;
    }
  }
}


/* return true when all images are loaded
 - no zero-width or failed images left in array */
boolean checkLoadStates(){
  for (int i=0; i<imgs.length; i++){
    if (imgs[i].width <= 0){
      return false;
    }
  }
  return true;
}
```

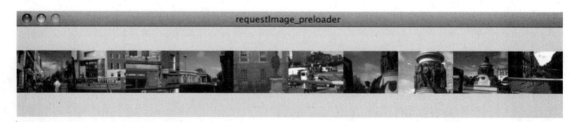

Figure 3-10. requestImage() with preloader

This last example was a bit long, although most of the code should be familiar. Processing doesn't come with any pre-built preloader functionality, nor does it expose image loading progress data, the way ActionScript does using something like

```
// ActionScript image loading progress code
imgLoader.contentLoaderInfo.addEventListener(ProgressEvent.PROGRESS, handleProgress);


function handleProgress(e:ProgressEvent):void {
        // get info about loading image
```

```
      trace("total bytes = " + e.bytesTotal);
      trace("bytes loaded = " + e.bytesLoaded);
      trace("percent loaded = " + e.bytesLoaded/e.bytesTotal*100);
}
```

My homespun preloading code used the checkLoadStates() function, which checked if any of the image widths were less than or equal to zero; it they were, the function returned false and the program kept running the preloader. When all the images are fully loaded—their widths evaluating to greater than zero— the checkLoadStates() function returned true, stopping the runLoaderAni() function and calling the drawImages() function. Notice also in the drawImages() function that I resized the ten images to evenly fill the sketch. Next, I'll discuss briefly what you can actually do now that you've got your image in Processing (other than look at it admiringly).

Pixels

Images on a computer screen are just a collection of color values. I realize that to experienced coders this isn't exactly big news. Earlier in the chapter, I discussed how color values are stored in Processing as packed 32-bit integers. Thus, one way to think of a loaded image in Processing is to think of it as a large collection of integer values. Processing includes two arrays for storing all these integers, and both of them are named pixels; one is a property declared in the PImage class that references all the pixel values in a PImage object, and the other is a global variable that references all the pixels in the sketch window.

Processing's approach to grabbing pixels is quite a bit simpler than ActionScript's, which relies on a series of classes. For example, to load an image in ActionScript and then duplicate its pixels, you could do something like this (using a frame script):

```
// actionscript load and pixels copy (clone) example
var url:String = "malahide.jpg";
startLoad();

function startLoad():void {
        var loader:Loader = new Loader();
        loader.contentLoaderInfo.addEventListener(Event.COMPLETE, completeHandler);
        var request:URLRequest = new URLRequest(url);
        loader.load(request);
        addChild(loader);
}

function completeHandler(event:Event):void {
        var img1:Bitmap = Bitmap(event.target.loader.content);
```

```
        var img2:Bitmap = new Bitmap(img1.bitmapData.clone());
        addChild(img2);
        img2.x+=img1.width;
}
```

In Processing, getting at the actual pixels in the sketch window, or within an image, is more direct (less abstract). For example, the next sketch loads and draws an image, then grabs the pixels of the entire sketch window and boosts the saturation of a third of the pixels; the sketch window is then updated with the edited pixels. The sketch, shown in Figure 3-11, includes a couple of new functions, which I'll discuss following the code.

```
/**
 * Boost saturation of screen pixels
 * Requires: malahide.jpg
 * in the data directory.
 * By Ira Greenberg <br />
 * The Essential Guide to Processing for Flash Developers
 * Friends of ED, 2009
 */


PImage img;

void setup(){
  size(600, 450);
  img = loadImage("malahide.jpg");
  image(img, 0, 0);
  // initialize pixels[] based on sketch window
  loadPixels();
  // boost saturation
  remapSaturation(2);
  // update value of sketch window from pixels[]
  updatePixels();
}


void  remapSaturation(float factor){
  colorMode(HSB, 255);
```

```
/* remap saturation of top third
 of sketch window pixels */
for (int i=0; i<pixels.length/3; i++){
  // extract saturation of ech pixel
  float sat = saturation(pixels[i]);
 // boost saturation
  sat *= factor;

  // rebuild pixel
  pixels[i] = color(hue(pixels[i]), sat, brightness(pixels[i]));
 }
}
```

Figure 3-11. Global pixels array variable example

Notice in the last example the command `loadPixels1()`. This call generates the `pixels` array of the entire sketch window. You can think of the command as taking a screen-shot of the sketch window and then storing all the pixel values (in a `pixels` array). After `loadPixels1()`, I call my custom `remapSaturation()` function, which initially changes the color mode of Processing from the default RGB format to HSB.

> *HSB stands for Hue, Saturation, and Brightness. This is another model for working with digital color. In addition to specifying the color mode, you can also set the range of value you want to use for the individual mode components. By passing a single 255 argument, each of the HSB color components will be mapped to 255 values. You can actually use any float or integer value as an argument for each component. And you can pass one, three, or four arguments (the fourth being for alpha, in either mode). For example, colorMode(HSB, 360, 1.0, 1.0, 1.0), colorMode(RGB, 100, 100, 50), and even colorMode(HSB, 200, 100, 50, 1.0) are all perfectly legal. In the last call, the range for Hue would be 0–200, for Saturation 0–100, for Brightness 0–50, and for alpha 0–1.0.*

After setting the color mode, I extracted the saturation of one-third of the pixels in the array. (Notice the sentinel value in the `for` loop: `i<pixels.length/3.`) Processing has seven functions for extracting individual color component values. In an earlier example in the chapter, I demonstrated the functions `red()`, `green()`, and `blue()()` and mentioned `alpha().()`. There are also component extraction functions for `hue()`, `brightness()`, and `saturation().()`.

Once I had retrieved the saturation values, I just increased them with the `factor` parameter value passed into the function—in this case 2. Finally, I updated the pixel values in the array with the new (more saturated) colors.

One thing I still haven't explained is how the `pixels` array stores the `int` values. Perhaps surprisingly, it doesn't store the values in a table structure (two-dimensional array), but rather uses a single array, storing pixel values in the order left-to-right, then working down the entire sketch window; that's why I was able to just change the saturation of the top third of the image using the `i<pixels.length/3` sentinel value. The last part of the sketch is the `updatePixels();` call, which reloads the more saturated `pixels` array and updates the screen.

Next, let's look at the `PImage pixels` array property. It works quite similarly to the sketch `pixels` global array variable, except you need to follow OOP syntax. The next example, shown in Figure 3-12, swaps pixels between images when the mouse is pressed. (This sketch requires images **dublin0.jpg** and **dublin1.jpg**, installed in the sketch's data directory.)

```
/**
 * PImage.pixels
 * Requires: dublin0.jpg & dublin1.jpg
 * in the data directory.
 * By Ira Greenberg <br />
 * The Essential Guide to Processing for Flash Developers
```

```
 * Friends of ED, 2009
 */
int imgCount = 2;
PImage[] imgs = new PImage[imgCount];
float sclFactor;

void setup(){
  size(600, 225);
  for (int i=0; i<imgCount; i++){
    // load images
    imgs[i] = loadImage("dublin"+i+".jpg");
  }
}

void draw(){
  for (int i=0; i<imgCount; i++){
    // scale image widths to 1/2 sketch window width
    sclFactor = width/float(imgCount)/imgs[i].width;
    // draw images
    image(imgs[i], width/float(imgCount)*i, 0, imgs[i].width*sclFactor,
          imgs[i].height*sclFactor);
  }
}

void mousePressed(){
  /* on mouse press toggles
   images left and right */
  // load pixels to make available
  imgs[0].loadPixels();
  imgs[1].loadPixels();

  // swap pixels
  color[] pxls0 = imgs[0].pixels;
  imgs[0].pixels = imgs[1].pixels;
```

```
imgs[1].pixels = pxls0;

// update sketch window
imgs[0].updatePixels();
imgs[1].updatePixels();
}
```

Figure 3-12. PImage.pixels property array example

The only new code in the example is in the mousePress() function, which is one of Processing's built-in event functions. Each time the mouse is pressed, the images swap their pixels. Notice I still needed to call loadPixels() and updatePixels(),(), but now as PImage methods (e.g., imgs[0].loadPixels()), as opposed to global function calls like in the previous example.

Events

Events are easy in Processing! (I guess I should probably say a bit more than that.) In ActionScript, a mouse press event can be handled like this (using a frame script):

```
// actionscript frame script, mouse down event
stage.addEventListener(MouseEvent.MOUSE_DOWN, handleMouseDown);


function handleMouseDown(me:MouseEvent) {
  // do stuff when the mouse is pressed
}
```

In Processing, as I illustrated earlier, you just need to include the mousePressed function:

```
void mousePressed(){
  // do stuff when the mouse is pressed
}
```

Well, you actually need to do one more thing—you need to include the draw() function in your sketch; without draw()() no events will be detected. Internally, Java uses a system quite similar to ActionScript's with a listening/broadcasting system, but Processing encapsulates it within very high-level, simplified function calls. In addition to mousePressed(), Processing includes mouseReleased(), mouseMoved(), mouseClicked(),(), and mouseDragged() events, and each works similarly to mousePressed(). The difference between mousePressed() and mouseClicked() is that the former registers an event when the mouse is pressed, and the latter requires a mouse press and release. mouseMoved() is invoked when the mouse is moved, but not pressed, while mouseDragged() requires the mouse to be pressed while moved. Next is an events example, shown in Figure 3-13, that demonstrates Processing's different mouse events (Warning: lots of code ahead).

```
/**
 * Mouse events
 * Requires: IGButton, RoundedRect classes
 * By Ira Greenberg <br />
 * The Essential Guide to Processing for Flash Developers
 * Friends of ED, 2009
 */
```

```
// declare custom buttons
int btnCount = 4;
IGButton[] btns = new IGButton[btnCount];

void setup(){
  size(400, 375);
  noStroke();
  smooth();
  int w = 150, h = 65, x=int(width*.25-w/2), y=int(height*.25-h/2);
  btns[0] = new IGButton("Press", x, y, w, h, color(50, 50, 85), 0, 2);
  w = 100;
  h = 100;
  x=int(width*.75-w/2);
  y=int(height*.25-h/2);
  btns[1] = new IGButton("Click", x, y, w, h, color(50, 90, 25), 1, 50);
  w = 100;
  h = 100;
  x=int(width*.25-w/2);
  y=int(height*.75-h/2);
  btns[2] = new IGButton("Move", x, y, w, h, color(60, 20, 60), 3, 12);
  w = 150;
  h = 65;
  x=int(width*.75-w/2);
  y=int(height*.75-h/2);
  btns[3] = new IGButton("Drag", x, y, w, h, color(80, 50, 10), 2, 28);
}

void draw(){
  background(100);
  for (int i=0;i<btnCount; i++){
    btns[i].create();
  }
}
```

```
// Begin Processing mouse events
void mousePressed(){
  if (btns[0].isOver(mouseX, mouseY)){
    btns[0].changeSize(-20, -20);
  }
}

void mouseReleased(){
  btns[0].reset();
  btns[2].reset();
  btns[3].reset();
}

void mouseClicked(){
  if (btns[1].isOver(mouseX, mouseY)){
    btns[1].reset();
    // make button bouncy
    //params are for dist and rate
    btns[1].setJitter(25, PI/15.0);
  }
}

void mouseMoved(){
  // set general hover states
  for (int i=0;i<4; i++){
    if (i!=2){
      if (btns[i].isOver(mouseX, mouseY)){
        btns[i].setColor(btns[i].hoverC);
      }
      else {
        btns[i].setColor(btns[i].initC);
      }
    }
  }
```

```
  // random color change on movement
  if (btns[2].isOver(mouseX, mouseY)){
    btns[2].setColor(color(random(255), random(255), random(255)));
  }
  else {
    btns[2].setColor(btns[2].initC);
  }
}

void mouseDragged(){
  if (btns[3].isOver(mouseX, mouseY)){
    btns[3].setLoc(mouseX-btns[3].w/2, mouseY-btns[3].h/2);
  }
}

class IGButton {

  // instance properties
  PImage img; // for gradient
  RoundedRect rr; //for mask
  // with some default values
  String label;
  int x, y, initX, initY;
  int w = 150, h = 60, initW, initH;
  color c = 0xff551122, initC;
  color hoverC;
  int border = 1;
  float cornerRadius = 15.0;
  int cornerDetail;
  // for label
  PFont font;

  // for jitter effect
  boolean isJittery = false;
```

```
float jitterTheta = 0.0;
float jitterDist = 25.0;
float jitterRate = PI/15.0;

// default constructor
IGButton(){
  init();
}


IGButton(String label){
  this.label = label;
  init();
}


// constructor
IGButton(String label, int x, int y, int w, int h, color c){
  this.label = label;
  this.x = x;
  this.y = y;
  this.w = w;
  this.h = h;
  this.c = c;
  init();
}


// constructor
IGButton(String label, int x, int y, int w, int h, color c, float cornerRadius){
  this.label = label;
  this.x = x;
  this.y = y;
  this.w = w;
  this.h = h;
  this.c = c;
  this.cornerRadius = cornerRadius;
```

```
    init();
}


// constructor
IGButton(String label, int x, int y, int w, int h, color c, int border, float cornerRadius){
  this.label = label;
  this.x = x;
  this.y = y;
  this.w = w;
  this.h = h;
  this.c = c;
  this.border = border;
  this.cornerRadius = cornerRadius;
  init();
}

void init(){
  img = createImage(w, h, RGB);
  cornerDetail = int(max(5, h*.2));
  // capture original values
  initX = x;
  initY = y;
  initW = w;
  initH = h;

  // color stuff
  initC = c;
  float btnR = red(c)*2;
  float btnG = green(c)*2;
  float btnB = blue(c)*2;
  hoverC = color(btnR, btnG, btnB);

  // label font
  font = loadFont("Helvetica-48.vlw");
```

```
  // for mask
  rr = new RoundedRect(x, y, w, h, cornerRadius, cornerDetail, border);
}


// reinitialize button
void reInit(){
  img = createImage(w, h, RGB);
  // ensure corner detail at least 5
  cornerDetail = int(max(5, h*.2));
  // for mask
  rr = new RoundedRect(x, y, w, h, cornerRadius, cornerDetail, border);
}


// create gradient
void create(){
  float r = red(c);
  float g = green(c);
  float b = blue(c);
  float deltaR = (255-r);
  float deltaG = (255-g);
  float deltaB = (255-b);
  float delta = (deltaR+deltaG+deltaB)/3;
  float theta = 0.0;
  float colRatio = 180.0/img.height;
  for (int i=0; i<img.height; i++){
    float tempR = r + sin(radians(theta))*delta;
    float tempG = g + sin(radians(theta))*delta;
    float tempB = b + sin(radians(theta))*delta;
    for (int j=0; j<img.width; j++){
      img.pixels[img.width*i+j] = color(tempR, tempG, tempB);
    }
    theta += colRatio;
  }
  PImage p = rr.getPImage();
```

```
      img.mask(p);
      image(img, x, y);
      // button outline
      noFill();
      if (border==0){
        noStroke();
      }
      else {
        strokeWeight(border+2);
        stroke(c);
      }

      rr.create();
      // label
      createLabel();
      // initialize jitter effect
      jitter();
  }

  void createLabel(){
    // fill col could be parameterized
    fill(10);
    // text sized based on button size
    textFont(font, w*.15+cornerDetail*.6);
    textAlign(CENTER);
    float ascent = textAscent();
    text(label, x, y + h/2-ascent/2, w, h);
  }

  /* detect mouse over button
   returns true or false */
  boolean isOver(float mx, float my){
    return (mx > x && mx < x+w && my > y && my < y+h);
  }
```

```
// put stuff back the way it started
void reset(){
  x = initX;
  y = initY;
  w = initW;
  h = initH;
  reInit();
}


// starts jitter
void setJitter(){
  isJittery = true;
}


// overloaded method with some params
void setJitter(float jitterDist, float jitterRate){
  isJittery = true;
  this.jitterDist = jitterDist;
  this.jitterRate = jitterRate;
}


// do the actual jitter
void jitter(){
  if (isJittery){
    // slows jitte-could be parameterized
    float damping = .975;
    x = int(initX+cos(jitterTheta)*jitterDist);
    y = int(initY+sin(jitterTheta)*jitterDist);
    w = int(initW+sin(jitterTheta*1.5)*jitterDist);
    h = int(initH+cos(jitterTheta*1.5)*jitterDist);
    jitterTheta+=jitterRate;
    jitterDist*=damping;
    // keep from running continuously
    if (jitterDist<.03){
```

```
        isJittery = false;
        jitterTheta = 0;
      }
     reInit();
   }
}

   void changeSize(int deltaW, int deltaH){
     x -=deltaW/2;
     y -=deltaH/2;
     w += deltaW;
     h += deltaH;
     reInit();
   }

   void setLoc(int mx, int my){
     x = mx;
     y = my;
     reInit();
   }

   void setLabel(String label){
     this.label = label;
   }

   void setColor(color c){
     this.c = c;
   }
}

class RoundedRect{
   // instance properties with default values
   int x, y;
   int w = 100, h = 50;
```

```
float radius = min(25.0, h/2.0);
int detail = 8;
int border = 1;

// default constructor
RoundedRect(){
}

// constructor
RoundedRect(int x, int y, int w, int h, float radius){
  this.x = x;
  this.y = y;
  this.w = w;
  this.h = h;
  // keep corner radius within bounds
  this.radius = min(radius, h/2.0);
}

// constructor
RoundedRect(int x, int y, int w, int h, float radius, int detail, int border){
  this.x = x;
  this.y = y;
  this.w = w;
  this.h = h;
  // keep corner radius within bounds
  this.radius = min(radius, h/2.0);
  this.detail = detail;
  this.border = border;
}

// draw rounded rect
void create(){
  float theta = 0.0;
  float px = 0, py = 0;
```

```
    beginShape();
    // right bottom corner
    for(int i=0; i<detail; i++){
      px = x+w-radius+cos(theta)*radius;
      py = y+h-radius+sin(theta)*radius;
      vertex(px, py);
      theta+=(PI/2)/detail;
    }
    // left bottom corner
    for(int i=0; i<detail; i++){
      px = x+radius+cos(theta)*radius;
      py = y+h-radius+sin(theta)*radius;
      vertex(px, py);
      theta+=(PI/2)/detail;
    }
    // left top corner
    for(int i=0; i<detail; i++){
      px = x+radius+cos(theta)*radius;
      py = y+radius+sin(theta)*radius;
      vertex(px, py);
      theta+=(PI/2)/detail;
    }
    // right top corner
    for(int i=0; i<detail; i++){
      px = x+w-radius+cos(theta)*radius;
      py = y+radius+sin(theta)*radius;
      vertex(px, py);
      theta+=(PI/2)/detail;
    }
    endShape(CLOSE);
  }

  /* return a PImage of the button
   - useful as an image mask */
```

```
PImage getPImage(){
  // create off-screen graphic
  PGraphics pg = createGraphics(w, h, JAVA2D);
  float theta - 0.0;
  float px = 0, py = 0;
  // draw into graphics object
  pg.beginDraw();
  pg.strokeWeight(border);
  pg.smooth();
  pg.beginShape();
  // right bottom corner
  for(int i=0; i<detail; i++){
    px = w-radius+cos(theta)*radius;
    py = h-radius+sin(theta)*radius;
    pg.vertex(px, py);
    theta+=(PI/2)/detail;
  }
  // left bottom corner
  for(int i=0; i<detail; i++){
    px = radius+cos(theta)*radius;
    py = h-radius+sin(theta)*radius;
    pg.vertex(px, py);
    theta+=(PI/2)/detail;
  }
  // left top corner
  for(int i=0; i<detail; i++){
    px = radius+cos(theta)*radius;
    py = radius+sin(theta)*radius;
    pg.vertex(px, py);
    theta+=(PI/2)/detail;
  }
  // right top corner
  for(int i=0; i<detail; i++){
    px = w-radius+cos(theta)*radius;
```

```
        py = radius+sin(theta)*radius;
        pg.vertex(px, py);
        theta+=(PI/2)/detail;
      }
    pg.endShape(CLOSE);
    pg.endDraw();

    return pg;
  }
}
```

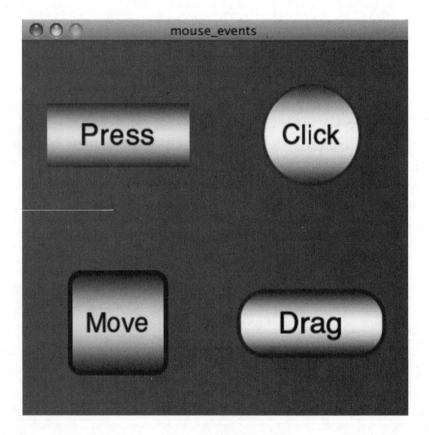

Figure 3-13. Mouse events

The next chapter is dedicated to OOP in Processing, so I thought I'd prime you with some custom classes in this final example. I began the sketch declaring four IGButton buttons, which I instantiated in setup(). The

IGButton constructor includes eight parameters for setting the button's label, position, size, color, border, and corner radius. The last property allows the button to be drawn from a rectangle to an ellipse and any shape in between. As mentioned earlier, Processing's event functions requires the draw() function to be included in the sketch. Within the draw() function I draw the actual buttons to the screen with the lines

```
for (int i=0;i<btnCount; i++){
    btns[i].create();
}
```

Since mouse events in Processing are globally detected (as opposed to ActionScript, where a mouse event can be connected to a specific object), I needed a system to distinguish what specific object was involved in the event. I created an isOver() method in the IGButton class that returns true if the mouse is currently over the object, or false if it is not. The detection is handled simply by checking the mouse coordinates in relation to the individual buttons. I won't say too much about the IGButton and RoundRect classes, as you'll get your OOP fill next chapter. There are a few points worth noting, though.

First of all, the two classes are fairly involved and worth taking your time playing with. I included functionality for drawing to an off-screen graphics object (rather than drawing directly to the screen), in the method PImage getPImage() of the RoundRect class, initiated with the line

```
PGraphics pg = createGraphics(w, h, JAVA2D);
```

Notice in this method that I use Processing's standard drawing functions, preceded with the PGraphics pg object I created. In the RoundRect class I included functionality to allow an image to function as a dynamic mask for another image, handled by the line

```
img.mask(p);
```

Finally, there are a number of good open-source, Processing, graphical-user-interface libraries at your disposal. You can learn more about them here: http://processing.org/reference/libraries/#interface (June 13, 2009, 5:12 EST). Even if you aren't going to use such a library *as is*, you'd still likely want to build off of it —to not reinvent the wheel, *or button*. Again, I definitely encourage you to read through the IGButton and RoundRect classes code, most of which is stuff I covered earlier in the chapter.

Tiny Taste of Typography

There is one other new topic I snuck into the example—typography, specifically the following lines of code in the IGButton class (*please note these lines are not all grouped together in the class*):

```
PFont font;
font = loadFont("Helvetica-48.vlw");
textFont(font, w*.15 + cornerDetail*.6);
```

```
textAlign(CENTER);
float ascent = textAscent();
text(label, x, y + h/2 - ascent/2, w, h);
```

Here, I'll just give you a very brief overview of how typography works in Processing. Later, in the projects section, I'll revisit the topic. PFont is a Processing class for working with typography. Like most of Processing's built-in classes, PFont objects are not instantiated using the *new* keyword. Instead, Processing utilizes two methods for creating fonts that return a PFont object: createFont() and loadFont().().

createFont(name, size) dynamically generates a bitmapped font, based on the font argument and size passed to the function. For the function to work, the machine running the sketch should have the designated font installed. Processing also includes a PFont.list() function that shows the names of the fonts installed on your system. (Please note that this function is not recommended for applets.) To learn more about createFont() and PFont.list(), check out http://processing.org/reference/createFont_.html (June 13, 2009, 5:21 EST) and http://processing.org/reference/PFont_list_.html (June 13, 2009, 5:21 EST).

loadFont(), as demonstrated in the last example, works in partnership with Processing's top menu bar command **Create Font**..., under the **Tools** menu. **Create Font**... pops open a **Create Font** dialog box, shown in Figure 3-14. In addition to the **font** and **size** selections, you can specify anti-aliasing by checking the **smooth** box, as well as including all the characters in the font. Please be aware that the conversion to **.vlw** involves bitmap data, and specifying larger font sizes and selecting all characters can greatly increase the size of your **.vlw** files (and thus negatively impact performance). The benefit of the **Create Font**... approach is that you can select a font installed in your system, and Processing then creates the font in its bitmapped **.vlw** format and writes it to the data directory of the current sketch. (If no data directory is found, one is created automatically.) The benefit of having the installed bitmapped **.vlw** font is that anyone can view your sketch as you intended it to be viewed, regardless of whether they have the actual (vector based) font installed on their system. To read more about loadFont(), check out http://processing.org/reference/loadFont_.html (June 13, 2009, 5:24 EST).

Figure 3-14. Create Font... dialog

Summary

Well, that sums up the primer section of the book. Of course, I didn't cover the Processing API in its entirety, but what I did include should provide a solid framework for creating (or at least starting) most projects in Processing. I hope that by now the consistency of the Processing API is also apparent. This consistency is one of the guiding principles in the overall design of the language, which the development team continues to refine. One of the wonderful benefits of the language design is a quick flattening of Processing's initial learning curve. I personally witness this at the beginning of each semester, as my students are able to get up and running in Processing almost immediately. Of course, once the students begin to write more sophisticated programs, new steep learning curves arise. In the next chapter I'll *class* things up a bit with a discussion on object-oriented programming in Processing.

Chapter 4

Object-Oriented Programming in Processing

Thus far in the book the majority of the code examples have been procedurally structured—relying on only variables and functions. Behind the scenes, through Processing's relationship to Java, Processing is object-oriented through and through. Though it is theoretically possible to avoid utilizing object-oriented syntax and structures when programming in Processing, it wouldn't be an especially sensible way to proceed as you build more sophisticated sketches. That being said, Processing was also not designed for industrial-grade, object-oriented development (though there are ways of using it for that as well). Confused? In this chapter I'll attempt to sort out some of these issues, as I ease you into OOP in Processing. Because of the wide range of readers' coding experiences, I'll take somewhat of a middle path in how I present OOP: I won't include a comprehensive introduction to OOP theory, though I will include some; nor will I go too deeply into advanced OOP concepts (but again I'll cover some of it). My main purpose here is to quickly get you up and coding with OOP in Processing and to also include a comparison between Processing and ActionScript's OOP approaches. For those of you completely new to OOP, it may be helpful to review some preliminary material. *Processing: Creative Coding and Computational Art* includes a comprehensive introduction to OOP in Processing, as do *Processing: A Programming Handbook for Visual Designers and Artists*, by Casey Reas and Ben Fry (MIT Press, 2007) and *Learning Processing: A Beginner's Guide to Programming Images, Animation, and Interaction*, by Daniel Shiffman (Morgan Kaufmann, 2008).

> *Although OOP brings an organizational framework to programming, making large-scale projects easier to manage, it also adds overhead. Thus OOP is not a solution for every type of problem. In fact, some old school programming purists decry programming languages such as Java as being too sluggish. My take on this issue is that with the speed of modern day processors, the relatively low cost of memory, and sophisticated compiling and executing processes, OOP and Java are capable of tackling most (really practically all) programming problems. That said, it is still important to consider how you use computing/memory resources when programming: does a value need to be set once or many times; is the benefit of that nth animated sprite really adding to the overall work; is there a simpler, more efficient way to do something?*

Some OOP Theory

A straightforward way to begin thinking in an object-oriented fashion is to model programming problems similarly to how you model problems in the "real" world. For example, let's say you were interested in hosting a dinner party at your home, you'd need to do certain things in preparation, such as: create a list of guests to invite, design a menu, purchase food and supplies, clean and organize your home, send out invitations, etc. Some of these tasks would be dependent on the results of other tasks—purchasing food only after you had designed the menu. Some of the tasks could be delegated to helpers, who don't even have a big picture view of the overall party planning (e.g., buy party hats and balloons). In addition, the overall plan you devise could be reused for future parties, or even for other non-party type events that require planning. Although these steps may sound simple and obvious, they also illustrate the fundamental principles behind OOP.

It may come as no surprise, even to new OOP coders, that the basic building block in **object**-oriented programming is the object. Objects, also known as instances, are composite data structures that reference a bunch of information. This information is defined for each object in a blueprint-like description called a class. One class can be used to create many objects. Any objects created from a specific class will contain the same internal structure, yet each object is still distinct. For example, if I have a class named Party, it might contain variables, also called properties or fields in OOP parlance, to keep track of a menu, budget, timeline, list of attendees, etc. Each object created based on the Party class could set different values for each of these properties. You can think of properties as internal variables defined within a class. For example, here's a description of the Party class as described thus far:

```
class Party {

    // properties
    String[] menu;
    float budget;
    float timeline;
    String[] attendees;
}
```

To create an object of the Party class, you would write an instantiation statement, as you would in ActionScript, only with slightly different syntax:

```
// create  myParty object of type Party
Party myParty = new Party();
```

Similar to ActionScript, in defining a class you use the **class** keyword, with curly braces defining the block of the class, where all the class members (properties and methods) need to reside. Class names, by convention, begin with a capital letter and adhere to camelback notation, where compound names use a capital letter for the nested names (e.g., ChickenBurrito, MyBigParty, etc.). One immediate difference between classes in Processing and ActionScript is the lack of a package block surrounding the class block, as is required in ActionScript. I'll discuss the package concept as it relates to Processing, when I discuss Processing and Java toward the end of the book.

Again, properties are simply variables declared within a class. In addition to properties, classes can also contain structures for interacting with the properties (e.g., setting the menu, getting the list of attendees, etc.). These structures are called methods and are simply functions defined within the class. Next is the Party class with two methods added:

```
class Party {

  // properties
  String[] menu;
  float budget;
  float time;
  float date;
  String[] attendees;

  // methods
  String[] getMenu(){
    return menu;
  }

  void setMenu(String[] menu){
    this.menu = menu;
  }
}
```

I hope the method syntax looks familiar, since again they are simply Processing functions declared within the class. Notice that I created a get and set method to work with the menu property declared in the class. This is a typical approach in OOP, to utilize get/set or more commonly separate getter and setter methods to both access and set property values. In classic OOP, you don't generally set object property values directly, such as

```
// create  myParty object of type Party
Party myParty = new Party();
```

```
// set menu property directly
myParty.menu = {"fried tofu", "leek soup", "sourdough bread"};
```

Rather you would normally use a setter method:

```
// create  myParty object of type Party
Party myParty = new Party();
```

```
// create String array
String[] menuItems = {"fried tofu", "leek soup", "sourdough bread"};
```

```
// Pass array as argument to setMenu method, which internally updates menu property
myParty.setMenu(menuItems);
```

Notice, similarly to ActionScript, that properties and methods are joined to objects using dot notation (object.property, object.method()).

In ActionScript the general rule is to not reference object properties directly, but instead to use get/set methods. ActionScript provides a way to enforce this through the use of the private access modifier. For example, to declare the menu property private in an .as class, you would write

```
// actionscript property declaration
private var menu:Array;
```

Java follows a similar convention to ActionScript (in actuality, ActionScript, based on ECMAScript, followed Java's lead on this), utilizing access modifiers, including private. Processing's convention is to not use access modifiers, in order to simplify coding and permit direct access to properties (by default assume everything is public in Processing). That being said, my suggestion, especially for experienced coders, is to keep using get and set style methods (even without the private keyword enforcing this behavior), but perhaps not exclusively. One of the main reasons for making properties private and requiring the get/set approach is to avoid strange (or worse) results from either faulty value assignments or internal code dependencies within a class. For example, if one property's value is dependent upon another property (e.g., the width of a detail in a graphic, based on the overall width of the graphic) you could get unexpected results if the width property value was changed directly, without the value of the detail width property also being recalculated. By using a set method, you can ensure these types of dependencies are handled internally within the method. Utilizing get/set methods reinforces good OOP practice and also prepares you for eventually integrating Java in your Processing projects (*better to develop good habits early on*).

> *Since Processing .pde classes are Java inner classes (also referred to as nested classes), the private modifier doesn't work as expected, preventing direct access to properties and methods declared with it. However, working in Processing's Java mode (a mode for advanced users that uses standard Java syntax) the modifiers do work as expected, which I'll discuss in Chapter 8. To learn more about Java nested classes, see:* `http://java.sun.com/docs/books/tutorial/java/javaOO/nested.html`.

Of course, not all methods in a class are simply used for getting or setting property values. Methods also handle other types of processes; for example, a Menu class could include a method that matched up side dishes with a main entrée, or gave seasonal suggestions. That said, classes should (ideally) not handle stuff out of their domain. This is actually a tricky (and important) part of good OOP design. In general, you don't want a class doing too much; they should be focused and logically structured. For example, in our Party class, we wouldn't want (or expect) the class to worry about checking if the date specified for the party is free from other conflicting events, or if the attendees' mailing addresses are up to date, or to know the cost of individual menu ingredients. However, we would expect the Party class to be able to tell us the day and time of the party, how many people will be at the party and the total cost of the menu. To get date conflicts, I'd refer to a calendar; to find attendees' addresses, I would refer to an address book; and to get menu ingredient prices, I'd go to the grocery store. Next is a getAttendeeCount() method you might add to the Party class:

```
// method returns an int value
int getAttendeeCount(){
    return attendees.length;
}
```

Again, when you are thinking about how to organize a program, the decisions should model how similar processes might occur in the real world. Referring back to the calendar, address book and grocery store, one sees that it makes sense that an overall program to help model a party would want a separate class to model each of these other entities, which would all work in conjunction with the Party class. Thus part of the challenge of good OOP design is in coordinating how to work with multiple classes to solve a problem collectively. This is actually a pretty complex issue, which I'll discuss further throughout the book.

Legs Class

Rather than go on and on about OOP theory, with little clever diagrams and lists of bulleted pearls of OOP wisdom—blah, blah, blah—I'd rather dive right into a Processing OOP example, including some visual elements and animation. I'll begin with the simplest approach to incorporating OOP in Processing and expand it in stages from there. Next is stage one of the program **Running Amuck**. The following code is for a **Legs.pde** class:

```
/**
 * Legs class, stage 01
 * Draw legs
 * By Ira Greenberg <br />
 * The Essential Guide to Processing for Flash Developers
 * Friends of ED, 2009
 */


class Legs{
  // instance properties with default values
  float w = 150, ht = 125;
  color col = #77AA22;


 // detail properties
  float detailW = w/6.0, detailHt = ht/8.0;
  float shoeBulge = detailHt*2.0;
  float legGap = w/7.0;


  // default constructor
  Legs(){
  }

// draw legs
  void create(){
    fill(col);
    // local variable ensures foot is within range
    float footWidth = (w - legGap)/2;
    beginShape();
    vertex(- w/2, - ht);
    vertex(- w/2, - ht + detailHt);
    vertex(- w/2 + detailW, - ht + detailHt);
```

```
  // left foot
  vertex(- w/2 + detailW,  0);
  curveVertex(- w/2 + detailW, 0);
  curveVertex(- w/2 + detailW, 0);
  curveVertex(- w/2 + detailW - shoeBulge,  detailHt/2);
  curveVertex(- w/2,  detailHt);
  curveVertex(- w/2,  detailHt);
  vertex(- w/2 + footWidth,  detailHt);
  // end left foot
  vertex(- w/2 + footWidth + legGap/2,  - ht + detailHt);
  vertex(- w/2 + footWidth + legGap/2,  - ht + detailHt);
  // right foot
  vertex(- w/2 + footWidth + legGap,  detailHt);
  vertex(w/2,  detailHt);
  curveVertex(w/2,  detailHt);
  curveVertex(w/2,  detailHt);
  curveVertex(w/2 - detailW + shoeBulge,  detailHt/2);
  curveVertex(w/2 - detailW,  0);
  vertex(w/2 - detailW,  0);
  // end right foot
  vertex(w/2 - detailW,  - ht + detailHt);
  vertex(w/2,  - ht + detailHt);
  vertex(w/2,  - ht);
  endShape(CLOSE);
  }
}
```

To create this example, open a new sketch and name it **running_amuck** (you can actually name it whatever you'd like, but that's what I called it). Next, enter the Legs class code in the text editor. If you read through the Legs class, hopefully the main structure looked familiar (class name, instance properties, constructor and methods). To keep things simple, I only included an empty default Legs() constructor. Technically, I wouldn't need to include an empty constructor if this was going to be the only constructor in the class. A default (empty) constructor is automatically invoked internally when objects are instantiated from a class, without any explicit constructor; this process occurs similarly in ActionScript. However, I'll eventualy add some additional constructors to the class, so I would need to explicitly include the default constructor if I wanted to give users the option of invoking it. (It's not a bad rule of thumb to always include a default constructor.)

> The approach of including multiple constructors, technically called **overloading**, is a common practice in Processing/Java, but is not permitted in ActionScript, where you are only permitted to include one copy of any constructor or method.

To make the empty `Legs` constructor actually useful in the class, I needed to include some default values for the instance properties, defined at the top of the class. Shortly, we'll move these initialization assignment operations to a better place.

The main crux of the `Legs` class that handles the actual drawing is a series of `vertex()` and `curveVertex()` calls. These calls may look confusing and not terribly comprehensible at first glance. I worked these drawing calls out primarily through trial and error, until I got a pair of legs that looked okay based on the default property values. I also wanted the main leg drawing algorithm to be cable of handling different argument values eventually passed in, allowing the legs to be customized. As an artist ("creative" coder) I tend to work out my drawing algorithms using this iterative ("numeric hunt and peck"?) approach. The `vertex()` function creates straight lines between consecutive calls, while the `curveVertex()` function creates smooth curves based on a Catmull-Rom spline. You can read more about Catmull-Rom splines at http://www.mvps.org/directx/articles/catmull/ (November 15, 2009, 19:11). Next, let's draw the default legs.

Directly above the `Legs` class code in the text editor, add the following code and then run the sketch.

```
/**
 * Running Amuck, stage 01
 * By Ira Greenberg <br />
 * The Essential Guide to Processing for Flash Developers
 * Friends of ED, 2009
 */


void setup(){
  size(600, 400);
  background(0);
  noStroke();
  translate(width/2, height/2);
  Legs legs = new Legs();
  legs.create();
}
```

If the sketch ran, you should have seen the image shown in Figure 4-1.

Figure 4-1. Running Amuck stage 01

If it wasn't obvious, instantiating and drawing the legs was handled in setup() by the two lines

```
Legs legs = new Legs();
legs.create();
```

The translate() call positions the legs at the center of the screen. It is common when working in computer graphics to draw geometry centered at the screen origin (0, 0) and then use translation to position the image. In later stages of the **Running Amuck** example, I'll define a separate location (x, y, and z) property to work in conjunction with the translate() call.

Before I improve the sketch, I want to restructure my code a bit. Although Processing allows you to put all your pde class code within the main tab (as long as you include Processing's setup() function), it's actually a much better idea to put each of your classes in their own separate tab. You can create a new tab by selecting the arrow at the top right of the environment (see Figure 4-2). This tab should be named the same name as your class—in this case, **Legs**. Please note that the suffix **.pde** will be appended automatically to **Legs**. Tabs in Processing allow you to conveniently organize your code. In reality, when you create new **.pde** classes in their own tables, such as **Legs.pde**, the code is eventually collapsed (during compilation) into a single main Java class file. The seperate .pde class files get converted into Java inner (also called nested) classes. Java (and Processing) allow an inner class to live within another class file, which is different from ActionScript, where each class is generally created within a separate document. Java inner classes follow slightly different rules from standard (outer) classes, especially with regard to scope (what can be accessed from where). For now, all that's critical to remember is that you can put the .pde class files either in their own tab or within the main tab (but again I recommend the separate tab route). Later in the book, when I discuss Java and Processing, I'll revisit the issue of scope and inner classes. Processing functions may also optionally be put in their own tabs, and these eventually also get collapsed into the main Java file during compilation as methods.

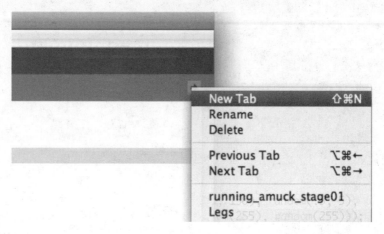

Figure 4-2. New tab arrow

Next, I'll add the ability to customize the sketch allowing for a range of potential legs to be created, as shown in Figure 4-3.

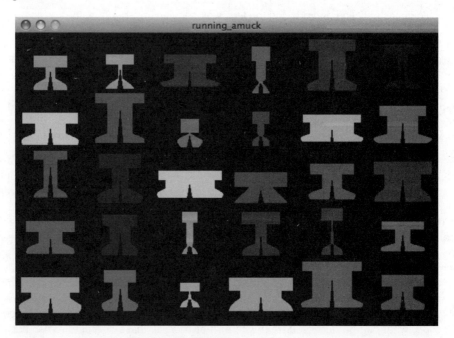

Figure 4-3. Running Amuck output of customized legs

I'll utilize two different strategies to add customization to the Legs class. First, I'll add a second Legs constructor with parameters. Second, I'll add a method to add even more detail.

Add the following overloaded constructor to the Legs class:

```
// standard constructor
  Legs(float w, float ht, color col){
    this.w = w;
    this.ht = ht;
    this.col = col;
    fill(col);
    detailW = w/6.0;
    detailHt = ht/8.0;
    shoeBulge = detailHt*2.0;
    legGap = w/7.0;
  }
```

This would likely be the "standard constructor," as it provides some level of customization while still being relatively simple to use (not too many arguments to pass). To try the new constructor, use the following instantiation call:

```
Legs legs = new Legs(random(20, 300), random(60, 200), ↵
    color(random(255), random(255), random(255)));
```

If you look at the Legs class, you'll notice that there are a number of additional instance properties that are not parameterized using one of the two constructors, and the astute reader may notice that there is now some redundancy in the code, with the same initialization assignment operations at the top of the class and in the standard constructor.

```
detailW = w/6.0;
detailHt = ht/8.0;
shoeBulge = detailHt*2.0;
legGap = w/7.0;
```

In general, in programming you want to eliminate redundant code. To this end I'll create an init() method and replace the redundant initialization code with calls to init(). Here's the revised standard constructor with init() call followed by the new init() method:

```
// standard constructor
  Legs(float w, float ht, color col){
    this.w = w;
    this.ht = ht;
    this.col = col;
    fill(col);
    // initialize
    init();
  }


// initializes advanced property values
  void init(){
    detailW = w/6.0;
    detailHt = ht/8.0;
    shoeBulge = detailHt*2.0;
    legGap = w/7.0;
  }
```

Next, I want to add a new setDetails() method to the Legs class that includes parameters for the instance properties not addressed by either constructor. I chose to do this in place of creating a third constructor that included parameters for all the properties. I think requiring too many paramters in a constructor or method is confusing. (That said, you could, of course, include both a setDetails() method and a third constructor chock-full of parameters.)

```
// set advanced instance property values
  void setDetails(float detailW, float detailHt, float shoeBulge, float legGap){
    this.detailW = detailW;
    this.detailHt = detailHt;
    this.shoeBulge = shoeBulge;
    this.legGap = legGap;
  }
```

To try the setDetails() method, simply invoke it before create(), as in

```
//  Running Amuck, stage 02
Legs legs = new Legs(random(150, 300), random(60, 200), ↵
    color(random(255), random(255), random(255)));
legs.setDetails(30, 50, 55, 75);
legs.create();
```

If you ran the sketch you should have seen some legs with nice fat feet and a wide stance. Obviously, there's plenty more you could do to the drawing algorithm to improve upon the legs, which I think would make an excellent exercise.

Before moving on there is one more method I want to add to the Legs class. Since the detailW and detailH properties are dependent on properties w and ht, I'll add a setSize() method for changing the values of these (as opposed to encouraging direct property assignments) that will ensure the other dependent instance properties are updated. (But remember without being able to specify w and ht as private using an access modifier this can't really be enforced.) Here's the setSize() method to add:

```
// update size and reinitialize
  void setSize(float w, float ht){
    this.w = w;
    this.ht = ht;
    init();
  }
```

Next, I'll expand the Legs class to allow you to animate our headless hero. The first step will be adding some additional properties for the striding calculations. Add the following instance properties at the top of the Legs class:

```
// stride properties
float strideL, strideR, strideRate, strideHt, fallOff, theta;
```

I'll follow the same procedure I used for earlier properties, by handling initialization of default property values in the init() method. Here's the updated init() method, with the new assignment statements in bold:

```
// initializes advanced properties with default values
  void init(){
    detailW = w/6.0;
    detailHt = ht/8.0;
    shoeBulge = detailHt*2.0;
    legGap = w/7.0;
    // init stride values
    strideRate = PI/30;
    strideHt = ht/2;
    fallOff = .9;
  }
```

I used the radian value PI/30 in the strideRate assignment because the striding motion will be calculated using simple trig expressions. If you'd prefer to work in degrees, you can replace the PI/30 value with radians(6). Next, add the following new stride() method to the class:

```
// make the legs run
void stride(){
  strideL = sin(theta)*strideHt;
  strideR = cos(theta)*strideHt;
  theta += strideRate;
}
```

The sine and cosine functions are mathematically out of phase by PI/2 (or 90 degrees). Thus, using them provides a relatively simple way to have a smooth, continuous, and synchronized alternating striding pattern. If you're a bit rusty on your trig, the real trick to using the functions is to keep incrementing the theta value (which needs to be in radians). The strideHt value controls the height of the stride (the amplitude of the curve).

Now that the Legs class can calculate stride values, you need to actually plug these values into the create() method, where the drawing occurs. Next is the updated method, with the new added properties in bold:

```
// draw legs
  void create(){
    fill(col);
    float footWidth = (w - legGap)/2;
    beginShape();
    vertex(- w/2, - ht);
    vertex(- w/2, - ht + detailHt);
    vertex(- w/2 + detailW, - ht + detailHt);
    // left foot
    vertex(- w/2 + detailW,  strideL);
    curveVertex(- w/2 + detailW, strideL);
    curveVertex(- w/2 + detailW, strideL);
    curveVertex(- w/2 + detailW - shoeBulge,  detailHt/2 + strideL);
    curveVertex(- w/2,  detailHt + strideL);
    curveVertex(- w/2,  detailHt + strideL);
    vertex(- w/2 + footWidth,  detailHt + strideL* fallOff);
```

```
    // end left foot
    vertex(- w/2 + footWidth + legGap/2,  - ht + detailHt);
    vertex(- w/2 + footWidth + legGap/2,  - ht + detailHt);
    // right foot
    vertex(- w/2 + footWidth + legGap,  detailHt + strideR* fallOff);
    vertex(w/2,  detailHt + strideR);
    curveVertex(w/2,  detailHt + strideR);
    curveVertex(w/2,  detailHt + strideR);
    curveVertex(w/2 - detailW + shoeBulge,  detailHt/2 + strideR);
    curveVertex(w/2 - detailW,  strideR);
    vertex(w/2 - detailW,  strideR);
    // end right foot
    vertex(w/2 - detailW,  - ht + detailHt);
    vertex(w/2,  - ht + detailHt);
    vertex(w/2,  - ht);
    endShape(CLOSE);
  }
```

Now, let's render the striding legs. To do so, you need to make some changes to the code in the main tab. First, I'll add Processing's draw() method, which will enable animation. I'll leave the legs instantiation and setDetails() calls up in setup(), and put the translate(), legs.create(), and legs.stride() calls down in draw():

```
/**
 * Running Amuck, stage 03

 * By Ira Greenberg <br />
 * The Essential Guide to Processing for Flash Developers
 * Friends of ED, 2009
 */

Legs legs;

void setup(){
  size(600, 400);
  background(0);
```

```
  noStroke();
  legs = new Legs(150, 160, #887733);
  legs.setDetails(30, 50, 55, 75);
}


void draw(){
  size(600, 400);
  background(0);
  noStroke();
  translate(width/2, height/2);
  legs.create();
  legs.stride();
  // saveFrame( "running_amok-###.jpg" );
}
```

If the code executed, you should have seen a pair of animated running legs, which I included as a series of stills in Figure 4-4. As an aside, the way I generated the stills for the figure was by using Processing's saveFrame() function, temporarily commented out at the bottom of draw(). You can read more about saveFrame() at http://processing.org/reference/saveFrame_.html.

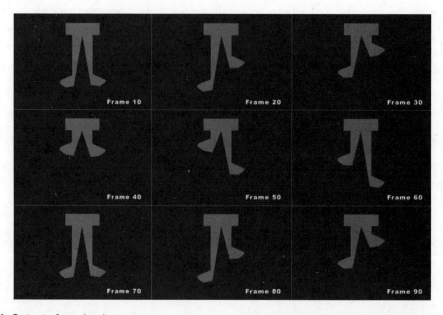

Figure 4-4. Output of running legs

Next, as with the other instance properties, I'll add a method to facilitate customizing the striding. I'll call this method setStride(), shown next:

```
// customize stride
  void setStride(float strideHt, float strideRate, float fallOff){
    this.strideHt = strideHt;
    this.strideRate = strideRate;
    this.fallOff = fallOff;
  }
```

To test the method, call setStride() in setup(), directly after setDetails(); both calls are below (with the new one in bold):

```
legs.setDetails(30, 50, 55, 75);
legs.setStride(190, PI/30, .49);
```

Running the sketch now, you should get a much longer stride, as shown in Figure 4-5. I suggest playing with the setStride() and setDetails() arguments, to better understand the range of legs you can draw with the class.

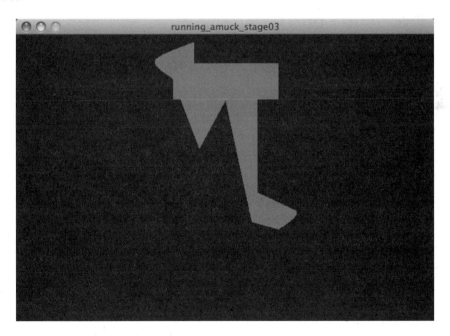

Figure 4-5. Legs with bent knee and high stride

Running Amuck

I suspect that you'd like to do something a bit more interesting with the Legs class (I know I would). To do so, I need to add some more code. In the next stage of the program, I'll introduce some loops to control an array of Legs objects, which will run through a virtual landscape, really just a defined ground plane. To create a more realistic view of the legs running in an actual space, I'll also introduce some very simple 3D, using Processing's P3D renderer.

At the top of the **Legs** class add the following property declarations:

```
// location properties
  PVector loc, initialLoc;
  // dynamics properties
  float speedX, speedZ, strideSpeed, damping;
```

I'll also create an additional constructor initializing the new loc property:

```
// constructor
  Legs(PVector loc, float w, float ht, color col){
    this.loc = loc;
    // get and keep initial location vector
    initialLoc = loc.get();
    this.w = w;
    this.ht = ht;
    this.col = col;
    fill(col);
    // initialize
    init();
  }
```

Processing's **PVector** class is convenient to use for storing an object's location, since it includes x, y, and z component float properties. If I didn't use the **PVector** class, I would have needed to create three separate x, y, and z float values. The **PVector** class also provides some convenient methods for working with vectors, such as the get() method I used to copy the data from loc **PVector** to initialLoc **PVector**, which I'll need later in the animation calculations.

> The **PVector** get() method copies the actual data from one **PVector** to another, returning a new PVector object initialized with that data. This is very different from what would happen using a simple assignment expression, such as initialLoc = loc. I hope you remember from Chapter 2 that variables that refer to objects are called reference variables, as opposed to primitive variables for values such as floats or ints. Reference variables refer (or point) to memory addresses, where the object data is stored. Assigning one object to another copies/assigns the memory address to both reference variables. It doesn't simply assign the object's property values. In other words, after object1 = object2 assignment, both variables now point to the same space in memory, so any changes made to either object will affect both of them. I included an example illustrating this in Chapter 2, and I'll return to the topic in chapter 8.

To initialize the dynamics properties with default values, I'll add some new assignment statements within init(), shown next with the new lines in bold:

```
void init(){
    detailW = w/6.0;
    detailHt = ht/8.0;
    shoeBulge = detailHt*2.0;
    legGap = w/7.0;
    // init stride values
    strideRate = PI/30;
    strideHt = ht/2;
    fallOff = .9;
    // init dynamics values
    speedX = 1.0;
    strideSpeed = 1.2;
    damping = .9;
}
```

Next, I need to plug the location properties into the drawing calls in the create() method. Both vertex() and curveVertex() can take an optional z-axis argument. Following is the updated create() method, with the new code in bold.

```
// draw legs
  void create(){
    fill(col);
    float footWidth = (w - legGap)/2;
    beginShape();
```

```
    vertex(loc.x - w/2, loc.y - ht, loc.z);

    vertex(loc.x - w/2, loc.y - ht + detailHt, loc.z);

    vertex(loc.x - w/2 + detailW, loc.y - ht + detailHt, loc.z);

    // left foot

    vertex(loc.x - w/2 + detailW,  loc.y + strideL, loc.z);

    curveVertex(loc.x - w/2 + detailW, loc.y + strideL, loc.z);

    curveVertex(loc.x - w/2 + detailW, loc.y + strideL, loc.z);

    curveVertex(loc.x - w/2 + detailW - shoeBulge,  loc.y + detailHt/2 + strideL, loc.z);

    curveVertex(loc.x - w/2,  loc.y + detailHt + strideL, loc.z);

    curveVertex(loc.x - w/2,  loc.y + detailHt + strideL, loc.z);

    vertex(loc.x - w/2 + footWidth,  loc.y + detailHt + strideL*fallOff, loc.z);

    // end left foot

    vertex(loc.x - w/2 + footWidth + legGap/2,  loc.y - ht + detailHt, loc.z);

    vertex(loc.x - w/2 + footWidth + legGap/2,  loc.y - ht + detailHt, loc.z);

    // right foot

    vertex(loc.x - w/2 + footWidth + legGap,  loc.y + detailHt + strideR*fallOff, loc.z);

    vertex(loc.x + w/2,  loc.y + detailHt + strideR, loc.z);

    curveVertex(loc.x + w/2,  loc.y + detailHt + strideR, loc.z);

    curveVertex(loc.x + w/2,  loc.y + detailHt + strideR, loc.z);

    curveVertex(loc.x + w/2 - detailW + shoeBulge,  loc.y + detailHt/2 + strideR, loc.z);

    curveVertex(loc.x + w/2 - detailW,  loc.y + strideR, loc.z);

    vertex(loc.x + w/2 - detailW,  loc.y + strideR, loc.z);

    // end right foot

    vertex(loc.x + w/2 - detailW,  loc.y - ht + detailHt, loc.z);

    vertex(loc.x + w/2,  loc.y - ht + detailHt, loc.z);

    vertex(loc.x + w/2,  loc.y - ht, loc.z);

    endShape(CLOSE);
  }
```

Staying consistent with the existing Legs class code, I'll add a method to modify the new dynamics properties, called setDynamics() and also a getStrideSpeed() method, both shown below:

```
// dynamics animation
  void setDynamics(float speedX, float strideSpeed, float damping){
```

```
    this.speedX = speedX;
    this. strideSpeed = strideSpeed;
    this.damping = damping;
  }


// return strideSpeed
  float getStrideSpeed(){
    return strideSpeed;
  }
```

Please note that I didn't include parameters for the speedYy or speedZy properties, as they will be determined by other calculations. The last thing to add to the Legs class is an actual method to move the legs, aptly named move():

```
// moves legs along x, y, z axes
  void move(float minZ, float maxZ){
    // move legs along y-axis
    loc.y = initialLoc.y+strideR*damping;
    /* move legs along x-axis and
     check for collision against frame edge */
    loc.x += speedX;
    if (screenX(loc.x, loc.y, loc.z) > width){
      speedX *= -1;
    }
    else if (screenX(loc.x, loc.y, loc.z) < 0){
      speedX *= -1;
    }
    /* move legs along z-axis based on speed of striding
     and check for collision against extremes */
    speedZ = strideRate*strideSpeed;
    loc.z += speedZ;
    if (loc.z > maxZ){
      strideSpeed *= -1;
    }
    else if (loc.z < minZ){
```

```
        strideSpeed *= -1;
    }
  }
```

This method is the most complex part of the Legs class and includes some new concepts. I hope the lines controlling the assignment/incrementation of the loc.x, loc.y, and loc.z properties are self-explanatory, the lines

```
loc.y = initialLoc.y+strideR*damping;
...
loc.x += speedX;
...
speedZ = strideRate*strideSpeed;
loc.z += speedZ;
```

The loc.y position will move up and down based on the striding speed of the legs, with a little damping of the strideR value. This will give the effect of a slight bounce of the body with each stride. loc.x and loc.z values will be incremented, causing the legs to move through space. The loc.x property is simply incremented by speedX, while loc.z, similarly to loc.y, is also dependent on strideRate. I did this to make faster striding legs move more quickly along the z axis. Because loc.x and loc.z are continually incremented, it is possible for the legs to move out of the screen, which I tried to correct for with the very simple if statements in the move() method.

In normal 2D boundary detection with the screen, you can simply check if an animated sprite's x and y properties are past the width or height of the screen (both global variables defined within Processing). However, in 3D things get more complicated, as perspective rendering along the z axis messes up these calculations. For example, if the legs are drawn at -150 on the z axis, they will be calculated (and rendered) to appear farther in space, thus the range of their x screen position will exceed the actual pixel width of the window. (Imagine how far a plane 30,000 feet above your head actually travels when it has visually moved an inch.) To enable you to find out where the 3D perspective calculations move your object on the screen, Processing includes three very handy functions: screenX(), screenY(), screenZ(). These, in a sense, collapse the 3D calculations back to actual 2D screen coordinates, flattening the sprite's 3D coordinate space to 2D screen space, which proved helpful in calculating the collision detection. In truth, this down and dirty solution is not very accurate or 100% reliable, but it will keep the legs from permanently disappearing off the screen.

The last step before executing the running amuck animation, shown in Figure 4-6, is updating the main tab, with the following. (Please note I used a lot of random() calls to create a nice variety of forms and motion. I strongly encourage you to mess around with the argument values in these calls.)

```
/**
 * Running Amuck, stage 04
 * By Ira Greenberg <br />
 * The Essential Guide to Processing for Flash Developers
 * Friends of ED, 2009
 */

int count = 350;
Legs[] legs = new Legs[count];

void setup(){
  size(600, 400, P3D);
  noStroke();
  for (int i=0; i<count; i++){
    PVector legsLoc = new PVector(random(-20, 20), 10, random(0, 150));
    legs[i] = new Legs(legsLoc, random(.5, 5), random(1, 8), color(random(255), ⏎
        random(255), random(255)));
    legs[i].setDetails(random(legs[i].w*.05, legs[i].w*.25), random(legs[i].ht*.05, ⏎
        legs[i].ht*.25), random(legs[i].w*.02, legs[i].w*.15), random(legs[i].w*.1, ⏎
        legs[i].w*.5));
    legs[i].setStride(random(.5, 2), random(PI/10, PI/5), random(.85, .95));
    legs[i].setDynamics(random(-.35, .35), random(.75, 2.5), random(.65, .95));
  }
}

void draw(){
  background(0);
  translate(width/2, height/2);
  fill(35);
  // draw ground plane
  beginShape();
  vertex(-width*2, 20, -1000);
  vertex(width*2, 20, -1000);
```

155

```
vertex(width/2, height/2, 400);
vertex(-width/2, height/2, 400);
endShape(CLOSE);
for (int i=0; i<count; i++){
  legs[i].create();
  legs[i].stride();
  // args set z bounds
  legs[i].move(-50, 400);
}
}
```

Figure 4-6. Running amuck animation

Composing Classes

One of the major benefits of OOP is its modularity, including a simulated black-box design. A well-designed class presents a public interface (its public members or API) and keeps its internal implementation (the black box part) hidden; this allows the guts of the class to be upgraded without impacting how the class is used. In good program design, classes work together, with individual classes encapsulating certain functionality and behavior. In an efficient system, each class is lean and specialized, with an effective interface for working in conjunction with other classes. Throughout the rest of this chapter, I'll build upon the Running Amuck program, creating a couple of new classes that work in concert with `Legs.pde`.

Head Class: More Than Just a Pretty Face

To give our running legs a bit more curb appeal, I'll add a head (which will also include a neck). The head will provide an opportunity to demonstrate how Processing works with images, while the neck will give me a chance to throw in some fun physics. Here's the finished Head class:

```
/**
 * Head class with customizable face
 * Running Amuck
 * By Ira Greenberg <br />
 * The Essential Guide to Processing for Flash Developers
 * Friends of ED, 2009
 */

class Head{
  // head faces
  PImage front, back, img;
  // head position
  PVector loc;
  float w, ht;
  int FRONT_FACE = 0, BACK_FACE = 1;
  // head rotation
  float headRot;

  // default constructor
  Head(){
  }

  // constructor - 2 images
  Head(PImage front, PImage back){
    this.front = front;
    this.back = back;
```

```
  img = front;
  init();
}

// constructor - 1 image
Head(PImage img){
  this.img = img;
  init();
}

// size vertices to image
void init(){
  loc = new PVector();
  w = img.width;
  ht = img.height;
}

// size vertices to image
void setScale(float scl){
  // based on width of legs
  float sclFctr = scl/w;
  w *= sclFctr;
  ht *= sclFctr;
}

// size shape vertices to image
void setSize(float w, float ht){
  this.w = w;
  this.ht = ht;
}

// update image
void setImg(PImage img){
  this.img = img;
```

```
    init();
  }

  // set position
  void setLoc(PVector loc){
    this.loc = loc;
  }

void setLoc( float x, float y, float z ){
    loc.x = x;
    loc.y = y;
    loc.z = z;
  }

  // set rotation
  void setRot(float headRot){
    this.headRot = headRot ;
  }

  // set head image based on z
  void setFace(int facing){
    if (facing == FRONT_FACE) {
      img = front;
    }
    else {
      img = back;
    }
  }

  // create and move head
  void create(){
    textureMode(NORMALIZED);
    pushMatrix();
    // move and rotate head
```

```
    translate(loc.x, loc.y, loc.z);
    rotateZ(headRot);
    // draw rect and texture map face image
    beginShape();
    texture(img);
    vertex(- w/2, 0, 0, 0, 1.0);
    vertex(-w/2, -ht, 0, 0, 0);
    vertex(w/2, -ht, 1.0, 0);
    vertex(w/2, 0, 0, 1.0, 1.0);
    endShape();
    popMatrix();
  }
}
```

The Head class is relatively simple, yet it introduces a couple of new Processing concepts. At the top of the class I declare three PImage properties:

```
PImage front, back, img;
```

PImage is a Processing class that encapsulates image handling, which I discussed briefly in Chapter 3. Image handling in Java is fairly involved, and Processing's PImage class greatly simplifies the process, while still enabling much of the same basic functionality offered in pure Java.

In order for you to work with external images in Processing, the images need to first be loaded into the sketch's data directory. You can do this by either literally dragging/copying images into the directory, or, better yet, using Processing's **Add File**... command found under the **Sketch** top menu. (Please note that a data directory will be created automatically when using the Add File... dialogue if one does not already exist.)

For the Head class, I'll use PImage to texture-map a face image onto head geometry. To keep things simple, the geometry will just be a rectangle, and I'll use a PNG image that includes an alpha component (for transparent pixels). This will allow the head to appear to be cut out or masked, shown in Figure 4.7, without revealing the actual rectangle geometry.

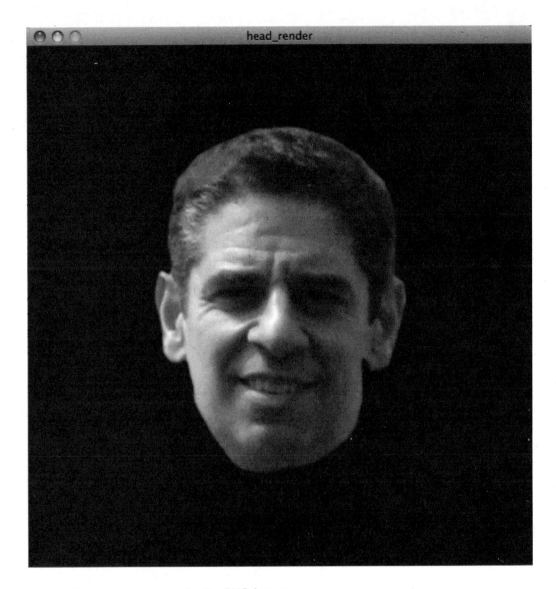

Figure 4-7. Cut out head image using the PNG format

The Head class includes three constructors, the default constructor, one with a single image parameter and one with two image parameters. I thought it would be amusing to have both a front and back image to texture map on the head geometry, with the image mapping selection determined by the direction the legs are moving along the z-axis. The other methods in the class should be self-explanatory, with the exception of the create() method, shown again next:

```
// create and move head
  void create(){
    textureMode(NORMALIZED);
    pushMatrix();
    // move and rotate head
    translate(loc.x, loc.y, loc.z);
    rotateZ(headRot);
    // draw rect and texture map face image
    beginShape();
    texture(img);
    vertex(- w/2, 0, 0, 0, 1.0);
    vertex(-w/2, -ht, 0, 0, 0);
    vertex(w/2, -ht, 0, 1.0, 0);
    vertex(w/2, 0, 0, 1.0, 1.0);
    endShape();
    popMatrix();
  }
}
```

This method both draws the rectangle geometry and texture-maps the loaded PImage onto it. As long as noStroke() is called somewhere before the drawing takes place, you won't see the outline of the actual rectangle. The textureMode(NORMALIZED); function sets the coordinate space for the texture mapping. The method can accept the arguments NORMALIZED or IMAGE. NORMALIZED utilizes values between 0 and 1. For example, in the image shown in Figure 4-7, I mapped the texture to fit 100% to the geometry, using the calls

```
vertex(- w/2, 0, 0, 0, 1.0);
vertex(-w/2, -ht, 0, 0, 0);
vertex(w/2, -ht, 0, 1.0, 0);
vertex(w/2, 0, 0, 1.0, 1.0);
```

Notice the vertex() calls take five arguments; the first three are the x, y, and z coordinate position, and the last two are for the texture mapping, commonly referred to as UV mapping. The U and V just represent a texture coordinate space. In the example, the UV coordinates map to the shape defined by the vertices, in that UV values of 0 would map to the left and top, while values of 1 would be to the right and down. However, you can alter these values. Figure 4-8 shows output of the same sketch with the UV values changed, listed next. (Notice also that the rectangle geometry reveals itself because of the image cropping.)

```
vertex(- w/2, 0, 0, .2, .8);
vertex(-w/2, -ht, 0, .2, .2);
vertex(w/2, -ht, 0, .8, .2);
vertex(w/2, 0, 0, .8, .8);
```

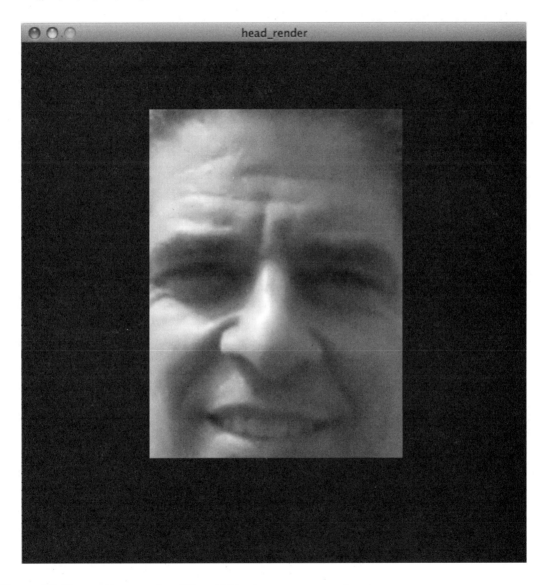

Figure 4-8. Cropped image using different UV values

Using the second argument option textureMode(IMAGE), the image map is created based on the actual image width and height values. For example, to map my 181 x 240 pixel face image, as illustrated in Figure 4-7, I'd use

```
texture(img);
vertex(- w/2, 0, 0, 0, 240);
vertex(-w/2, -ht, 0, 0, 0);
vertex(w/2, -ht, 0, 181, 0);
vertex(w/2, 0, 0, 181, 240);
```

Note also that the texture(img); call needs to precede the vertex() calls (for either NORMALIZED or IMAGE argument option), with the img argument obviously being the PImage used for the texture map.

Finally, I just want to be sure you're clear on the use of pushMatrix() and popMatrix(), which I also discussed last chapter. Using these calls has the result of isolating individual transformation calls (e.g., translate(), rotate()) from the overall transformation state. In other words, whatever the overall transformation state was previous to the pushMatrix() call, it will be the same after the popMatrix() call, regardless of the transformations performed between the two calls; these calls must be used together, and they may be nested for more complex sorts of transformations, which you can see an example of here: http://processing.org/learning/3d/cubicgrid.html.

Neck Class: Spring-Loaded

The next step involves connecting the head to the legs. There are a number of ways you could approach this. One way would be to add a Head object reference property within the Legs class and have the legs internally size and position the head. This is a pretty good approach, as it encapsulates some aspects of the head's context in relation to the legs. However, it also locks the Head object to the Legs class, which perhaps doesn't make the most sense semantically. I'd also like to try to work with the Legs class "as is" and not be forced to add stuff to the class. A different approach would be to create another composing class, say a Person class that maintained object references for the different body parts. This approach is much more object-oriented in that it supports modular design. In addition, a Person class would allow a very high level approach to creating virtual characters, such as (theoretically) through simple instantiation—new Person(); and you've got an avatar walking about.

The solution I'll apply will be a hybrid approach to the two potential scenarios discussed. I'll create a Neck class that will contain a Head object reference, and I'll also create a new Schlemiel class (Schlemiel is a Yiddish term for a clumsy, foolish person) that will take care of composing the Neck and Leg objects, through internal references to the two classes. Next is the finished Neck class. To add the code to your current sketch, create a new tab named **Neck:**

```
/**
 * Neck class
 * Running Amuck
```

```
 * - manages Head object
 * By Ira Greenberg <br />
 * The Essential Guide to Processing for Flash Developers
 * Friends of ED, 2009
 */

class Neck{
  // drawing properties
  PVector loc;
  int segs;
  float w, ht;
  // bones are drawn based on spine vertices
  PVector[] spine;
  PVector[] bones;
  // controls neck/head bobble physics
  PVector[] springs;
  // springs in neck follow this
  float bobbleLead;
  // control range and rate of bobble
  float bobbleRangeMin, bobbleRangeMax, bobbleRateMin, bobbleRateMax;
  float theta, damping;

  // internal Head object property
  Head head;

  // default constructor
  Neck(Head head){
    this.head = head;
    loc = new PVector();
    segs = 12;
    // set defaults
    init();
  }
```

```
// constructor
Neck(PVector loc, int segs, float w, float ht, Head head){
  this.loc = loc;
  this.segs = segs;
  this.w = w;
  this.ht = ht;
  this.head = head;
  // scale head based on width of neck
  head.setScale(w*4);
  init();
}

void setSegments(int segs){
  this.segs = segs;
  init();
}

void setSize(float w, float ht){
  this.w = w;
  this.ht = ht;
  // scale head based on width of neck
  head.setScale(w*4);
  init();
}

void init(){
  // structure
  spine = new PVector[segs];
  bones = new PVector[segs*2];
  // set default dynamics
  springs = new PVector[spine.length];
  setDynamics(2.0, 12.0, PI/90.0, PI/60.0, .96);
  // create spine and instantiate springs
  float segHt = ht/segs;
```

```
    for (int i=0; i<segs; i++){
      spine[i] = new PVector(0, segHt*i, 0);
      springs[i] = new PVector();
    }
  }


  // calculate and draw neck
  void create(){
    // calculate neck vertices
    for (int i=0; i<segs; i++){
      bones[i] = new PVector(loc.x+spine[i].x+w/2, loc.y+spine[i].y, loc.z+spine[i].z);
        bones[bones.length-1-i] = new PVector(loc.x+spine[i].x-w/2, loc.y+spine[i].y, ↵
            loc.z+spine[i].z);
    }
    // draw neck shape
    beginShape();
    for (int i=0; i<bones.length; i++){
      vertex(bones[i].x, bones[i].y, bones[i].z);
    }
    endShape(CLOSE);
  }


  // set neck position
  void setLoc(PVector loc){
    this.loc = loc;
  }


  // make neck/head bobble
  void bobble(){
    bobbleLead = sin(theta)*random(bobbleRangeMin, bobbleRangeMax);
    float[] deltaX = new float[spine.length];
    for (int i=0; i<spine.length; i++){
      deltaX[i] = (bobbleLead-spine[i].x)*(1.0/dist(spine[i].x, spine[i].y, bobbleLead, ht));
```

```
    springs[i].x += deltaX[i];
    spine[i].x += springs[i].x;
    springs[i].x *= damping;
  }
  theta += random(bobbleRateMin, bobbleRateMax);
  // position and rotate head
  head.setLoc(new PVector((bones[0].x+bones[1].x)/2, bones[0].y+ht/10, bones[0].z));
  head.setRot(radians(spine[spine.length-1].x));
  head.create();
}


void setFacing(float zSign){
  if (zSign>0){
    head.setFace(head.FRONT_FACE);
  }
  else {
    head.setFace(head.BACK_FACE);
  }
}


// controls bobble
void setDynamics(float bobbleRangeMin, float bobbleRangeMax, ⏎
    float bobbleRateMin, float bobbleRateMax, float damping){
  this.bobbleRangeMin = bobbleRangeMin;
  this.bobbleRangeMax = bobbleRangeMax;
  this.bobbleRateMin = bobbleRateMin;
  this.bobbleRateMax = bobbleRateMax;
  this.damping = damping;
}
}
```

The Neck class enables you to produce a spring-loaded neck that will take care of positioning, scaling and bobbling a passed-in Head object. The neck will eventually move based on the legs' motion, but that dependency is not explicitly built into the class, as is the one between the Head object reference within the

Neck class. The Neck class includes a setLoc() method for resetting the position of the neck. Because the relationship between Neck and Legs classes is not hard coded, a Neck object could eventually also be controlled by some other class or agent. Again, in OOP, it's worth thinking about class usage beyond a specific solution, including any internal dependencies that could potentially limit the classes' more general use. (That said, I personally don't believe these types of organizational issues should ever squelch innovation, or even the joy of programming, especially in terms of creative coding projects.)

Returning to the Neck class, it begins with the standard declaration of instance properties, followed by constructors and then additional methods. I hope that, even if the OOP stuff is new to you, you're beginning to recognize a repeating pattern to how classes in Processing (and also Java) are structured. The Neck class includes three PVector[] (array) properties, including ones for both a spine and bones. The neck will be built by defining a spine of certain length and number segments; then the neck shape will be calculated based on the spine geometry and a specified width. The calculated vertex data will be stored in the bones[] array. This approach will allow the spine geometry to be calculated once in setup() and function as an armature, while the bones vertices and spine location can be recalculated in real time (each frame) to allow for organic animation, which is precisely what this class does.

The class design basically follows the Legs class with multiple constructors and an init() method to handle redundant code common to the constructors. I'll assume you can make sense of most of the class code. One method that may be less clear is create(). Following is the first for loop in this method:

```
// calculate neck vertices
    for (int i=0; i<segs; i++){
      bones[i] = new PVector(loc.x+spine[i].x+w/2, loc.y+spine[i].y, loc.z+spine[i].z);
      bones[bones.length-1-i] = new PVector(loc.x+spine[i].x-w/2, loc.y+spine[i].y, ↩
            loc.z+spine[i].z);
    }
```

What's potentially confusing about this loop is that I'm calculating both the right and left side of the neck geometry each iteration of the loop. The first bones[i] assignment handles the right side of the neck, based on the on the i++ incrementation through the array. The second bones[] assignment statement handles the left side of the neck and works from the end of the array backwards (bones[bones.length-1-i]), subtracting the value of i. I chose to do this so that the next loop in the create() method handling the actual drawing (shown next),

```
// draw neck shape
    beginShape();
    for (int i=0; i<bones.length; i++){
      vertex(bones[i].x, bones[i].y, bones[i].z);
    }
    endShape(CLOSE);
```

could simply run through the `bones[]` array connecting each vertex in succession, shown in Figure 4-9. (Please note I rendered the vertices as small circles to help illustrate how the drawing works.)

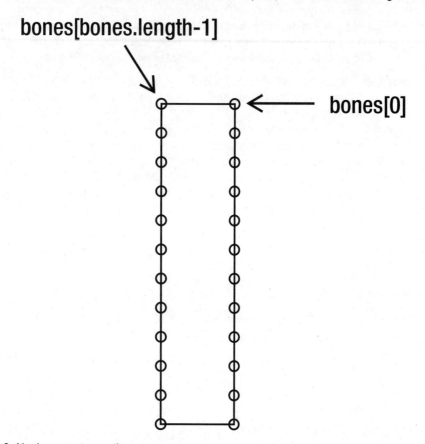

Figure 4-9. Neck geometry vertices

In addition to `create()`, I suspect the `bobble()` method needs some elucidation as well. This method creates a cool wave effect that runs through the neck, shown in Figure 4-10, and updates the head's position as well as adding some dynamic rotation to it (the head bobbling). The basic springing algorithm is inspired by Keith Peters's excellent book *Foundation ActionScript 3.0 Animation: Making Things Move!* (`http://www.friendsofed.com/book.html?isbn=1590597915`).

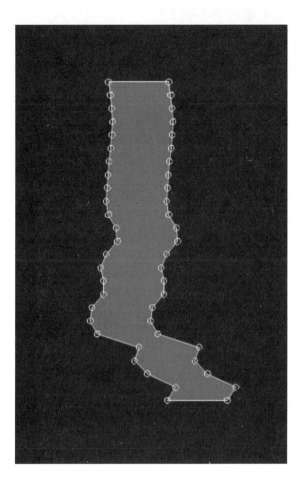

Figure 4-10. Springing neck

Here's the basic springing algorithm in pseudo code, followed by a line-by-line description.

Pseudo code:

```
#   deltaX = leadingSprite.x - followingSprite.x
#   springVelocity += deltaX
#   followingSprite.x += springVelocity
#   springAmount *= damping
```

Description:

```
#   Local variable deltaX is assigned the difference (each frame) between
```

```
                the leading sprite.x - following sprite.x
    #    Increment the global variable springVelocity by deltaX each frame
    #    Move the following sprite.x by spring force
    #    Dampen the spring force so it doesn't grow forever
```

The springing in the bobble() method is a bit more complicated than the pseudo code, as I added a fall-off to the springing effect based on the distance of the vertices from the bobbleLead (the invisible leading sprite); in addition, I needed to inverse this distance value. The best way to understand this abstract math stuff is to simply play with the values and watch what happens (empirical math rules!). The rest of the bobble() method is for positioning the head on the neck, so it feels attached yet appropriately bobbly.

The last method I want to just highlight is

```
void setFacing(float zSign){
    if (zSign>0){
      head.setFace(head.FRONT_FACE);
    }
    else {
      head.setFace(head.BACK_FACE);
    }
}
```

This method simply swaps the image used to texture-map the head, based on the sign of the zSign parameter. Again, the images used for the texture mapping must be in the sketch's data directory. The last new class to add to finish the Running Amuck program is the Schlemiel class.

Schlemiel Class: Putting All the Pieces Together

```
/**
 * Schlemiel class
 * Running Amuck
 * - composite class manages components
 * By Ira Greenberg <br />
 * The Essential Guide to Processing for Flash Developers
 * Friends of ED, 2009
 */
class Schlemiel{

  PVector loc;
  Legs legs;
```

```
Neck neck;
PVector minBounds, maxBounds;

// default constructor
Schlemiel(){
}

// constructor
Schlemiel(Neck neck, Legs legs){
  this.legs = legs;
  this.neck = neck;
  init();
}

// set some defaults
void init(){
    neck.setSize(legs.w/4.0, legs.ht/2.0);
    minBounds = new PVector(0, 0, -1000);
    maxBounds = new PVector(0, 0, 600);
    neck.setDynamics(legs.w/4, legs.w/2, PI/180, PI/60, .97);
}

void setLoc(PVector loc){
  this.loc = loc;
}

void setLegs(Legs legs){
  this.legs = legs;
}

void setNeck(Neck neck){
  this.neck = neck;
}
```

```
// set limits of movement
void setMotionBounds(PVector minBounds, PVector maxBounds){
  this.minBounds = minBounds;
  this.maxBounds = maxBounds;
}

void create(){
  legs.create();
  neck.create();
}

void move(){
  // move legs
  legs.stride();
  legs.move(minBounds.z, maxBounds.z);
  // position neck on legs
  neck.setLoc(legs.loc.x, legs.loc.y-legs.ht-neck.ht+neck.ht/5, legs.loc.z);
  // make neck wave
  neck.bobble();
  // change face based on direction legs are moving
  neck.setFacing(legs.getStrideSpeed());
}
}
```

The main function of this class is to compose the neck and legs into a single character. Really, this could be considered a high-level convenience class, as the functionality of this class could have been handled in the main tab. However, if the character had more parts, it could get unwieldy to have to worry about manually rigging all the parts together. Schlemiel is really an unfinished class, used primarily as an example of an OOP approach for organizing multiple classes together. It would be an excellent exercise to try to add another component to the Schlemiel character, such as arms perhaps.

To view the final Running Amuck animation you just need to update the code in the main tab, shown next:

```
/**
 * Running Amuck, stage 05
 * By Ira Greenberg <br />
 * The Essential Guide to Processing for Flash Developers
```

```
 * Friends of ED, 2009
 */


PImage front, back;
int count = 50;
Neck[] necks = new Neck[count];
Legs[] legs = new Legs[count];
Schlemiel[] schlemiels = new Schlemiel[count];


void setup(){
  size(800, 500, P3D);
  noStroke();
  // images for head (same 2 for all heads)
  front = loadImage("face_front.png");
  back = loadImage("face_back.png");
  for (int i=0; i<count; i++){
    // create local Head object per neck
    Head head = new Head(front, back);
    necks[i] = new Neck(head);
    necks[i].setSegments(int(random(12, 25)));
    // legs position
    PVector legsLoc = new PVector(random(-20, 20), 10, random(-450, -200));
    legs[i] = new Legs(legsLoc, random(5, 30), random(8, 60), color(random(255), ⬅
        random(255), random(255)));
    legs[i].setDetails(random(legs[i].w*.05, legs[i].w*.25), random(legs[i].ht*.05,⬅
        legs[i].ht*.25), random(legs[i].w*.02, legs[i].w*.15), random(legs[i].w*.1, ⬅
            legs[i].w*.5));
    legs[i].setStride(random(5, 12), random(PI/20, PI/10), random(.85, .95));
    legs[i].setDynamics(random(-.35, .35), random(.75, 2.5), random(.65, .95));
    // pass Neck and Leg objects to Schlemiel constructor
    schlemiels[i] = new Schlemiel(necks[i], legs[i]);
    // set z-bounds
    schlemiels[i].setMotionBounds(new PVector(0, 0, -1000), new PVector(0, 0, 425));
```

```
    }
}

void draw(){
  background(10);
  translate(width/2, height/2);
  // draw ground plane
  createGround(color(50));
  // draw the bobbling schlemiels
  for (int i=0; i<count; i++){
    schlemiels[i].create();
    schlemiels[i].move();
  }
}


// ground plane
void createGround(color col){
  fill(col);
  beginShape();
  vertex(-width*2, 20, -1000);
  vertex(width*2, 20, -1000);
  vertex(width/2, height/2, 400);
  vertex(-width/2, height/2, 400);
  endShape(CLOSE);
}
```

One of the strategies I tried to follow in designing the Running Amuck program was giving users a high-level approach for creating a character, while also providing ample room for customization. It would have been possible to fully encapsulate the Leg and Neck objects inside the Schlemiel class, without giving users the ability to instantiate these objects explicitly and pass them into the class. However, this convenience would come at the expense of reduced customization, not to mention a perhaps too-specialized class, which wouldn't be very usable for future projects. As I mentioned earlier, this is a guiding strategy in object-oriented programming, (but one that—in regard to Processing—does not need to be blindly followed).

In the Running Amuck example, there are some redundant structures common to the different classes, as well as some highly specific object references internal to the classes. An OOP way to improve the program would be to eventually make the classes less specific (more abstract in OOP thinking) and thus ultimately more reusable. With regard to redundant structures between the classes, one common OOP approach is to create a parent-type class (superclass) that the other classes would build upon, or extend. This last point, called inheritance, is a central feature of OOP and is implemented similarly in Processing and ActionScript. That said, this has been a long enough chapter, so I'll introduce inheritance next chapter. First, though, I strongly recommend that you run the finished Running Amuck sketch and experiment with the wide array of parameters for customization. I'd also try some different head images. Next are some screen shots of the program executing, as it's written, shown in Figures 4-11 through 4-14, as well as one other screen shot, shown in Figure 4-15, that includes a programmatically-generated checkered floor I added. (I'll leave the checkered floor as a fun coding challenge.)

Figure 4-11. Running Amuck, screenshot 1

Figure 4-12. Running Amuck, screenshot 2

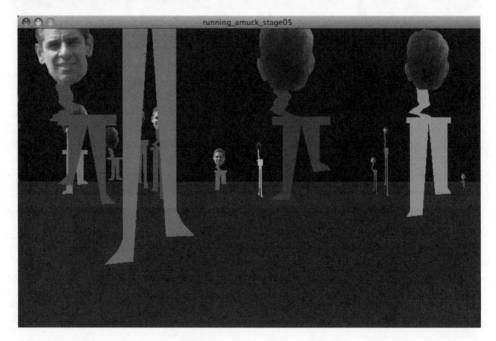

Figure 4-13. Running Amuck, screenshot 3

Figure 4-14. Running Amuck, screenshot 4

Figure 4-15. Running Amuck, screenshot with checkered floor

Summary

My hope is that this chapter provided something for everyone: for those new to OOP, I hope you were able to begin to grasp what OOP is and how it is implemented; for more experienced ActionScript coders, I hope you now have a better sense of Processing's approach to OOP as compared to ActionScript; and for very experienced OOP'sters, I hope the Running Amuck program provided a good example of what's possible with OOP in Processing—really I just scratched the surface.

OOP takes time to fully digest, so I wouldn't worry if you found some of the material in this chapter challenging. Throughout the book I'll be revisiting all of these concepts. I hope that the Running Amuck example gave you food for thought and perhaps will inspire your own variations. This was not a simple example, but one that touched upon a number of topics in graphics programming, which I'll also be discussing in more detail in later chapters. Finally, this chapter was really a very cursory introduction to OOP in Processing. I'll be building upon the concepts introduced, including exploring in detail the OOP concepts of inheritance and polymorphism, as well as discussing these principles in regard to Processing's relationship and integration with Java. Next chapter, I'll apply many of the concepts covered thus far in the book in developing an object-oriented particle engine in Processing.

Chapter 5

I Like Particle Engines!

It's mid-November in North Dallas, and there are dramatic migratory flocks of birds everywhere. The birds move as a giant swarm, billowing like an organic mass. Yet, in spite of this seemingly orchestrated behavior, there is no flock leader or central organizing structure. Rather, the individual birds' behavior en masse creates this beautiful, emergent phenomenon. This is a wonderful real-world example of a particle system. In addition to bird flocks, particle systems can model things as literal as falling snow, or as complex as virtual armies on a battlefield. Combining surfacing and sophisticated rendering techniques, particle systems can also model non-object-like things such as water, fire, and explosions.

It's true, I definitely have a thing for particle engines. In fact, when I give Processing workshops, more than likely my example will be a simple particle system. I think what I like about them is the scale of their complexity coupled with the aesthetic payoff; it's basically an even exchange. By contrast, I've definitely worked on projects throughout my career where the pain/fun ratio was less balanced (ahh, corporate websites come to mind).

That said, the definition of a particle engine (or system) is quite broad and can specify something extremely complex or, by contrast, quite simple. For example, if you were trying to precisely describe the accurate interactions of gas molecules for a scientific experiment, you'd need to use pretty rigorous mathematics. However, if you were trying to simulate randomly moving insects, you could use much simpler calculations that roughly described the physics. My goal with this example is to shoot somewhere toward the middle of this complexity scale—*rigorously simple math*—and to also extend the conversation about object-oriented programming in Processing.

Some Principles and Terms

There are some principles worth examining before we begin letting the code fly—especially since the engine we'll construct will require a fair amount of it. As mentioned earlier, particle engines are used for lots of problems, from the soft body dynamics in a waving flag, to the flowing grass in Shrek. Some systems use complex structures, including springs, emitters, attractors/repellors, colliders, as well as other environmental forces: wind, gravity, friction, etc. Really, these systems can be as complex as you can conceive of them. Although the feature set can get very large, in principle—precise scientific applications not withstanding—most of the math behind these systems is relatively straightforward. The example I'll discuss uses basic simulated physics, which is sufficient for most aesthetically-oriented projects. If you do want to learn about more accurate systems, I suggest checking out Keith Peters's excellent book *AdvancED ActionScript 3.0 Animation* (friends of ED, 2009).

I'll include **emitters** and **colliders** in our particle engine. In addition, the system will include gravity, friction, wind, resistance, turbulence, damping, and both orthogonal and non-orthogonal collision detection, the latter being the most complex math we'll tackle. Beyond the simulated physics and dynamics, I'll also demonstrate a slightly more advanced object-oriented structure than the Running Amuck example discussed in Chapter 4. Specifically, I'll utilize inheritance to allow classes to build upon one another and to add polymorphic structure to the engine.

> *Polymorphism is a core principle in OOP, which fosters flexibility and a more open type of system. Literally, polymorphism means occurring in multiple forms. In object-oriented programming, this translates to occurring in multiple types (a class defines a type). Through inheritance, an object can appear as both its own type and also any types it inherits from. For more information on polymorphism, check out http://en.wikipedia.org/wiki/Polymorphism_in_object-oriented_programming (November 16, 2009, 10:37).*

I'll begin the engine by defining some terms:

- Emitters—You can think of these as nozzles that emit the actual particles. They typically will include properties such as location, emission vector (direction and emission speed), emission birthrate, particle population size, and spray radius.
- Colliders—Particles will collide with these objects based on some collision rules. In our example the particles will simply deflect off these as if they are rigid immovable objects. These can be as simple as static blocks or ellipses or as complex as organic, moving shapes.
- Attractors/Repellors—You can think of these as polarized magnets moving around a container full of other magnets (though the principle of magnetism is not the point here). When a magnet gets within a certain distance to another magnet, they are either attracted or repelled. In a dynamic system, such as swarming, an attractor (such as prey or a food source) could be one force acting on an organism, while wind, gravity, repelling, and collisions might be other competing forces. Particle systems are especially interesting when you program these varied forces and watch the behavior dynamically emerge, sometimes in unexpected configurations.
- Birthrate—The amount of particles that emit from the emitter each frame
- Lifespan—How long the particle exists

In addition to the terms, there are some motion principles, shown in bold, worth reviewing. Again, my approach will be to keep things as simple as possible. Simple motion can be thought of as a change in position over some period of time, where speed is the rate of that change. However, speed doesn't tell us in what direction you're heading. Thus it's possible (and helpful) to break motion down into **speed** and **direction** (more commonly referred to as **velocity**). There is a very handy mathematical structure used to store this type of composite information, called a **vector**.

A vector can be visualized as an arrow, as shown in Figure 5-1. Notice in the figure that the vectors v1 and v2 have the same values, yet are in different places on the coordinate system; this is because the values shown don't refer to a specific vertex, but rather the change (or delta) between the components (x, y) of the two terminal vertices. This way of specifying vectors allows them to be independent of any coordinate system, which is really helpful when you perform actual calculations on them.

To account for the different positions of the vectors on the graph, you can think of that difference being an overall **translation** (or shift along the coordinate system) of the vector. Again, the vector's value doesn't change, just its relative position does. It is also common to refer to the length of a vector as its **magnitude**, a value we'll use shortly when we begin using vectors to calculate motion. The way you can separate the direction from the magnitude is to treat a vector as if it had a length of 1 multiplied by a specific magnitude. You can think of a vector with a length of 1 (referred to as a `unit vector`) as representing the base direction of the vector. **Normalizing** is the term used to describe the process of converting a vector to a unit vector, which is included in the code to follow.

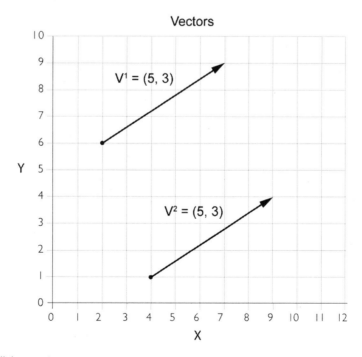

Figure 5-1. Visualizing vectors

Designing a Solution

I'll use an object-oriented design to construct the engine, as opposed to a procedural approach using only variables and functions. Last chapter you looked at OOP, but for a relatively simple example. The particle engine is more complex and thus would benefit from a bit more work up front, before coding. In general, it's a good idea to put time in the planning and/or design stage of an object-oriented solution. And, in fact, this is one of the more challenging (and important) aspects of OOP—how best to design a solution. There are countless ways of programming to reach the same results, and of course there are far less and more efficient ways. And I guess, if you're a hardcore algorithmic efficiency expert, there is ultimately (at least in theory) *THE* way. Needless to say, I've never been known for my efficiency (as my 1000-page previous Processing book is a testament to), so my approach is to describe a *good enough* way.

As discussed last chapter, in thinking about an object-oriented solution, it helps to impose a real-world framework on a virtual problem: if I were to actually build a physical particle system, how would I do it? There are highly structured approaches, methodologies, and even a language, called UML (Unified Modeling Language), used in software engineering to deal with program design. To learn more about UML see http://en.wikipedia.org/wiki/Unified_Modeling_Language (November 16, 2009, 10:42). I'll utilize some of these approaches in designing my solution. My goal here is to create a simple enough OOP design that you don't need another book to decode my design solution.

I'm not going to include user interaction in the example, something I'll discuss next chapter when we build a game. This example will assume once the program executes that the end-user simply sits back, latte in hand, and experiences the awe. Of course, that said, I will describe the program from a programmer's perspective, including how the program can be customized, extended, and reused.

Engine Description

Next is a basic narrative about the engine:

> The particle engine will allow emitters and colliders to be added, with each emitter containing a population of particles. Ideally, the particles and colliders can be customized allowing for different types of each. The system should be smart enough to automatically handle collisions between the particles and the frame boundaries and colliders. In addition, the particles should be capable of interacting with emission and environmental forces. Finally, the system should be open and reusable enough that new particle and collider types can be added to the system, without the need to expose the source code of the core engine.

Wow, that's a lot to ask for, but I think it is a good example of a simple narrative project specification. Next, I'll break the project into component parts, which will help define what classes need to be created. Based on the narrative, the logical components include

- Engine
- Emitters
- Colliders

- Particles
- Environmental Forces

Before we build a class for each of these, it will also be helpful to think about how the components relate to one another. Figure 5.2 shows a diagram connecting them into one integrated system.

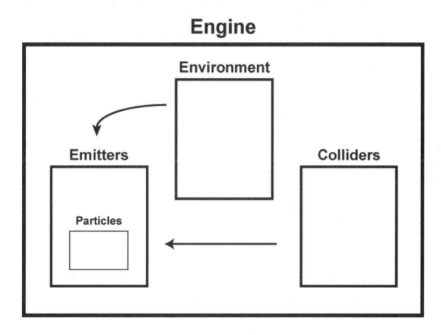

Figure 5-2. Particle engine interactions diagram

The engine encapsulates all of its component parts. The arrows in the diagram simply illustrate what engine component has influence over another component. The environment component will influence the behavior of the particles, which are encapsulated inside the emitters. The colliders will also influence the particles, but (in this engine design) will not be influenced by either the environment or the particles. I chose this strategy primarily to keep the engine complexity to a minimum. Another design could have included additional influence(s) on the colliders, which, in fact, would make for an interesting engine and an excellent follow-up exercise.

Next, I'll turn the components into classes, adding properties and methods. As I do this, I'll also create some updated class diagrams and, when applicable, create some interim sketches to test out the individual components.

Engine Class

The Engine class will handle the heavy lifting for the entire particle system, allowing a single point of command and control. One of the main design decisions to consider when building an OOP project of any scale is how much customization should the code framework allow versus how high-level, or turnkey, should it be. It's possible to design an engine that a user would simply instantiate (e.g., `new Engine()`) and away you'd go, without any need (or room) for customization. The other extreme would be to allow users to customize every possible detail in the engine, down to how all the individual algorithms function. My approach will be a middle path, enabling sufficient room for customization without requiring a user to have to quit her day job to understand the framework (if any day jobs actually remain in the current economy).

I'll build the `Engine` class in a few stages. Figure 5-3 shows a diagram of an initial class. The diagram doesn't adhere to any strict UML styles but is a simplified (common sense) approach. The top part of the diagram lists the instance properties, while the bottom includes the instance methods. For multiple methods, including the constructors, I'll use a '+' sign to specify that there are overloaded methods (methods having the same name, but with different method signatures). The bullets in the diagram are just a visual aid for reading and don't have any specific functional meaning.

Engine

- Emitter emitter
- Emitter[] emitters
- Collider[] colliders
- Environment environment

+ constructors
- void init()
- void run()
+ object setter methods

Figure 5-3. Engine class diagram

Notice in the diagram that the main `Engine` class properties are object references to other classes (`Collider`, `Emitter`, `Environment`) shown in the initial diagram. To keep things simpler in the diagrams, I'm also not spelling out the individual setter methods or individual constructors, although you, of course, could. Next is the initial `Engine` class code:

```
/**
 * Engine class
 * Particle Engine - stage 01
 * By Ira Greenberg <br />
 * The Essential Guide to Processing for Flash Developers,
 * Friends of ED, 2009
 */
```

```
class Engine {

  // properties
  Emitter emitter;
  Emitter[] emitters;
  Collider[] colliders;

  // create default environment
  Environment environment = new Environment();

  // default constructor
  Engine(){
  }

  // constructor
  Engine(Emitter emitter, Environment environment){
    this.emitter = emitter;
    this.environment = environment;
    init();
  }

  // constructor
  Engine(Emitter[] emitters, Environment environment){
    this.emitters = emitters;
    this.environment = environment;
  }

  // constructor
  Engine(Emitter emitter, Collider[] colliders, Environment environment){
    this.emitter = emitter;
    this.colliders = colliders;
    this.environment = environment;
    init();
  }
```

```
// constructor
Engine(Emitter[] emitters, Collider[] colliders, Environment environment){
  this.emitters = emitters;
  this.colliders = colliders;
  this.environment = environment;
}


// If only 1 emitter added to engine,
// add to emitters array
void init(){
  emitters = new Emitter[1];
  emitters[0] = emitter;
}


// called in draw function to run engine
void run(){
  if (emitters != null && emitters.length > 0){
    for (int i=0; i<emitters.length; i++){
      emitters[i].emit();
    }
  }

  if (colliders != null && colliders.length>0){
    for (int i=0; i<colliders.length; i++){
      colliders[i].create();
    }
  }
}


// setters
void setEmitter(Emitter emitter){
  this.emitter = emitter;
  // create emitters array and adds emitter at [0]
  init();
```

```
  }

  void setEmitter(Emitter[] emitters){
    this.emitters = emitters;
  }

  void setColliders(Collider[] colliders){
    this.colliders = colliders;
  }

  void setEnvironment(Environment environment){
    this.environment = environment;
  }
}
```

> To begin building the Particle Engine project, create a new sketch named "particle_engine," and then create a new tab named "**Engine**." Within the new **Engine** tab, enter the Engine class code. Please note that the Engine class code will **NOT** execute yet, but will live happily within its tab, as we construct the rest of the engine. We'll eventually add more code to the Engine class, later in the chapter.

The `Engine` class will delegate control to its embedded component objects (`Emitter`, `Collider`, and `Environment`). Again, this will provide a central command/control structure, while still providing room for customization. Reading through the code, you'll notice I followed the same class structure used throughout Chapter 4: I begin the class with instance properties, then include multiple constructors and then instance methods. I utilized a bunch of (overloaded) constructors, to allow for different ways of instantiating an Engine object, and as usual I included a default constructor.

> The Engine class design does include one design flaw, in a pure OOP sense, in that it will be possible for a user of the class to create more than one Engine object. Most likely we wouldn't want that to be possible, and we'd want to structure the code to prevent it. There is an OOP approach (commonly referred to as a design pattern) called a Singleton Pattern that is used to precisely enforce this. In pure Processing there is no way to pull this off, as you'd need to use the Java keywords *static* and *private*, which don't work as expected. However, later in the book when we look at Java and Processing, this solution will be viable. Here's a link about the Singleton Pattern (in Java): *http://www.javacoffeebreak.com/articles/designpatterns/index.html* (November 17, 2009, 14:17). This pattern is also problematic in ActionScript, which you can read more about here: *http://www.darronschall.com/weblog/2007/ 11/actionscript-3-singleton-redux.cfm* (November 17, 2009, 14:17).

I don't think the Engine code as it stands right now needs much clarification. One minor detail that might not be immediately clear is the init() method. I wanted to allow users to be able to pass in either a single Emitter object or an array of Emitter objects. I could have simply forced an array to be used, as I did with the colliders. However, I assumed in some applications you'd only use one emitter (a fountain perhaps), so I added the option. The init() method simply creates an emitters array of length 1, assigning the single Emitter object to the first slot of the array (emitters[0]). I did this so that regardless if a single Emitter object or array of Emitter objects is passed to the Engine, they are handled internally by the class in a consistent and centralized way, while still providing users some level of customization. Next, I'll discuss the Particle class, which is where things will begin to get more interesting.

Particle Class

The Particle class will be a base class for all particles in the engine. This is a classic OOP approach, where functionality is passed on (inherited), allowing classes to be both distinct single entities and also powerful high-level composite structures. If you're not an experienced OOP coder, inheritance is one of the pillars of object-oriented programming, allowing for a complex class system (a framework) to much more easily be developed, while also providing a high level of abstraction to the framework. We'll explore these points more specifically throughout the example.

In thinking about the Particle class, it will be helpful to update the **Particle** diagram, adding some properties and methods. Figure 5-4 shows an initial attempt at doing this.

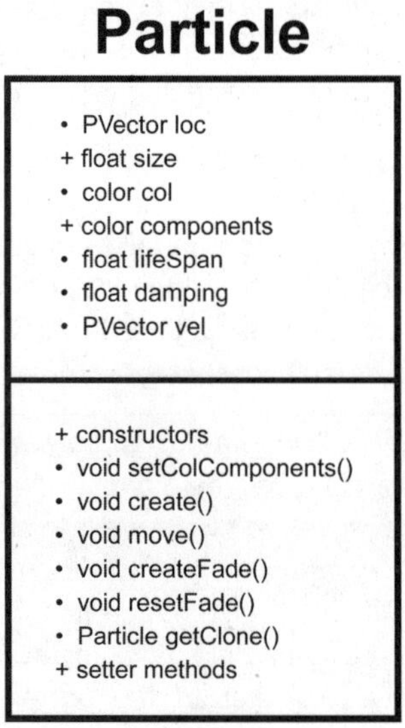

Particle

```
• PVector loc
+ float size
• color col
+ color components
• float lifeSpan
• float damping
• PVector vel
```

```
+ constructors
• void setColComponents()
• void create()
• void move()
• void createFade()
• void resetFade()
• Particle getClone()
+ setter methods
```

Figure 5-4. Particle class diagram

This set-up could work fine in developing the base `Particle` class. Don't worry about what the specific properties and methods do quite yet; we'll look at that in the code shortly. However, before we lock down the class design, it is worth asking a few questions:

1. Will any other non-particle class in the framework share any of these class members (OOP speak for the instance properties and methods)?
2. Will the design work for any particle?
3. Can I simplify the class?

The reason for asking these questions is both to attempt to simplify the class (always a good idea) and also to see if there is any common lineage that other classes would benefit from sharing (inheriting). With regard to question 1, the `Collider` class will likely also need location, size, and color properties. Since our colliders will be stationary, they won't need any velocity or the other dynamics properties, like the particles will require. By the same standard, the static colliders can use a `create()` method, but won't need `move()`. In terms of the other questions, I'll go out on a limb and say the `Particle` class is both simple enough and will work for all the different types of particles I'll be creating. But, of course, as you likely realize, there are no right answers here, just better ones.

To deal with the common class members between `Particle` and `Collider`, there are a couple of options: one would be to have `Collider` extend `Particle`, which translates to the `Collider` class inheriting the members of `Particle`. This solution would allow `Collider` objects access to the location, size, and color properties in `Particle`, but, of course, it would also give colliders access to the particle dynamics stuff, which would be unnecessary and, more importantly, potentially confusing to users of the class (if in fact the colliders are supposed to be stationary).

Sprite Class

A better solution would be to have both `Particle` and `Collider` inherit from a common ancestor that includes only the duplicated members. This design would not lock the `Particle` and `Collider` classes together, nor would it add extraneous members to either class. Thus, before we go any further with the `Particle` class, we need look at its antecedent class, which we'll name (in tribute to ActionScript) `Sprite`. Next is a diagram of the `Sprite` class, shown in Figure 5-5.

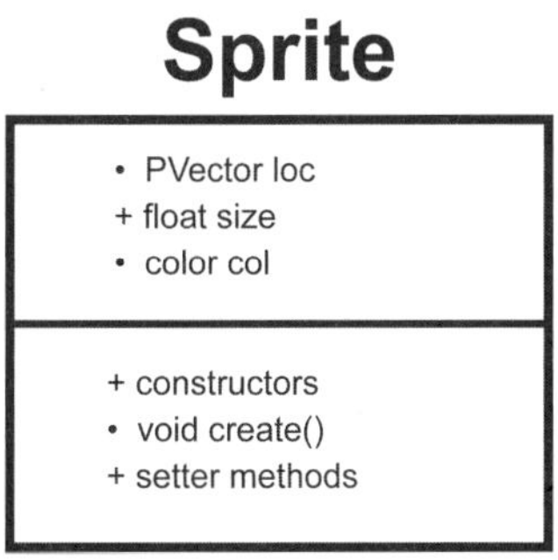

Sprite

• PVector loc
+ float size
• color col
+ constructors
• void create()
+ setter methods

Figure 5-5. Sprite class diagram

And here's the Sprite class code:

```
/**
 * Particle Engine
 * By Ira Greenberg <br />
 * The Essential Guide to Processing for Flash Developers,
 * Friends of ED, 2009
 */

// Base class for Particles and Colliders
class Sprite {

  // instance properties
  // location
  PVector loc = new PVector();
  // size
  float w = 1.0;
  float h = 1.0;
  float radius = 1.0;

  // color
  color col;

  // default constructor
  Sprite(){
  }

  // constructor
  Sprite(float w, float h){
    this.w = w;
    this.h = h;
  }
```

```
// constructor
Sprite(float radius){
  this.radius = radius;
}


// constructor
Sprite(float w, float h, color col){
  this.w = w;
  this.h = h;
  this.col = col;
}


// constructor
Sprite(PVector loc, float radius, color col){
  this.loc = loc;
  this.radius = radius;
  this.col = col;
}


// constructor
Sprite(float radius, color col){
  this.radius = radius;
  this.col = col;
}


// constructor
Sprite(color col){
  this.col = col;
}


// instance methods
// this will most likely be overridden in child classes
```

```
void create(){
  fill(col);
  rectMode(CENTER);
  rect(0, 0, radius*2, radius*2);
}

// setters
void setLoc(PVector loc){
  this.loc.set(loc);
}

void setSize(float radius){
  this.radius = radius;
}

void setSize(float w, float h){
  this.w = w;
  this.h = h;
}

void setCol(color col){
  this.col = col;
}
}
```

This is the completed Sprite class code, and it should be entered within its own tab, named "**Sprite**," in the current **particle_engine** sketch. There is nothing too fancy in this class, mostly just a bunch of constructors and setter methods. I do include size options based on radius and also width/height, which we'll need eventually. Also, I include a create() method that just draws a default rectangle particle. You'll see when we get to the specfic particle classes that we'll override this method (and remember in Processing, unlike ActionScript, we don't need to use the **override** keyword to do this). One last subtle point: you'll notice I instantiated the PVector loc = new PVector(); property when I declared it at the top of the class. We'll need this object instantiated for the engine to function properly, so I thought it was easier to do it this way, rather than declare the variable at the top of the class and instantiate it in a separate init() method. Next, let's return to the Particle class diagram and update it accordingly, shown in Figure 5-6. You'll notice the Particle class is leaner now, with an arrow pointing from **Particle** to

`Sprite` in the diagram. This is how I'll visualize the inheritance relationship in the eveloving diagram: the hollow-tipped arrow points from the inheriting (subclass) to the inherited (superclass).

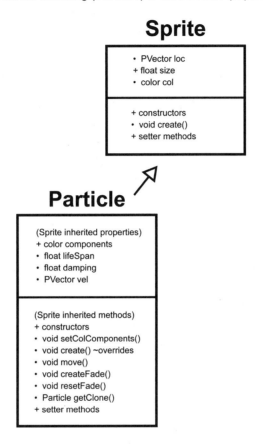

Figure 5-6. Updated Particle class diagram

And here's the `Particle` class code. Please note this code is complete and should be entered into a separate tab (named **Particle**) in your current sketch, which should already include a tab for the Sprite class.

```
/**
 * Particle Engine
 * By Ira Greenberg <br />
 * The Essential Guide to Processing for Flash Developers,
 * Friends of ED, 2009
 */
```

```
// This class should be extended by other particle types
class Particle extends Sprite{

// color components to calculate fade
  float colR;
  float colG;
  float colB;
  float colA;
  // capture inital alpha value
  float initAlpha;

  // particle dynamics
  float lifeSpan = 1000;
  float damping = .825;
  // velocity
  PVector vel = new PVector();

  // default constructor
  Particle(){
    super();
    setColComponents();
  }

  // constructor
  Particle(float radius, color col, float lifeSpan, float damping){
    super(radius, col);
    this.lifeSpan = lifeSpan;
    this.damping = damping;
    // get color component values
    setColComponents();
  }

  // constructor
  Particle(color col, float lifeSpan, float damping){
```

```
  super(col);
  this.lifeSpan = lifeSpan;
  this.damping = damping;
  // get color component values
  setColComponents();
}

// instance methods
void setColComponents(){
  // collects color component values
  colR = red(col);
  colG = green(col);
  colB = blue(col);
  colA = initAlpha = alpha(col);
}

// overrides method in Sprite class
// allowing custom particle to be created
// in Sprite descendant classes
void create(){
  fill(col);
  noStroke();
  ellipse(0, 0, radius*2, radius*2);
}

void move(){
  loc.add(vel);
  translate(loc.x, loc.y);
}

// decreases alpha component
void createFade(float val){
  colA -= val;
  col = color(colR, colG, colB, colA);
```

```
  }

  // resets alpha component
  void resetFade(){
    // put alpha back to original value
    colA = initAlpha;
    col = color(colR, colG, colB, colA);
  }

  void setVel(PVector vel){
    this.vel = vel;
  }

  // used by engine for collision detection
  Particle getClone(){
    Particle p = new Particle();
    p.loc.set(loc);
    p.vel.set(vel);
    p.radius = radius;
    p.damping = damping;
    return p;
  }
}
```

This class is a bit more complex than Sprite, though it follows a very similar structure. Right off the bat you'll notice the introduction of the extends keyword in the class declaration statement:

```
class Particle extends Sprite{
```

This is the same extends keyword in ActionScript with the same basic meaning: *inheritence*. Also, notice that I did not need any package or import statements, as we would in ActionScript. Of course, it is essential that the Sprite and Particle classes are in the same direcory, which is precisely what happens when you create a new tab in Processing. Figure 5-7 shows a screenshot of the sketchbook directory of my finished particle engine sketch, with all the classes. You can quickly access your current sketch directory by selecting **Show Sketch Folder**, in the Processing Sketch menu.

Figure 5-7. Particle engine sketchbook directory screenshot (of completed engine)

The first major difference you'll notice in the Particle class, compared to Sprite, is the use of the super keyword in the Particle constructor blocks. As with the extends keyword, Processing and ActionScript both utilize super in a similar way. If you're not very experienced with OOP, super refers to the superclass of the Particle class, in this case Sprite. In OOP-speak we use the terms superclass and subclass to refer to the contextual relationship between a parent class (superclass) and a child class that extends it (subclass). I say contextual, because any class you create in Processing can be both a parent class as well as a child class. When I create the Arrow class shortly, you'll see this contextual dynamic come into play.

Using an explicit call to super in a child class calls the constructor in the parent class; thus there needs to be a constructor with a matching signature to the call. Remember, a method/constructor signature relates to the type and number of parameters defined in the head of the method, which must match by the number/type of arguments passed in the call. Based on this, looking at the default Particle constructor,

```
// default constructor
  Particle(){
    super();
    setColComponents();
  }
```

there would need to be a default constructor declared in the Sprite class, which there is, of course. The only other way to get around this would be to not explicitly include any constructors in the Sprite class. The reason this would work is that every class always includes a default constructor, regardless of whether you explicitly include one. However, if you do include any constructors at all, the default (internal) constructor is overridden. Thus, an important rule of thumb I try to always follow is to (at least) include a default constructor in all classes. One other more subtle but very related point is that if you extend a class, the subclass constructor will automatically call the parent class constructor during instantiation, regardless of whether you invoke it with a call to super(). You might want to read that again. My recommendation to deal with these more subtle OOP intricacies is to, as I just mentioned, always include a default constructor in your class and explicitly invoke a superclass constructor, **as the first line** in the subclass constructors. I put "**as the first line**" in **bold** because any explicit calls to super **MUST** be the first call in the subclass constructor, or you'll get a compiler error.

This Processing sketch illustrates the relationship between the superclass and subclass constructors, also sometimes referred to as constructor chaining. I recommend playing with this to better understand the inheritance relationship.

```
// superclass constructor chaining example
void setup(){
  new Child();
  new Child("ira");
}


class Parent{
  //default constructor
  Parent(){
    println("Parent default constructor called");
  }
    //default constructor
```

```
  Parent(String n){
    println("Parent constructor called for " + n);
  }
}


class Child extends Parent{
  //default constructor
  Child(){
    // explicitly call a superclass constructor 1st
    super();
    println("Child default constructor called");
  }
  // constructor
  Child(String name){
    // explicitly call a superclass constructor 1st
    super(name);
    println("Child constructor called");
  }
}
```

Returning to the Particle class, one of the benefits of utilizing a superclass is the ability to build off existing classes, rather than having to continually reimplement existing functionality. This reuse includes the subclass accessing the properties and methods of its parent superclass. Thus, in Particle, I don't need to redeclare the loc, size (w, h and radius), or col properties at the top of the class, yet I can use them as if they were declared within the class; I can do the same with the Sprite class methods. (In the Arrow class I'll develop next, I'll take this one step further.) In the calls to super in the Particle constructors, notice I'm passing through argument values received by the constructors; this is how the superclass properties are initialized, allowing the subclass to reference these values.

I'm not yet going to go through all the details with regard to how the Particle objects are actually created, moved, fade, etc.; this will become more apparent as we begin testing the engine. However, there are a few additional points worth noting about this class before moving on.

The method call setColComponents() is made at the bottom of each of the constructors. I did this to facilitate access to the individual color components of each particle. Eventually, when I fade the particle, it will be necessary to change each particle's alpha setting and then update the col property. The last point I want to make is about the create() method:

```
void create(){
    fill(col);
    noStroke();
    ellipse(0, 0, radius*2, radius*2);
}
```

The Particle class includes a create() method, as does Sprite. This may seem to fly in the face of my earlier comment about inheritance preventing redundant code. Sometimes in a parent class a method functions more as a template for an implementation in a subclass. Implementation refers to the method's block of code (between the curly braces). There are ways of formally enforcing this relationship, for example using the abstract keyword, which we'll look at later in the book. Instead, I included a base particle implementation within the Sprite create() method, which will generate simple square particles. However, each of the Particle subclasses will be expected to reimplement this method. By reimplementing it, I simply mean including their own create() method (using the same method signature as in Sprite). In OOP, when a subclass has a method with the same signature as a method in the superclass, the subclass implementation is used. As we get further along in the example, you'll see how this design allows for a very convenient and flexible abstraction in terms of designing a family of related classes, such as a set of custom particle classes.

Arrow Class

I'll return to the Particle class when I rev up the engine. Next I'll discuss the Arrow class; Figure 5-8 shows an updated class diagram.

Sprite

• PVector loc + float size • color col
+ constructors • void create() + setter methods

Particle

(Sprite inherited properties) + color components • float lifeSpan • float damping • PVector vel
(Sprite inherited methods) + constructors • void setColComponents() • void create() ~overrides • void move() • void createFade() • void resetFade() • Particle getClone() + setter methods

Arrow

(Sprite inherited properties) (Particle inherited properties) • int tailFinCount • float len
(Sprite inherited methods) (Particle inherited methods) + constructors • void create() ~overrides • void move() ~overrides + setter methods

Figure 5-8. Updated class diagram, including the Arrow class

Notice the inheritance chain in the diagram, and how the Arrow class inherits both the members of Particle and Sprite. This allowed me to add few new members to Arrow, but still infuse it with lots of functionality. Also, since Arrow objects will point in the direction they are moving, I needed to implement both the move() and create() methods in the class. You'll remember that this means the subclass implementations of the two methods override the implementations in the superclass (of the methods with the same signatures). Next is the Arrow class code:

```
/**
 * Arrow class
 * Particle Engine
 * By Ira Greenberg <br />
 * The Essential Guide to Processing for Flash Developers,
 * Friends of ED, 2009
 */


class Arrow extends Particle{
 // properties with defaults
 int tailFinCount = 4;
 float len = 20.0;


 // default constructor
 Arrow(){
   // pass some defaults
   super(#0000DD, 5000, .875);
   // required for accurate collision detection
   radius = len/2;
 }


 // constructor
 Arrow(float w, color col, float lifeSpan, float damping, int tailFinCount){
   super(w, col, lifeSpan, damping);
   len = w;
   this.tailFinCount = tailFinCount;
   // required for accurate collision detection
   radius = len/2;
```

```
}

// overrides Particle create()
// draw arrow
void create(){
  float gap = 0.0;
  stroke(col);
  noFill();
  // draw arrow at 0 degrees on unit circle (facing right)
  // arrow shaft
  beginShape();
  vertex(-len/2, 0);
  vertex(len/2, 0);
  // tail
  if (tailFinCount > -1){
    // add tail feathers to last quarter of arrow shaft
    if (tailFinCount > 1){
      gap = len*.25/(tailFinCount-1);
    }
    for (int i=0; i<tailFinCount; i++){
      // top
      vertex(-len/2 + gap*i, 0);
      vertex(-len/2 - len/10.0 + gap*i, -len/10.0);
      //bottom
      vertex(-len/2 + gap*i, 0);
      vertex(-len/2 - len/10.0 + gap*i, len/10.0);
    }
    endShape();
    // head
    float theta = 0;
    float radius = len/8.0;
    fill(col);
    beginShape();
    for (int i=0; i<3; i++){
```

```
      vertex(len/2.0 + cos(theta)*radius, sin(theta)*radius);
      theta += PI/1.5;
    }
    endShape(CLOSE);
  }
}


// override Particle move()
// - arrow requires rotation alignment
void move(){
  loc.add(vel);
  translate(loc.x, loc.y);
  rotate(atan2(vel.y, vel.x));
}


// setters
void setTailFinCount(int tailFinCount){
  this.tailFinCount = tailFinCount;
}


void setLen(float len){
  this.len = len;
  radius = len/2;
}
}
```

This is completed class code, which you should add to the current sketch in a new tab named **Arrow**. The arrow particles require a bit more drawing than the simple particles, and I also added a rotation to them, ensuring they always point in the direction they're moving. The drawing code in the create() method should be self-explanatory, simply utilizing a series of vertex() calls. I created a len property in Arrow. Its value is shared (through an assignment operation) to the radius property in Shape. I only added len for the purpose of semantic consistency; we think of an arrow having a length, not a radius. The move() method is probably the most complex part of the Arrow class. Here it is again isolated:

```
void move(){
    loc.add(vel);
    translate(loc.x, loc.y);
    rotate(atan2(vel.y, vel.x));
}
```

Although this is a pretty short method, it's utilizing some sophisticated principles. Notice I'm moving the `Arrow` particles using Processing's `translate()` function, rather than directly incrementing, say, an x and y property, as you might do in ActionScript. The `move()` method does increment the `PVector loc` property (inherited from `Sprite`), but this property is then fed into the `translate()` function, not directly assigned to x and y properties utilized in the actual drawing of the arrows. The reason for doing this, which I've discussed in other places in the book, is to be able to draw the `Arrow` objects centered at the origin (0, 0). By drawing objects around the origin, you can rotate them around their center point (the way a propeller is supposed to rotate). When we call `translate()` in Processing, we're moving the entire contents (technically the drawing context) of the window, including the origin; everything drawn after translation is shifted over by this distance. It is common to refer to this space as world coordinate space. If instead of translation I did move the arrows some distance, relative to the origin, then they would appear to rotate around the origin the distance they were moved (the way an object tied to a string would rotate).

In the short code example that follows, shown in Figure 5-9, the rectangle on the left is drawn centered at the origin and then translated along the world coordinate space, allowing it to both rotate around its center point while also being moved to the center of the screen. The rectangle on the right, by comparison, is drawn offset of the origin. Do you think this rectangle will rotate like a propeller or an object tied to a string?

```
// transformations in world space
float x, y, w = 120, h = 10;
void setup(){
  size(800, 400);
  smooth();
  rectMode(CENTER);
}
void draw(){
  // paint background
  fill(0, 5);
  rect(width/2-1, height/2-1, width+2, height+2);
  // divide canvas
```

```
line(width/2, 0, width/2, height);
stroke(255);
fill(0);
// rotate around object origin
pushMatrix();
// translate world space
translate(width*.25, height/2);
rotate(frameCount*PI/180);
// center at object origin
x = 0;
y = 0;
rect(x, y, w, h);
popMatrix();
// rotate with object offset
pushMatrix();
// translate world space
translate(width*.75, height/2);
rotate(-frameCount*PI/180);
// offset object space by 100, 100
x = 100;
y = 100;
rect(x, y, w, h);
popMatrix();
}
```

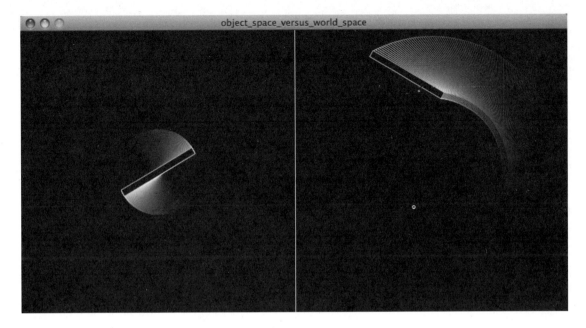

Figure 5-9. Object coordinate space versus world coordinate space

The rotation of the arrows is handled by the line `rotate(atan2(vel.y, vel.x))`, in the `move()` method. `vel` is an instance property (of type `PVector`) declared within the `Particle` class, assigned the particle's velocity. If you haven't programmed something (such as a game perhaps) that involved firing or steering, this function call may seem pretty mysterious.

`atan2()` is a math function that is included in most programming language math libraries, including ActionScript, Java, and Processing, just to name a few. It's actually a variant of the trigonometry arctangent function modified for computer graphics—again, to help with things like aiming and steering. Arctangent is considered an inverse function to the tangent function that returns an angle of rotation in the range of –Pi/2 to Pi/2. However, for rotating the arrow (or anything else that would need to be able to rotate fully) we need a value returned in the range of -Pi to Pi; this is precisely the sort of thing `atan2()` corrects for. I suspect this information still doesn't shed much light on why `atan2()` works. To understand it, you may want to consider how the sine and cosine functions are used in rotation. I've discussed this in other places in the book already, so hopefully the following two expressions look familiar:

```
x = cos(theta) * radius;
y = sin(theta) * radius;
```

These powerful, yet simple, lines of code convert polar coordinate values (where location is defined by an angle of rotation and a radius) to the Cartesian coordinate system (the standard x, y grid) of our screens. Using the two trig expressions, as we increment or decrement the value of theta (expressed in radians), we can move clockwise or counterclockwise around a circular path respectively. How these expressions directly connect to the atan2() function is more apparent when you consider the following relationship between tangent, sine, and cosine:

$$\tan gent(\theta) = \frac{Sine(\theta)}{cosine(\theta)}$$

Therefore, arctangent (written in the equation as arctan) can be expressed as

$$\theta = \arctan\left(\frac{y}{x}\right)$$

If you're still scratching your head about all this, don't worry; understanding the math is not a prerequisite for using the atan2() function. Figure 5-10 illustrates how atan2() relates to sin() and cos(), as it applies to our purpose—finding an angle of rotation. If, however, you'd like to explore more of the math behind the inverse trig functions, check out http://www.euclideanspace.com/maths/geometry/trig/inverse/index.htm (November 17, 2009, 15:33).

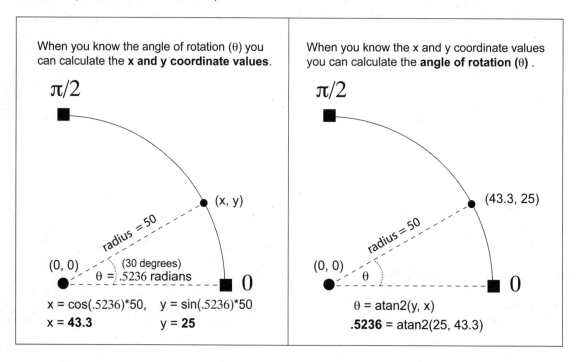

Figure 5-10. atan2() illustrated

We'll run some initial tests soon with the evolving engine, but prior to that it might be helpful to see atan2() in action. Next is a very simple example that uses the mouse to control the rotation of a triangle, shown in Figure 5-11.

```
/**
 * atan2() Example
 * By Ira Greenberg <br />
 * The Essential Guide to Processing for Flash Developers,
 * Friends of ED, 2009
 */


float theta = 0.0, radius = 20.0, offset = 0.0;
PVector[] tri = new PVector[3];

void setup(){
  size(400, 400);
  background(255);
  smooth();
  for (int i=0; i<tri.length; i++){
    if (i==0){
      offset = 80.0;
    }
    else {
      offset = 0.0;
    }
    tri[i] = new PVector(cos(theta)*(radius+offset), sin(theta)*(radius+offset));
    theta += PI/1.5;
  }
}

void draw(){
  fill(255, 32);
  rect(-1, -1, width+1, height+1);
  fill(165);
  translate(width/2, height/2);
  rotate(atan2(mouseY - height/2, mouseX - width/2));
  beginShape();
  for (int i=0; i<tri.length; i++){
```

211

```
    vertex(tri[i].x, tri[i].y);
  }
  endShape(CLOSE);
}
```

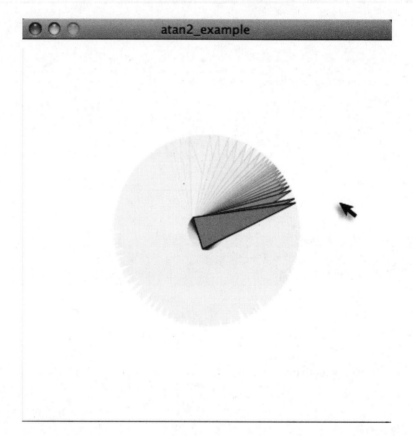

Figure 5-11. atan2() example

Emitter Class

To begin to rev up our engine, we'll need a way of projecting the particles. There are numerous ways you could do this, including by simply calling the move() method on the Particle objects directly. However, this approach will be more limiting (and ultimately more confusing) in the long run. A better approach is to encapsulate this process, by delegating the actual firing of the particles to an Emitter class. This approach will give us more high-level control, while concealing the less friendly-looking emission calculations. Next is an updated diagram including an Emitter class, shown in Figure 5-12.

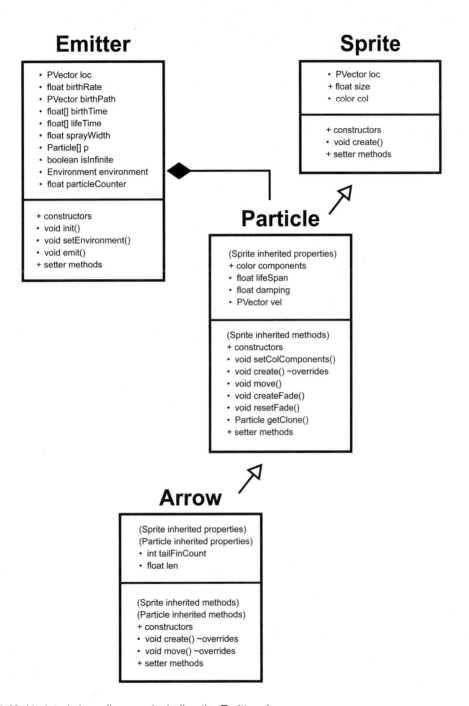

Figure 5-12. Updated class diagram, including the Emitter class

I included a new symbol in the updated diagram, the filled-in diamond, with a line connecting the Emitter class to the Particle class. The diamond represents a compositional relationship between Emitter and Particle. Composition, like inheritance, is an OOP technique for creating relationships between classes, allowing them to work together. Where inheritance involves one class extending another class, composition involves embedding a reference to a class within another class—in our case, embedding a reference to the Particle class within the Emitter class. In OOP parlance, we speak of composition being a "**has a**" relationship (the Emitter object **has an** Arrow particle) and inheritance being an "**is a**" (the Arrow object **is a** type of Particle). Composition relationships can be further granularly defined, including an aggregate relationship, which I won't cover here, but you can read more about at http://en.wikipedia.org/wiki/Object_composition (November 17, 2009, 15:33).

The Emitter class is more complicated than the classes discussed thus far. However, as expected, it follows an identical class structure to the other classes shown. The following code should be put within its own tab in the current sketch, named **Emitter**.

```
/**
 * Emitter class
 * Particle Engine
 * By Ira Greenberg <br />
 * The Essential Guide to Processing for Flash Developers,
 * Friends of ED, 2009
 */


class Emitter {

  // Properties
  // emitter position
  PVector loc = new PVector(0, 0);
  // rate particles are created
  float birthRate;
  // 3D path particles are projected
  PVector birthPath;
  // keep track of particle lifespan
  float[] birthTime;
  float[] lifeTime;
  // frame rate of the sketch, default is 60fps
  float sketchFrameRate;
  // radius the particles spray from the emitter at birth
  float sprayWidth;
```

```
// ammo
Particle[] p;

// By default emitter runs infinitely
boolean isInfinite = true;

// Environment reference with default instantiation
Environment environment = new Environment();

// used to control particle birth rate
float particleCounter = 0.0;

// default constructor
Emitter(){
}

// constructor for infinite emission
Emitter(PVector loc, float sketchFrameRate, PVector birthPath, ↵
   float sprayWidth, Particle[] p){
  this.loc = loc;
  this.sketchFrameRate = sketchFrameRate;
  birthRate = p.length/((p[0].lifeSpan/1000.0) * (sketchFrameRate));
  this.birthPath = birthPath;
  this.sprayWidth = sprayWidth;
  birthTime = new float[p.length];
  lifeTime = new float[p.length];
  this.p = p;
  for (int i=0; i<p.length; i++){
    init(i);
  }
}

// constructor for single emission with birthRate param
// (good for explosions, etc)
```

```
Emitter(PVector loc, PVector birthPath, float birthRate, ⏎
    float sprayWidth, Particle[] p){
  this.loc = loc;
  // ensure birthRate max is particleCount-1
  this.birthRate = min(birthRate, p.length-1);
  this.birthPath = birthPath;
  this.sprayWidth = sprayWidth;
  birthTime = new float[p.length];
  lifeTime = new float[p.length];
  this.p = p;
  for (int i=0; i<p.length; i++){
    init(i);
  }
  isInfinite = false;
}


// called at the beginning of each emission cyle
// (and initially by the constructor)
void init(int i){
  float theta = random(TWO_PI);
  float r = random(sprayWidth);
  p[i].vel = new PVector(birthPath.x + cos(theta)*r, birthPath.y + sin(theta)*r);
}


void setEnvironment(Environment environment){
  this.environment = environment;
}


// general methods
void emit(){
  for (int i=0; i<particleCounter; i++){
    pushMatrix();
    //move each particle to emitter location
    translate(loc.x, loc.y);
    // draw/move particle
```

```
  p[i].move();
  p[i].create();
  popMatrix();

  // capture time at particle birth
  if (birthTime[i] == 0.0){
    birthTime[i] = millis();
  }
  if (lifeTime[i] < p[i].lifeSpan){
    // accelerate based on gravity
    p[i].vel.y += environment.gravity;

    p[i].vel.y += random(-environment.turbulence, ↩
      environment.turbulence) + environment.wind.y;

    p[i].vel.x += random(-environment.turbulence, ↩
      environment.turbulence) + environment.wind.x;
    p[i].vel.mult(environment.resistance);
    // fade particle
    p[i].createFade(p[i].initAlpha/(frameRate*(p[i].lifeSpan/1000)));
  }
  else {
    if (isInfinite){
      // keep emitter going
      p[i].loc.mult(0.0);
      init(i);
      birthTime[i] = millis();
      p[i].resetFade();
    }
  }
  lifeTime[i] = millis() - birthTime[i];
}

// controls rate of emission
if (particleCounter < p.length - birthRate){
  particleCounter += birthRate;
}
```

```
  }

  // set methods
  void setLoc(PVector loc){
    this.loc = loc;
  }

  void setBirthRate(float birthRate){
    this.birthRate = birthRate;
  }
}
```

I'll discuss this code in manageable chunks, beginning with the properties defined at the top of the class. I've added comments for most of the properties, which I think provide a fairly clear picture as to what each property does. I think a general overview of the particle emission process will be most helpful.

The Emitter class allows particles to either be born in a single burst without repeat, like in an explosion, or for the emitter to run infinitely, like a replenishing fountain. The birthrate of the emitter relates to the total number of particles added to the emitter as well as the frame rate of the sketch. In addition, there is a property for controlling how long the particles live, before they fade away. There are properties for controlling where the emitter is located in the world space and also the direction the particles are initially emitted. To this latter point, the particles will be initially controlled by an emission vector that shoots the particles out, until environmental and particle-specific dynamics take over. Also, notice that a few of the properties are declared with initial values, including a couple that are instantiated at the top of the class. I did this to allow the emitters to be used with minimal setup, which I'll demonstrate shortly.

The Emitter constructors are also a bit more complex than others we've looked at previously. For example, in the first constructor, the line

```
birthRate = p.length/((p[0].lifeSpan/1000.0) * (sketchFrameRate));
```

calculates the emitter's birthrate, taking into account the total particle count, the particle lifespan (of the first particle in the array), and the frame rate of the sketch. This last factor needs some additional clarification. By default, Processing's frame rate is 60 frames per second, and Processing includes the global variable frameRate, which should report back the current frame rate of the sketch. However, it takes a couple of frames for this rate to stabilize. For example, when I run the following code:

```
void setup(){}
void draw(){
  println(int(frameRate));
}
```

I get the following output (through 39 values):

11	15	20	24	27	31	34	36	39	41	43	44	46
47	49	50	50	51	52	53	54	54	55	55	56	56
56	57	57	57	58	58	58	58	58	58	58	58	59

This delay prevented me from referencing frameRate in the constructor in the birthRate calculation. To solve this, I explicitly passed in the frame rate using the sketchFrameRate parameter. The birthRate calculation ensures that the emitter keeps shooting particles continuously.

In the second constructor, used for single-burst emissions, I just needed to ensure that the birth rate didn't exceed the length of the particle array.

At the bottom of both constructors I pass the individual particles to an init() method:

```
for (int i=0; i<p.length; i++){
      init(i);
}
```

The init() method calculates the initial particle velocity based on the birth Path vector and a random rotational offset.

The emit() method is where all the particle dynamics are calculated. Notice that the calculations rely heavily on the environment object. At the top of the Emitter class I declared and instantiated this object. However, this default instantiation of the Environment class is not the final one that you'll utilize with the Emitter. Eventually, when we use an encompassing Engine class, we'll pass in a more customized Environment object to the engine, along with the emitters and colliders. The engine will then manage this relationship between the emitters and environment. By including a default Environment instantiation in the Emitter class, though, I provide a simple way of using the Emitter class without the Engine class, with default Environment property values. I'll discuss the Environment class next, but before I do, I just want to mention one last thing about the emit() method, specifically the following snippet (please note I left out the code in the if block):

```
if (lifeTime[i] < p[i].lifeSpan){

   ...

}
else {
        if (isInfinite){
          // keep emitter going
          p[i].loc.mult(0.0);
          init(i);
```

```
        birthTime[i] = millis();
        p[i].resetFade();
      }
    }
  lifeTime[i] = millis() - birthTime[i];
```

The else block only runs for perpetually running emitters, when the dynamic lifeTime value of the particle becomes equal to its preset lifeSpan value; this causes a reinitialization, putting the particle back in the emitter and resetting its lifeSpan and alpha values. You'll notice I'm using Processing's millis() function to calculate each particle's lifeTime. millis() returns the time the Processing sketch has been running in milliseconds since executed. In addition to millis(), Processing also includes the time/calendar functions: second(), minute(), hour(), day(), month(), year().(), year().

> *I want to make one last point about the Emitter class, which is honestly a bit of a disclaimer. I chose to make this class handle the complete motion of particles—controlling the particles' emission (really birth) through acceleration and ultimate fading. This decision was based primarily on how I wrote and structured the chapter. My technical reviewer, David Wicks, felt the Emitter should be less involved and the Engine class should handle more of the load. In pure OOP terms, David is right. (As David is a former student of mine, his being right makes me quite proud, bruised ego and all.) That said, I've decided to offer both engine examples as a download on the book's site. I'm honored to present David's improved OOP design right alongside my own.*

Environment Class

Figure 5-13 shows an updated class diagram, including the Environment class.

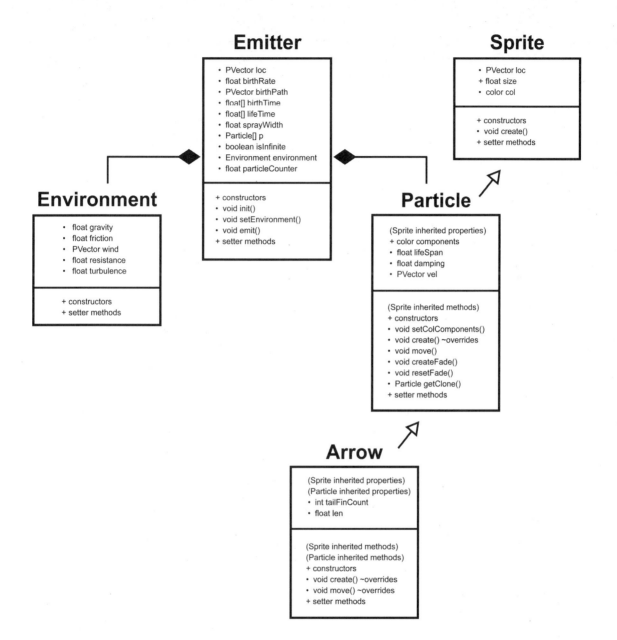

Figure 5-13. Updated class diagram, including the Environment class

This is a pretty simple class consisting of some constructors and setter methods. Next is the class code, which should be put in a new tab in the current sketch, named **Environment**:

```
/**
 * Environment class
 * Particle Engine
 * By Ira Greenberg <br />
 * The Essential Guide to Processing for Flash Developers,
 * Friends of ED, 2009
 */


class Environment{
  // props with some defaults
  float gravity =.05;
  float friction = .875;
  PVector wind = new PVector(0, 0);
  float resistance = .985;
  float turbulence = .04;

  // default constructor
  Environment(){
  }

  // constructor
  Environment(float gravity, float friction, PVector wind, float resistance, ↩
    float turbulence){
    this.gravity = gravity;
    this.friction  = friction;
    this.wind = wind;
    this.resistance = resistance;
    this.turbulence = turbulence;
  }

  // constructor
  Environment(float gravity, float friction, PVector wind){
    this.gravity = gravity;
```

```
    this.friction  = friction;
    this.wind = wind;
  }


  // setter methods
  void setGravity(float gravity){
    this.gravity = gravity;
  }


  void setFriction(float friction){
    this.friction  = friction;
  }


  void setWind(PVector wind){
    this.wind = wind;
  }


  void setResistance(float resistance){
    this.resistance = resistance;
  }


  void setTurbulence(float turbulence){
    this.turbulence = turbulence;
  }
}
```

I don't think this class needs any elucidation, as it's basically a convenience class that encapsulates a bunch of dynamics property values with some constructors and setters.

We're almost ready to test out the particle system. However, since the initial Engine class code included a reference to a Collider object, we just need to create a Collider stub class for now to get our code to compile properly; we'll shortly fill the rest of it in. A stub class is just a skeleton of a class, usually with just a class declaration and some message signatures; mine will be really simple, including only the class declaration and one method signature. Add the following code to a new tab named "**Collider**":

```
/**
 * Collider class
 * Particle Engine
```

```
* By Ira Greenberg <br />
* The Essential Guide to Processing for Flash Developers,
* Friends of ED, 2009
*/


class Collider{
  void create(){
  }
}
```

It is now possible to test the system. If you've been following along, adding to the current **particle_engine** sketch throughout the chapter, you should now have a sketch tab structure that looks something like the image shown in Figure 5-14. Notice that I haven't added any code to the main tab yet; I'll do that next.

Figure 5-14. Current screenshot of particle _engine sketch

To test the engine, we just need to create some particles and an emitter and then call the Emitter emit() method. Here's some code to add to the main sketch tab, to try the engine:

```
/**
 * Particle Engine
 * By Ira Greenberg <br />
 * The Essential Guide to Processing for Flash Developers,
 * Friends of ED, 2009
 */


// create particle population
int particleCount = 300;
// instantiate particle array
Particle[] particles = new Particle[particleCount];
// declare emitter
Emitter emitter;
// explicitely set frameRate;
float myFrameRate = 60.0;

void setup(){
  size(600, 400);
  background(0);
  smooth();
  frameRate(myFrameRate);
  // instantiate particles
  for (int i=0; i<particleCount; i++){
    particles[i] = new Particle(random(1, 3), color(255, random(90, 128), 10), 2000, .85);
  }
  // instantiate emitter
  //emitter = new Emitter(new PVector(300, 100), new PVector(0, 0), 20, 10, arrows);
  emitter = new Emitter(new PVector(width/2, 100), myFrameRate, new PVector(0, -1), ↩
    .5, particles);
}
```

```
void draw(){
  background(0);
  emitter.emit();
}
```

Figure 5-15 shows a screenshot of the running sketch.

Figure 5-15. Screenshot of the running sketch with base particles

Again, I'll eventually encapsulate the emitter objects and emit() calls within the Engine class, but I've structured the code so you can test the emitters independently of the Engine class. Before finishing up the Engine and Collider classes, I suggest playing with the argument values passed in the Particle and Emitter instantiations, in the lines

```
particles[i] = new Particle(random(1, 3), color(255, random(90, 128), 10), 2000, .85);
...

emitter = new Emitter(new PVector(width/2, 100), myFrameRate, new PVector(0, -1), ↵
  .5, particles);
```

Figure 5-16 shows a screenshot of the running sketch using Arrow particles and a larger spray width.

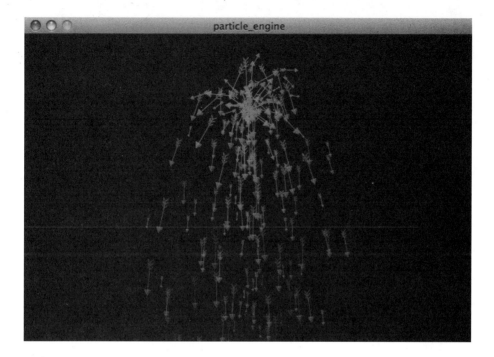

Figure 5-16. Screenshot of the running sketch with Arrow particles

Collider Class

Collision detection, especially accurate collision detection, is not a simple subject; in fact, there are entire equation-filled books devoted to it. My approach is an attempt to create a relatively simple collision response, based on collisions between the particles and simple circular objects, as opposed to more accurate detection between, say, individual polygons and/or even line segments. Yet, in spite of trying to keep this basic collision as simple as possible, I still needed to incorporate the most complex math I've discussed thus far in the book. There are two problems in collision handling that contributed to this: accurate detection of the collision and a physically realistic response. On both these fronts, my solutions are *good enough* for aesthetically-oriented applications, but probably not approaches you'd want to use to, say, land a rover on Mars.

The first step in implementing collision will be finishing up the Collider class. Figure 5-17 shows an updated class diagram incorporating Collider.

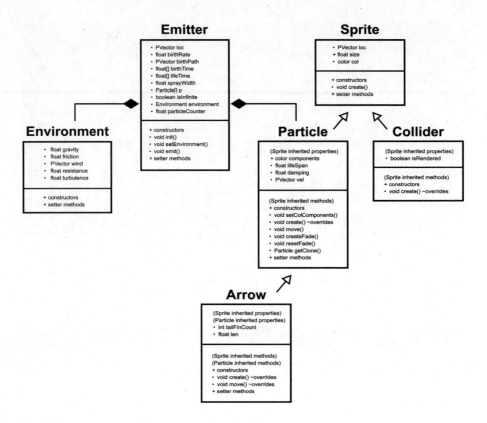

Figure 5-17. Updated class diagram, including the Collider class

I left the Collider class very simple, essentially just including the option of drawing the colliders or leaving them invisible. (The more gnarly collision calculations will occur in the Engine class, which I'll discuss next.) Again, a lot more could be done with this class, to greatly increase the sophistication of collision response in the particle engine—which would make another great expanded project for the more mathematically inclined reader. Next is the final Collider class code, which should replace the stub code currently in the **Collider** tab.

```
/**
 * Collider class
 * Particle Engine
 * By Ira Greenberg <br />
 * The Essential Guide to Processing for Flash Developers,
 * Friends of ED, 2009
 */
```

```
class Collider extends Sprite{

  // use to control collider visibility
  boolean isRendered;

  // default constructor
  Collider(){
  }

  // constructor - smooth circle
  Collider(PVector loc, float radius, color col, boolean isRendered){
    super(loc, radius, col);
    this.isRendered = isRendered;
  }

  void create(){
    noStroke();
    // only draw if true
    if (isRendered){
      fill(col);
      pushMatrix();
      translate(loc.x, loc.y);
      ellipse(0, 0, radius*2, radius*2);
      popMatrix();
    }
  }
}
```

This code should be self-explanatory; just remember that Collider extends Sprite and so has access to both the Sprite and Collider class members.

Engine Class

We're almost there! The final step is completing the Engine class. As mentioned earlier, the Engine class provides centralized command and control, managing (through composition) the Emitter, Collider, and Environment classes. Because Engine owns a lot of tasks, it's also chock-full of code, some of which is fairly dense. Figure 5-18 shows the finalized class diagram, including the Engine class.

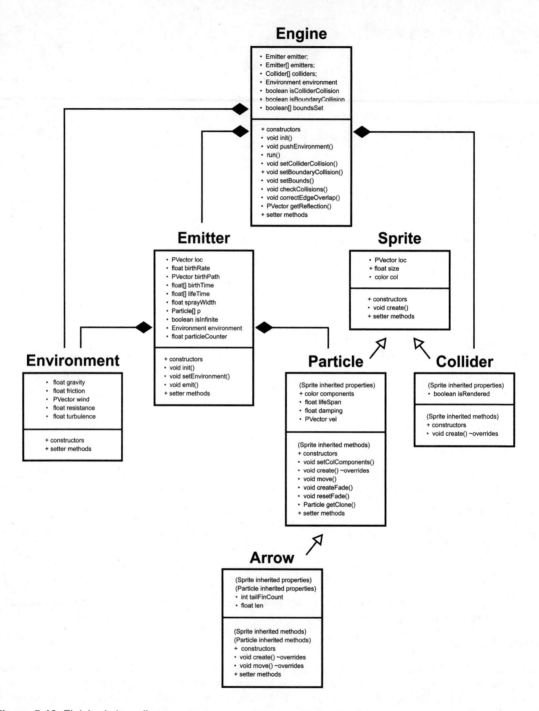

Figure 5-18. Finished class diagram

Next is the finished Engine class. I've put in **bold** the new code, not included in the original Engine class shown near the beginning of the chapter. If you've been following along, building the particle engine incrementally, you just need to add the code in bold to the existing code in the Engine tab. However, it might be simpler to replace all the code in the **Engine** tab with the finished code.

```
/**
 * Engine class
 * Particle Engine
 * By Ira Greenberg <br />
 * Processing for Flash Developers,
 * Friends of ED, 2009
 */


class Engine {

  // properties
  Emitter emitter;
  Emitter[] emitters;
  Collider[] colliders;

 // create default environment
  Environment environment = new Environment();

  // engine states
  boolean isColliderCollision;
  boolean isBoundaryCollision;

  // for individual boundary collisions
  boolean[] boundsSet = {false, false, false, false};

  // default constructor
  Engine(){
  }

  // constructor
  Engine(Emitter emitter, Environment environment){
```

```
    this.emitter = emitter;
    this.environment = environment;
    init();
    pushEnvironment();
}


// constructor
Engine(Emitter[] emitters, Environment environment){
  this.emitters = emitters;
  this.environment = environment;
  pushEnvironment();
}


// constructor
Engine(Emitter emitter, Collider[] colliders, Environment environment){
  this.emitter = emitter;
  this.colliders = colliders;
  this.environment = environment;
  init();
  pushEnvironment();
}


// constructor
Engine(Emitter[] emitters, Collider[] colliders, Environment environment){
  this.emitters = emitters;
  this.colliders = colliders;
  this.environment = environment;
  pushEnvironment();
}


// If only 1 emitter added to engine,
// add to emitters array
void init(){
  emitters = new Emitter[1];
```

```
    emitters[0] = emitter;
  }


  // pass through environment object to emitter objects
  // - emitters handle controlling particles, not engine
  void pushEnvironment(){
    for (int i=0; i<emitters.length; i++){
      emitters[i].setEnvironment(environment);
    }
  }


  // called in draw function to run engine
  void run(){
    if (emitters != null && emitters.length > 0){
      for (int i=0; i<emitters.length; i++){
        emitters[i].emit();
      }
      checkCollisions();
    }

    if (colliders != null && colliders.length>0){
      for (int i=0; i<colliders.length; i++){
        colliders[i].create();
      }
    }
  }


  void setColliderCollision(boolean isColliderCollision){
    this.isColliderCollision =  isColliderCollision;
  }


  // overloaded setBoundaryCollision method - individual boundaries set
  void setBoundaryCollision(boolean isBoundaryCollision, boolean[] boundsSet){
```

```
    this.isBoundaryCollision =  isBoundaryCollision;
    this.boundsSet = boundsSet;
}


// overloaded setBoundaryCollision method - all boundaries set
void setBoundaryCollision(boolean isBoundaryCollision){
    this.isBoundaryCollision =  isBoundaryCollision;
    for (int i=0; i< boundsSet.length; i++){
        boundsSet[i] =true;
    }
}


// set individual boundary collisions to true
void setBounds(boolean[] boundsSet){
    this.boundsSet = boundsSet;
}


// collision detection
void checkCollisions(){
    // boundary collisions
    if (isBoundaryCollision){
        for (int i=0; i<emitters.length; i++){
            for (int j=0; j<emitters[i].p.length; j++){
                Particle part = emitters[i].p[j];
                // right bounds collision
                if (boundsSet[0] && part.loc.x > width - emitters[i].loc.x -↵
                part.radius){
                    part.loc.x = width - emitters[i].loc.x - part.radius;
                    part.vel.x *= -1;
                }
                // left bounds collision
                else if (boundsSet[1] && part.loc.x < -emitters[i].loc.x +↵
```

```
      part.radius){
        part.loc.x = -emitters[i].loc.x + part.radius;
        part.vel.x *= -1;
      }


      // bottom bounds collision
      if (boundsSet[2] && part.loc.y > height-emitters[i].loc.y -↵
      part.radius){
        part.loc.y = height-emitters[i].loc.y - part.radius;
        part.vel.y *= -1;
        part.vel.y *= part.damping;
        part.vel.x *= environment.friction;
      }
      // top bounds collision
      else if (boundsSet[3] && part.loc.y < -emitters[i].loc.y +↵
      part.radius){
        part.loc.y = -emitters[i].loc.y + part.radius;
        part.vel.y *= -1;
      }
    }
  }
}
// collider collision
if (colliders != null && colliders.length>0){
  for (int i=0; i<emitters.length; i++){
    for (int j=0; j<emitters[i].p.length; j++){
      // get shallow clone of current particle
      Particle part = emitters[i].p[j].getClone();
      // add emitter offset
      part.loc.add(emitters[i].loc);


      // check each particle against colliders
```

```
            for (int k=0; k<colliders.length; k++){
              Collider cldr = colliders[k];
              if (dist(part.loc.x, part.loc.y, cldr.loc.x, cldr.loc.y) <↵
              part.radius + cldr.radius){
                // set particle to collider bounds to avoid overlap
                correctEdgeOverlap(emitters[i].p[j], cldr, emitters[i].loc);
                // get reflection vector
                PVector rv = getReflection(part, cldr);
                emitters[i].p[j].setVel(rv);
                // damping  slows particles upon collisions
                emitters[i].p[j].vel.y*=emitters[i].p[j].damping;
              }
            }
          }
        }
      }
    }

// reset to boundary edges
void correctEdgeOverlap(Particle part, Collider collider, PVector↵
  emitterOffset){
  // temporarily add emitter location to particle
  part.loc.add(emitterOffset);
  // get vector between object centers
  PVector collisionNormal = PVector.sub(part.loc, collider.loc);
  // convert vector to Unit length
  collisionNormal.normalize();
  // set to perfect distance (sum of both radii)
  collisionNormal.mult(collider.radius + part.radius);
  // put particle precisely on collider edge
  part.loc.set(PVector.add(collider.loc, collisionNormal));
  // subtract emitter location
```

```
    part.loc.sub(emitterOffset);
}


//Non-orthogonal Reflection, using rotation of coordinate system
PVector getReflection(Particle particle, Collider collider){
    // get vector between object centers
    PVector collisionNormal = PVector.sub(particle.loc, collider.loc);
    // calculate reflection angle by rotating vectors to 0 on unit circle
    // inital theta of collisionnormal
    float theta = atan2(collisionNormal.y, collisionNormal.x);

    // rotate particle velocity vector by -theta (to bring 0 on unit circle)
    float vx = cos(-theta)*particle.vel.x - sin(-theta)*particle.vel.y;
    float vy = sin(-theta)*particle.vel.x + cos(-theta)*particle.vel.y;

    // reverse x component and rotate velocity vector back to original position
    PVector temp = new PVector(vx, vy);
    vx = cos(theta)*-temp.x - sin(theta)*temp.y;
    vy = sin(theta)*-temp.x + cos(theta)*temp.y;
    return new PVector(vx, vy);
}


// setters
void setEmitter(Emitter emitter){
    this.emitter = emitter;
    // create emitters array and adds emitter at [0]
    init();
    // pass environment to emitters
    pushEnvironment();
}


void setEmitter(Emitter[] emitters){
    this.emitters = emitters;
```

```
  // pass environment to emitters
  pushEnvironment();
}

  void setColliders(Collider[] colliders){
    this.colliders = colliders;
  }

  void setEnvironment(Environment environment){
    this.environment = environment;
    // ensures particles have been added to engine
    // before calling pushEnvironment()
    if (emitters != null){
      pushEnvironment();
    }
  }
}
```

If you skim quickly through the code in bold, you'll see it primarily involves integration of the environment object and collision detection—the latter being the bulk of the complexity. Near the top of the class I included three new properties:

```
boolean isColliderCollision;
boolean isBoundaryCollision;
boolean[] boundsSet = {false, false, false, false};
```

These assist in collision detection—the first between particles and colliders and the second and third between particles and the boundaries of the running sketch window. isColliderCollision and isBoundaryCollision are boolean flags that set the state of collision response. In other words, if these are set to true, the engine should calculate the respective type of collision. Using flags is a relatively simple way to control a program state: on or off. The boundsSet array includes four flags used to control which boundaries should have collision detection enabled; they correspond to boundsSet[0] (right), boundsSet[1] (left), boundsSet[2] (bottom), boundsSet[3] (top).

The next new code is the pushEnvironment() call added to the constructors, followed by the same named method. The environment object is used by the emitters in calculating particle motion. I chose not to pass the environment object directly to the individual emitters during their instantiation. Instead, I chose to have the engine accept the environment argument and then push it through to the emitters. This was really more of a design decision than anything else; it could have been handled the other way as well, with each emitter object being passed an environment object directly. However, I think it is simpler to just have the Engine class receive and manage the Environment object.

Next, I added the checkCollisions() method call to the run() method. This simple call begins a chain reaction of lots of collision checking, which I'll get to shortly.

Following run(), I added four new methods (please note that I only reproduced their signatures here):

```
void setColliderCollision(boolean isColliderCollision)

void setBoundaryCollision(boolean isBoundaryCollision, boolean[] boundsSet)

void setBoundaryCollision(boolean isBoundaryCollision)

void setBounds(boolean[] boundsSet)
```

These are setter methods for the collision flags I mentioned earlier. Notice that the setBoundaryCollision() calls are overloaded, allowing boundaries to be set both individually or all together.

Returning now to the checkCollsions() method, I'll discuss it in sections. The code that handles the boundary collision is the most straightforward, shown next:

```
// boundary collisions
    if (isBoundaryCollision){
      for (int i=0; i<emitters.length; i++){
        for (int j=0; j<emitters[i].p.length; j++){
          Particle part = emitters[i].p[j];
          // right bounds collision
          if (boundsSet[0] && part.loc.x > width - emitters[i].loc.x - part.radius){
            part.loc.x = width - emitters[i].loc.x - part.radius;
            part.vel.x *= -1;
          }
          // left bounds collision
          else if (boundsSet[1] && part.loc.x < -emitters[i].loc.x + part.radius){
            part.loc.x = -emitters[i].loc.x + part.radius;
            part.vel.x *= -1;
          }

          // bottom bounds collision
          if (boundsSet[2] && part.loc.y > height-emitters[i].loc.y - part.radius){
```

```
        part.loc.y = height-emitters[i].loc.y - part.radius;
        part.vel.y *= -1;
        part.vel.y *= part.damping;
        part.vel.x *- environment.friction;
      }
      // top bounds collision
      else if (boundsSet[3] && part.loc.y < -emitters[i].loc.y + part.radius){
        part.loc.y = -emitters[i].loc.y + part.radius;
        part.vel.y *= -1;
      }
    }
  }
}
```

The boundary collision code is nested in a conditional block controlled by the isBoundaryCollision flag; the block is executed only if the flag evaluates to true. The code here does get a little dense, due to the level of encapsulation of the actual particles within the engine; each particle is part of an array of particles, contained within an individual emitter, which is then referenced within an array of emitters within the engine. The actual conditional collision test of a particle with the boundaries should look familiar, as we've done this before. The two if/else blocks check all four boundaries.

The basic algorithm for the detection is

1. check if the particle has passed through the boundary
2. place the particle on the collision edge
3. reverse the particle's velocity vector

Notice within the bottom collision if statement—the one that begins if (boundsSet[2] && part.loc.y > height-emitters[i].loc.y - part.radius)—that I'm using damping and friction for some simulated physics when the particles hit the bottom boundary.

Below the boundary collision code, I check for collider collision, which is where things get more complex. Here again is the block I'm referring to:

```
// collider collision
    if (colliders != null && colliders.length>0){
      for (int i=0; i<emitters.length; i++){
        for (int j=0; j<emitters[i].p.length; j++){
          // get shallow clone of current particle
          Particle part = emitters[i].p[j].getClone();
```

```
      // add emitter offset
      part.loc.add(emitters[i].loc);

      // check each particle against colliders
      for (int k=0; k<colliders.length; k++){
        Collider cldr = colliders[k];
        if (dist(part.loc.x, part.loc.y, cldr.loc.x, cldr.loc.y) < part.radius + ⏎
          cldr.radius){
          // set particle to collider bounds to avoid overlap
          correctEdgeOverlap(emitters[i].p[j], cldr, emitters[i].loc);
          // get reflection vector
          PVector rv = getReflection(part, cldr);
          emitters[i].p[j].setVel(rv);
          // damping  slows particles upon collisions
          emitters[i].p[j].vel.y*=emitters[i].p[j].damping;
        }
      }
    }
  }
}
```

As just shown, when colliding against an orthogonal surface, like the ground or wall, we just need to reverse the sign of the velocity vector (on one axis) to give a realistic-looking reaction. However, when the collision response is against a non-orthogonal surface we need a little more math to solve the problem.

The collider collision block of code begins with a conditional check to ensure that the colliders array exists (!=null) and that it has some length; obviously, there is no reason to execute collision testing if there are no colliders. The next line

```
Particle part = emitters[i].p[j].getClone();
```

calls a custom cloning method I wrote. I did this because I needed a simple way to get a copy of the current Particle object being evaluated. To less experienced programmers, you may be wondering about the reasons to go through all the cloning, when you can simply assign the current particle to a new particle variable, like this:

```
Particle part = emitters[i].p[j];
```

Unfortunately, this won't work. Processing and Java (and ActionScript) pass objects by reference, not value. What this means in a practical sense is that when objects are assigned to a reference variable (such as `Particle part` in the previous problematic expression), their contents (property values) are not actually assigned; instead, the memory location of the object is assigned. Saying this another way, after assignment both the original object reference variable and the (assigned to) reference variable now point to the same memory location, and if you subsequently change any value in the object (using either of the object references) the change will be reflected for both references to the object. (There is only one memory location for the object regardless of the amount of references to it.) Next is a simple example that proves this point. I also discus reference variables in greater detail in Chapter 3 and Chapter 8.

```
void setup(){
  Obj o1 = new Obj();
  println("o1.prop before = " + o1.prop);
  Obj o2 = o1;
  Obj o3 = o2;
  Obj o4 = o3;
  Obj o5 = o4;
  o5.prop = 3;
  println("o1.prop after = " + o1.prop);
  println("o2.prop after = " + o2.prop);
  println("o3.prop after = " + o3.prop);
  println("o4.prop after = " + o4.prop);
  println("o5.prop after = " + o5.prop);
}


class Obj{
  int prop = 2;
}
```

Returning to the collider code and my `clone()` method, Java actually includes its own `clone()` method (http://java.sun.com/j2se/1.5.0/docs/api/java/lang/Object.html#clone()) that we could theoretically use (with some effort), but I felt it was simpler for our purposes to write my own. Cloning in Java can get fairly complex when deep inheritance chains are involved and many object references are composed within classes. Fortunately, my `clone()` method (which lives in the `Particle` class) is quite simple; here it is again:

```
Particle getClone(){
    Particle p = new Particle();
    p.loc.set(loc);
    p.vel.set(vel);
    p.radius = radius;
    p.damping = damping;
    return p;
}
```

The reason I chose to clone the particle was to be able to more simply account for its translation, which is a coordinate space issue I discussed earlier in the chapter—local versus global coordinate systems. The particles are born from an emitter, which has a location in the world coordinate space (relative to the Processing window). In contrast, the Particles each exist at their local origin (0,0), which allows them to rotate around their center point. When calculating particle collisions with the colliders, I needed a way to account for the emitter translation of each particle; it was easiest to clone the existing particle and add the emitter translation, with the line

```
part.loc.add(emitters[i].loc);
```

Then, I'll eventually pass the translated particle clone to the getReflection() function. This is the function that handles some of the fancy math, returning a new updated velocity vector, based on the collision. Before we actually pass the particle clone, though, we need to check that it actually collided with the collider. To do so I used a conditional with the distance formula:

```
if (dist(part.loc.x, part.loc.y, cldr.loc.x, cldr.loc.y) < part.radius + cldr.radius){
```

The algorithm for the particle/collider collisions is as follows:

1. check if the distance between the particle and collider is less than their combined radii
2. place the particle precisely on the collider's edge, along the collision vector
3. reverse the particle's velocity vector

The process is similar to the boundary collision detection, but because of the non-orthogonal surface, we need the fancy math. The first step after detection is placing the particle on the collider edge, handled by the correctEdgeOverlap() method, shown again next:

```
void correctEdgeOverlap(Particle part, Collider collider, PVector emitterOffset){
    // temporarily add emitter location to particle
    part.loc.add(emitterOffset);
    // get vector between object centers
    PVector collisionNormal = PVector.sub(part.loc, collider.loc);
```

```
// convert vector to Unit length
collisionNormal.normalize();
// set to perfect distance (sum of both radii)
collisionNormal.mult(collider.radius + part.radius);
// put particle precisely on collider edge
part.loc.set(PVector.add(collider.loc, collisionNormal));
// subtract emitter location
part.loc.sub(emitterOffset);
}
```

Unlike the getReflection() method previously discussed, I will not use the cloned particle. Instead, I'll pass the actual particle to the correctEdgeOverlap() method and then add the emitter translation inside the method (which I'll eventually also subtract out). This sort of coordinate accounting is necessary, as mentioned earlier, because the particles are born at the emitter location in the global coordinate system. The next step in the method is calculating the collision vector, shown in Figure 5-19. This is the path of the collision between the center of the particle and the collider. Once you have this vector, you can normalize it (creating a unit vector of length 1) to get the base direction of the collision vector, (which would be even more helpful if the colliders were actually dynamic). Next, you multiply the normalized collision vector by the sum of the two radii, giving you the precise distance to place the particle along the vector, in relation to the collider. Finally, you subtract the emitter translation back out. I do realize this is somewhat involved. My recommendation, if it's still unclear, is to comment out individual lines of code in the method when you test the engine; the immediate impact on the collision detection should hammer home the individual line's meaning. Also—this may be obvious, but I'll state it anyway—there are other approaches you could take to handle the edge correction, and if/when you come up with a better way, please send it along.

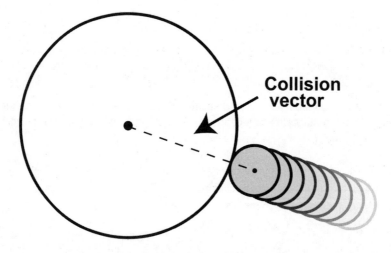

Figure 5-19. Particle and collider collision vector

Next, we'll look at the actual reflection of the particle, now that it's sitting nicely on the edge of the collider. Referring back to the collider collision code, in the checkCollisions() method, the next step (after correcting for edge overlap) is calculating the accurate reflection of the particle off the collider, invoked by the line

```
PVector rv = getReflection(part, cldr);
```

And here's the getReflection() method again. Notice this method returns a reflection vector (using the particle clone in the reflection calculations), while the correctEdgeOverlap() method directly updated the (actual) particle's loc property.

```
//Non-orthogonal Reflection, using rotation of coordinate system
  PVector getReflection(Particle particle, Collider collider){
    // get vector between object centers
    PVector collisionNormal = PVector.sub(particle.loc, collider.loc);
    // calculate reflection angle by rotating vectors to 0 on unit circle
    // inital theta of collisionnormal
    float theta = atan2(collisionNormal.y, collisionNormal.x);

    // rotate particle velocity vector by -theta (to bring 0 on unit circle)
    float vx = cos(-theta)*particle.vel.x - sin(-theta)*particle.vel.y;
    float vy = sin(-theta)*particle.vel.x + cos(-theta)*particle.vel.y;

    // reverse x component and rotate velocity vector back to original position
    PVector temp = new PVector(vx, vy);
    vx = cos(theta)*-temp.x - sin(theta)*temp.y;
    vy = sin(theta)*-temp.x + cos(theta)*temp.y;
    return new PVector(vx, vy);
  }
```

The basic algorithm for handling the rotation is as follows:

1.   get the angle of the collision vector
2.   rotate the velocity vector by –angle, to make the collision (temporarily) orthogonal
3.   reverse the velocity vector's x coordinate value
4.   rotate the velocity vector back to its original position

The first step again is to get the collision vector between the particle and collider. Again, I didn't need to add (and then subtract) the emitter location as with the correctEdgeOverlap() method, as that was added to the particle clone earlier, which gets passed to this method. Since this method will return a vector, I didn't make any changes to the actual particle, just its clone. Next, I find the angle of rotation of the collision vector using Processing's atan2() function, which we looked at earlier in the chapter. I then use the negative value of this angle to temporarily rotate the particle velocity vector back to 0. Now the particle is in an orthogonal orientation to the collider, so to reflect it all I need to do is reverse the x component of the velocity vector. Then I rotate the velocity vector back to its original angle of rotation and update the actual particle velocity vector with the returned rotated vector. (You'll notice I also add some damping to the y-component of the velocity vector after collision for good measure.)

There are three handy sets of trig expressions for handling vector rotations around any of the coordinate axes (x, y, z). We'll use these in other places throughout the book as well. They are as follows:

rotation around the x axis

$vec2.y = vec.y*cos(\theta) - vec.z*sin(\theta)$

$vec2.z = vec.y*sin(\theta) + vec.z*cos(\theta)$

$vec2.x = vec.x$

rotation around the y axis

$vec2.z = vec.z*cos(\theta) - vec.x*sin(\theta)$

$vec2.x = vec.z*sin(\theta) + vec.x*cos(\theta)$

$vec2.y = vec.y$

rotation around the z axis

$vec2.x = vec.x*cos(\theta) - vec.y*sin(\theta)$

$vec2.y = vec.x*sin(\theta) + vec.y*cos(\theta)$

$vec2.z = vec.z$

That pretty much does it for the Engine class code, as well as the entire particle engine project. The last thing I want to do is run some tests on the engine. Next is a setup for a burst pattern. To try it, replace the code in the main (left) tab in your project with the following. (I also included some additional screen-shots, shown in Figures 5-20 to 5-23.) Enjoy playing with the engine!

```
/**
 * Particle Engine  - Burst Test 01
 * By Ira Greenberg <br />
 * The Essential Guide to Processing for Flash Developers,
 * Friends of ED, 2009
```

```
*/


 // create particle populations
int particleCount = 5000;


// instantiate particle arrays
Particle[] particles = new Particle[particleCount];


// instantiate collider arrays
int colliderCount = 1;
Collider[] colliders = new Collider[colliderCount];
// instantiate emitter arrays
int emitterCount = 1;
Emitter[] emitters = new Emitter[emitterCount];
// declare rest of global variables
Environment environment;
Engine engine;


void setup(){
  size(800, 600, P2D);
  background(0);
  smooth();
  // instantiate base particles
  for (int i=0; i<particleCount; i++){
    particles[i] = new Particle(random(1, 2), color(255, random(80, 150), 10, random(255)), ⏎
      8000, .85);
  }


   // instantiate colliders
  for (int i=0; i<colliderCount; i++){
    colliders[i] = new Collider(new PVector(width/2, height/2), 200, #323332, false);
  }
  // instantiate emitters
```

```
    emitters[0] = new Emitter(new PVector(width/2, height/2), new PVector(0, 0), ⏎
      particles.length, 5, particles);

    // instantiate Environment
    environment = new Environment(.01, .785, new PVector(0, 0), .995, .01);
    // instantiate engine
    engine = new Engine(emitters, colliders, environment);

    //set boundary collisions
    boolean[] bounds =  {true, true, true, false};
    engine.setBoundaryCollision(true, bounds);
}

void draw(){
 // uncomment next line to see animated particles
 // background(0);
  // required to make engine do its thing
  engine.run();
}
```

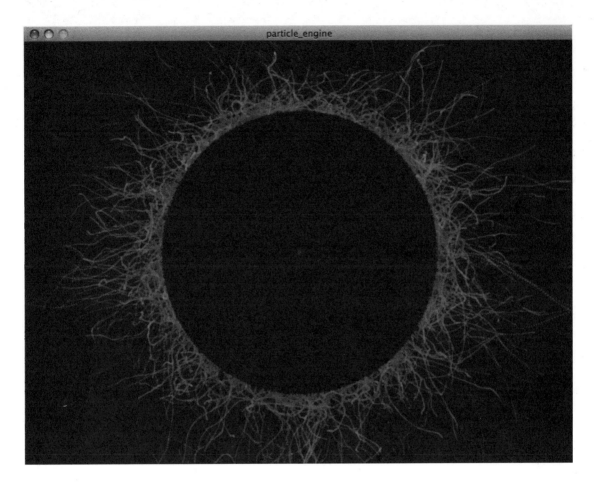

Figure 5-20. Particle engine output 1

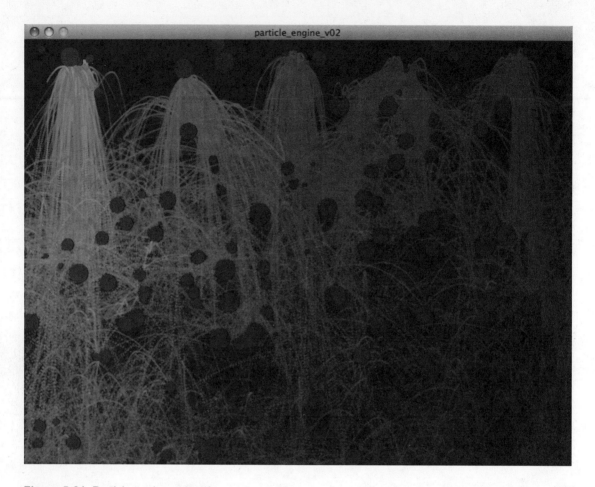

Figure 5-21. Particle engine output 2

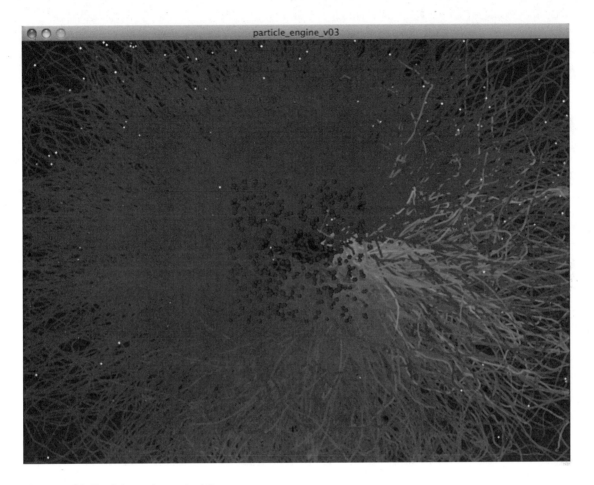

Figure 5-22. Particle engine output 3

Figure 5-23. Particle engine output 4

Summary

This chapter kicked off the project section of the book, *where you learn by doing*. One of Processing's strengths is its performance, which we were able to exploit in creating a dynamic particle engine. Extending our conversation about object-oriented programming, begun in Chapter 4, we looked at inheritance in Processing and applied it in the creation of a flexible code framework for the engine—supporting efficient modular design. In addition, you also learned about class compositional relationships, a complimentary building strategy to inheritance employed in OOP. Using an UML-inspired diagramming system, we also looked at some theory and techniques for conceptualizing and designing an object-oriented programming solution. Next chapter we'll continue this conversation as we create a game and also explore some new areas of the Processing core API.

Chapter 6

A "Serious" Game

To my 10-year-old son, all computer games are serious. In academic circles, "serious" games are those that teach in the context of play. A broader definition, according to Wikipedia, is games with "...a primary purpose other than pure entertainment." Of course, if you find learning stuff highly entertaining then you may need to find a new definition. In this chapter, you'll construct a game with Processing, and YES, it will fall under the category of a serious game (though, I, of course, hope you also find it entertaining!)

Now for a second disclaimer: *I am not a gamer*. This is not for any philosophical reasons—I don't believe today's youth are being corrupted by games (television already did that, right?). Rather, I find creative coding more fun than playing games, or said another way: I find *programming* games more fun than *playing* them.

"You Can't Create a Game Using Processing"

I can hear this argument being put forth by hardcore gamers—some of my own students even! Although it's true that Processing was not designed primarily for creating games, it is perfectly equipped for doing so, and I use it for such in my own Processing classes. In this sense, Processing and Flash are quite similar, as my students also build games using Flash. That said, I'd make the argument that Processing is best used for prototyping games, permitting very fast development, with a minimal amount of code. I'd argue that as a prototyping language, especially for graphics-intensive applications, Processing is without compare.

The Game Origin

The game that we'll build is based on a concept I came up with a number of years ago and even began prototyping in Flash, but never finished. I was excited to revisit the idea and finally realize it. The original core principle behind the idea actually goes back even further to a freshman seminar on game theory I took in college. I was a pretty lost student back then, so I don't remember too much about the class. However, I do remember a lecture the professor gave on zero-sum games, which essentially means one player's gain is another player's loss—think chess, ping-pong, or poker. I actually find these sorts of games stressful (especially since my brother always beat me at them). There are also non-zero-sum games, as illustrated by a classic problem I learned about in the class: The Prisoner's Dilemma, described next.

http://en.wikipedia.org/wiki/Prisoner%27s_dilemma (May 7, 2009, 2:56 EST):

> *Two suspects are arrested by the police. The police separate both prisoners so they have no contact, and offer them the same deal. If one testifies against the other and the other remains silent , the betrayer goes free and the silent accomplice receives the full 10-year sentence. If both remain silent, both prisoners are sentenced to only six months in jail. If each betrays the other, each receives a five-year sentence. How should the prisoners act?*

I'll leave it to you figure out the answer to the prisoner's dilemma (which I hope doesn't happen through personal experience). What's different about this game from a classic zero-sum game is that both players can win or lose together—introducing the concept of cooperation. What's interesting about games, and game theory in general, is that they tell us much more about human nature and the way our brains work than you might initially think. For example, if you switch around the characters in the prisoner's dilemma from criminals to investors (yes, there is a difference), the basic theory underlying the game carries over to economics theory. Mathematicians and computer scientists have found clever ways of formally describing the logic behind specific game theories and have even developed formal approaches (heuristics) for solving them.

> *There are certain problems that are very difficult to solve, as they may be too complex (too many unknowns) or require too much time (computationally) to calculate a solution. However, there are ways at getting at usable (if not absolutely optimal) solutions to these problems. You might think of this as an (highly) educated guess approach. A heuristic is the term used to describe this type of strategy. This is not to say that a heuristic solution will be ineffective; they can be highly effective and are used widely for solving real-world problems. However, the solution may not be provable (in mathematical terms) as being the optimal solution.*

Two of the more colorful characters to do work in game theory were John Von Neumann and John Nash. Von Neumann was also known for his heavy drinking, reckless driving, and practical jokes, among other "interesting" quirks. He was one of the most brilliant mathematicians of his age who made major contributions across numerous fields, including game theory—supposedly inspired by his interest in poker. You can learn more about Von Neumann at http://cse.stanford.edu/class/sophomore-college/ projects-98/game-theory/neumann.html (May 19, 2009). John Nash was portrayed by Russell Crowe in *A*

Beautiful Mind, the academy-award-winning film that chronicled the brilliant Nash's struggles with schizophrenia. Nash's interest in game theory was inspired by Von Neumann's, and his work in this area contributed to him receiving the Nobel Prize in 1994. To learn more about Nash, check out `http://nobelprize.org/nobel_prizes/economics/laureates/1994/nash-autobio.html` (May 19, 2009).

The Concept

As I mentioned, I'm not personally a fan of playing zero-sum games. However, they make excellent programming exercises. A classic zero-sum programming problem you might be assigned in a computer science class is programming tic-tac-toe (also known as noughts and crosses). Tic-tac-toe is a relatively easy game to program, if it's designed for two human players. However, it is quite a bit more difficult to program if one of the players is a computer (and you don't want it to always lose).

> *Although tic-tac-toe is a relatively simple game, easily mastered by children, it still involves a fairly large possible game state, or possible moves and game configurations. According to Wikipedia (May 10, 2009) there are "...765 different positions (the state space complexity)...26,830 possible games...(the game tree complexity)...and 362,880 (i.e. 9!) ways of placing Xs and Os on the board."*

In our game, we'll construct tic-tac-toe with a computer player that has variable playing ability—from essentially guessing to playing perfectly. Even in a zero-sum game, like tic-tac-toe, there is often a draw position, or tie. Generally, this outcome is treated as a do-over—keeping the contest going. However, in our game, we'll make the draw state the desired outcome, which we'll reinforce with a reward, or pay-off. (Yes, I realize I'm turning a classic American game into an exercise in socialism.)

The draw state in tic-tac-toe will always occur if both players play properly. In our game, it will be possible to tell the computer to play variably—from poorly to perfectly (heuristically speaking). When playing poorly, the computer will mark any open square, without any concern for strategic position, blocking, or winning; when playing perfectly, the computer can't be beaten. Where the game becomes most interesting, I think, is when the computer plays less than perfectly, but not purely randomly. In other words, sometimes the computer moves strategically and other times randomly; this forces the human player to concentrate on not inadvertently winning or losing—again, if the desired outcome is a draw.

The Pay-off

I wanted a cooperative pay-off that reflected the effort of both players—machine and human. I also wanted a pay-off that was integrally tied to the play of the game. Of course, being an artist, I also thought it would be interesting if the pay-off had aesthetic interest. Taking all of this into account, I designed the pay-off as an automatically generated work of human-machine art, based on the play of the game. To pull this off, I took some liberties with the visual elements of classic tic-tac-toe—the X's and O's. Rather than only work with standard and uniform letters (which we will work with as well), I abstracted them into more general curvilinear and linear forms; some examples are shown in Figure 6-1.

Figure 6-1. Example curvilinear and linear forms

Class Design

I'll begin with a class overview and, as in the last chapter, I will develop a UML-style diagram of the program structure. In terms of the OOP solution, this example doesn't add many new principles to what I covered in Chapters 4 and 5. However, the class composition and overall program design is a bit more complex. I've continued to try to keep my classes lean and focused—creating a new class only when the functionality and semantics demand it. The classes are

- TTTBoard class—main organizing class
- Shape class—base data structure for geometry
- Cell class—data structure for each cell of tic-tac-toe board
- Line class—composes cell objects
- Pen class—for drawing
- Style class—base drawing algorithm
- IraStyle class—custom drawing algorithm
- Tri class—base data structure
- ShallowGreen class—for game logic (AI)
- Pattern class—for the final artwork creation

TTTBoard Class

TTTBoard is the main organizing class that encapsulates many of the complexities of the program. As with the particle engine in Chapter 5, I've tried to find a balance between ease of use (using default constructors) and customization (setting lots of instance property values). Figure 6-2 provides a class diagram, beginning with TTTBoard. I'll slowly fill in the diagram, like we did last chapter, as I introduce the other classes. I also encourage you to build the project iteratively as I introduce the classes/code.

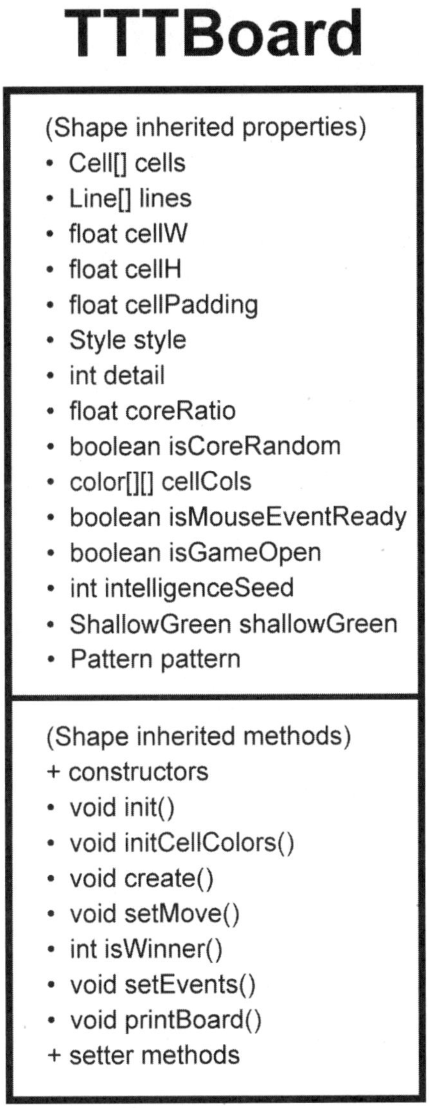

TTTBoard

(Shape inherited properties)
• Cell[] cells
• Line[] lines
• float cellW
• float cellH
• float cellPadding
• Style style
• int detail
• float coreRatio
• boolean isCoreRandom
• color[][] cellCols
• boolean isMouseEventReady
• boolean isGameOpen
• int intelligenceSeed
• ShallowGreen shallowGreen
• Pattern pattern
(Shape inherited methods)
+ constructors
• void init()
• void initCellColors()
• void create()
• void setMove()
• int isWinner()
• void setEvents()
• void printBoard()
+ setter methods

Figure 6-2. TTTBoard class diagram

I followed the same conventions and structure with the class diagram as I did last chapter: class properties up top with methods below the line; the '+' sign being used to denote multiple (overloaded) constructors/methods; bullets preceding each class member, just to denote a new line; and individual getters/setters methods generally omitted. Next is the complete TTTBoard code, which I'll discuss in smaller sections. I recommend at this point that you create a new sketch (titled whatever you like) and add a new tab titled "**TTTBoard**," where you should add the following code:

```
/**
 * Draw Game
 * TTTBoard class - main organizing class
 * By Ira Greenberg <br />
 * The Essential Guide to Processing for Flash Developers,
 * Friends of ED, 2009
 */

class TTTBoard extends Shape{

  // Instance Properties
  // table cell structure and cell style properties
  Cell[] cells = new Cell[9];
  Line[] lines = new Line[8];
  float cellW, cellH, cellPadding;
  /* default Style instantiation - encapsulates drawing algorithm
  that the cell uses to draw the computer/human player's mark.
  It is possible to pass in a custom Style object as well */
  Style style = new Style();
  // controls articulation of cell shapes
  int detail = 1;
  // ratio of inner cell shape core to cell shape
  float coreRatio = .75;
  // flag to control random size of cell shape core
  boolean isCoreRandom = false;
  // each cell has a 3 color array (background, main form and core of the form)
  color[][] cellCols;

  // events
  // used to set mouse pressed/released events on cells
  boolean isMouseEventReady = true;

  // flag is false when a win, loss or draw occurs
  boolean isGameOpen = true;
```

```
// controls AI - level of intelligence (1-5)
int intelligenceSeed = 2;


// composed helper objects
ShallowGreen shallowGreen; // AI
Pattern pattern;  // final artwork

// default constructor
TTTBoard(){
  super(0, 0, width, height);
  initCellColors();
  init();
}


// constructor
TTTBoard(float x, float y, float w, float h){
  super(x, y, w, h);
  initCellColors();
  init();
}


// constructor
TTTBoard(int detail, float coreRatio, boolean isCoreRandom, color[][] cellCols){
  super(0, 0, width, height);
  this.detail = detail;
  this.coreRatio = coreRatio;
  this.isCoreRandom = isCoreRandom;
  this.cellCols = cellCols;
  init();
}


// constructor
```

```
TTTBoard(float x, float y, float w, float h, int detail, ↵
    float coreRatio, boolean isCoreRandom, color[][] cellCols){
  super(x, y, w, h);
  this.detail - detail;
  this.coreRatio = coreRatio;
  this.isCoreRandom = isCoreRandom;
  this.cellCols = cellCols;
  init();
}


// set critical initialization values
void init(){
  cellW = w/3;
  cellH = h/3;

  //instantiate individual cell objects
  for (int i=0; i<cells.length; i++){
    float coreW = cellW;
    float coreH = cellH;
    if (isCoreRandom){
      coreW = random(max(cellW*.1, cellW*coreRatio));
      coreH = random(max(cellH*.1, cellH*coreRatio));
    }
    else {
      coreW *= coreRatio;
      coreH *= coreRatio;
    }
    cells[i] = new Cell(this, 0, 0, cellW, cellH, detail, ↵
      new Dimension(int(coreW), int(coreH)), cellCols[i], cellPadding, style);
  }

  // map cells to lines
```

```
  // rows
  lines[0] = new Line(cells[0], cells[1], cells[2]);
  lines[1] = new Line(cells[3], cells[4], cells[5]);
  lines[2] = new Line(cells[6], cells[7], cclls[8]);
  // cols
  lines[3] = new Line(cells[0], cells[3], cells[6]);
  lines[4] = new Line(cells[1], cells[4], cells[7]);
  lines[5] = new Line(cells[2], cells[5], cells[8]);
  // diags
  lines[6] = new Line(cells[0], cells[4], cells[8]);
  lines[7] = new Line(cells[6], cells[4], cells[2]);
  shallowGreen = new ShallowGreen(this);

  // default pattern instantiation
  pattern = new Pattern();
}


// ensure cell color initialized if default/minimal constructor used
void initCellColors(){
  cellCols = new color[cells.length][3];
  // set default colors
  for (int i=0; i<cellCols.length; i++){
    // cell background col
    cellCols[i][0] = 0xff222222;
    // cell shape  col
    cellCols[i][1] = 0xffbbbbbb;
    // cell shape core  col
    cellCols[i][2] = 0xff666666;
  }
}


// construct board
void create(){
```

```
    for (int i=0; i<3; i++){
      for (int j=0; j<3; j++){
        // array incrementation variable
        int k - i*3 + j;
        cells[k].x = x + j*cells[k].w;
        cells[k].y = y + i*cells[k].h;
        // individual cells manage their own drawing
        cells[k].create();
      }
    }
    // enable user events
    setEvents();
  }


  // start game move procedure
  void setMove(){
    for (int i=0; i<cells.length; i++){
      if(cells[i].isClicked()){
        if (cells[i].getValue()==0){
          cells[i].setValue(-1);
          if (isWinner() == 0){
            shallowGreen.setNextMove();
          }
        }
      }
    }
  }


  // check for computer and human winner
  int isWinner(){
    for (int i=0; i<lines.length; i++){
      if (lines[i].cells[0].getValue() +
        lines[i].cells[1].getValue() +
```

```
          lines[i].cells[2].getValue() == -3){
            // highlight players win
            for (int j=0; j<lines[i].cells.length; j++){
              lines[i].cells[j].cellCols[0] = 0xff000000;
              lines[i].cells[j].cellCols[1] = 0xff777777;
              lines[i].cells[j].cellCols[2] = 0xffffffff;
            }
            return -1;
          }
        else if (lines[i].cells[0].getValue() +
            lines[i].cells[1].getValue() +
            lines[i].cells[2].getValue() == 3){
            // highlight ShallowGreen's win
            for (int j=0; j<lines[i].cells.length; j++){
              lines[i].cells[j].cellCols[0] = 0xffffffff;
              lines[i].cells[j].cellCols[1] = 0xff777777;
              lines[i].cells[j].cellCols[2] = 0xff000000;

            }
            return 1;
        }
      }
      return 0;
}


// hacked together mouse pressed/released function
void setEvents(){
  if (mousePressed && isGameOpen){
    if (isMouseEventReady){
      setMove();
      isMouseEventReady = false;
    }
  }
```

```
    else {
      // mouse released stuff here
      if (!isMouseEventReady){
        // check for win here
        if(isWinner() == 1){
          isGameOpen = false;
          println("shallowGreen Won");
        }
        else if (isWinner() == -1){
          isGameOpen = false;
          println("Player Won");
        }
        else if (shallowGreen.isDraw()){
          isGameOpen = false;
          println("DRAW\n");
          println("Pattern Created");
          // generate pattern output
          pattern.create();
        }
        isMouseEventReady = true;
      }
    }
  }


// print matrix of current board values
void printBoard(){
  for (int i=0; i<lines.length; i++){
    if (i==0){
      println(" rows");
    }
    else if (i==3){
      println("\n columns");
    }
```

```
    else  if (i==6){
      println("\n Diagonals");
    }
    print("[ ");
    for (int j=0; j<lines[i].cells.length; j++){
      print(lines[i].cells[j].getValue()+"  ");
    }
    print("]\n");
  }
}


// setter methods
// set style of table cells
void setCellStyle(int detail, float coreRatio, boolean isCoreRandom, ↵
    color[][] cellCols, float cellPadding, Style style){
  this.detail = detail;
  this.coreRatio = coreRatio;
  this.isCoreRandom = isCoreRandom;
  this.cellCols = cellCols;
  this.cellPadding = cellPadding;
  this.style = style;
  init();
}


  // overloaded set style of table cells -no Style object parameter
void setCellStyle(int detail, float coreRatio, boolean isCoreRandom,↵
    color[][] cellCols, float cellPadding){
  this.detail = detail;
  this.coreRatio = coreRatio;
  this.isCoreRandom = isCoreRandom;
  this.cellCols = cellCols;
  this.cellPadding = cellPadding;
```

```
    init();
}

void setPattern(Pattern pattern){
  this.pattern = pattern;
}

// controls ShallowGreen's intelligence
void setIntelligence(int intelligenceSeed){
  this.intelligenceSeed = intelligenceSeed;
}

void setLines(Line[] lines){
  this.lines = lines;
}

}
```

I realize that's a lot of code. (As I mentioned, this is the main organizing class in the program.) However, most of it is pretty straightforward.

The first thing to notice is that TTTBoard extends Shape. The Shape class is a very simple class that defines some block geometry. (The Cell class will also extend Shape.) The TTTBoard class begins with instance property declarations (including some default value initialization). I've commented the code, so this section of the class should be pretty self-explanatory. Notice that I include references to both Cell[] and Line[] arrays. These classes are used to structure the tic-tac-toe board: eight lines will make up the board, with three cells per line. Figure 6-3 illustrates this. I could have written the program without a Line class—used to conveniently group the individual cells—but it proved very handy during game position evaluations, which I'll discus further when we look at the ShallowGreen class.

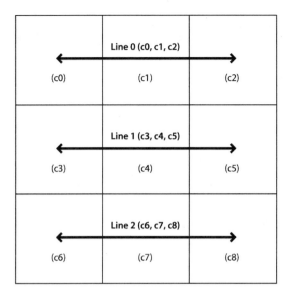

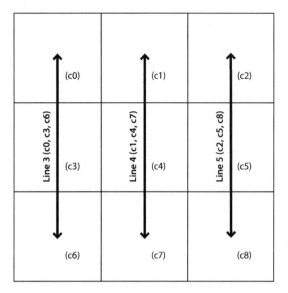

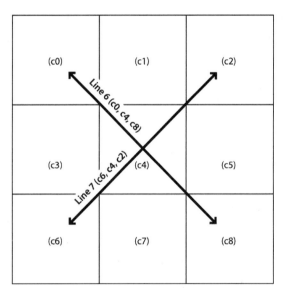

Figure 6-3. Lines, including Cells diagram

TTTBoard includes a bunch of constructors, providing different options for initializing the TTTBoard object. When we eventually run the program, I'll illustrate some of these different approaches. The init() method is used to initialize the size of the individual board spaces, which I'll refer to as cells. The cell sizes are based on the overall size of the board, which, by default, is based on the size of the sketch; this can be overridden as well, which I'll again demonstrate when we run the sketch. init() also builds the Line objects, which encapsulate the individual cells, into logical groupings, as illustrated in Figure 6-3. Finally, init() also builds a default Pattern object, which can also be overridden for a more customized object. The Pattern object is used to create the final artwork, generated when the two players (computer and human) reach a draw state.

initCellColors() creates default color values for the cells. In most instances you'll override this, unless you simply love grayscale patterns.

create() is where the board is drawn and will need to be called from within Processing's draw() function. Notice that create() contains another nested call to cells[k].create(). TTTBoard really just delegates here, creating a single high-level command/control interface that internally hands procedures off to its helper classes, such as the individual Cell objects. The final call in the create() method—setEvents();— is what initializes the event behavior in the program, which I'll say more about shortly.

setMove() functions as part of the event handling process. When a cell is clicked, if it is empty (evaluated by the call: cells[i].getValue()==0) the cell is filled with the (human) user's mark (O or curvilinear form). In addition, if the game hasn't been won, the computer user then moves, controlled by the line shallowGreen.setNextMove();

isWinner() checks for a winner, either human or computer. When either player places their mark in an open cell, a value is set (-1 for human and 1 for machine). When a win is determined (a line evaluates to -3 or 3), the method highlights the line won. (In addition to adding up the marks per line, there is also a check to ensure that all the marks are either the computer or human player's exclusively.) We'll look more specifically at this when we look at the Line and Cell classes.

setEvents() is honestly a bit of a convoluted and hacked event-handling method, but it works quite well. Compared to Flash (and Java), Processing's event handling system is extremely simple and very, very high level. In addition, Processing lacks any pre-built components that have built-in event behavior, such as Flash's Button component. However, there are user-submitted Processing libraries that approximate the event-handling models/components found in Flash and Java. Current libraries can be viewed and downloaded here: http://processing.org/reference/libraries/#interface.

For this program, I just needed very simple mouse detection, enabling mouse-pressed and released detection on the individual board cells. Processing includes a global mousePressed boolean property, which I used. However, it lacks a mouseReleased property. Processing does include both mousePressed() and mouseReleased() functions, though. A simple calligraphic drawing example using these two methods is shown next, in Figure 6-4. (Please note, Processing's pmouseX and pmouseY properties include the mouse coordinate values from 1 frame in the past.)

```
/**
 * Mouse event detection functions example
 * Calligraphic drawing with Processing
 * By Ira Greenberg <br />
 * The Essential Guide to Processing for Flash Developers,
 * Friends of ED, 2009
```

```
    */

boolean isDrawable = false;
void setup(){
  size(400, 400);
  background(255);
  smooth();
}


// need to include draw() for event detection
void draw(){
  // stroke weight based on angle of drawing
  float wt = abs(degrees(atan2((mouseX-pmouseX), (mouseY-pmouseY)))*.1);
  strokeWeight(wt);
  if (isDrawable){
    line(pmouseX, pmouseY, mouseX, mouseY);
  }
}


void mousePressed(){
  isDrawable = true;
}
void mouseReleased(){
  isDrawable = false;
}
```

Figure 6-4. Mouse event calligraphic example

Returning to the TTTBoard class, one other solution I could have pursued, but chose not to, would have been to handle the event detection using the aforementioned mouse event functions in the main sketch tab, and not encapsulating them within the TTTBoard class. However, I felt it would be simpler, and better OOP design, to encapsulate the main tic-tac-toe board event handling within the TTTBoard class.

To encapsulate the event handling, I used the global mousePressed property and designed my own mouse-released procedure using a conditional statement and the boolean property isMouseEventReady. Notice that the setEvents() method, called every draw() cycle, includes calls to both isWinner() and setMove(), which I discussed earlier; it also assigns false to the Boolean flag isGameOpen when a win or draw occurs, disabling further event behavior. Finally, the method prints information to the Processing IDE text area when a win or draw occurs.

printBoard() simply prints a matrix of values, showing the current state of the game board. For example, Figure 6-5 shows three printBoard() outputs: the computer player wins (left), the human player wins (middle). and a draw state is reached (right).

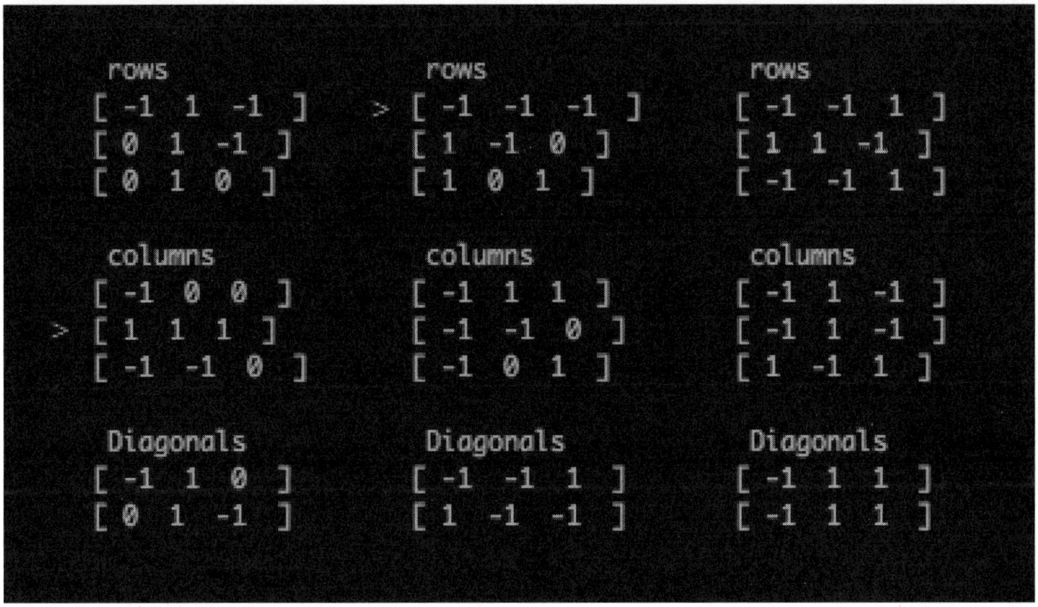

Figure 6-5. printBoard() example

The remaining methods in the TTTBoard class are standard setter methods, most of which are self-explanatory. Notice that I used two setCellStyle() methods, which, in OOP speak, are called overloaded methods, methods of the same name, but with different parameter lists. The only difference between the methods is that the second version doesn't include a final Style style parameter. This parameter is used to pass in a custom drawing algorithm to the class, which I'll discuss later in the example.

Shape Class

Since the TTTBoard class extends the Shape class, I'll discuss it next. However, there's not much to discuss, as it's a very simple class. Figure 6.6 shows an updated class diagram, including Shape.

Shape

• float x
• float y
• float w
• float h
+ constructors
+ setter methods

TTTBoard

(Shape inherited properties)
• Cell[] cells
• Line[] lines
• float cellW
• float cellH
• float cellPadding
• Style style
• int detail
• float coreRatio
• boolean isCoreRandom
• color[][] cellCols
• boolean isMouseEventReady
• boolean isGameOpen
• int intelligenceSeed
• ShallowGreen shallowGreen
• Pattern pattern
(Shape inherited methods)
+ constructors
• void init()
• void initCellColors()
• void create()
• void setMove()
• int isWinner()
• void setEvents()
• void printBoard()
+ setter methods

Figure 6-6. Updated class diagram including the Shape class

Here's the finished Shape class code, which should be put into its own tab, named `Shape`.

```
/**
 * Draw Game
 * Shape class - convenience class
 * By Ira Greenberg <br />
 * The Essential Guide to Processing for Flash Developers,
 * Friends of ED, 2009
 */


class Shape {

  // instance properties
  float x;
  float y;
  float w;
  float h;

  // default constructor
  Shape(){
  }

  // constructor
  Shape(float x, float y, float w, float h){
    this.x = x;
    this.y = y;
    this.w = w;
    this.h = h;
  }

  // setters
```

```
void setLoc(float x, float y){
  this.x = x;
  this.y = y;
}

void setSize(float w, float h){
  this.w = w;
  this.h = h;
}

}
```

Next we'll look at the Cell and Line classes, which are the main organizing structural classes encapsulated within the TTTBoard class.

Cell Class

Figure 6-7 shows the updated class diagram, including the Cell class.

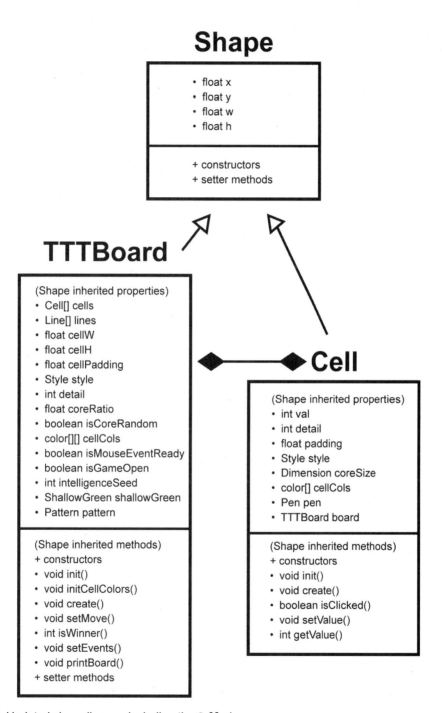

Figure 6-7. Updated class diagram including the Cell class

Create a new tab named `Cell` and add the following code to it:

```
/**
 * Draw Game
 * Cell class
 * By Ira Greenberg <br />
 * The Essential Guide to Processing for Flash Developers,
 * Friends of ED, 2009
 */


class Cell extends Shape{
  /* value associated with the cell
   based on what is in the cell:
   empty=0, human mark=-1, computer mark=1 */
  int val;
  /* the level of detail in the curvilinear (human)
   and linear(computer) marks */
  int detail;
  /* controls the space between the mark
   and the edges of the cell */
  float padding;
  //controls Pen's drawing algorithm
  Style style;
  /* Java's Dimension class
   -includes public width and height properties */
  Dimension coreSize;
  /*Reference to color array of length 3
   cellCols[0] = cell background
   cellCols[1] = cell main mark color
   cellCols[2] = cell mark core color */
  color[] cellCols;
  // composed helper class delegates drawing
  Pen pen;
```

```
// reference to main organizing class
TTTBoard board;

// default constructor
Cell(){
  init();
}
// constructor
Cell(TTTBoard board, float x, float y, float w, float h,int detail, Dimension coreSize, ↩
    color[] cellCols, float cellPadding, Style style){
  super(x, y, w, h);
  this.board = board;
  this.detail = detail;
  this.coreSize = coreSize;
  this.cellCols = cellCols;
  padding = cellPadding;
  // returns copy of style argument
  this.style = style.getClone();
  init();
}

// ensure pen is instantiated
void init(){
  pen = new Pen(this, style);
}

// draw the cells
void create(){
  fill(cellCols[0]);
  stroke(100);
  // hide cell outlines before pattern is created
  if (board.shallowGreen.isDraw()){
    noStroke();
```

```
  }
  // draw cell background
  rect(x, y, w, h);
  // draw cell contents
  pen.create();
}

// detect mouse click on cell
boolean isClicked(){
  return (mouseX > x && mouseX < x+w && mouseY>y ⏎
    && mouseY < y+h);
}

// setter/getter
void setValue(int val){
  this.val = val;
}

int getValue(){
  return val;
}


}
```

The Cell class is used to model the individual board spaces. I heavily commented the instance properties, which should be self-explanatory. However, I did sneak in a new data structure, Dimension, lifted directly from Java. Java's Dimension class is a convenient and simple data type that encapsulates publicly accessible width and height properties (normally in Java and ActionScript, properties are declared private); since Processing compiles to Java, it is legal to include Java data types. There are three object reference properties (Style style, Pen pen, TTTBoard board) that need a little explanation.

Style style and Pen pen are references to objects that will handle the drawing of the content in the cells. Utilizing an approach like this—isolating the cell content from the cell structure—makes good OOP sense as it allows you to change the drawing implementation, without affecting the Cell structure. Later in the example we'll do just this, creating a custom drawing algorithm.

TTTBoard board is a reference to the main organizing class we looked at earlier. The Cell class is designed to manage structural aspects of the individual cells, including—through delegation to some helper classes—cell content creation. The Cell object will also need to communicate back to the TTTBoard object during game play, which is what the encapsulated TTTBoard board property enables. Notice also in the diagram that the line connecting the TTTBoard and Cell classes together has diamonds at both ends. This denotes a bi-directional compositional relationship, which simply means that each class contains a reference to the other. This is done to facilitate communication between the two classes, allowing messages between the classes to flow in both directions. This will be especially important as additional classes are added that contain a reference variable to one of the classes but not the other. Through the bi-directional relationship the TTTBoard or Cell class will be able to pass information between outer classes lacking any direct reference to itself. These types of delegation relationships become more important as programs get more complex.

Next, we'll look at Cell's organizing partner class, Line.

Line Class

The updated class diagram, including Line, is shown in Figure 6-8.

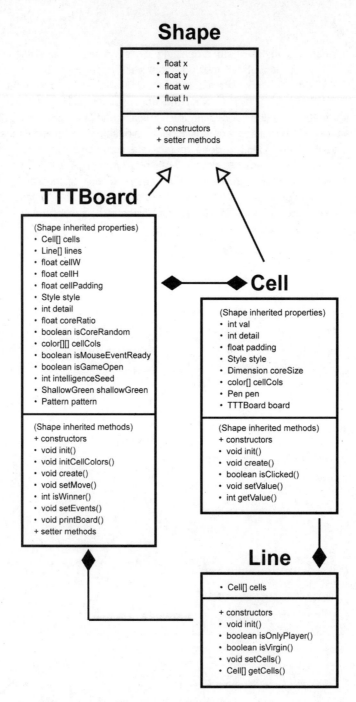

Figure 6-8. Updated class diagram including the Line class

Next is the complete Line code, which should be put in a new tab named "**Line.**"

```
/**
 * Draw Game
 * Line class - organizes cells
 * By Ira Greenberg <br />
 * The Essential Guide to Processing for Flash Developers,
 * Friends of ED, 2009
 */


class Line{

  // reference to its internal cells
  Cell[] cells = new Cell[3];

  // default constructor
  Line(){
    init();
  }

  // constructor
  Line(Cell c1, Cell c2, Cell c3){
    cells[0] = c1;
    cells[1] = c2;
    cells[2] = c3;
  }

  // used by default constructor
  void init(){
    for (int i=0; i<cells.length; i++){
      cells[i] = new Cell();
```

```java
        }
    }


    // used by AI for assessing strategic position
    boolean isOnlyPlayer(){
      // ensure no shallowGreen marks
      for (int i=0; i<3; i++){
        if (cells[i].getValue() == 1){
          return false;
        }
      }
      // if only 1 human player mark in line return true
      if (cells[0].getValue() + cells[1].getValue() + cells[2].getValue() == -1){
        return true;
      }
      return false;
    }


    // returns true if no human player marks in line yet
    boolean isVirgin() {
      boolean isSafe = true;
      for (int i=0; i<cells.length; i++){
        if (cells[i].getValue() == -1){
          isSafe =  false;
        }
      }
      return isSafe;
    }


    // setter/getter
    void setCells(Cell c1, Cell c2, Cell c3){
```

```
    cells[0] = c1;

    cells[1] = c2;

    cells[2] = c3;

  }


  Cell[] getCells(){

    return cells;

  }


}
```

Line is a relatively simple class that organizes the individual cells in the context of a line. This is helpful for checking the state of the game, since tic-tac-toe is evaluated per line. The two methods isOnlyPlayer() and isVirgin() provide information about the game state of the lines, which we'll look more closely at when we get to the ShallowGreen class, which handles the game logic. In addition to Cell and Line, two additional classes are involved in the creation of cell content Pen and Style; we'll look at each next.

Pen Class

Figure 6-9 shows the updated class diagram including the Pen class.

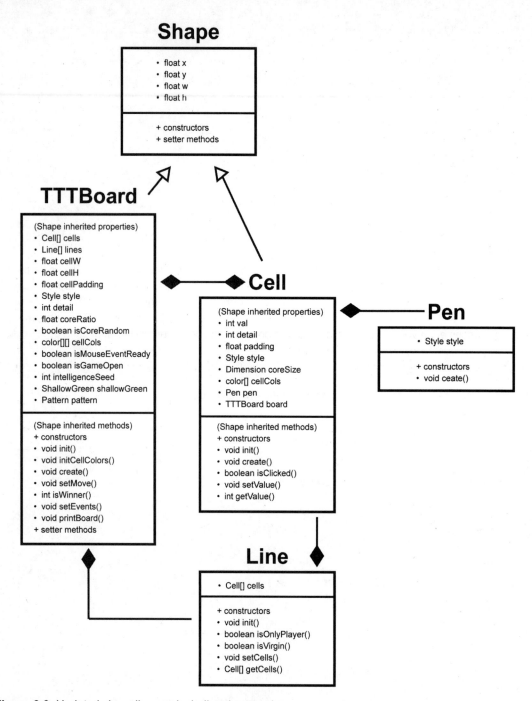

Figure 6-9. Updated class diagram including the Pen class

This is a very simple class that is used to delegate the cell content creation. Here's the complete code, which should be added to a new tab named "**Pen**."

```
/**
 * Draw Game
 * Pen class - delegates drawing to its style object
 * By Ira Greenberg <br />
 * The Essential Guide to Processing for Flash Developers,
 * Friends of ED, 2009
 */


class Pen{
  // controls pen's drawing algorithm
  Style style;

  // default constructor
  Pen(){
  }

  // constructor
  Pen(Cell c, Style style){
    this.style = style;
    style.init(c);
  }

  // delegate's drawing to its Style object
  void create(){
    style.create();
  }

}
```

Each Cell object will have its own Pen object. The Pen objects will create the actual cell content using a Style object, which encapsulates the drawing algorithm. This approach, which may seem overly abstract, allows new drawing algorithms to be easily added to the system without going into existing class code, which I'll demonstrate later in the chapter. Figure 6-10 shows the updated class diagram, including the Style class. Please note that I've created quite a number of compositional links in this example—

specifically in regard to the Style class—primarily for convenience. There are certainly other ways this example could be structured, including eliminating some of these embedded object references.

Style Class

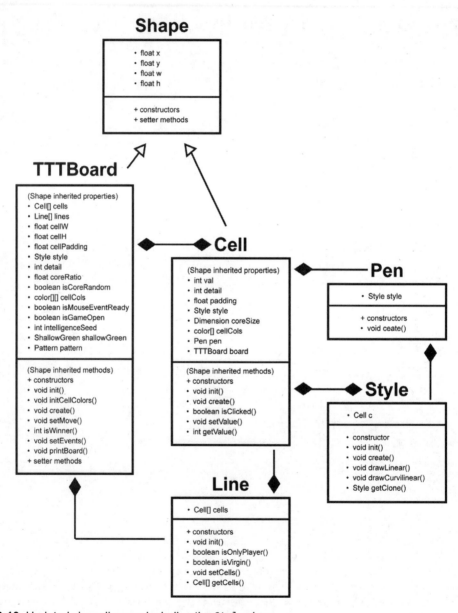

Figure 6-10. Updated class diagram including the Style class

The following Style code should be added to a new tab named "`Style`."

```
/**
 * Draw Game
 * Style base class - drawing algorithms
 * - extend Style for custom drawing algorithms
 * By Ira Greenberg <br />
 * The Essential Guide to Processing for Flash Developers,
 * Friends of ED, 2009
 */


class Style {
  Cell c;

  // only a default constructor
  Style(){
  }

  // pass in reference to Cell object
  void init(Cell c){
    this.c = c;
  }

  //draw geometry based on cell value:
  void create(){
    // human player
    if (c.getValue()==-1){
      drawCurvilinear();
    }   // computer player
    else if (c.getValue()==1){
      drawLinear();
    }
  }
```

```
/* default linear drawing algorithm creates an X
  - generally this will be overrided by subclass*/
void drawLinear(){
  float cx = c.x + c.padding + c.w/2-c.padding;
  float cy = c.y + c.padding + c.h/2-c.padding;
  float r1 = c.w/2 - c.padding/2;
  float r2 = r1*.15;
  float theta = PI/4.0;
  float phi = TWO_PI/5;
  float px_in1=0, py_in1=0, px_out1=0, py_out1=0;
  float px_out2=0, py_out2=0, px_in2=0, py_in2=0;
  int legs = 3 + c.detail;

  fill(c.cellCols[1]);
  noStroke();
  beginShape();
  for (int i=0; i<legs; i++){
    px_in1 = cx + cos(theta-phi)*r2;
    py_in1 = cy + sin(theta-phi)*r2;
    vertex(px_in1, py_in1);
    px_out1 = cx + cos(theta-phi*.1)*r1;
    py_out1 = cy + sin(theta-phi*.1)*r1;
    vertex(px_out1, py_out1);
    px_out2 = cx + cos(theta+phi*.1)*r1;
    py_out2 = cy + sin(theta+phi*.1)*r1;
    vertex(px_out2, py_out2);
    px_in2 = cx + cos(theta+phi)*r2;
    py_in2 = cy + sin(theta+phi)*r2;
    vertex(px_in2, py_in2);
    theta+=TWO_PI/legs;
  }
  endShape(CLOSE);
}
```

```
/* default curvilinear drawing algorithm,
 generally this will be overrided by subclass*/
void drawCurvilinear(){
   float px = c.x+c.padding/2;
   float py = c.y+c.padding/2;
   float diam = c.w-c.padding;
   noStroke();
   float r = red(c.cellCols[1]);
   float g = green(c.cellCols[1]);
   float b = blue(c.cellCols[1]);
   ellipseMode(CORNER);
   int rings = constrain(c.detail, 1, 6);
   float interval = diam/c.detail/2;
   for (int i=0; i<rings; i++){
      fill(r, g, b));
      ellipse(px, py, diam, diam);
      px += interval/2*(i+1);
      py += interval/2*(i+1);
      diam -= interval*(i+1);
      r = min(225, r += 20);
      g = min(225, g += 20);
      b = min(225, b += 20);
   }
   ellipseMode(CENTER);
}


/* returns new instance of this class
 need to do this so each Cell has it's own Style object*/
Style getClone(){
   return new Style();
}

}
```

This is really a base class to be extended for creating customized drawing algorithms. However, I included a default style implementation that creates a standard 'X' and 'O,' with some variations I'll demonstrate at the end of the chapter.

The Style class includes a single Cell cell instance property. It will use this to reference the specific board cell that it is drawing into (with the help of the cell's Pen object). Style only includes a default constructor, with the Cell object argument being passed in using the init() method. I needed to do this (rather than pass in the argument during instantiation) to allow the Style object to be instantiated without the Cell object argument dependency. The reasoning behind this will become clearer shortly, when we create a custom Style subclass.

The create() method simply delegates drawing to either the drawLinear() (computer player) or drawCurvilinear() (human player) methods. In the Style subclasses these methods will be overridden with custom drawing implementations.

The final getClone() method returns a new object of the current class type. This may seem like an odd thing to do, but each cell will need its own Style object, as opposed to a reference to a shared object (which is why return this doesn't work, but return new Style() does). When we look next at the Style subclass IraStyle the reasoning behind this will become clearer (if it's not already).

IraStyle Class

Figure 6-11 shows the updated class diagram, including the IraStyle class.

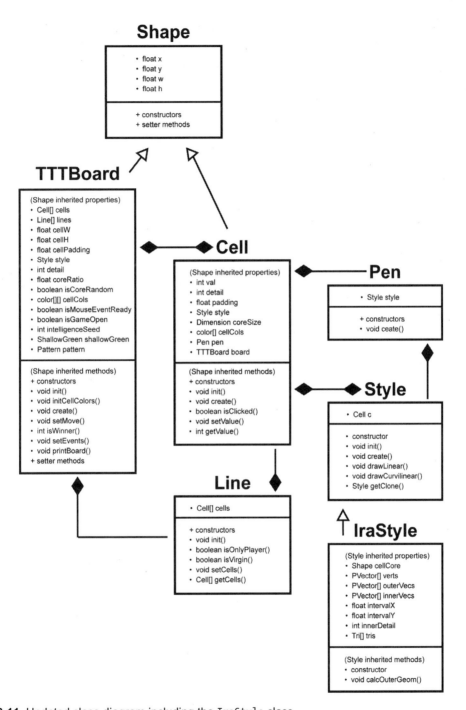

Figure 6-11. Updated class diagram including the IraStyle class

The following code should be put into a new tab named "IraStyle."

```
/**
 * Draw Game
 * IraStyle class —extends Style
 * - for custom drawing algorithm
 * By Ira Greenberg <br />
 * The Essential Guide to Processing for Flash Developers,
 * Friends of ED, 2009
 */


class IraStyle extends Style{

  // instance properties for  geometry
  Shape cellCore;
  PVector[] verts;
  PVector[] outerVecs;
  PVector[] innerVecs;
  float intervalX, intervalY;
  int innerDetail;
  // Tri is a helper class that creates triangle data types
  Tri[] tris;

  // default constructor
  IraStyle(){
  }

  // overrides init() in Style
  void init(Cell c){
    super.init(c);
    // initialize geometry
    verts = new PVector[c.detail*4];
    outerVecs = new PVector[c.detail*4];
```

```
  innerVecs = new PVector[4 + (c.detail-1)*4];
  intervalX = (c.w-c.padding)/(c.detail+1);
  intervalY = (c.h-c.padding)/(c.detail+1);
  innerDetail = c.detail - 1;
  tris = new Tri[c.detail*4];
}


// overrides create()in Style
void create(){
  // instantiate inner shape
  cellCore = new Shape((c.x+c.padding/2) + (c.w-c.padding)/2-c.coreSize.width/2,↵
     (c.y+c.padding/2) + (c.h-c.padding)/2-c.coreSize.height/2, c.coreSize.width,↵
      c.coreSize.height);
  // calculate internal geometry
  calcOuterGeom();
  // draw internal geometry
  if (c.getValue()==-1){
    // human player
    drawCurvilinear();
  }
  else if (c.getValue()==1){
    // computer player
    drawLinear();
  }
}


// unique method to this Style subclass
void calcOuterGeom(){
  int counter = 0;
  // top
  for (int i=0; i<c.detail; i++){
```

```
    outerVecs[counter++] = new PVector ((c.x+c.padding/2)+intervalX + intervalX*i, ⮐
      (c.y+c.padding/2));
  }
  // right
  for (int i=0; i<c.detail; i++){
    outerVecs[counter++] = new PVector ((c.x+c.padding/2)+(c.w-c.padding), ⮐
      (c.y+c.padding/2)+intervalY + intervalY*i);
  }
  //bottom
  for (int i=0; i<c.detail; i++){
    outerVecs[counter++] = new PVector ((c.x+c.padding/2)+ ⮐
      (c.w-c.padding)-intervalX - intervalX*i, (c.y+c.padding/2)+(c.h-c.padding));
  }
  //left
  for (int i=0; i<c.detail; i++){
    outerVecs[counter++] = new PVector ((c.x+c.padding/2), ⮐
      (c.y+c.padding/2)+(c.h-c.padding)-intervalY - intervalY*i);
  }
}


// overrides drawCurvilinear()in Style
void drawCurvilinear(){
  // calculate inner edge points
  float radius = (cellCore.w + cellCore.h)/4;
  float theta = -HALF_PI*1.5;
  float px = 0.0;
  float py = 0.0;

  for (int i=0; i<innerVecs.length; i++){
    px = (c.x+c.padding/2)+(c.w-c.padding)/2 + cos(theta)*radius;
    py = (c.y+c.padding/2)+(c.h-c.padding)/2 + sin(theta)*radius;
    innerVecs[i] = new PVector (px, py);
```

```
  theta += TWO_PI/innerVecs.length;
}


// cell core shape
fill(c.cellCols[2]);
noStroke();
curveTightness(0);
beginShape();
for(int i=0; i<innerVecs.length; i++){
  vertex(innerVecs[i].x, innerVecs[i].y);
}
endShape(CLOSE);
//
noStroke();
// cell internal shape
fill(c.cellCols[1]);
for(int i=0; i<outerVecs.length; i++){
  beginShape();
  if (i == outerVecs.length-1){
    curveVertex(innerVecs[0].x, innerVecs[0].y);
    curveVertex(innerVecs[i].x, innerVecs[i].y);
    curveVertex(outerVecs[i].x, outerVecs[i].y);
    curveVertex(innerVecs[0].x, innerVecs[0].y);
    curveVertex(innerVecs[i].x, innerVecs[i].y);
  }
  else {
    curveVertex(innerVecs[i+1].x, innerVecs[i+1].y);
    curveVertex(innerVecs[i].x, innerVecs[i].y);
    curveVertex(outerVecs[i].x, outerVecs[i].y);
    curveVertex(innerVecs[i+1].x, innerVecs[i+1].y);
    curveVertex(innerVecs[i].x, innerVecs[i].y);
  }
  endShape(CLOSE);
```

```
    }
    // optional draw vertices
    //fill(255, 255, 0);
    for(int i=0; i<innerVecs.length; i++){
      //ellipse(innerVecs[i].x, innerVecs[i].y, 5, 5);
    }
    for(int i=0; i<outerVecs.length; i++){
      //ellipse(outerVecs[i].x, outerVecs[i].y, 5, 5);
    }
  }


// overrides drawLinear()in Style
void drawLinear(){
    // calculate inner edge points
    // **1 less than outer per edge)
    float intervalX = cellCore.w/c.detail;
    float intervalY = cellCore.h/c.detail;
    int counter = 0;

    // top
    innerVecs[counter++] = new PVector (cellCore.x, cellCore.y);
    for (int i=0; i< innerDetail; i++){
      innerVecs[counter++] = new PVector (cellCore.x+intervalX + intervalX*i, cellCore.y);
    }
    // right
    innerVecs[counter++] = new PVector (cellCore.x+cellCore.w, cellCore.y);
    for (int i=0; i< innerDetail; i++){

      innerVecs[counter++] = new PVector (cellCore.x+cellCore.w, ↵
      cellCore.y+intervalY + intervalY*i);
    }
    //bottom
    innerVecs[counter++] = new PVector (cellCore.x+cellCore.w, cellCore.y+cellCore.h);
    for (int i=0; i< innerDetail; i++){
```

```
    innerVecs[counter++] = new PVector (cellCore.x+↵
      cellCore.w-intervalX - intervalX*i, cellCore.y+cellCore.h);
}
//left
innerVecs[counter++] = new PVector (cellCore.x, cellCore.y+cellCore.h);
for (int i=0; i< innerDetail; i++){
  innerVecs[counter++] = new PVector (cellCore.x, cellCore.y+↵
  cellCore.h-intervalY - intervalY*i);
}


// calculate triangles
for(int i=0; i<tris.length; i++){
  if (i == tris.length-1){
    tris[i] = new Tri(innerVecs[i], outerVecs[i], innerVecs[0]);
  }
  else {
    tris[i] = new Tri(innerVecs[i], outerVecs[i], innerVecs[i+1]);
  }
}


// cell core shape
noStroke();
fill(c.cellCols[2]);
rect(cellCore.x, cellCore.y, cellCore.w, cellCore.h);
// cell internal shape
fill(c.cellCols[1]);
for(int i=0; i<tris.length; i++){
  beginShape();
  vertex(tris[i].vecs[0].x, tris[i].vecs[0].y);
  vertex(tris[i].vecs[1].x, tris[i].vecs[1].y);
  vertex(tris[i].vecs[2].x, tris[i].vecs[2].y);
  endShape(CLOSE);
}
```

```
// optional draw vertices
//fill(255, 255, 0);
for(int i=0; i<innerVecs.length; i++){
  //ellipse(innerVecs[i].x, innerVecs[i].y, 5, 5);
}
for(int i=0; i<outerVecs.length; i++){
  //ellipse(outerVecs[i].x, outerVecs[i].y, 5, 5);
}
}


// overrides getClone()in Style
Style getClone(){
  /*returns new object of this class type.
   polymorphism allows more generic Style
   return type to handle all Style subclasses*/
  return new IraStyle();
}
}
```

Although this class is a bit long, it's the drawing algorithm that makes up the bulk of the code. I primarily created this class as an example, with the hope that you might be inspired to create your own custom style. Notice IraStyle adheres to Style's structure, overriding all of Style's methods. IraStyle does add a bunch of its own properties involved in the custom drawing procedures, and the class adds one new method, calcOuterGeom(), also used in the drawing calculations. Notice also how the overridden getClone() method returns a new object of its own subclass type: return new IraStyle(); Through inheritance in Processing/Java it's perfectly legal for the method signature Style getClone() to return either a Style object or an object of the class that extends Style, such as IraStyle(). This is a great example of polymorphism, where an object that has ancestors through inheritance can assume the type of any of them.

Tri Class

Before we get to the most complex class in the example, which handles the actual tic-tac-toe logic, we'll look at the simplest: Tri. The IraStyle class declared the instance property reference Tri[] tris;, which proved useful during the drawing procedure. The Tri class is so simple, it needs no elucidation. Figure 6-12 shows the updated class diagram, including Tri.

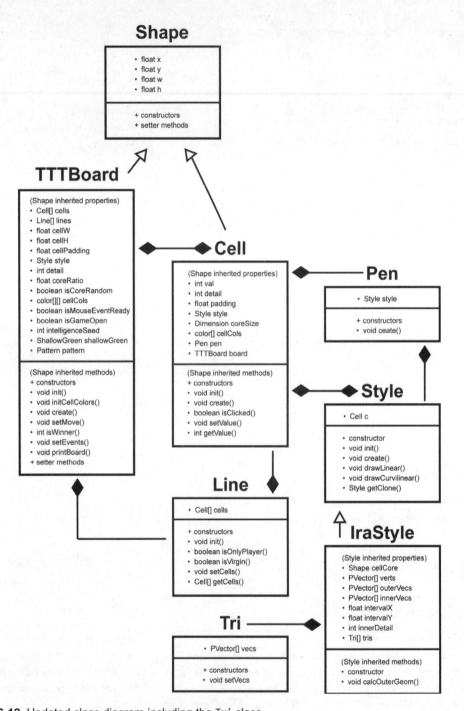

Figure 6-12. Updated class diagram including the Tri class

The following code should be put in a new tab, named "Tri."

```
/**
 * Draw Game
 * Tri class - convenience triangle class
 * By Ira Greenberg <br />
 * The Essential Guide to Processing for Flash Developers,
 * Friends of ED, 2009
 */

class Tri{
  PVector[] vecs = new PVector[3];

  // default constructor
  Tri(){
  }

  // constructor
  Tri(PVector v0, PVector v1, PVector v2){
    vecs[0] = v0;
    vecs[1] = v1;
    vecs[2] = v2;
  }

  // setter
  void setVecs(PVector[] vecs){
    this.vecs = vecs;
  }
}
```

ShallowGreen Class

Here's where things get a bit more complex. The ShallowGreen class encapsulates most of the game logic. If you're curious, the silly name is a tribute to IBM's "Deep Blue," a specialized computer IBM developed to beat the reigning world chess champion, which it did in 1997, against Gary Kasparov. You can read more about Deep Blue at http://www.research.ibm.com/deepblue/ (November 16, 2009, 00:16). Figure 6-13 shows the updated class diagram, including the ShallowGreen class.

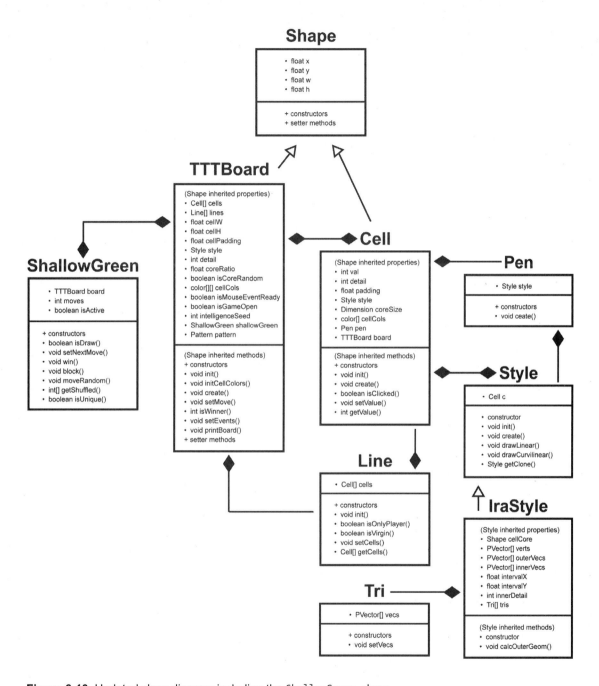

Figure 6-13. Updated class diagram including the ShallowGreen class

The following code should be put in a new tab, named "ShallowGreen."

```
/**
 * Draw Game
 * ShallowGreen class:  tic-tac-toe ai class
 * By Ira Greenberg <br />
 * The Essential Guide to Processing for Flash Developers,
 * Friends of ED, 2009
 */

class ShallowGreen{

  // instance properties
  TTTBoard board;
  int moves;
  boolean isActive = true;

  // default constructor
  ShallowGreen(){
  }

  // constructor
  ShallowGreen(TTTBoard board){
    this.board = board;
  }

  // return true if game is a draw
  boolean isDraw(){
    for (int i=0; i<board.cells.length; i++){
      if (board.cells[i].getValue()==0){
        return false;
      }
    }
```

```
      return true;
   }


   /* rules:
    1. Try to win
    2. Try to block
    3. Take a strategic position
    4. Take best remaining position
    5. Take any remaining position
   */
   void setNextMove(){
     // keep track of number of moves
     moves++;
     int shallowGreen = 0;
     int player = 0;
          int intelligence = 0;
     if (board.intelligenceSeed > 4){
       intelligence = 2;
     }
     else {
       intelligence = round(random(board.intelligenceSeed));
     }
     // flag that controls evaluation flow
     isActive = true;
     if (intelligence > 1){
       win();
       block();
       moveRandom();
     }
     else {
       moveRandom();
     }
   }
```

```
// Try to WIN
void win(){
  int shallowGreen = 0;
  int player = 0;
  for (int i=0; i<board.lines.length; i++){
    if (isActive){
      // reset tally
      shallowGreen = 0;
      player = 0;
      // tally each line
      for (int j=0; j<board.lines[i].cells.length; j++){
        if (board.lines[i].cells[j].getValue() == 1){
          shallowGreen += 1;
        }
        else if (board.lines[i].cells[j].getValue() == -1){
          player += 1;
        }
      }
      // 1. Try to WIN
      // line has 2 o's and no x's
      if (shallowGreen == 2 && player == 0){
        // set line to all o's
        for (int j=0; j<board.lines[i].cells.length; j++){
          board.lines[i].cells[j].setValue(1);
        }
        isActive = false;
      }
    }
  }
}


// block player win or strategic position
void block(){
```

```
// 2. Try to BLOCK win
for (int i=0; i<board.lines.length; i++){
  if (isActive){
    // reset tally
    int shallowGreen = 0;
    int player = 0;
    // tally each line
    for (int j=0; j<board.lines[i].cells.length; j++){
      if (board.lines[i].cells[j].getValue() == 1){
        shallowGreen += 1;
      }
      else if (board.lines[i].cells[j].getValue() == -1){
        player += 1;
      }
    }
    // Block win
    if (player == 2 && shallowGreen == 0){
      isActive = false;
      for (int j=0; j<board.lines[i].cells.length; j++){
        if (board.lines[i].cells[j].getValue() == 0){
          board.lines[i].cells[j].setValue(1);
        }
      }
    }
  }
}


// 2. BLOCK traps
// check diagonal traps
// take non-corner
/*
 |0|  |  |     |  |  |0|
 |  |X|  |  or |  |X|  |
```

```
   |  |  |0|      |0|  |  |
   */
   if (isActive && moves == 2){
      if (board.lines[0].cells[0].getValue() == -1 && ↵
          board.lines[2].cells[2].getValue() == -1 || ↵
          board.lines[2].cells[0].getValue() == -1 && ↵
          board.lines[0].cells[2].getValue() == -1){
               board.lines[1].cells[0].setValue(1);
               isActive = false;
        }
   }
   // check more diagonal traps
   // take blocked corner
   /*
    |0|  |  |
    |  |X|  | or similar variations
    |  |0|  |
    */
   if (isActive && board.lines[0].cells[0].getValue() == 0){
      if (board.lines[0].isOnlyPlayer() && board.lines[3].isOnlyPlayer()){
         board.lines[0].cells[0].setValue(1);
         isActive = false;
      }
   }
   if (isActive && board.lines[0].cells[2].getValue() == 0){
      if (board.lines[0].isOnlyPlayer() && board.lines[5].isOnlyPlayer()){
         board.lines[0].cells[2].setValue(1);
         isActive = false;
      }
   }
   if (isActive && board.lines[2].cells[0].getValue() == 0){
      if (board.lines[2].isOnlyPlayer() && board.lines[3].isOnlyPlayer()){
```

```
      board.lines[2].cells[0].setValue(1);
      isActive = false;
   }
}
if (isActive && board.lines[2].cells[2].getValue() == 0){
   if (board.lines[2].isOnlyPlayer() && board.lines[5].isOnlyPlayer()){
      board.lines[2].cells[2].setValue(1);
      isActive = false;
   }
}


// check diagonal traps 2
// take available corner
/*
 |X| | |    | | |X|
 | |O| | or | |O| |
 | | |O|    |O| | |
 */
if (isActive && moves == 2){
   if (board.lines[1].cells[1].getValue() == -1 && board.lines[2].cells[2].getValue() ==↩
      -1 ||
      board.lines[0].cells[0].getValue() == -1 && board.lines[1].cells[1].getValue() ==↩
      -1){
      board.lines[2].cells[0].setValue(1);
      isActive = false;
   }
}
if (isActive && moves == 2){
   if (board.lines[2].cells[0].getValue() == -1 && board.lines[1].cells[1].getValue() ==↩
      -1 ||
      board.lines[0].cells[2].getValue() == -1 && board.lines[1].cells[1].getValue() == -1){
      board.lines[0].cells[0].setValue(1);
      isActive = false;
```

```
    }
  }


  // 3. check for center square
  if (board.lines[1].cells[1].getValue() == 0 && isActive){
    board.lines[1].cells[1].setValue(1);
    isActive = false;
  }


  // 4. take best remaining
  // check for line with win potential(free of human player mark)
  for (int i=0; i<board.lines.length; i++){
    if (board.lines[i].isVirgin() && isActive){
      for (int j=0; j<board.lines[i].cells.length; j++){
        if (board.lines[i].cells[j].getValue() == 0 && isActive){
          board.lines[i].cells[j].setValue(1);
          isActive = false;
        }
      }
    }
  }
}


// 5. place mark randomly in any available cell
void moveRandom(){
  int[] shuffledCells = getShuffled();
  for (int i=0; i<board.cells.length; i++){
    if (board.cells[shuffledCells[i]].getValue() == 0 && isActive){
      board.cells[shuffledCells[i]].setValue(1);
      isActive = false;
      break; //go ahead and stop looping
    }
  }
```

```
    }

    // shuffles cell array to avoid predictable moves
    int[] getShuffled(){
      // local shuffled array
      int[] shuffledArr = {
      };
      while(shuffledArr.length<board.cells.length){
        int val = floor(random(board.cells.length));
        //  pass random value to helper method
        if (isUnique(val, shuffledArr)){
          shuffledArr = append(shuffledArr, val);
        }
      }
      return shuffledArr;
    }

    // helper method for getShuffled() method
    boolean isUnique(int val, int[] arr){
      for (int i=0; i<arr.length; i++){
        if (arr[i] == val){
          return false;
        }
      }
      return true;
    }

}
```

Like the Cell class, ShallowGreen has a bi-directional compositional relationship with the TTTBoard class, as each class includes a reference to the other. Again, this is useful to allow classes to have two-way communication. For example, the isDraw() method in the ShallowGreen class needs to reference the Cell's value, to determine what type of mark (computer or human) occupies the cell. However, ShallowGreen doesn't include a reference to Cell, which is encapsulated in the TTTBoard class. By including a reference to TTTBoard in ShallowGreen, the value can be accessed like this:

board.cells[i].getValue(). How the TTTBoard reference value was originally passed to ShallowGreen was in the line shallowGreen = new ShallowGreen(this); at the bottom of the TTTBoard init() method.

setNextMove() is the method that begins a chain of game logic evaluation, utilizing the win(), block(), and moveRandom() methods. I created the game logic with the following rules:

1. Try to win
2. Try to block
3. Take a strategic position
4. Take best remaining position
5. Take any remaining position

Winning and blocking are simple to solve, since the solutions are obvious—if the computer player has two marks in any line, place your mark in the third open cell in the line to win; if the human player has two marks in any line, place your mark in the third open cell in the line to block. Obviously, as described, you should attempt to win before you attempt to block.

Taking a strategic position is a bit more complex, requiring relatively complicated math or some good educated guesses (heuristic approach). I opted for the heuristic approach, and I approached the problem iteratively, changing up my algorithm until the computer seemed to be unbeatable. The approach that I settled on is as follows:

Block traps, as illustrated in Figures 6-14, 6-15 and 6-16. I refer to traps as positions where a player has a winning position in two lines, guaranteeing a victory. Figure 6-14 shows a trap where a move to either free corner guarantees a victory by the human player. A successful counter is a move to any side position, as illustrated in Figure 6-14. This position can also be recreated by rotating the board 90 degrees.

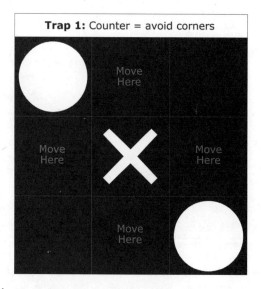

Figure 6-14. Trap example 1

Figure 6-15 illustrates another trap where a successful counter is moving to the blocked corner; by blocked I mean a corner that has an opponent's mark on both lines forming the corner. This position also has numerous potential configurations, such as by rotating the board 90 degrees or by 180 degrees, among others.

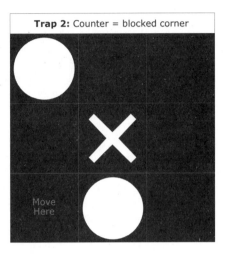

Figure 6-15. Trap example 2

Figure 6-16 illustrates another trap where a successful counter is moving to either open corner. This position also has numerous configurations, such as by rotating the board by 90 degrees.

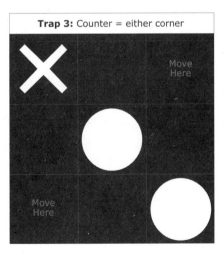

Figure 6-16. Trap example 3

After checking for traps, the algorithm attempts to take the center position, which is very strategic as it can be used by any line; next it checks for any lines still free of a human player mark, using the method call board.lines[i].isVirgin(). If this evaluates to true, then there is still a possibility of victory on that line. Finally, after all wins/blocks and strategic positions have been exhausted, the algorithm randomly takes any available cell.

The methods moveRandom(), getShuffled(), and isUnique() are all involved in generating a random move. Generating a random move might initially seem like a relatively simple thing to do, but it's actually a bit involved. The basic algorithm is to take an array of integers from 0 to 9, representing the nine cells, and randomly shuffle the array. Then check free cells in the order of the shuffled integer array. The main challenge is shuffling an array of values, without duplicating or excluding any values.

The moveRandom() procedure is also used by the variable intelligence feature built into the program. This feature is controlled by the setIntelligence() method and intelligenceSeed property in the TTTBoard class. The intelligence of ShallowGreen can be set between 1 and 5, where 1 (no intelligence) means that the moveRandom() procedure will handle nearly all moves, while 5 (pure intelligence) ensures the optimal logic algorithm will be followed, as outlined in this chapter. Values between 1 and 5 will use varying degrees of intelligence, with higher values evaluating to higher intelligence (using less random moves).

Next we'll look at the final class of the example, Pattern.

Pattern Class

The Pattern class generates the final artwork created whenever a draw state occurs. The artwork is saved in a **patterns** subdirectory, in the main sketch directory. As the name implies, the artwork generated is a pattern, based on the configuration of the board at the time of the draw.

Figure 6-17 shows an updated and final class diagram that includes the Pattern class. As mentioned, pattern artwork is automatically generated when a draw state is detected; this is controlled by the Boolean value returned from the call shallowGreen.isDraw(), in the TTTBoard class; here's the snippet of code:

```
else if (shallowGreen.isDraw()){
    isGameOpen = false;
    println("DRAW\n");
    println("Pattern Created");
    // generate pattern output
    pattern.create();
}
```

Although the Pattern and ShallowGreen classes are not directly linked, their common compositional relationship to TTTBoard allows their inter-class communication.

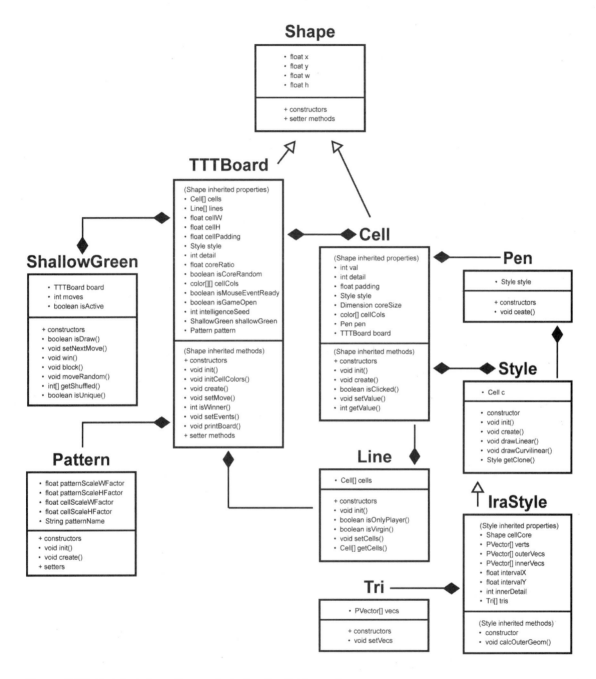

Figure 6-17. Updated class diagram including the `Pattern` class

Next is the Pattern class code, which should be put in a new tab named "Pattern."

```
/**
 * Draw Game
 * Pattern class - outputs pattern jpg
 * By Ira Greenberg <br />
 * The Essential Guide to Processing for Flash Developers,
 * Friends of ED, 2009
 */

class Pattern{

  // properties with defaults
  float patternScaleWFactor = 2;
  float patternScaleHFactor = 2;
  float cellScaleWFactor = .5;
  float cellScaleHFactor = .5;
  String patternName;

  // Default constructor
  Pattern(){
    init();
  }

  // constructor
  Pattern(float patternScaleWFactor, float patternScaleHFactor, float cellScaleWFactor, ⏎
      float cellScaleHFactor, String patternName){
    this.patternScaleWFactor = patternScaleWFactor;
    this.patternScaleHFactor = patternScaleHFactor;
    this.cellScaleWFactor = cellScaleWFactor;
    this.cellScaleHFactor = cellScaleHFactor;
    this.patternName = patternName;
  }
```

```
// constructor (with auto naming)
Pattern(float patternScaleWFactor, float patternScaleHFactor, float cellScaleWFactor, ⏎
    float cellScaleHFactor){
  this.patternScaleWFactor = patternScaleWFactor;
  this.patternScaleHFactor = patternScaleHFactor;
  this.cellScaleWFactor = cellScaleWFactor;
  this.cellScaleHFactor = cellScaleHFactor;
  init();
}


// ensure pattern name is unique
void init(){
  patternName = "pattern_"+year()+month()+day()+hour()+minute()+second();
}


// make beautiful pattern
void create(){
  //Create PImage to output
  PImage img = createImage(int(width*patternScaleWFactor), ⏎
    int(height*patternScaleHFactor), RGB);
  // create PImage based on current sketch dimension
  PImage imgC = createImage(width, height, RGB);
  // populate global(screen) pixel array
  loadPixels();
  // copy pixels
  imgC.pixels = pixels;
  // scale image
  imgC.resize(width*=cellScaleWFactor, height*=cellScaleHFactor);
  int[] pixelsRev = reverse(imgC.pixels);

  int tileWidthCount = img.width/imgC.width;
```

```
      int tileHeightCount = img.height/imgC.height;
      // create tiled pattern
      // nested loops based on tiled count and source tile dimensions
      for (int g=0; g<tileHeightCount; g++){
        for (int h=0; h<tileWidthCount; h++){
          for (int i=0; i<imgC.height; i++){
            for (int j=0; j<imgC.width; j++){

              img.pixels[img.width*i + img.width*imgC.height*g + j + imgC.width*h] = ↵
                imgC.pixels[i*imgC.width + j];

            }
          }
        }
      }
      // save file to current sketch directory/patterns
      img.save("patterns/"+patternName);
    }


    // getters/setters
    void setPatternScale(float patternScaleWFactor, float patternScaleHFactor){
      this.patternScaleWFactor = patternScaleWFactor;
      this.patternScaleHFactor = patternScaleHFactor;
    }


    void setCellScale(float cellScaleWFactor, float cellScaleHFactor){
      this.cellScaleWFactor = cellScaleWFactor;
      this.cellScaleHFactor = cellScaleHFactor;
    }


    void setPatternName(String patternName){
      this.patternName = patternName;
    }
  }
```

Pattern includes instance properties that can be set to control variations in the artwork.

The properties patternScaleWFactor and patternScaleHFactor control the size of the output image, allowing the size of the final artwork to be independent from the sketch size. For example, Figure 6-18 shows a draw state with a sketch whose size was set to 200 pixels (width) by 600 pixels (height). Figure 6-19 shows the output pattern image generated for this sketch using the values patternScaleWFactor = 6 and patternScaleHFactor = 2. Notice the horizontal (compression) distortion, as the ratio of the width and height (of the sketch window) was not 1/1. However, using patternScaleWFactor and patternScaleHFactor, I was able to generate a pattern image with a near 1/1 relationship, in regard to the image's outer dimensions.

Figure 6-18. Draw state, size(200, 600)

Figure 6-19. Pattern image generated using `patternScaleWFactor` = 6 and `patternScaleHFactor` = 2

`cellScaleWFactor` and `cellScaleHFactor` control the scale of the cells to the whole. The image in Figure 6-19 had `cellScaleWFactor` and `cellScaleHFactor` both set to 1. The image in Figure 6-20 was generated with the values both changed to `.25`.

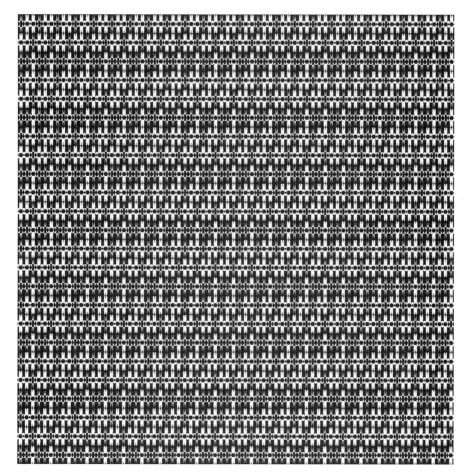

Figure 6-20. Pattern image generated using `patternScaleWFactor = 6`, `patternScaleHFactor = 2`, `cellScaleWFactor = .25`, and `cellScaleHFactor = .25`

Pattern includes three constructors, one that calls the `init()` method that handles auto-naming:

```
void init(){
    patternName = "pattern_"+year()+month()+day()+hour()+minute()+second();
  }
```

I used Processing's calendar functions, concatenating them into a long string, to ensure the name for each pattern would be unique.

Where the `Pattern` class gets complex is in its `create()` method, shown again next:

```
void create(){
    //Create PImage to output
    PImage img = createImage(int(width*patternScaleWFactor), int↵
    (height*patternScaleHFactor), RGB);
    // create PImage based on current sketch dimension
    PImage imgC = createImage(width, height, RGB);
    // populate global(screen) pixel array
    loadPixels();
    // copy pixels
    imgC.pixels = pixels;
    // scale image
    imgC.resize(width*=cellScaleWFactor, height*=cellScaleHFactor);
    // calculate ratio of external image to tile
    int tileWidthCount = img.width/imgC.width;
    int tileHeightCount = img.height/imgC.height;
    // create tiled pattern
    // nested loops based on tiled count and source tile dimensions
    for (int g=0; g<tileHeightCount; g++){
      for (int h=0; h<tileWidthCount; h++){
        for (int i=0; i<imgC.height; i++){
          for (int j=0; j<imgC.width; j++){
            img.pixels[img.width*i + img.width*imgC.height*g + j + ↵
              imgC.width*h] = imgC.pixels[i*imgC.width + j];
          }
        }
      }
    }
    // save file to current sketch directory/patterns
    img.save("patterns/"+patternName);
  }
```

The create() method creates two PImages, one a size specified by the patternScaleWFactor and patternScaleHFactor properties, looked at earlier, and one the same size of the existing sketch. I used Processing's createImage() method to do this, which creates an off-screen PImage of a certain size and color format, in this case RGB; it is also possible to specify ARGB and ALPHA color format arguments. The method then copies a reference to the pixels array of the sketch window (which contains the draw state) to the newly created PImage (imgC) and then resizes the imgC based on the cellScaleWFactor and cellScaleHFactor properties. Next, the ratio of the external pattern image to the individual tiles is calculated and assigned to the properties tileWidthCount and tileHeightCount. And—this is where the really eye-crossing stuff happens—the deeply nested for loops then calculate the final pattern image.

I do realize the expression

```
img.pixels[img.width*i + img.width*imgC.height*g + j + imgC.width*h] =
imgC.pixels[i*imgC.width + j];
```

is pretty nasty looking, but it is a very efficient line of code that builds the final pixel array. The best way to understand how it processes the final pixel array is to change some of the sentinel values (the values after <) in the for loops to see how they affect output. The last line in the method (img.save("patterns/"+patternName);) saves the image in the **patterns** subdirectory of the sketch directory. The rest of the Pattern class just includes some standard setters.

Well, that completes all the classes needed for the Draw game. The last thing we need to do to try out the game is to add some code to the main (leftmost) tab.

Running the Game

Add the following code to the main sketch tab:

```
/**
 * Draw Game
 * Main Tab
 * By Ira Greenberg <br />
 * The Essential Guide to Processing for Flash Developers,
 * Friends of ED, 2009
 */


TTTBoard board;

void setup(){
  size(400, 400);
  background(0);
  smooth();
  board = new TTTBoard();
}
```

```
void draw(){
  board.create();
}
```

This is the simplest way to execute the game, using the default `TTTBoard` instantiation and a call to its `create()` method. This approach will only use internally predefined default values, and the cell contents will be O's and X's. Also, the computer player will essentially guess for most of its moves. Figure 6-21 shows the pattern image generated using these settings (after a draw state was reached).

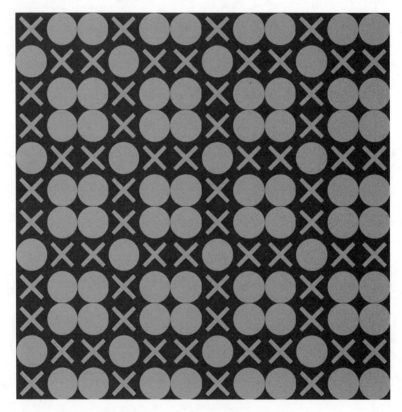

Figure 6-21. Pattern artwork generated using predefined default values

Obviously, you can generate more interesting output with user-defined values. Figure 6-22 shows an image generated with the following code in the main tab:

```
/**
 * Draw Game
```

```
 * Main Tab
 * By Ira Greenberg <br />
 * The Essential Guide to Processing for Flash Developers,
 * Friends of ED, 2009
 */


TTTBoard board;

void setup(){
  size(800, 800);
  background(20, 80, 30);
  smooth();
  board = new TTTBoard(30, 30, 740, 740);

  //manually set board colors
  color[][] cellCols = {
   {0xffff8800, 0xff2233ff, 0xff000000},
   {0xff550055, 0xff999900, 0xff000000},
   {0xffff8800, 0xff2233ff, 0xff000000},
   {0xff550055, 0xff999900, 0xff000000},
   {0xffff8800, 0xff2233ff, 0xff000000},
   {0xff550055, 0xff999900, 0xff000000},
   {0xffff8800, 0xff2233ff, 0xff000000},
   {0xff550055, 0xff999900, 0xff000000},
   {0xffff8800, 0xff2233ff, 0xff000000}
   };

  // set board style values
  //board.setCellStyle(6, .35, true, cellCols, 0);
}

void draw(){
  board.create();
}
```

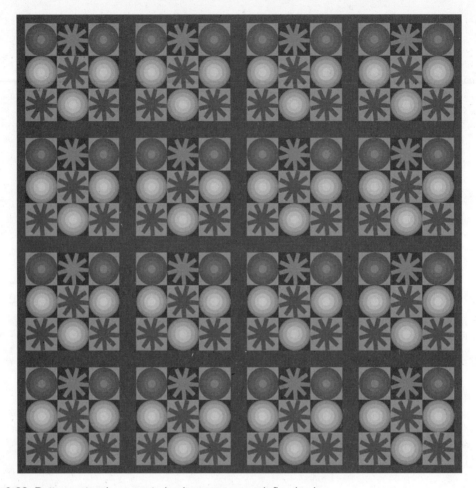

Figure 6-22. Pattern artwork generated using some user-defined values

I suggest playing with these values a bit to see the expressive range of the default base `Style` class. That said, you'll have much more freedom for experimentation if you create a custom style (`Style` subclass), as I did with the `IraStyle` class. The following code utilizes `IraStyle` and also includes more explicit style parameter settings. Notice also that I included the call `board.setIntelligence(5);`, which sets `ShallowGreen`'s intelligence to the maximum, making him unbeatable. Figures 6-23 through 6-26 demonstrate just a tiny sample of possible variations.

```
/**
 * Draw Game
 * Main Tab
 * By Ira Greenberg <br />
```

```
 * The Essential Guide to Processing for Flash Developers,
 * Friends of ED, 2009
 */

TTTBoard board;

void setup(){
  size(400, 400);
  background(20, 80, 30);
  smooth();
  board = new TTTBoard(0, 0, 400, 400);


  // randomly assign board colors
  color[][] cellCols = new color[9][3];

  // random RGB
  for (int i=0;i<9; i++){
    for (int j=0;j<3; j++){
      cellCols[i][j] =  color(random(255), random(255), random(255));
    }
  }

  // set optional styles (drawing algorithms)
  Style style = new IraStyle();
  // set board style values
  board.setCellStyle(6, .85, true, cellCols, 6, style);

  // set pattern values
  Pattern pattern = new Pattern(6, 6, .5, .5);
  board.setPattern(pattern);

  board.setIntelligence(5);

}
```

```
void draw(){
  board.create();
  // prints board values
  board.printBoard();
}
```

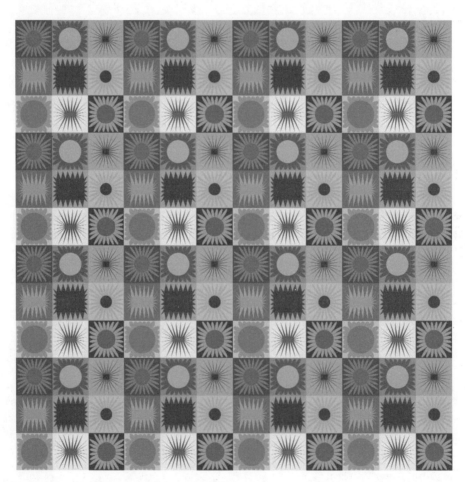

Figure 6-23. Pattern artwork generated using IraStyle

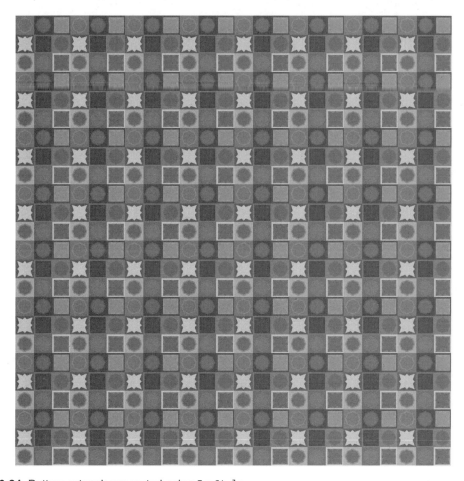

Figure 6-24. Pattern artwork generated using `IraStyle`

Figure 6-25. Pattern artwork generated using `IraStyle`

Figure 6-26. Pattern artwork generated using `IraStyle`

Summary

So perhaps this wasn't a "serious" game as defined by my 10-year-old son and his peers. However, the approach I adopted, especially with regard to combining numerous classes together, could be utilized for many other types of programs, including less serious games. One of the challenges of building more complex programs, such as games, is managing the communication between classes. In the Draw game example, I utilized the TTTBoard class as the main organizing class, which included numerous object references (composition relationships) to different components of the program. In addition, each program component was responsible for managing its own functionality, such as the Cell object controlling the structural aspects of the individual cells and the Pen and Style objects together handling the creation of cell content. We also looked at how to encapsulate game logic, using the ShallowGreen class, and also how to incorporate both vector and raster drawing operations in final pattern artwork creation, including how to directly manipulate the pixel buffer arrays. Next chapter we'll explore one of my favorite topics, artificial life and how to create simulations in Processing.

Chapter 7

Hacking Life

I suspect, if you're like me, that you find the idea of modeling aspects of the natural world a bit more interesting than, say, creating an accounting program (no disrespect to accountants intended). I first got excited by programming precisely because I (finally) made the connection between math and life and glimpsed the potential of code to actually model this relationship. As a painter I used to look at nature and try to deconstruct it visually: *what colors could I see in the leaves*; *how did the horizon recede into the distance*; *what made highlights and shadows appear*. When I moved to code I asked many of the same questions, but could now go much deeper, beneath the surface to the very forces that created what I was looking at: what determined a tree's branch structure; how do migrating birds organize themselves into a V; what causes the patterns in tree bark, marble, clouds, etc. And when I first began to be able to code small examples of some of these things, it was incredibly exciting—like discovering a magic box of paints. I continue to be awed and inspired by this potential of code to literally *hack* life.

Emergence and Complexity

One of the most interesting aspects of coding natural processes is that many seemingly organized, complex structures are actually created by extremely simple rules. Using really basic math, we can quickly glimpse how simple rules create vastly massive structures. For example, by beginning with the number 1 and simply doubling it 70 times, we reach the estimated number of stars in the universe, 10^{21} (according to Astrophysicist Laura Whitlock of NASA's Goddard Space Flight Center). Using some code and a few simple rules you can simulate colonies of insects organizing their surroundings, flocking and swarming behaviors, and all sorts of physical dynamic systems. The key to simulating these types of emergent phenomena is iteration. When simple rules are allowed to be executed hundreds or even thousands of times, unpredictable complex structures can emerge. One classic mathematical model that reveals this potential is Cellular Automata, which also lends itself quite well to programming.

Cellular Automata

Cellular Automata (plural of cellular automaton) or CA were first conceived of in the 1950s by mathematicians John von Neumann and Stanislaw Ulam, when both men were working at Los Alamos National Laboratory, New Mexico. At first, CA were more of a mathematical abstraction that held the promise of developing self-replicating structures—theoretically even the fundamental structures of life itself. Von Neumann and Ulam's pioneering work didn't really impact the wider scientific community until the 1970s, when their work was expanded (and popularized), due in large part to advances in and increased accessibility to computation, including the capability to more easily create computer-generated graphics.

In 1971 Princeton mathematician John Conway created arguably the most famous CA, "Conway's Game of Life," which brought CA to the popular imagination through an article written about it in Scientific American. A decade later, Steven Wolfram, founder of the Mathematica software package, continued the CA charge, eventually publishing a massive tome related to the subject: *A New Kind of Science*. For a wonderful history about CA, check out this article in the CellLab manual, by authors Rudy Rucker and John Walker: http://www.fourmilab.ch/cellab/manual/chap5.html (June 23, 2009, 23:01).

In spite of the rather lofty aspirations of CA originators von Neumann and Ulam, the basic concepts behind CA are quite simple:

> *Create a finite set of cells in a grid-like configuration, where each cell has a set of states (most commonly two, for "on" or "off") that is controlled by its surrounding cells (its neighborhood) from the previous generation.*

The simplest type of CA is one-dimensional (1D), meaning that a single cell's state is controlled only by neighboring cells along one axis. The classic 1D CA uses three contiguous cells, shown in Figure 7-1.

Figure 7-1. Cell with controlling contiguous cells

Since there are three cells—defined as the neighborhood—each with an on or off state, there is a total of eight possible configurations (2^3), shown in Figure 7-2. In running a simulation, you apply very simple rules that change the pixel values (turn them off or on) based on the neighborhood configuration. Figure 7-3 shows the previous figure updated with some simple rules. Please note these rules are arbitrary and can thus be changed, as I'll demonstrate later in the chapter.

Figure 7-2. Three cell (on/off) configurations

Figure 7-3. CA visual rules table

Programming a simple 1D CA is fairly straightforward. As discussed earlier, each pixel's state will be determined by three contiguous pixels (itself and the pixels to its left and right). These new calculated pixel values will, in a sense, represent pixel values in the next generation. Thus, in a programming implementation it is helpful to use two separate arrays (named `bits` and `pixels` in the upcoming example) representing the preset and future pixels. The initial simple 1D Cellular Automata program is listed next.

```
/**
 * Simple 1D Cellular Automata
 * By Ira Greenberg <br />
 * The Essential Guide to Processing for Flash Developers,
 * Friends of ED, 2009
 *
 * Good CS article
 * http://www.generation5.org/content/2003/caIntro.asp
 */

// array for bit values
int[] bits;
/* CA rules, 4th val is new bit state
(0=off, 1 = On), based on each rule */
int[][] rules = {
    {0,0,0,0},
    {1,0,0,1},
    {0,1,0,1},
    {0,0,1,1},
    {1,1,0,1},
    {0,1,1,1},
    {1,0,1,1},
    {1,1,1,0}
};
```

```
void setup(){
  size(400, 400);
  // map color values between 0-1.0
  colorMode(RGB, 1.0);
  // access pixels array of sketch window
  loadPixels();
  // instantiate bits array to size of sketch
  bits = new int[width*height];
  // initialize starting bit state
  initNeighborhood();
}



// create initial state
void initNeighborhood(){
  // turn bottom middle bit on
    bits[width*(height-1) + width/2] = 1;
}


// update bits based on CA rules
void createGeneration(){
  for(int i=0; i<height-1; i++){
    for(int j=0; j<width; j++){



        // 1st and last columns use each other as neighbors in calculation
            int firstCol = (j==0) ? width-1 : j-1;
            int endCol = (j>0 && j<width-1) ? j+1 : 0;


        // check rules
        for(int k=0; k<rules.length; k++){
          if (bits[width*(i+1)+firstCol] == rules[k][0] &&
            bits[width*(i+1)+j] == rules[k][1] &&
            bits[width*(i+1)+endCol] == rules[k][2]){
```

```
            bits[width*i+j] = rules[k][3];
        }
      }
    }
  }
}


// paint screen pixels based on stored values in bits
void setCells(){
  for (int i=0; i<bits.length; i++){
    // casts int to color data type for pixel value
    pixels[i] = color(bits[i]);
  }
    // call whenever changing pixels array
  updatePixels();
}


void draw(){
  // calculates CA
  createGeneration();
  // copies bit values to PImage pixels[]
  setCells();
}
```

In this first CA example, I tried to create a very simple implementation, with the trade-off for the simplicity being a lack of parameterization to easily customize the program. But don't worry, in the CA examples to follow, I'll provide lots of opportunity for customization (with, of course, the requisite increased complexity).

In the **simple 1D CA** example, I used int arrays (bits[] and rules[][]) as the main data structures. You'll see shortly why this provided for both an efficient and simple solution. The basic program execution proceeds with the creation of a single on/off state, followed by a rules analysis and then the creation of the next generation. In this implementation the initial state is simply turning the bottom center pixel to "on" (painted white), while all the other pixels are initialized to "off" (painted black). The main execution happens repeatedly within draw(), which allows the CA to proceed across the entire screen, until a steady state is reached. Later in the chapter, we'll look at some two-dimensional CA examples that actually never reach this type of (static) steady-state and continually show the genesis of later generations. If you haven't yet, try running the example. A screen-shot of the final steady-state of the CA is shown in Figure 7-4.

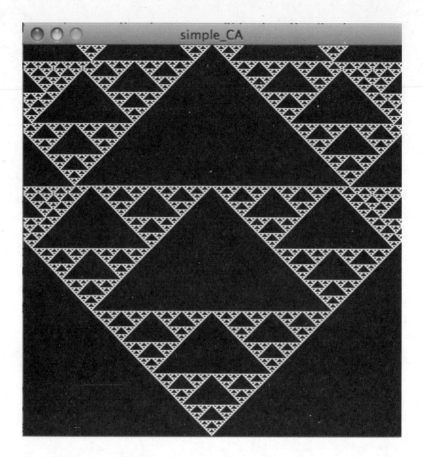

Figure 7-4. Simple_1D_CA screen-shot

If you haven't seen CA before, perhaps the order (and beauty) of the output surprised you. You'll see shortly that this example demonstrates just the very tip of the iceberg of what's possible with CA.

Returning to the example code, I want to clarify why I chose to use int arrays. Processing structures its color data type as a packed 32-bit integer, in the format aaaaaaaa rrrrrrrr gggggggg bbbbbbbb, with 8-bits for alpha, red, green, and blue respectively. Because of this relationship between the int and color types in Processing, it's possible to cast a plain old integer into a specific pixel value, as I do in the setCells() function, with the line

```
pixels[i] = color(bits[i]);
```

Casting again is the converting of one data type into another. There are specific rules about type casting, and not all types can be converted to one another. I cover type casting in Processing in Chapter 2. The **simple_1D_CA** example will only use an off or on state for each pixel, so I utilized a 0 and 1 to record these two states respectively, which obviously fit well within the range of the int type.

> *It might seem more efficient to try to utilize a smaller data structure than a 32-bit integer to record 1 bit of information, such as Processing's char type, which is 16 bits; or byte, which is only 8 bits; or best of all perhaps Processing's Boolean type, which presumably would be a 1-bit data structure, only needing to account for* true *or* false. *Because Processing (really Java) has an internal memory management scheme in conjunction with a virtual machine, it turns out these seemingly smaller data types internally utilize more memory than assumed, and in some cases would also require additional casting to work as a valid color type.*

Returning to the **simple_1D_CA** example, the rules[][] array (shown again next)

```
int[][] rules = {
    {0,0,0,0},
    {1,0,0,1},
    {0,1,0,1},
    {0,0,1,1},
    {1,1,0,1},
    {0,1,1,1},
    {1,0,1,1},
    {1,1,1,0}
};
```

functions as a look-up table of the CA rules. rules[][] is a 2D array, or an array of arrays, with an overall length of eight, with each internal array having a length of four. The first three values in the internal arrays account for the neighborhood states I discussed earlier, and the fourth value has the rule for that state. For example, when one is looking at the first internal array, {0,0,0,0}, if the neighborhood is all off (all 0's), then the pixel being evaluated will be turned/remain off. In the second array {1,0,0,1}, if the pixel on the left is on and the next two pixels to its right are off, then the pixel being evaluated will be turned/remain on. The reason I wrote "turned/remain" is because the evaluation will occur on the pixel row directly below the pixel affected, so the affected pixel could either be on or off. Please note also the rule (the fourth value in each array) is hard-coded in this initial example, but in later examples in the chapter, you'll be able to pass arguments to create variations to the rules, and thus output.

The main work in the example is handled by the createGeneration() function, listed again next:

```
void createGeneration(){
  for(int i=0; i<height-1; i++){
    for(int j=0; j<width; j++){

      // 1st and last columns use each other as neighbors in calculation
        int firstCol = (j==0) ? width-1 : j-1;
        int endCol = (j>0 && j<width-1) ? j+1 : 0;
```

```
      // check rules
      for(int k=0; k<rules.length; k++){
        if (bits[width*(i+1)+firstCol] == rules[k][0] &&
          bits[width*(i+1)+j] == rules[k][1] &&
          bits[width*(i+1)+endCol] == rules[k][2]){
          bits[width*i+j] = rules[k][3];
        }
      }
    }
  }
}
```

Using nested for loops, the function moves through the bits[] array, where each value in the array represents a specific pixel in the sketch window. The actual pixels are stored in another array aptly named "pixels."

> *Please remember that to access the sketch window's global pixels array, you need to first call Processing's loadPixels() function, which I did up in the setup() function.*

The actual CA rules evaluation occurs within the conditional block, within the nested for loops. In regard to program flow, createGeneration() is called from within draw(), which executes at Processing's default frame rate (60 FPS). Each draw cycle, the nested for loops process the entire bits array checking for matches against the rules. As I mentioned earlier the analysis occurs on the row directly beneath the actual bit (ultimately pixel) affected. You can think of the rows as representing different generations (present and future respectively).

> *Nesting three for loops is bit confusing at first glance (alright, even on later glances), and in truth is not terribly efficient, performance-wise speaking. You could conceivably use at least one less loop and treat the bits and pixels arrays as single-dimensional arrays (which of course they really are). However, I personally find it easier to think about (and process) arrays that represent 2D data (a table structure) using a procedure that accounts for rows and columns, which is what the extra loop provides.*

With regard to the rules table, within the nested conditional block when all three statements evaluate to true, then the rule (the fourth value in the same nested array) is applied. Since the rules look-up table accounts for all possible neighborhood configurations, every pixel's state is accounted for this way. A final point about this function refers to the two rather ugly lines

```
int firstCol = (j==0) ? width-1 : j-1;

int endCol = (j>0 && j<width-1) ? j+1 : 0;
```

If you're not familiar with this syntax, it uses the ternary operator ?: (The same one exists in ActionScript.) I have to admit to not really being a big fan of it, but in this case it seemed to keep the function from getting too pudgy. The ternary operator allows you to do terse if/else expressions, but, some would say, with decreased readability—until (I guess) you get really used to it. If it isn't obvious, the ternary operation is (Boolean condition) ? (stuff to do if true) : (stuff to do if false). The reason I included these two expressions in the first place was to account for the first and last pixel in each column. Since the CA neighborhood in this example includes three contiguous pixels (used to evaluate every pixel) there will be an edge problem (a missing third pixel) on the first and last pixel in each row. To account for this I wrap the window pixels, by using the pixels on the opposite edge of the sketch window as the third pixel. In other words, when a right column edge pixel is evaluated, the pixel to its left and the first pixel on the left side of the screen are used for the rules evaluation. (If you're wondering, I didn't invent this idea, but saw it implemented in numerous other CA implementations.)

Again, this initial sketch was intended to give you a down-and-dirty look at CA; more interesting variations are coming. However, if you simply can't wait for the next example, you can create some variation in this example by altering the initial starting state in the initNeighborhood() function. For example, Figure 7-5 shows a screen-shot created using the following starting position: bits[width*(height-1) + width/8] = 1. You can also easily adjust the rules by changing which conditions result in on or off pixels—just be prepared for some funky results.

Figure 7-5. Simple_1D_CA screen-shot based on altered initial state

In considering a more robust and creative application of CA, it will help to create a well-structured program, so I'll utilize an OOP approach. (I hope you feel refreshed after the brief procedural respite.) The next example will function as both a framework for extended 1D and 2D CA development, as well as a small showcase of their creative potential.

1D CA Framework

There were a number of issues I tried to address in this example. I wanted users to be able to

- customize the CA, including altering color
- zoom-in to see the CA at different pixel resolutions
- use the CA as part of a larger image
- create their own CA subclasses

To follow along with the example, create a new sketch named whatever you like, and then add a new tab to the sketch named "Shape." Here's the Shape class code.

```
/**
 * Cellular Automata
 * Shape class - convenience class
 * By Ira Greenberg <br />
 * The Essential Guide to Processing for Flash Developers,
 * Friends of ED, 2009
 */


class Shape {

  // instance properties
  PVector loc = new PVector();
  float w;
  float h;



  // default constructor
  Shape(){
  }
```

```
Shape(float w, float h){
  this.w = w;
  this.h = h;
}


// constructor
Shape(float x, float y, float w, float h){
  loc.x = x;
  loc.y = y;
  this.w = w;
  this.h = h;
}


// setters
void setLoc(float x, float y){
  loc.x = x;
  loc.y = y;
}


void setLoc(PVector loc){
  this.loc = loc;
}


void setSize(float w, float h){
  this.w = w;
  this.h = h;
}


}
```

This Shape class is very straightforward with concepts I've covered throughout the book. It will serve as a base class, encapsulating a location and size, which other classes will extend. Next, create a tab named "Cell," including the following code:

```
/**
 * Cellular Automata
 * Cell class
 * - encapsulates drawing to pixel buffer
 * By Ira Greenberg <br />
 * The Essential Guide to Processing for Flash Developers,
 * Friends of ED, 2009
 */

class Cell extends Shape{

  color c;
  // reference to CA obj
  CA ca;

  Cell(float x, float y, float w, float h, CA ca){
    super(x, y, w, h);
    this.ca = ca;
  }

  void setColor(color c){
    this.c = c;
  }

  // draw to pixels buffer
  void create(){
    float origin = int(loc.y) * ca.w + int(loc.x);
    for (int i=0; i<w; i++){
      for (int j=0; j<h; j++){
          // - pretty nasty pixls[index] expression
        ca.p.pixels[int(min(origin + j*ca.w + i, ca.w*ca.h))] = c;
      }
    }
  }
}
```

The `Cell` class, which you'll notice extended Shape, will function primarily as a utility class that allows pixels to be grouped into a larger block or cell. The class is also straightforward, with the exception of its `create()` method, which converts the **cell** construct, from a higher-level 2D component, to specific index values in a pixel buffer. I'll return to this method later in the chapter.

Next, create a new tab named "**CA**," which will be the base class for **1D** (and some **2D**) CA. Add the following code to the CA tab:

```
/**
 * Cellular Automata
 * CA class (base class)
 * By Ira Greenberg <br />
 * The Essential Guide to Processing for Flash Developers,
 * Friends of ED, 2009
 */


abstract class CA extends Shape{
  // instance properties, including default values
  int cellScale = 3;
  int rows = 10, cols = 10;
  float rowSpan, colSpan;
  Cell[][] cells;
  PImage p;
  color[] pixls;
  color[] nextPixls;
  int[] state;

  // default start colors
  color onC = 0xff000000;
  color offC = 0xffffffff;

  // default constructor
  CA(){
    super(200.0, 200.0);
    initCA();
  }
```

```
// constructor
CA(float w, float h, int cellScale){
  super(w, h);
  this.cellScale = cellScale;
  rows = ceil(h/cellScale);
  cols = ceil(w/cellScale);
  initCA();
}

// initialize
void initCA(){
  pixls = new color[rows*cols];
  nextPixls = new color[rows*cols];
  // record current pixel on/off state as integer array
  state = new int[pixls.length];
  colSpan = w/cols;
  rowSpan = h/rows;

  cells = new Cell[rows][cols];
  for (int i=0; i<rows; i++){
    for (int j=0; j<cols; j++){
      // instantiate cells
      cells[i][j] = new Cell(colSpan*j, rowSpan*i, colSpan, rowSpan, this);
    }
  }
  p = createImage(int(w), int(h), RGB);
}

// set starting state (single pixel)
void setInitState(int id){
  resetState();
  // turn initial pixel on
  pixls[id] = onC;
  recordState();
```

```
  paintInitState();
}


// set starting state (array of pixels)
void setInitState(int[] ids){
  resetState();
  for (int i=0; i<ids.length; i++){
    pixls[ids[i]] = onC;
  }
  recordState();
  paintInitState();
}


// set starting state (single pixel using 2D coord)
void setInitState(int row, int col){
  resetState();
  pixls[row*(cols-1) + (col-1)] = onC;
  recordState();
  paintInitState();
}


// record pixel state in integer array (1 = on, 0 = off)
void recordState(){
  for (int i=0; i<pixls.length; i++){
    if (pixls[i] == onC){
      state[i] = 1;
    }
    else {
      state[i] = 0;
    }
  }
}


// update pixels based on state integer array
```

```
void updateState(){
  for (int i=0; i<state.length; i++){
    if (state[i] == 1){
      pixls[i] = onC;
    }
    else {
      pixls[i] = offC;
    }
  }
}


// ensure starting pixel state is rendered
void paintInitState(){
  arrayCopy(pixls, nextPixls);
  paint();
}


// reset all pixels to off
void resetState(){
  for (int i=0; i<pixls.length; i++){
    pixls[i] = offC;
  }
}


// paint "dem perty" cells
void paint(){
  p.loadPixels();
  for (int i=0; i<rows; i++){
    for (int j=0; j<cols; j++){
      cells[i][j].setColor(nextPixls[cols*i + j]);
      cells[i][j].create();
    }
  }
  p.updatePixels();
```

```
    image(p, -w/2+loc.x, -h/2+loc.y);
    arrayCopy(nextPixls, pixls);
  }


  // must be implemented in subclass (or subclass will be abstract)
  abstract void init();
  abstract void createGeneration();


}
```

CA is an abstract class, meaning that it can't be instantiated directly. Abstract classes can include properties and methods like in a standard class, as well as abstract method stubs, or unimplemented methods such as

```
abstract void init();
abstract void createGeneration();
```

These methods are declared with the `abstract` **keyword** and do not include a method block (are unimplemented).

> Abstract methods must be implemented in any class that extends the abstract class, or the subclass automatically becomes abstract as well.

One of the main benefits of an abstract class is an enforced common interface. For example, it is safe to assume that any (non-abstract) class that extends CA will include implemented `init()` and `createGeneration()` methods. Each CA subclass can implement these methods to suit its own needs. In other words, the method interfaces will be common (between CA subclasses) but the implementation of the methods will not. Abstract classes help enforce good black-box design, where the interface to the box, not what happens inside the box, is what's known (accessible).

Even though abstract classes can't be directly instantiated, they can still contain constructors that are invoked by subclass constructors. This provides the same benefit of a standard superclass in regard to being able to efficiently initialize an object though chained constructors. The CA subclasses we'll create will use the CA constructor for this purpose.

Next we'll look at the instance property arrays (`cells`, `pixls`, `nextPixls`, `state`) in CA declared at the top of the class,

- `cells` references the higher level component constructs I mentioned earlier. The number and size of the Cell objects will be based on the overall size of the CA object and the `cellScale` property; larger scale values will create fewer but larger cells.
- `pixls` and `nextPixls` will directly reference the CA object's pixel buffer—present and next generation respectively.

- state will help with bookkeeping of a sort, keeping track of the pixel on/off state, without having to worry about the specific pixel color values (since the pixels will not only be black and white as with the previous example).

The initCA() method initializes the arrays and instantiates the Cell objects. Notice in the instantiation call I pass a reference to the CA object, as the last argument

```
cells[i][j] = new Cell(colSpan*j, rowSpan*i, colSpan, rowSpan, this);
```

Finally, with line p = createImage(int(w), int(h), RGB); I create an off-screen image that contains a pixel buffer (pixels array). Unlike the simple_1D_CA example, I will not write directly to the sketch window pixels array. Instead, I'll write to the pixel array of the off-screen image; then when I want to render the CA to the screen, I'll draw the off-screen image using image(p, x, y). Also, remember that Processing includes both a pixels array global variable and a PImage pixels array instance property (this was one of the reasons I chose to name my color array pixls in the example.)

In the simple_1D_CA example, the starting state was limited to a single pixel. Here, we can also use an array of pixels. The overloaded setInitState() methods provide a public interface for initiating the neighborhood state. There are also a number of component utility methods, including recordState(), updateState(), paintInitState(), and resetState(). These will allow us to both run the CA in real time, as well as to step through each generation, using, for example, a mouse event.

Finally the paint() method, included again next, coordinates the drawing of the pixels to the screen. This is a bit more involved than perhaps at initial glance, so I'll walk through the process.

```
// paint "dem perty" cells
  void paint(){
    p.loadPixels();
    for (int i=0; i<rows; i++){
      for (int j=0; j<cols; j++){
        cells[i][j].setColor(nextPixls[cols*i + j]);
        cells[i][j].create();
      }
    }
    p.updatePixels();
    image(p, -w/2+loc.x, -h/2+loc.y);
    arrayCopy(nextPixls, pixls);
  }
```

The first step is to "safely" load the p.pixels array using the p.loadPixels() call. Honestly, I find this step a bit of a clunky implementation and inconsistent with standard OOP. And in truth, it may even be possible to access the PImage pixels array without this call. However, it is strongly advised in the language reference that this call always be used to ensure the array is properly created/loaded. Here's what the reference has to say about it:

> "Certain renderers may or may not seem to require loadPixels() or updatePixels(). However, the rule is that any time you want to manipulate the pixels[] array, you must first call loadPixels(), and after changes have been made, call updatePixels(). Even if the renderer may not seem to use this function in the current Processing release, this will always be subject to change."

Next in paint(), within the for loops, the cells' colors are updated based on the nextPixls array, and then the cells.create() method is invoked. To see again what happens in the create() method, click on the **Cell** tab. I've copied the method again next:

```
// From Cell.pde
// draw to pixels buffer
  void create(){
    float origin = int(loc.y) * ca.w + int(loc.x);
    for (int i=0; i<w; i++){
      for (int j=0; j<h; j++){
          // - pretty nasty pixls[index] expression
        ca.p.pixels[int(min(origin + j*ca.w + i, ca.w*ca.h))] = c;
      }
    }
  }
```

The create() method draws a block of pixels, based on the width and height specified for the Cell object. This block is drawn directly into the p.pixels array, which, you'll remember, was instantiated back in CA; this was the reason I needed to pass a reference to CA when I instantiated the Cell objects. Drawing the block of pixels in the right place in the p.pixels array was tricky, especially since the pixels arrays in Processing are one-dimensional. The full-length expression I needed for targeting each pixel in the correct order based on the nested for loops was

```
ca.p.pixels[int(min(int(loc.y) * ca.w + int(loc.x) + j*ca.w + i, ca.w*ca.h))] = c;
```

That is one scary-looking line of code that should make your head hurt; it really did mine while I was trying to figure it out. The int() casting and min() calls are needed to ensure rounding errors do not allow the index value to go out of (array length) bounds. In the create() method, you'll notice, I broke the expression into two lines to make it a bit more comprehensible.

Returning to the paint() method in CA, after p.pixels is written to, I call p.updatePixels() to ensure the pixels array is properly updated, and then I draw the image to the sketch window with image(p, -w/2+loc.x,

349

-h/2+loc.y). The last step, arrayCopy(nextPixls, pixls) copies the nextPixls array values to pixls, updating the pixel state (previous generation) to current generation values. arrayCopy() is an efficient Processing function for copying the contents (or part of the contents) of one array into another. You can read more about the function at http://processing.org/reference/arrayCopy_.html.

To use CA, we need to create a subclass that extends it. The first I'll show will build upon what we looked at in the simple_1D_CA example, with added parameterization; then we'll look at an interesting variation on the 1D CA.

Create a new tab named "**CA_1D**" and copy the following code into it:

```
/**
 * Cellular Automata
 * CA_1D class
 * neighborhood:    | ? |
 *                * | * | *
 * By Ira Greenberg <br />
 * The Essential Guide to Processing for Flash Developers,
 * Friends of ED, 2009
 */


class CA_1D extends CA{
  // instance properties

  // CA rules
  boolean[] rules = new boolean[8];
  color[][] table = new color[8][4];

  // default constructor
  CA_1D(){
    super();
    init();
  }

  // constructor
  CA_1D(int w, int h, int cellScale){
    super(w, h, cellScale);
    init();
```

```
}

// REQUIRED implementation - initializes stuff
void init(){
  // initialize 1D rules
  initRules();
  // build rules table
  buildTable();
  //set default pixel starting state - bottom center pixel set to on
  int middleBottomCell = (rows-1)*(cols) + (cols)/2;
  setInitState(middleBottomCell);
  // record pixel on/off state in integer state table
}

// initialize rules
void initRules(){
  rules[0] = false;
  rules[1] = true;
  rules[2] = true;
  rules[3] = true;
  rules[4] = true;
  rules[5] = true;
  rules[6] = true;
  rules[7] = false;
}

// build rules table
void buildTable() {
  table[0][0] = offC;
  table[0][1] = offC;
  table[0][2] = offC;
  table[0][3] = rules[0] ? onC : offC;
  table[1][0] = offC;
  table[1][1] = offC;
  table[1][2] = onC;
```

```
    table[1][3] = rules[1] ? onC : offC;
    table[2][0] = offC;
    table[2][1] = onC;
    table[2][2] = offC;
    table[2][3] = rules[2] ? onC : offC;
    table[3][0] = offC;
    table[3][1] = onC;
    table[3][2] = onC;
    table[3][3] = rules[3] ? onC : offC;
    table[4][0] = onC;
    table[4][1] = offC;
    table[4][2] = offC;
    table[4][3] = rules[4] ? onC : offC;
    table[5][0] = onC;
    table[5][1] = offC;
    table[5][2] = onC;
    table[5][3] = rules[5] ? onC : offC;
    table[6][0] = onC;
    table[6][1] = onC;
    table[6][2] = offC;
    table[6][3] = rules[6] ? onC : offC;
    table[7][0] = onC;
    table[7][1] = onC;
    table[7][2] = onC;
    table[7][3] = rules[7] ? onC : offC;
  }


  // REQUIRED implementation
  void createGeneration(){
    for (int i=0; i<rows-1; i++){
      for (int j=0; j<cols; j++){
        for (int k=0; k<rules.length; k++){
          // 1st and last columns use each other as neighbors in calculation
          int firstCol = (j==0) ? cols-1 : j-1;
          int endCol = (j>0 && j<cols-1) ? j+1 : 0;
```

```
        // rules determined by binary table: 0 = offCol, 1 = onC.
        // [111][110][101][100][011][010][001][000]
        if (pixls[cols*(i+1) + firstCol] == table[k][0] &&
          pixls[cols*(i+1) + j] == table[k][1] &&
          pixls[cols*(i+1) + endCol] ==  table[k][2]){
            nextPixls[(cols)*i + j] = table[k][3];
        }


      }
    }
  }
  // paint pixels on screen
  paint();
}


// update rules - requires 8 boolean values
void setRules(boolean[] rules) {
  this.rules = rules;
  buildTable();
}


void setOnColor(color onC){
  this.onC = onC;
  buildTable();
  updateState();
  paintInitState();
}


void setOffColor(color offC){
  this.offC = offC;
  buildTable();
  updateState();
  paintInitState();
}
}
```

Although this example will follow rules similar to those of the `simple_1D_CA` example, the implementation will be different. Rather than using `int` arrays to store 0's and 1's only, I used `color[]` arrays, to refer to actual pixel values; I did this to allow for display of a full range of color.

The `CA_1D` constructors, as discussed earlier, call the `CA` constructors for initialization. In addition, the subclass has its own initialization routine, `init()`, which, you'll remember, must be implemented since the method was declared abstract in `CA`. The `init()` implementation includes the call `setInitState(middleBottomCell)`, for setting a default starting on/off state (the first generation).

Reading through the rest of the class, I split the `rules` table into two methods, `initRules()` and `buildTable()`, to allow users to be able to set custom rules, which I'll demonstrate shortly. The `createGeneration()` method, like `init()`, was required to be implemented since it was also declared abstract in CA. Its implementation is quite similar to the same named function in the `simple_1D_CA` example. However, now the conditional block is comparing actual pixel color values, instead of just 0's and 1's. This method also includes a call to `paint()`, defined in CA. The rest of the class code consists of setter methods, which I'll assume are self-explanatory. Next, we'll generate some sample CA, using the new classes.

In the main tab, which should still be blank if you've been following along, add the following code and run the sketch:

```
/**
 * Cellular Automata Main Tab - 01
 * By Ira Greenberg <br />
 * The Essential Guide to Processing for Flash Developers,
 * Friends of ED, 2009
 */


CA_1D ca;

void setup(){
  size(600, 600);
  background(255);
  ca = new CA_1D(600, 600, 1);
}


void draw(){
  translate(ca.w/2, ca.h/2);
  ca.createGeneration();
}
```

If the sketch ran successfully you should see output, shown in Figure 7-6, similar to the simple_1D_CA example, only with the black and white colors reversed.

Figure 7-6. 1D Cellular Automata screen-shot, stage 1

Obviously if all we wanted to do was this, the simple-1D-CA implementation would have sufficed. In the next step we'll change the colors of the cells as well as the scale. Here's the updated main tab code, with the changes in **bold**.

```
/**
 * Cellular Automata Main Tab - 02
 * By Ira Greenberg <br />
 * The Essential Guide to Processing for Flash Developers,
 * Friends of ED, 2009
 */

CA_1D ca;
color onC = 0xff22ee33;
color offC = 0xff772299;

void setup(){
  size(600, 600);
  background(255);
  ca = new CA_1D(600, 600, 5);
  ca.setOnColor(onC);
  ca.setOffColor(offC);
}

void draw(){
  translate(ca.w/2, ca.h/2);
  ca.createGeneration();
}
```

Figure 7-7. 1D Cellular Automata screen-shot, stage 2

Notice in the purple and green output how the larger scale factor turns each pixel into a block, creating, in a sense, a magnified bitmap of the image. In this implementation, save for memory limitations, there is no maximum limit for the scale factor.

As we briefly looked at earlier, you can change the initial on/off start state to influence the final output. In this implementation you can specify a single cell as we did earlier, or an array of cells, which I'll demonstrate next, shown in Figure 7-8; again the new code is **bold**.

```
/**
 * Cellular Automata Main Tab - 03
 * By Ira Greenberg <br />
 * The Essential Guide to Processing for Flash Developers,
 * Friends of ED, 2009
 */


CA_1D ca;
color onC = 0xff221166;
color offC = 0xffffff00;

void setup(){
  size(600, 600);
  background(255);
  ca = new CA_1D(600, 600, 12);
  ca.setOnColor(onC);
  ca.setOffColor(offC);

  //add multiple starting states
  int seedCount = 50;
  int[] cells = new int[seedCount];
  for (int i=0; i<seedCount; i++){
    cells[i] = int((ca.rows-1) * (ca.cols) + random(ca.cols));
  }
  ca.setInitState(cells);
}

void draw(){
  translate(ca.w/2, ca.h/2);
  ca.createGeneration();
}
```

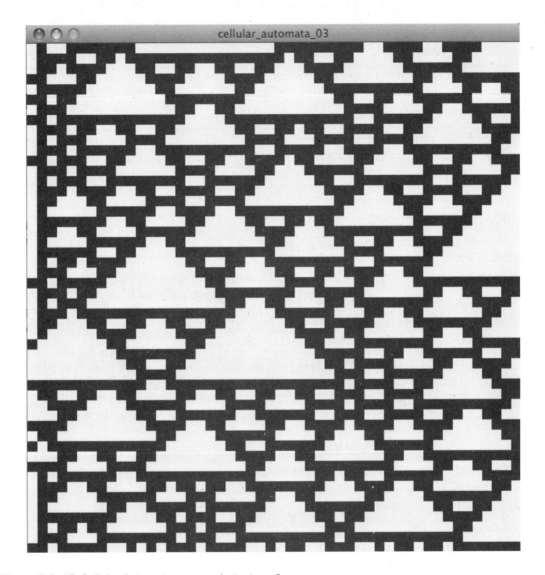

Figure 7-8. 1D Cellular Automata screen-shot, stage 3

The next variation, shown in Figures 7-9 and 7-10, demonstrates how changing the rules affects the output. The example creates a table of 16 CA, each with a different rule set. Replace your main tab code with the following to run the example:

```
/**
 * Cellular Automata Main Tab - 04
 * By Ira Greenberg <br />
```

```
 * The Essential Guide to Processing for Flash Developers,
 * Friends of ED, 2009
 */


CA_1D[] cas = new CA_1D[16];
boolean[] rules = new boolean[8];
color onC = 0xff000000;
color offC = 0xff111111;

void setup(){
  size(800, 800);
  background(255);
  for (int i=0; i<cas.length; i++){
    cas[i] = new CA_1D(200, 200, 2);
    // calculate random rules
   for (int j=0; j<8; j++){
      rules[j] = boolean(round(random(1)));
    }
    cas[i].setRules(rules);
  }
}


void draw(){
  translate(cas[0].w/2, cas[0].h/2);
  int step = cas.length/4;
  for (int i=0; i<step; i++){
    for (int j=0; j<step; j++){
      pushMatrix();
      translate(cas[step*i + j].w*i, cas[step*i + j].h*j);
      cas[step*i + j].createGeneration();
      popMatrix();
    }
  }
}
```

Figure 7-9. 1D Cellular Automata screen-shot, stage 4, screenshot 1

Figure 7-10. 1D Cellular Automata screen-shot, stage 4, screenshot 2, (cellScale = 10)

You may want to run this example a number of times to see the range of potential output. You can also be more selective in specifying the rules—not making them all random. I randomized the rules using the expression `rules[j] = boolean(round(random(1)))`.

> *Although the boolean type in Processing evaluates to the constants true or false, it is possible to cast a 1 and 0 to these respective constants; this also works the other way around (e.g., `int(true)` evaluates to 1).*

Finally, I include one more variation that puts all the aspects discussed thus far together and adds random rotation as well (see Figures 7-11 and 7-12). The new code is in **bold**.

```
/**
 * Cellular Automata Main Tab - 05
 * By Ira Greenberg <br />
 * The Essential Guide to Processing for Flash Developers,
 * Friends of ED, 2009
 */


CA_1D[] cas = new CA_1D[16];
boolean[] rules = new boolean[8];
// for random rotation
float[] rots = new float[cas.length];

void setup(){
  size(800, 800);
  background(255);
  for (int i=0; i<cas.length; i++){
    cas[i] = new CA_1D(200, 200, round(random(1, 20)));
    // calculate random rules
    for (int j=0; j<8; j++){
      rules[j] = boolean(round(random(1)));
    }
    cas[i].setRules(rules);
    // calculate random color
    cas[i].setOnColor(color(random(255), random(255), random(255)));
    cas[i].setOffColor(color(random(255), random(255), random(255)));
```

```
    // calculate random rotation
    rots[i] = HALF_PI*round(random(1, 3));
  }
}


void draw(){
  translate(cas[0].w/2, cas[0].h/2);
  int step = cas.length/4;
  for (int i=0; i<step; i++){
    for (int j=0; j<step; j++){
      pushMatrix();
      translate(cas[step*i + j].w*i, cas[step*i + j].h*j);
      rotate(rots[i]);
      cas[step*i + j].createGeneration();
      popMatrix();
    }
  }
}
```

Figure 7-11. 1D Cellular Automata screen-shot, stage 5, screenshot 1

Figure 7-12. 1D Cellular Automata screen-shot, stage 5, screenshot 2

Using very simple rules, the CA_1D class allowed you to create somewhat complex patterns based on discrete on/off cell states. You saw by changing the rules you could create some interesting variations. It would, of course, also be possible to change the evaluation neighborhood and rules structure further to create other variations. However, one of the limiting factors in this approach is the use of discrete cell states, either being on or off. In the next example, I'll extend our discussion of one-dimensional CA using a continuous (versus discrete) method of cell genesis.

(Almost) Continuous CA

Rather than flipping cells on or off, the continuous CA will average the actual color values of cells in its neighborhood to determine the cell's color in the next generation. However, averaging alone is not enough to create something very interesting. Figure 7-13 illustrates a CA output using just the averaging process.

Figure 7-13. 1D Continuous Cellular Automata screenshot

To get more interesting results, we need to introduce some chaos into the process. This will involve a two-stage process. First, I'll introduce a constant value that will be added to each averaged color component (r, g, b). Second, I'll introduce a threshold, or maximum, that I'll use as a constraint for each component value. Here's an example of the process using pseudo code with cells *C1*, *C2*, and *C3* representing the neighborhood and *CN* as the new cell.

```
// pseudo code
c = constant
t = threshold
CN.r = (C1.r + C2.r + C3.r)/3 + c
CN.g = (C1.g + C2.g + C3.g)/3 + c
CN.b = (C1.b + C2.b + C3.b)/3 + c
if (CN.r > t) then CN.r -= t
if (CN.g > t) then CN.g -= t
if (CN.b > t) then CN.b -= t
Create next generation using CN
```

In truth, my Continuous CA implementation will not be technically continuous. This has not only to do with my pathological inability to follow directions (even my own), but also the results I'll generate, which will be essentially indistinguishable from a "real" continuous CA. The term continuous perhaps evokes real numbers for you. (Yes, you probably are a geek if this is true.) In a continuous system, pretty much every value can be represented using the range 0.0 to 1.0. Most continuous CA examples that I've seen do in fact use this range. However, my system will be a little simpler and based on integers in the range of 0–255. Next is a Continuous CA class.

Using the existing sketch, add a new tab named "**CA_1DC**" and add the following class code to it:

```
/**
 * Cellular Automata
 * CA_1DC class
 * neighborhood:   | ? |
 *                * | * | *
 * By Ira Greenberg <br />
 * The Essential Guide to Processing for Flash Developers,
 * Friends of ED, 2009
 */

class CA_1DC extends CA{
```

```
//instance properties
float[] consts = {
  23, 23, 23  };
float[] thresholds = {
  255, 255, 255  };


// default constructor
CA_1DC(){
  super();
  init();
}


// constructor
CA_1DC(int w, int h, int cellScale){
  super(w, h, cellScale);
  init();
}


void init(){
  int middleBottomCell = (rows-1)*cols + cols/2;
  setInitState(middleBottomCell, onC);
}


// set starting state (single pixel)
void setInitState(int id, color c){
  resetState();
  pixls[id] = c;
  paintInitState();
}


// set starting state (array of pixels)
void setInitState(int[] ids, color[] c){
```

```
  // reset();
  resetState();
  for (int i=0; i<ids.length; i++){
    pixls[ids[i]] = c[i];
  }
  paintInitState();
}


// set starting state
void setInitState(int row, int col, color c){
  // reset pixels
  resetState();
  pixls[row*(cols-1) + (col-1)] = c;
  paintInitState();
}


/* rules:
  1. average 3 neighboring colors, e.g. (c[j-1] + c[j] + c[j+1])/3
  2. add a constant, e.g. c + const
  3. if color components > 255 subtract 255 */
void createGeneration(){
  for (int i=0; i<rows-1; i++){
    for (int j=0; j<cols; j++){
      // use 1st colum as j+1, for end pixel in each column
      int firstCol = (j==0) ? cols-1 : j-1;
      int endCol = (j>0 && j<cols-1) ? j+1 : 0;
      int row = cols*(i+1);
      float r =  ((pixls[row + firstCol] >> 16 & 0xFF) + (pixls[row + j] >> ↩
        16 & 0xFF) + (pixls[row + endCol] >> 16 & 0xFF))/3 + consts[0];
      float g =  ((pixls[row + firstCol] >> 8 & 0xFF) + (pixls[row + j] >> ↩
        8 & 0xFF) + (pixls[row + endCol] >> 8 & 0xFF))/3 + consts[1];
```

```
        float b =  ((pixls[row + firstCol] & 0xFF) + (pixls[row + j] & 0xFF) + ⏎
          (pixls[row + endCol] & 0xFF))/3 + consts[2];
        if (r>thresholds[0]){
          r-=thresholds[0];
        }

        if (g>thresholds[1]){
          g-=thresholds[1];
        }

        if (b>thresholds[2]){
          b-=thresholds[2];
        }
        nextPixls[(cols)*i + j] = int(r) << 16 | int(g) << 8 | int(b);
      }
    }
    // paint pixels on screen
    paint();
  }


  // pass custom rules
  void setconsts(float[] consts) {
    this.consts = consts;
  }


  void setThresholds(float[] thresholds) {
    this.thresholds = thresholds;
  }
}
```

Since the class extends CA it follows a structure very similar to CA_1D. Again, one of the nice things about a consistent framework is that it allows you to almost intuit how to work with a class. Thus, I'll assume you can make your way through most of this source code on you own. Where I think I can offer some clarification is in the createGeneration() method. You'll remember as a CA subclass, both init() and createGeneration() need to be implemented. Next is the snippet of code in the function again that handles the main CA calculation.

```
float r =  ((pixls[row + firstCol] >> 16 & 0xFF) + (pixls[row + j] >> ↵
    16 & 0xFF) + (pixls[row + endCol] >> 16 & 0xFF))/3 + consts[0];

float g =  ((pixls[row + firstCol] >> 8 & 0xFF) + (pixls[row + j] >> ↵
    8 & 0xFF) + (pixls[row + endCol] >> 8 & 0xFF))/3 + consts[1];

float b =  ((pixls[row + firstCol] & 0xFF) + (pixls[row + j] & 0xFF) + ↵
    (pixls[row + endCol] & 0xFF))/3 + consts[2];


    if (r>thresholds[0]){
r-=thresholds[0];
}


    if (g>thresholds[1]){
  g-=thresholds[1];
}


if (b>thresholds[2]){
    b-=thresholds[2];
}
nextPixls[(cols)*i + j] = int(r) << 16 | int(g) << 8 | int(b);
```

I chose to use bitwise operators to work with the components, as they are substantially faster than using Processing's red(), green(), blue(), and color() functions; to see this for yourself try substituting Processing's color component functions in the expressions. For example, the red expression would look like this:

```
float r =  (red(pixls[row + firstCol]) + red(pixls[row + j]) + red(pixls[row + endCol]))/3 +
consts[0];
```

I covered bitwise operations in Chapter 2 and more extensively in *Processing Creative Coding and Computational Art*, *Appendix B*.

To allow for more variation in the CA I created three constants, as well as three threshold values. Again, the constants are simply added to each averaged color component, and then the new component value is reduced to the amount greater than the threshold (or if the value is less than the threshold it remains unchanged). Finally, the color is put back together. To try out the new CA_1DC class, enter the following code in the main tab:

```
/**
 * Continuous Cellular Automata Main Tab - 01
 * By Ira Greenberg <br />
 * The Essential Guide to Processing for Flash Developers,
 * Friends of ED, 2009
 */


// global variables
CA_1DC cca;
void setup(){
  size(600, 600);
  cca = new CA_1DC(600, 600, 1);
}


void draw(){
  translate(cca.w/2, cca.h/2);
  cca.createGeneration();
}
```

This first example, shown in Figure 7-14, is grayscale as the three constants are all the same values, and the onC and offC colors are black and white by default. Notice, though, the interesting pattern that's generated.

Figure 7-14. 1D Continuous Cellular Automata screen-shot, stage 1

In the next example, shown in Figures 7-15, 7-16, and 7-17, I'll create a table of CA varying the constants and thresholds in each CA, but keeping the three values in each array the same. Here's the code:

```
/**
 * Continuous Cellular Automata Main Tab - 02
 * By Ira Greenberg <br />
 * The Essential Guide to Processing for Flash Developers,
 * Friends of ED, 2009
 */

// global variables
int rows = 4, cols = 4;
int rowSpan, colSpan;
int cellScale = 1;
float threshMin = 128, threshMax = 255;
float constMin = 2, constMax = 127;
// for random seed placement
int seedCount = 2;

// declare arrays
CA_1DC[] cacs;
int[] seeds;
color[] clrs;

void setup(){
  size(800, 800);
  initialize();
}

void initialize(){
  this.rows = rows;
  this.cols = cols;
  rowSpan = height/rows;
  colSpan = width/cols;

  cacs = new CA_1DC[rows*cols];
  seeds = new int[seedCount];
  clrs = new color[seedCount];
```

```
  for (int i=0; i<cacs.length; i++){
    cacs[i] = new CA_1DC(colSpan, rowSpan, cellScale);

    for (int j=0; j<seedCount; j++){
      seeds[j] = int((cacs[i].rows-1)*(cacs[i].cols) + int(random(cacs[i].cols)));
      clrs[j] = color(random(255), random(255), random(255));
    }
    cacs[i].setInitState(seeds, clrs);

    float t = random(threshMin, threshMax);
    cacs[i].setThresholds(new float[] { t, t, t });
    float c = random(constMin, constMax);
    cacs[i].setconsts(new float[] { c, c, c });
  }
}


void draw(){
  for (int i=0; i<rows; i++){
    for (int j=0; j<cols; j++){
      pushMatrix();
      // simplify stuff
      int index = cols*i + j;
      float x = cacs[index].w*j;
      float y = cacs[index].h*i;
      float w = cacs[index].w;
      float h = cacs[index].h;
      // move top left corner to 0,0
      translate(w/2, h/2);
      // move into position in table
      translate(x, y);
      // do CA magic
      cacs[index].createGeneration();
      popMatrix();
    }
  }
}
```

Figure 7-15. 1D Continuous Cellular Automata screen-shot, stage 2

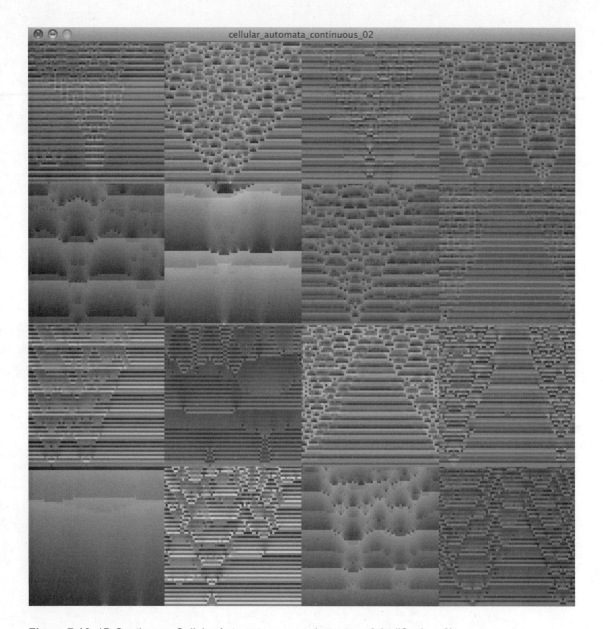

Figure 7-16. 1D Continuous Cellular Automata screen-shot, stage 2 (cellScale = 3)

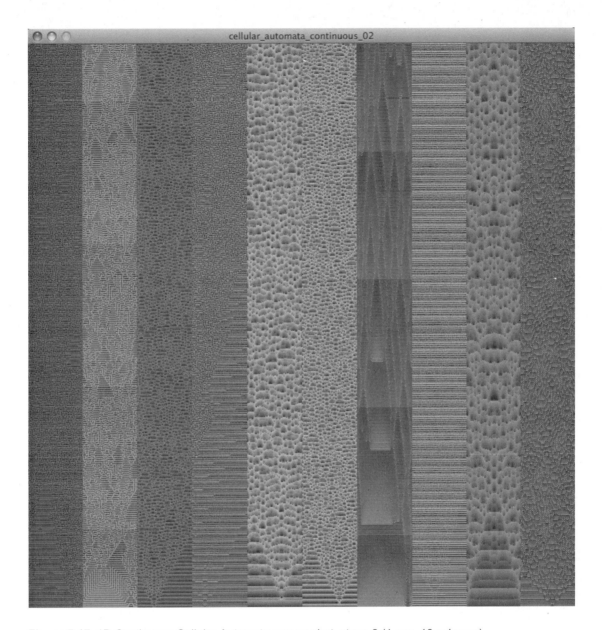

cellular_automata_continuous_02

Figure 7-17. 1D Continuous Cellular Automata screen-shot, stage 2 (1 row, 10 columns)

There is nothing really new in this code. I suggest messing around with the values a bit to see what's possible. I'm sure you'll agree that the continuous approach yields much more interesting images than the straight 1D discrete CA discussed earlier. You might also try creating your own CA rules, maybe using trig functions in the continuous calculations, for example; there is a lot of untapped aesthetic potential here. Before I move on to 2D CA, I want to include one more interactive continuous CA example.

One of the benefits of being able to see a table of smaller CA is the increased rate of exploration. However, the small images make it difficult to fully see all the detail (or perhaps output an image for a tee-shirt). It would be nice if you could enlarge any image without sacrificing detail and/or resolution. In the last continuous CA example, I'll code interactivity to allow us to do this. I'll also add some additional functionality to create even more variation, shown in Figures 7-18, 7-19, 7-20, and 7-21. Additions/changes to the existing code are **bold**.

```
/**
 * Continuous Cellular Automata Main Tab - 03
 * By Ira Greenberg <br />
 * The Essential Guide to Processing for Flash Developers,
 * Friends of ED, 2009
 */


// global variables
int rows = 8, cols = 8;
int rowSpan, colSpan;
int cellScale = 1;
float threshMin = 128, threshMax = 255;
float constMin = 2, constMax = 127;
// for random seed placement
int seedCount = 1;


// declare arrays
CA_1DC[] cacs;
float[][] thresholds;
float[][] consts;
int[][] seeds;
color[][] clrs;


// for interactivity
int overID = 0;
boolean iSFirstClick = true;
```

```
void setup(){
  size(800, 800);
  initialize();
}

void initialize(){
  this.rows = rows;
  this.cols = cols;
  rowSpan = height/rows;
  colSpan = width/cols;

  cacs = new CA_1DC[rows*cols];
  thresholds = new float[cacs.length][3];
  consts = new float[cacs.length][3];
  seeds = new int[cacs.length][seedCount];
  clrs = new color[cacs.length][seedCount];

  for (int i=0; i<cacs.length; i++){
    cacs[i] = new CA_1DC(colSpan, rowSpan, cellScale);

    for (int j=0; j<seedCount; j++){
      seeds[i][j] = int((cacs[i].rows-1)*(cacs[i].cols) + int(random(cacs[i].cols)));
      clrs[i][j] = color(random(255), random(255), random(255));
    }
    cacs[i].setInitState(seeds[i], clrs[i]);

    for (int j=0; j<thresholds[0].length; j++){
      thresholds[i][j] = random(threshMin, threshMax);
      consts[i][j] = random(constMin, constMax);
    }
    cacs[i].setThresholds(thresholds[i]);
    cacs[i].setconsts(consts[i]);
  }
```

```
}

// draw selected CA full screen with original values
void calcCA(int i){
  // factor to scale the initial pixel state
  float widthFctr = width/cacs[i].w;
  // get original rows and cols value before updated
  float oldRows = cacs[i].rows;
  float oldCols = cacs[i].cols;

  // new output will fill the sketch window
  rows = cols = 1;
  int scl = cacs[0].cellScale;
  // reinitialize cacs
  cacs = new CA_1DC[1];
  cacs[0] = new CA_1DC(width, height, scl);
  // updates initial seeds, if originally set
  for (int j=0; j<seedCount; j++){
    if (seeds[i][j] !=0){
      seeds[i][j] = int((cacs[0].rows-1)*cacs[0].cols + (seeds[i][j]- ↵
        (oldRows-1)*oldCols)*widthFctr);
    } else {
      // if default centered seed was used
      seeds[i][j] = (cacs[0].rows-1)*cacs[0].cols + cacs[0].cols/2;
    }
  }
  // set with original values
  cacs[0].setInitState(seeds[i], clrs[i]);
  cacs[0].setThresholds(thresholds[i]);
  cacs[0].setconsts(consts[i]);
}
```

```
void draw(){
  for (int i=0; i<rows; i++){
    for (int j=0; j<cols; j++){
      pushMatrix();
      // simplify stuff
      int index = cols*i + j;
      float x = cacs[index].w*j;
      float y = cacs[index].h*i;
      float w = cacs[index].w;
      float h = cacs[index].h;
      // move top left corner to 0,0
      translate(w/2, h/2);
      // move into position in table
      translate(x, y);
      // do CA magic
      cacs[index].createGeneration();
      popMatrix();

      // check which cell mouse is over
      if (mouseX > x && mouseX < x + w &&
        mouseY > y && mouseY < y + h){
        overID = index;
      }
    }
  }
}


// if the first time clicking on sketch, select CA to enlarge
void mouseClicked(){
  if (iSFirstClick){
    calcCA(overID);
    iSFirstClick = false;
  }
}
```

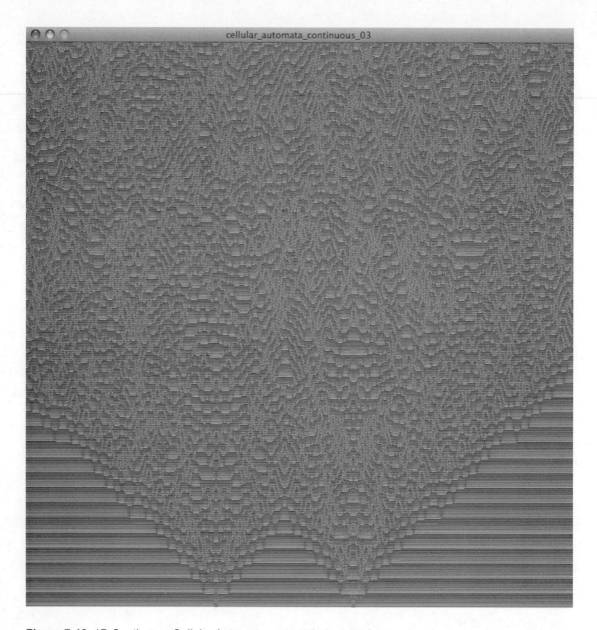

Figure 7-18. 1D Continuous Cellular Automata screen-shot, stage 3

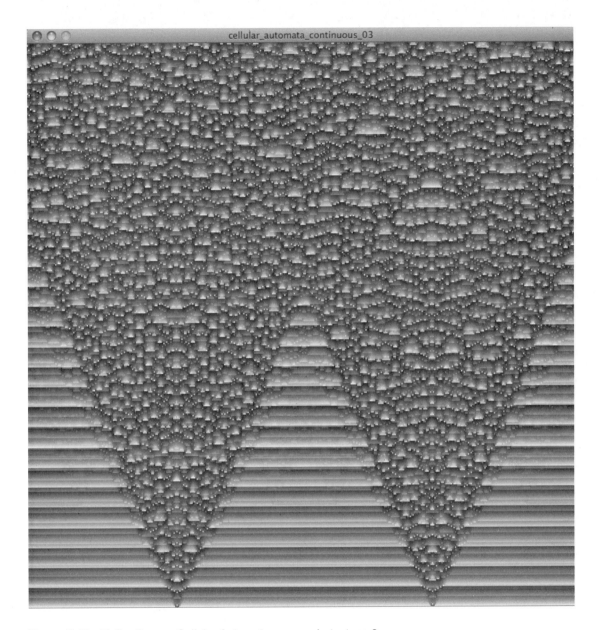

Figure 7-19. 1D Continuous Cellular Automata screen-shot, stage 3

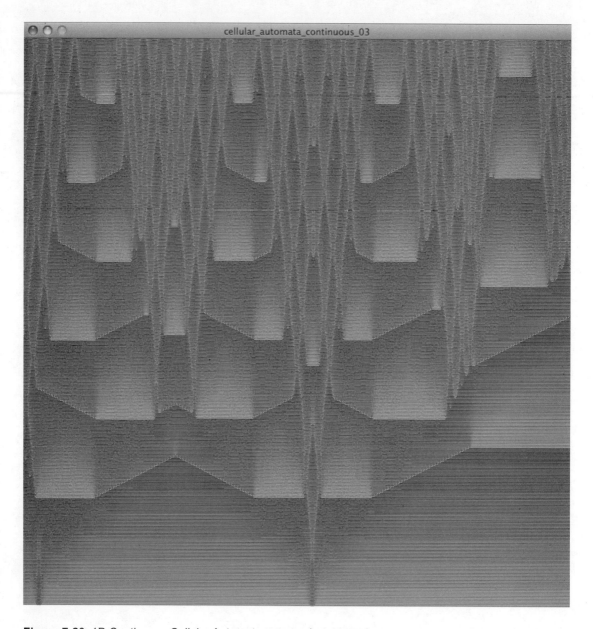

Figure 7-20. 1D Continuous Cellular Automata screen-shot, stage 3

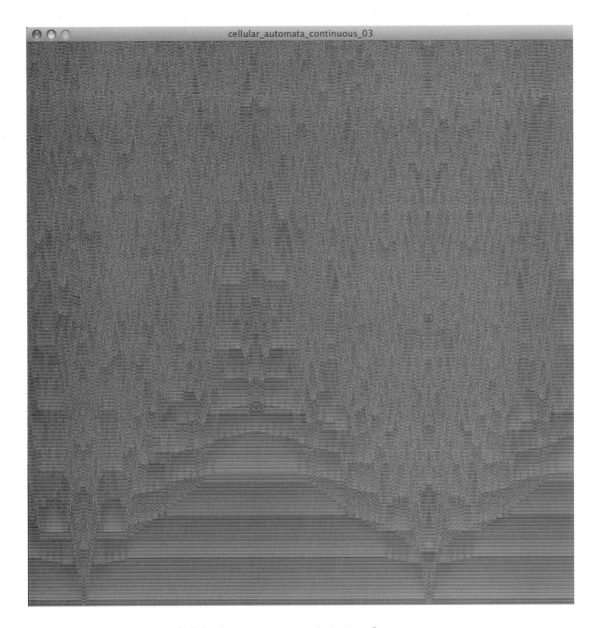

Figure 7-21. 1D Continuous Cellular Automata screen-shot, stage 3

Looking at the code in the example, you'll notice I added a bunch of 2D arrays. The main coding challenges I had to deal with were retaining all the critical data for each thumbnail (i.e., colors, constants, and threshold values) and coming up with an event detection method that would know which thumbnail had been clicked on.

I found it easiest to create the new calcCA() method to isolate the redrawing of the large image from the initial drawing of the thumbnails. The calcCA() method is called from within the mouseClicked() function, which is one of Processing's built-in event functions. Each time calcCA(overID) is called an index value is passed to the function representing the thumbnail clicked on. Within draw() notice the home-brewed detection block:

```
if (mouseX > x && mouseX < x + w &&
  mouseY > y && mouseY < y + h){
  overID = index;
}
```

Admittedly this approach is neither elegant nor efficient, as the detection check happens every draw cycle, and I needed to create the overID global variable. However, a more OOP'ish solution would have required doing a bit of tinkering with the base CA class, which, at this point in the chapter, wasn't going to happen. Of course, adding detection to the CA class and rewiring this example (even adding interactivity to all the previous examples) would be an excellent thing to try on your own. One other point that might be confusing is the expression I used to scale the seeds in the original thumbnail to the larger image, the line

```
seeds[i][j] = int((cacs[0].rows-1)*cacs[0].cols + (seeds[i][j]-↩
  (oldRows-1)*oldCols)*widthFctr);
```

This is a pretty ornery-looking line of code. Since the seeds are all on the bottom row of cells (which you'll remember are stored in a 1D array), it was simplest to only deal with the last row in calculating the scaling. Thus, I simply added the scaled index positions to the rest of the array. To get a clearer sense of why I handled it this way, try scaling a table and seeing how specific index values shift within the table; it's messy!

One-dimensional CA offered a glimpse into how simple rules can lead to remarkable complexity. By adding an additional dimension and generating two-dimensional CA, we can blow open the doors of this fascinating potential. That said, 2D CA is a pretty large area of research (and this has already been a long chapter), so I'll just introduce the topic here and provide examples that both reveal interesting aspects of this research area and also create the beginnings of a 2D CA framework for studying them further.

2D CA

Going from 1D to 2D CA is not very difficult. However, as I mentioned earlier, it opens up lots of new possibilities; from a coding standpoint it's simply a matter of incorporating a second axis in the rules analysis. You can also create 3D CA by adding a third axis, which I won't be covering here, but you can learn more about here: http://risais.home.comcast.net/~risais/3dca/3dca.htm (November, 15, 2009 14:08). The examples to follow will be based on the most famous 2D CA, *Game of Life ("Life")*, developed by John Conway in 1970.

Conway developed Life based on the earlier work of John von Neumann, one of the originators of CA mentioned at the beginning of the chapter. What is so interesting about Conway's Life CA is the range of output it's capable of producing, In fact, Life "theoretically" has the capacity to function as a computer, or more precisely the capacity to calculate any algorithm. You can read more theoretical information about Life at http://en.wikipedia.org/wiki/Conway%27s_Game_of_Life (August, 6, 2009 11:38 am).

In spite of Life's computational power, it is pretty simple to code, which is perhaps the most fascinating aspect of this whole area of research—from simple steps can emerge incredible complexity. As previously mentioned, implementing Life will involve two axes (x and y), and each cell's neighborhood will be defined by its eight surrounding cells (see Figure 7-22).

Figure 7-22. 2D CA Game of Life neighborhood

The rules of Life are as follows (taken directly from the Wikipedia page previously referenced, http://en.wikipedia.org/wiki/Conway%27s_Game_of_Life):

1. Any live cell with fewer than two live neighbors dies, as if caused by under-population.
2. Any live cell with more than three live neighbors dies, as if by overcrowding.
3. Any live cell with two or three live neighbors lives on to the next generation.
4. Any dead cell with exactly three live neighbors becomes a live cell.

The basic coding structure we'll follow will be very similar to what we've done throughout the chapter. In fact, we'll use our current CA framework. To get started, create a new tab in the existing sketch used for the continuous CA example, or you can use any sketch that includes the Shape, Cell, and CA classes. Name the new tab "**CA_2D**" and enter the following code into the tab:

```
/**
 * Cellular Automata
 * CA_2D class
 * neighborhood: * | * | *
 *               * | ? | *
 *               * | * | *
 * By Ira Greenberg <br />
 * The Essential Guide to Processing for Flash Developers,
 * Friends of ED, 2009
 */


class CA_2D extends CA{
  // instance properties

  // default constructor
  CA_2D(){
    super();
    init();
  }

  // constructor
  CA_2D(int w, int h, int cellScale){
    super(w, h, cellScale);
    init();
  }

  // REQUIRED implementation - initializes stuff
  void init(){
    // set default starting state
    /* R-pentomino pattern
    **
   **
    *
    */
```

```
    int[] initState = {
                        ((rows)/2-1)*(cols) + (cols-1)/2+1,
                        ((rows)/2-1)*(cols) + (cols-1)/2,
                        (rows)/2*(cols) + (cols-1)/2,
                        (rows)/2*(cols) + (cols-1)/2-1,
                        ((rows)/2+1)*(cols) + (cols-1)/2
                    };
    setInitState(initState);
  }


  // set starting state (array of pixels)
  void setInitState(int[] ids){
    resetState();
    for (int i=0; i<ids.length; i++){
      pixls[ids[i]] = onC;
    }
    paintInitState();
  }


// set starting state (single pixel)
  void setInitState(int row, int col){
    resetState();
    pixls[row*(cols-1) + (col-1)] = onC;
    paintInitState();
  }


  // REQUIRED implementation
  void createGeneration(){
    for (int i=0; i<rows; i++){
      for (int j=0; j<cols; j++){
        // 1st and last columns use each other as neighbors in calculation
        int firstCol = (j==0) ? cols-1 : j-1;
        int endCol = (j>0 && j<cols-1) ? j+1 : 0;
        // 1st and last rows use each other as neighbors in calculation
```

```
int firstRow = (i==0) ? rows-1 : i-1;
int endRow = (i>0 && i<rows-1) ? i+1 : 0;

int sum = 0;
if (pixls[cols*(firstRow) + firstCol] == onC){
  sum+=1;
}
if (pixls[cols*(firstRow) + j] == onC){
  sum+=1;
}
if (pixls[cols*(firstRow) + endCol] == onC){
  sum+=1;


}
if (pixls[cols*i + endCol] == onC){
  sum+=1;


}
if (pixls[cols*(endRow) + endCol] == onC){
  sum+=1;


}
if (pixls[cols*(endRow) + j] == onC){
  sum+=1;


}
if (pixls[cols*(endRow) + firstCol] == onC){
  sum+=1;
}
if (pixls[cols*i + firstCol] == onC){
  sum+=1;
}


if (pixls[cols*i + j] == onC){
```

```
        if (sum < 2 || sum > 3){
          nextPixls[cols*i + j] = offC;
        }
        // if sum is 2 or 3
        else {
          nextPixls[cols*i + j] = onC;
        }
      }
      // if pixel is offC
      else {
        if (sum == 3){
          nextPixls[cols*i + j] = onC;
        }
      }
    }
  }
  // paint pixels on screen
  paint();
}

void setOnColor(color onC){
  this.onC = onC;
}

void setOffColor(color offC){
  this.offC = offC;
}


}
```

The class is very similar to the CA_1D class, although the init() and createGeneration() methods are implemented differently. The rules analysis in createGeneration() is a bit lengthier than in the 1D examples, but it should still be pretty self-explanatory as it follows the Life rules enumerated earlier. Before discussing the init() method, let's try out the new code. In the main tab enter the following and then run the sketch:

```
/**
 * Cellular Automata 2D _ main tab - 01
 * By Ira Greenberg <br />
 * The Essential Guide to Processing for Flash Developers,
 * Friends of ED, 2009
 */

CA_2D ca2;

void setup(){
  size(600, 600);
  background(255);
  ca2 = new CA_2D(600, 600, 1);
}

void draw(){
  translate(ca2.w/2, ca2.h/2);
  ca2.createGeneration();
}
```

If the code ran okay, you should have seen a bunch of white pixels growing and moving about the sketch window. Figure 7-23 shows the sketch after 1000 frames. To be more specific, albeit cryptic, the sketch screenshot shows the R-pentomino pattern after 1000 generations following Life's rules.

Figure 7-23. 2D CA Game of Life R-pentomino pattern after 1000 frames

Returning to the CA_2D code, here's the init() method again.

```
// REQUIRED implementation - initializes stuff
  void init(){
    // set default starting state
    /* R-pentomino pattern
    **
    **
```

```
    *
    */
    int[] initState = {
                          ((rows)/2-1)*(cols) + (cols-1)/2+1,
                          ((rows)/2-1)*(cols) + (cols-1)/2,
                          (rows)/2*(cols) + (cols-1)/2,
                          (rows)/2*(cols) + (cols-1)/2-1,
                          ((rows)/2+1)*(cols) + (cols-1)/2
                      };
    setInitState(initState);
  }
```

This method creates a default starting on/off pixels state, which we've also done in earlier examples. However, rather than beginning with a single pixel or random array of pixels, we're beginning with a very specific pixel pattern, in this case one named "R-pentomino" (also sometimes referred to as F-pentomino). To better see this pattern, we'll modify our example sketch, increasing the scale of the pixels and also adding an interactive element. Replace the code in the main tab with the following:

```
/**
 * Cellular Automata 2D _ main tab - 02
 * By Ira Greenberg <br />
 * The Essential Guide to Processing for Flash Developers,
 * Friends of ED, 2009
 */

CA_2D ca2;

void setup(){
  size(600, 600);
  background(255);
  ca2 = new CA_2D(600, 600, 20);
  translate(ca2.w/2, ca2.h/2);
  ca2.paint();
}

void draw(){
}
```

```
void mousePressed(){
  translate(ca2.w/2, ca2.h/2);
  ca2.createGeneration();
}
```

When you run the sketch, click anywhere within the sketch window to iteratively move through the sketch one iteration at a time. Figures 7-24, 7-25, and 7-26 show the sketch at iterations 0, 30, and 100 respectively.

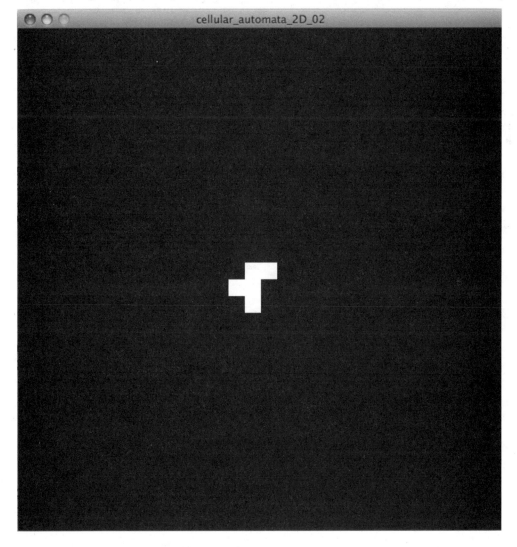

Figure 7-24. 2D CA Game of Life R-pentomino pattern at start, cellScale = 20

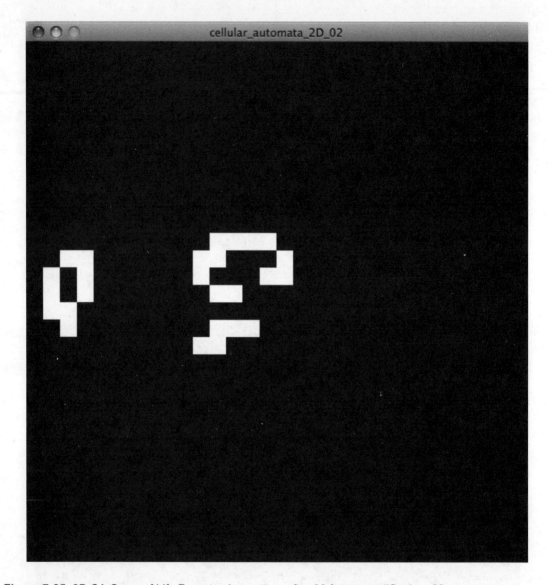

Figure 7-25. 2D CA Game of Life R-pentomino pattern after 30 frames, cellScale = 20

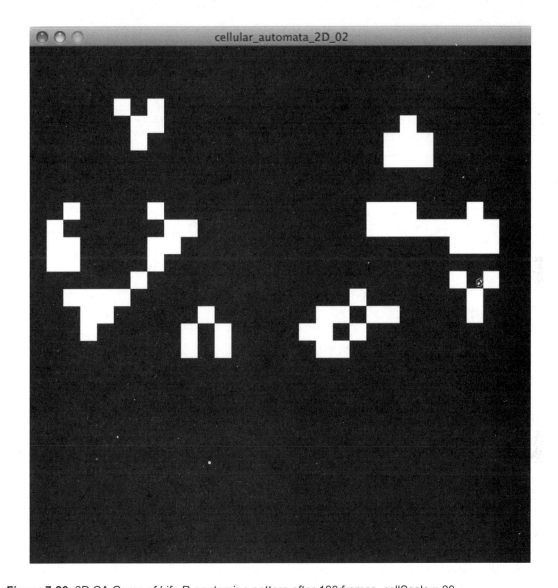

Figure 7-26. 2D CA Game of Life R-pentomino pattern after 100 frames, cellScale = 20

A pentomino is simply a shape composed of five symmetrical squares that are all connected orthogonally. You can read more about them at http://en.wikipedia.org/wiki/Pentomino (August, 6, 2009 14:00). Based on Life's rules, the R-pentomino pattern creates some unexpected results, which was indeed what Conway discovered when he first tried inputting the pattern, by *hand* mind you! It turns out that the R-pentomino pattern doesn't reach a stable state until a little over 1100 iterations (certainly a lot of work to try to do by hand). It also turns out that many of the sub-patterns created during these 1000 iterations of R-pentomino reveal many of the other classic patterns that Life produces, including ones formally classified as still-lifes, gliders, oscillators, guns, and puffers among others. Here is a nice link that discusses some of these interesting patterns: http://www.math.com/students/wonders/life/life.html (August, 6, 2009 14:12).

Although it would be interesting to try to create new patterns, there is already a treasure trove of them, with many creative hybrid patterns that combine multiple sub-patterns; some of these can be very complex. For example, Figure 7-27 shows a pattern called "c/3 long spaceships," by Hartmut Holzwart and David Bell, which is composed of about 40,000 characters.

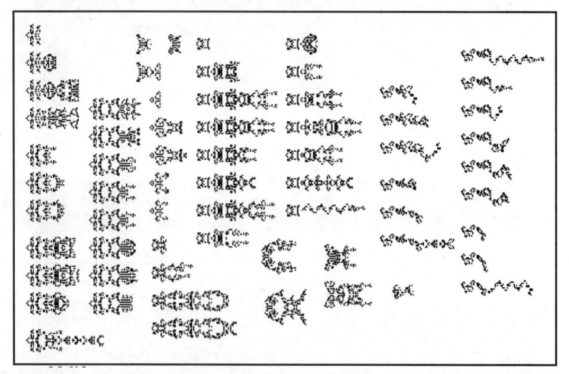

Figure 7-27. "c/3 long spaceships" pattern, by Hartmut Holzwart and David Bell

You probably wouldn't want to try to code the *c/3 long spaceships* pattern by hand; loading it (like you would an image) would obviously be a much better solution. Fortunately, this loading problem has been solved—*well, sort of.* There have been file formats created for storing Life patterns (see http://psoup.math.wisc.edu/mcell/ca_files_formats.html#Life%201.05, August 6, 2009 14:56) enabling people to load and distribute them. A common Life pattern format is "Life 1.05," which uses the .lif suffix (you'll also see .life suffixes). It's a very simple ASCII format that lists on/off pixels as a series of *'s and .'s respectively; in addition, each block of characters is preceded by a point location, specifying where on a Cartesian coordinate system to draw the block of pixels. For example, to draw the R-pentomino pattern at coordinate 100, 100, the .lif file would look like this. (Please note the #D is for file descriptions/comments. Some files also include a #N or #R for specifying rules, which we'll ignore.)

```
#Life 1.05
#D R-pentomino
#D Adapted by Ira Greenberg
#D The Essential Guide to Processing for Flash Developers
#D Friends of ED, 2009
#P 100 100
.**
**.
.*.
```

I mentioned earlier that the Life pattern format *sort of* solved the problem; the other part is being able to parse the .lif file. As you might suspect, a Google search did not turn up a Processing .lif parser, so I decided to write one. My parser takes a URL address argument (as a link to a .lif file), which can be local, in the sketch's data directory, or on the web. In my example, the URL will be on the web, within a freely accessible Life patterns catalog.

> *If you're running an example online (as an applet), and the .lif file is on the web, it needs to reside on the same server as your applet or the applet must be **signed**; this is for security reasons. To learn how to sign an applet, check out this Processing hack I wrote a while back: http://processing.org/hacks/hacks:signapplet (August 7, 2009 15:05).*

I've coded the parser as a Processing class that will work within our CA framework. In the existing CA sketch (that includes the CA_2D class) create a new tab named "**LIF_PARSER**." I'll state in advance that this class is pretty dense, BUT it will be our last example, so you'll be able to rest your brain shortly. Also, in the next chapter we'll look at Processing's XML implementation, so this final example will also be a good data loading primer. Add the following to the **LIF_PARSER** tab:

```
/**
 * Cellular Automata
 * LIF_Parser class
 * By Ira Greenberg <br />
 * The Essential Guide to Processing for Flash Developers,
 * Friends of ED, 2009
 */
class LIF_Parser{
  // stores symbols (. *)
  String[] symbs = {};
  // path to .lif file
```

```
String url;
// stores all lines in .lif file
String[] lines;
// stores number of lines of symbols within each coord group
int[] indices;
// utility counter to increment coords[][] array
int coordsCounter = 0;
// stores origin in a sense of each symbol group
int[][] coords;
// bits buffer for pattern
int[] bits;
// bits array size (w, h)
int w, h;


// constructor
LIF_Parser(String url){
  this.url = url;
  // load .lif file
  lines = loadStrings(url);
  // get numbers of lines within each coord group
  indices = getIndices();
  // instantiate coords array values of where to draw each part of pattern
  coords = new int[indices.length][2];
  // isolate coords and reformat as int[][]
  parseCoords();
  //shift coords to remove negative values and isolate symbols
  shiftCoords();
  // create bits array based on pattern
  calcBits();
}

/* parses initial line strings, creating
 int[][] of coord data and isolates symbols*/
```

```
void parseCoords(){
  for (int i=0; i<lines.length; i++){
    String tempStr = "";
    // detect coords
    if (lines[i].charAt(0) == '#' && lines[i].charAt(1) == 'P'){
      // collect coord locs
      for (int j = 2; j<lines[i].length(); j++){
        tempStr += lines[i].charAt(j);
      }
      String tempStr2 = "";
      for (int j=0; j<tempStr.length(); j++){
        if (j>0 && tempStr.charAt(j) == ' '){
          tempStr2 += ',';
        }
        else if (tempStr.charAt(j) != ' '){
          tempStr2 += tempStr.charAt(j);
        }
      }
      coords[coordsCounter][0] = int(split(tempStr2, ','))[0];
      coords[coordsCounter][1] = int(split(tempStr2, ','))[1];
      coordsCounter ++;
    }
    else {
      // collect symbols
      if (lines[i].charAt(0) != '#'){
        symbs = append(symbs, lines[i]);
      }
    }
  }
}


/* add offset to x and y coords, based on lowest
 values, to avoid negative values */
```

```
void shiftCoords(){
  int xMin = 0, yMin = 0;
  // get lowest values
  for (int i=0; i<coords.length; i++){
    if (coords[i][0] < xMin){
      xMin = coords[i][0];
    }
    if (coords[i][1] < yMin){
      yMin = coords[i][1];
    }
  }
  // shift all coords
  for (int i=0; i<coords.length; i++){
    coords[i][0] += abs(xMin);
    coords[i][1] += abs(yMin);
  }
}


/* structure of data
 * stores number of symbols within each group
 * delimited by #P coordX coordY  in .lif file */
int[] getIndices(){
  int j = 0;
  int[] indices = {};

  for (int i=0; i<lines.length; i++){
    if(lines[i].charAt(0) != '#'){
      j++;
    }
    else {
      if (j!= 0){
        indices = append(indices, j);
      }
      j = 0;
```

```
    }
  }
  // get last group
  indices = append(indices, j);
  return indices;
}


// calculate bits
void calcBits(){
  // counter
  int ctr = 0;
  for (int i=0; i<indices.length; i++){
    for (int j=0; j<indices[i]; j++){
      // calculate max horizontal dimension
      if (coords[i][0] + symbs[ctr].length() > w){
        w = coords[i][0] + symbs[ctr].length();
      }
      // calculate max vertical dimension
      if (coords[i][1] + indices[i] > h){
        h = coords[i][1] + indices[i];
      }
      ctr++;
    }
  }
  // instantiate bits array
  bits = new int[w*h];
  // reset counter
  ctr = 0;
  //fill bits array
  for (int i=0; i<indices.length; i++){
    for (int j=0; j<indices[i]; j++){
      for (int k=0; k<symbs[ctr].length(); k++){
        if (symbs[ctr].charAt(k) == '.'){
          bits[w*(coords[i][1] + j) + (coords[i][0]+k)] = 0;
```

```
            }
          else if (symbs[ctr].charAt(k) == '*'){
            bits[w*(coords[i][1] + j) + (coords[i][0]+k)] = 1;
          }
        }
      }
      ctr++;
    }
  }
}


}
```

Rather than break down all this code in detail, I'll discuss the class in a top-level way, which I think will more quickly help demystify it; really it's not that complicated (it just looks that way). Here's the basic algorithm:

1. Load the URL using Processing's `loadStrings()` function. `loadStrings()` brings in an external file as a `String` array, delimited by line breaks.
2. Calculate and store the number of lines of symbols within each coordinate group. It's possible that the file will contain only one coordinate group.
3. Isolate and store the coordinate values where to place each symbol group.
4. Shift the coordinate values so they are all positive.
5. Calculate and store an array of bits based on the symbols '*' = 1 or '.' = 0.

I strongly suggest going through the class to see how I coded each part of the algorithm. If you come across a Processing function you haven't seen before, be sure to highlight it and hit command+shift+f (Mac) or control+shift+f (Win), to read about it in the Processing reference.

We're almost ready to test out the new parser. First, though, we need to add one more method to the CA_2D class. At the bottom of the class, add the following method (be sure to put it above the final closing curly brace of the class):

```
// put pattern array into pixls as initial on/off state
  void setPattern(LIF_Parser lp){
    resetState();
    float deltaW = (cols - lp.w)/2.0;
    float deltaH = (rows - lp.h)/2.0;
    int ctr = 0;
    for (int i=0; i<rows; i++){
      for (int j=0; j<cols; j++){
```

```
        if (i >= deltaH && i < lp.h+deltaH &&
          j >= deltaW && j < lp.w+deltaW){
          if (lp.bits[ctr] == 0){
            pixls[int(i*cols+j)] = offC;
          }
          else if (lp.bits[ctr] == 1){
            pixls[int(i*cols+j)] = onC;
          }
          // pixls[int(i*cols+j)] = lp.pixls[ctr];
          ctr++;
        }


    }
  }
  paintInitState();
}
```

This method enables the CA_2D object to accept a .lif pattern and embed the pattern in the pixls array. As with most things relating to pixels in Processing, the only challenging part was accounting for the two-dimensional structure of the pattern in the one-dimensional arrays. I used the local variables deltaW and deltaH to help center the pattern bits in the pixls array.

The last step is running the new parser. Replace what's in the main tab with the following to give it a test drive:

```
/**
 * Cellular Automata 2D Parser - main tab
 * By Ira Greenberg <br />
 * The Essential Guide to Processing for Flash Developers,
 * Friends of ED, 2009
 */


LIF_Parser lp;
String url = "http://www.radicaleye.com/lifepage/patterns/aqua50.lif";
CA_2D ca2;
```

```
void setup(){
  size(800, 600);
  background(255);
  ca2 = new CA_2D(width, height, 1);
  ca2.setOnColor(0xffff9900);
  ca2.setOffColor(0xff112233);
  lp = new LIF_Parser(url);
  ca2.setPattern(lp);
}

void draw(){
  translate(ca2.w/2, ca2.h/2);
  ca2.createGeneration();
}
```

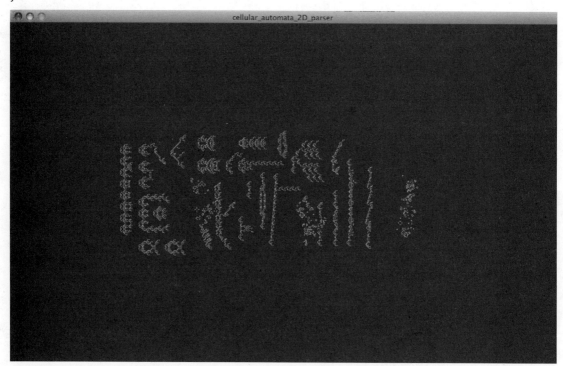

Figure 7-28. "p2 c/2 spaceships" pattern, by Hartmut Holzwart and Dean Hickerson

If it worked you should have seen something that looked like Figure 7-28. I recommend trying a bunch more patterns, which you can find around the web. There is a good pattern catalog at `http://radicaleye.com/lifepage/#browse` (August 7, 2009, 17:41). Just replace the quoted `String` address part of the line, `String url = "http://www.radicaleye.com/lifepage/patterns/aqua50.lif";`, with the new address. One last thing I suggest you also try is building a table structure of all the different CA discussed this chapter. Since they all work with the CA framework, you should be able to run them all simultaneously; then send me an email of what you get at `processing@iragreenberg.com`.

Summary

This chapter introduced the exciting concepts of emergence and complexity showcasing cellular automata. Building a CA framework, we looked at 1D, Continuous and 2D implementations, including an interactive example that allowed us to select CA thumbnails for enlargement (for our burgeoning tee-shirt business). CA reveal how simple rules can lead to very unexpected emergent complexity. This idea has much broader implications than for simply making cool images (not to knock cool images), but relates to how large complex systems, across many disciplines, emerge, grow, transform, and even perish. CA is just one computational approach for simulating and "playing" with complexity. Processing is a great environment for exploring this area because of its robustness, and ease, in handling pixel operations. Next chapter we'll build upon some of the concepts we looked at during this chapter, as well as earlier in the book, as we explore creative data visualization in Processing.

Chapter 8

Creative Information Visualization

Hiding out in the ivory tower most of my career, primarily in art departments, I've had the luxury of not having to worry about many "real world" problems—other than say the occasional apathetic student (alright, maybe not so occasional). This self-induced cloistering has greatly influenced the types of projects I've worked on, which can be generically categorized as things that seem cool and fun. This approach is in contrast to some of my colleagues in computer science, who often need to prove or apply something beyond their own whimsical wondering. More recently, I (and even some of them) have been making forays across this whimsical-utilitarian divide into the space of data visualization.

According to Wikipedia, data or information visualization is a relatively new field of study:

> *"The recent emphasis on visualization started in 1987 with the special issue of Computer Graphics on Visualization in Scientific Computing" (http://en.wikipedia.org/wiki /Information_visualization, October 29, 2009, 12:18 pm).*

On the art side of the academy, arguments could be made that information visualization is not new at all, but dates back to when people first began recording nature (perceptual data); don't worry—I won't press this argument. Statistician-turned-information-guru Edward Tufte is the most well-known figure to bring information visualization into the mainstream and onto the radar screen of designers and artists. Through his teachings, books, and lectures, Tufte helped create a groundswell of new research, academic centers, and artwork related to the visualization of quantitative information—or more simply put, data. And, languages like ActionScript and Processing have become two of the environments of choice for creative information visualization, which is, of course, the direction I'll pursue in this chapter.

Java on the Cheap, and It's 3D

Since this is the last chapter in the book, I've taken the liberty of structuring the example a little differently than in earlier chapters. Thus far we've looked at Processing's procedural (function-based) approach and simplified object-oriented syntax; this chapter we'll explore Processing's Java mode. For very experienced ActionScript coders, this approach may actually seem more familiar than the other coding style used throughout the book. For less experienced coders though, this new approach may initially seem overly complicated (even unnecessarily so), but rest assured there is a method to the madness. Learning Java mode also has the added benefit of teaching you something that you can apply back to ActionScript.

As a refresher, Processing classes (using a `.pde` suffix) are technically Java inner classes. Java, unlike ActionScript, allows classes to be nested. For example, this is perfectly legal in Java:

```
public class Outer {

  // legal inner class in Java

  class Inner {

  // do inner class stuff

  }

}
```

> *Nested classes are used when a class only needs to be referred to once and are especially useful for handling events.*

In ActionScript things work a bit differently: only one class can be defined in a package declaration. Although, you can include additional classes outside the package scope; to read more about this see `http://probertson.com/articles/2006/07/28/one-file-many-as3-classes/` (October 30, 2009, 10:34am).

Java inner classes act pretty much like standard Java classes, with some subtle differences that are beyond the scope of this discussion. You can learn more about Java inner classes here: `http://java.sun.com/docs/books/tutorial/java/java00/nested.html` (October 29, 2009, 12:10pm).

In Java mode, you use standard Java classes (outer classes), which utilize a `.java` suffix. Processing makes it pretty simple to introduce pure Java right alongside Processing's procedure code and inner (`.pde`) classes—all in the same environment.

> *Processing's clever approach to integrating multiple coding styles in the same environment has been noticed by departments of Computer Science at leading universities. Since many of these departments teach Java in their introductory classes, Processing can be easily integrated into the curriculum.*

The final benefit of Java mode is that you can eventually package your code as a Processing Library or Tool, which can be then distributed to other users. Libraries and Tools represent the future growth of Processing, where users like you can extend the overall Processing API (beyond the core) as well as the development environment. For the most current snapshot of available Processing Libraries, see:

`http://processing.org/reference/libraries/` (October 29, 2009, 11:12am); notice the number of user-submitted libraries far exceeds the core ones.

Beyond Java, I'll also include a more in-depth look at 3D in Processing. This is one of Processing's sweet spots with a wonderfully simple approach, far less cryptic than the way 3D is implemented and exposed in ActionScript. Of course, with all this 3D coolness does come a bit of math, even in Processing's gentler approach. But don't worry, most of the math is closely related to what you've looked at before, with minor variations. The chapter example includes classes for creating 3D geometry and a relatively simple custom transformation routine, which we'll use to avoid some issues using Processing's built-in system. As I've tried to do in earlier chapters in the book, there is a lot of development space in the chapter example, allowing you to build onto it with your own classes as well as mess around with tons of parameters.

Popularity of Widget Colors

The example we'll code is inspired by a prototype visualization I created a couple years back, based on the constitution of the Czech Republic; that data source proved to be a bit too large and complex for the current example, so I decided to combine the basic aesthetic part of the project with a simpler, albeit far more prosaic, data source—popularity of widget colors. I can't really take credit for the widget choice either, as this was inspired by Dupont Corporation's annual list of the most popular automobile colors.

The basic approach I took in structuring the example was to create a visualization system, as compared to a single visualization solution. This, again, will enable motivated readers to extend the system for their own purposes, as well as facilitate the creation of a visualization library. In creating a system, I tried to develop the beginnings of a framework, rather than simply a coded example. The difference between a framework and an example is that the former should include a level of general abstraction allowing you to create a greater range of different types of work, than, say, beginning with just a specific example. I also tried to encapsulate certain common behavior, such as mouse event handling, while still exposing enough of the framework to allow some of the code to be overridden, etc. The basic steps I took in developing the example (not actually in this order, though) are as follows:

1. Structure the data so it can be read into Processing and then parsed. I created an XML document based on the data. Processing, like ActionScript, includes a straightforward way of importing and processing XML.
2. Create a base object class that can be extended for creating different geometric objects. The basic object class will be 3D and include properties for location, size, color, and mouse handling (picking), which is trickier in 3D than in 2D. I named this class `VizObj.java.`
3. Create a lower-level geometry handling-type class that will manage vertices and also encapsulate the interactive events in the piece. This class is the real engine and encapsulates some of the gnarliest math and algorithms. This class enables the framework to be used with a minimal amount of code and complexity (if so desired). I named this class `Interactor.java.`
4. Create a specific Visualization class that will function as an organizing class for the individual geometric components and also as a delegation class, communicating between the user's Processing code and the `Interactor.java` class just discussed. I named this class: `Visualizer.java.`

5. Create the individual geometry classes. The example includes four such classes: `Block.java`, `Cylinder.java`, `Helix.java`, and `Icosahedron.java`. Other geometry classes can be created by extending `VizObj.java`.

Enough Talk, Let's Build

As I mentioned earlier, I didn't actually build the example in the order I outlined. However, I felt it was easier to understand the overall process presented in that order. I'll begin building with the core `VizObj.java` class. To follow along, which I recommend, create a new Processing sketch. Next, create a new tab named "`VizObj.java`" and enter the following code into it.

```java
/**
 * Data Visualizer
 * VizObj.java class
 * By Ira Greenberg <br />
 * The Essential Guide to Processing for Flash Developers,
 * Friends of ED, 2009
 */


import processing.core.*;


abstract class VizObj{

  protected PVector[] vecs, finalVecs;
  protected PApplet p;
  protected PVector loc = new PVector();
  protected int r, g, b, upR, upG, upB, hoverR, hoverG, hoverB;
  protected int[] arrR, arrG, arrB;
  protected float radius, w, h;
  protected boolean isMouseEnabled;
  protected String info;
  // where things can attach
  protected PVector joint;


  // default constructor
  protected  VizObj(){
```

```
}

// constructor
public VizObj(PApplet p){
  this.p = p;
}

// constructor
public VizObj(PApplet p, float radius){
  this.p = p;
  this.radius = radius;
}

// constructor
public VizObj(PApplet p, float w, float h){
  this.p = p;
  this.w = w;
  this.h = h;
  radius = (w+h)/4.0f;
}

// init Color
public void initRGB(float r, float g, float b){
  this.r = upR = p.round(r);
  this.g = upG = p.round(g);
  this.b = upB = p.round(b);
  hoverR = p.round(r*=2.0f);
  hoverG = p.round(g*=2.0f);
  hoverB = p.round(b*=2.0f);
}

// for gradient rendering option
public void initRGB(int[] arrR, int[] arrG, int[] arrB){
  this.arrR = arrR;
```

```
    this.arrG = arrG;
    this.arrB = arrB;
  }


  // update Color
  public void updateRGB(int r, int g, int b){
    this.r = r;
    this.g = g;
    this.b = b;
  }


  // rotate vertices
  public void setRot(PVector rot){
    // pre calc trig vals
    // x-axis rotation
    float cx = p.cos(rot.x);
    float sx = p.sin(rot.x);

    // y-axis rotation
    float cy = p.cos(rot.y);
    float sy = p.sin(rot.y);

    // z-axis rotation
    float cz = p.cos(rot.z);
    float sz = p.sin(rot.z);

    PVector[] tempVecs = new PVector[vecs.length];
    for (int i=0; i<vecs.length; i++){
      // x-axis rotation
      tempVecs[i] = new PVector (vecs[i].x, cx*vecs[i].y -  ⏎
          sx*vecs[i].z, sx*vecs[i].y + cx*vecs[i].z);
      // y-axis rotation
      vecs[i] = new PVector (sy*tempVecs[i].z + cy*tempVecs[i].x,  ⏎
          tempVecs[i].y, cy*tempVecs[i].z - sy*tempVecs[i].x);
```

```
    // z-axis rotation
    tempVecs[i] = new PVector (cz*vecs[i].x - sz*vecs[i].y, ↩
        sz*vecs[i].x + cz*vecs[i].y, vecs[i].z);
  }
  p.arrayCopy(tempVecs, vecs);
}


// returns if mouse is currently over object
// - this is bare bones and not very accurate picking
public boolean isOver(){
  float mx = p.mouseX;
  float my = p.mouseY;

  float tempX = 0.0f;
  float tempY = 0.0f;
  float tempZ = 0.0f;
  for (int i=0; i<finalVecs.length; i++){
    tempX += finalVecs[i].x;
    tempY += finalVecs[i].y;
    tempZ += finalVecs[i].z;
  }
  tempX /= finalVecs.length;
  tempY /= finalVecs.length;
  tempZ /= finalVecs.length;
  if(mx>p.screenX(tempX, tempY, tempZ)-radius && ↩
    mx<p.screenX(tempX, tempY, tempZ)+radius && ↩
    my>p.screenY(tempX, tempY, tempZ)-radius && ↩
    my<p.screenY(tempX, tempY, tempZ)+radius){
    return true;
  }
  return false;
}
```

```
// add location to vertices
protected void update(){
  for (int i=0; i<vecs.length; i++){
    vecs[i].add(loc);
  }
}


// more setters below
public void setPApplet(PApplet p){
  this.p = p;
}


public void setLoc(PVector loc){
  this.loc = loc;
  update();
}


// sets String info used in screen output
public void setInfo(String info){
  this.info = info;
}


public PVector getJoint(){
  return joint;
}


protected void setMouseEnabled(boolean isMouseEnabled){
  this.isMouseEnabled = isMouseEnabled;
}


// abstract methods to be implemented in subclasses
abstract void init();
abstract void create(PVector[] finalVecs);
}
```

The class begins with an import statement that I haven't used before. This statement isn't automatically added to the sketch by importing a library, as with OPENGL. Instead, this import statement is for the core classes in Processing. Because we're working in Java now, Processing won't convert the `VizObj.java` class to an inner nested class. Normally, a .pde class is automatically converted to an inner class, giving it access to the Processing core classes (which make up the majority of the Processing language). Simply by using the .java suffix, the class is treated as an external independent class and thus doesn't by default have access to the Processing core commands. Using the `import processing.core.*;` statement, and then passing in a reference to the main `PApplet` object (which we'll look at in a moment), we can seamlessly integrate Java classes directly into Processing.

Notice I declared the `VizObj` class `abstract`, as it will only be used as a superclass for individual geometry classes; it will never be instantiated directly. Another new element I added to the class members is the `protected` keyword, used as an access modifier when declaring the default constructor and instance properties. ActionScript also includes access modifiers, so this should look familiar to experienced coders. In Java, the `protected` keyword limits access to the marked method or property to subclasses (in any package) and classes within the same package. To keep things simple I won't create any explicit packages, but will keep all the classes together in the sketch directory (which will function as a default package). By convention in OOP, for both ActionScript and Java, instance properties should be declared `private`, which we'll (mostly) adhere to in the rest of the classes. However, since the `VizObj` class is only used for inheritance, it's fine in this context to allow its subclasses to directly access properties declared with the `protected` modifier, which still provides some level of access control. Please also note that by providing no modifier in Java, you automatically get some access control, with only classes within the same package having access; this is similar to ActionScript's `internal` modifier, which Java does not have.

One last point with the property declarations is the statement: `protected PApplet p;`. PApplet is the main Processing object that includes most of the methods (that act like functions) in the language. You can view the reference to this class at: `http://dev.processing.org/reference/core/index.html`. Since `VizObj` is a Java class we'll need a reference to the current `PApplet` object to be able to access Processing commands from within the class; this will become clearer shortly, if it isn't already.

Next are the constructors, which are overloaded. Notice that aside from the default constructor, each includes a `PApplet` parameter. Looking next at the `initRGB()` method, notice how the `PApplet` reference ("p") is used in the line `this.r = upR = p.round(r);`. What this reveals is how Processing's function calls are actually methods of the `PApplet` class. When we work in Java mode, we need to explicitly call these commands as methods using the `PApplet` reference. The `initRGB()` method initializes color values for the objects. I chose to treat color in the example as individual r, g, b components. Processing's `color` pseudo data type doesn't work properly in Java mode, since it's not really a full-fledged data type. Another option would have been to use Java's `Color` data type, but I decided to keep it simple and just use individual color components. The example includes a hover and up state for each object. Notice that for the hover state I'm multiplying each component by `2.0f` to make it brighter. You may also be wondering what the heck the "f" is in `2.0f`. In Processing all floating point values (numbers with an explicit fractional part) are 32-bits long (single precision). In Java, floating points values can also be 64-bits, referred to as "double"; this is also the default floating point size in Java. Processing normally handles the conversion from double to float internally. However, in Java mode, we need to do this explicitly by appending the "f" to the end of our floating point values.

Two other methods in this class that may need some elucidation are setRot(PVector rot) and isOver(). Processing includes very easy-to-use transformation functions, which we've used throughout the book, such as translate() and rotate(). However, these are also very high-level calls, deeply encapsulating the actual transformed vertices. There are times when it is helpful to have more low-level control and specifically handle the transformations on the actual vertices manually; this is the strategy I pursued in this example. There are two different transformations I'll do to the objects. The first is to rotate vertices during the actual constructing of the object(s), which is what setRot(PVector rot) is for, and the second is to control the overall rotation of all the objects' vertices, which we'll look at in the Interactor.java class later in the chapter. Notice again in setRot(PVector rot) the use of p. in front of standard Processing calls.

Within the setRot(PVector rot) method, the actual rotating of the vertices relies on relatively simple trig equations, shown next around all three axes:

X-Axis Rotation

y' = y*cos q - z*sin q

z' = y*sin q + z*cos q

x' = x

Y-Axis Rotation

z' = z*cos q - x*sin q

x' = z*sin q + x*cos q

y' = y

Z-Axis Rotation

x' = x*cos q - y*sin q

y' = x*sin q + y*cos q

z' = z

> *If you have trouble memorizing the rotations around all three axes, notice the equations follow a pattern, where x-axis rotation is y', z', x' and then you move to the next consecutive letter for y-axis rotation: z', x', y' (after z' you go back to x'). I assume you now can figure out how to get the z-axis rotation. Also, the shorter and more common 2D equations around the z axis: x' = cos q, y' = sin q are just shortened forms, based on simplifying the equations.*

The last line in the method, p.arrayCopy(tempVecs, vecs); is an efficient way of copying data between arrays in Processing.

The isOver() method returns true if the mouse is over the object. In 3D, mouse event detection is more complicated than in 2D because of spatial rendering. 3D renderers include calculations to simulate the effects of binocular perception and perspectival distortion—how we see the three-dimensional world with our two eyes. As an art student, I formally studied this effect and also learned how to simulate it—think railroad tracks converging into the distance—which is similar to what Processing does, only using some fancy math. In *Processing: Creative Coding and Computational Art*, I constructed a simple 3D renderer that includes these perspective calculations. The challenge with mouse detection in 3D is that there is no mouseZ value, as the mouse is always on the surface. When Processing renders geometry using perspective, the coordinate values of the vertices don't actually change value—rather, the renderer, or virtual camera, handles the math transformations for displaying the vertices in the right scale and space. Thus, we need a way, in a sense, of flattening out the perspective rendering to the surface of the screen. This would allow us to check the mouse against these new flattened vertex values, along the x and y axes. Fortunately, we don't need to hack our way through this sort of solution, as Processing includes the methods screenX, screenY, and screenZ, which do the flattening calculations for us.

The rest of the class should be self-explanatory, with a bunch of setter methods and the two abstract methods

```
abstract void init();
abstract void create(PVector[] finalVecs);
```

which need to be implemented by any classes that extend VizObj, one of which we'll look at next.

Block.java

To use VizObj.java, we'll create a simple block class, named Block.java. Create a new tab named "**Block.java**" in the current sketch and enter the following code:

```
/**
 * Data Visualizer
 * Block.java class
 * By Ira Greenberg <br />
 * The Essential Guide to Processing for Flash Developers,
 * Friends of ED, 2009
 */

import processing.core.*;

public class Block extends VizObj{

  private float d = 1.0f;

  // default constructor
  public Block(){
  }
```

```
  // constructor
  public Block(PApplet p){
    super(p);
    init();
  }

  // constructor
  public Block(PApplet p, float sz){
    super(p, sz, sz);
    d = sz;
    init();
  }

// constructor
  public Block(PApplet p, float w, float h, float d){
    super(p, w, h);
    this.d = d;
    init();
  }

  // required implementation - calculates geometry
  protected void init(){
    vecs = new PVector[8];
    vecs[0] = new PVector(loc.x-w/2, loc.y-h/2, loc.z+d/2);
    vecs[1] = new PVector(loc.x+w/2, loc.y-h/2, loc.z+d/2);
    vecs[2] = new PVector(loc.x+w/2, loc.y+h/2, loc.z+d/2);
    vecs[3] = new PVector(loc.x-w/2, loc.y+h/2, loc.z+d/2);

    vecs[4] = new PVector(loc.x-w/2, loc.y-h/2, loc.z-d/2);
    vecs[5] = new PVector(loc.x+w/2, loc.y-h/2, loc.z-d/2);
    vecs[6] = new PVector(loc.x+w/2, loc.y+h/2, loc.z-d/2);
    vecs[7] = new PVector(loc.x-w/2, loc.y+h/2, loc.z-d/2);
  }

  // required implementation - draws geometry
  public void create(PVector[] finalVecs){
```

```
this.finalVecs = finalVecs;
p.fill(r, g, b);
p.beginShape(p.QUADS);
// front
p.vertex(finalVecs[0].x, finalVecs[0].y, finalVecs[0].z);
p.vertex(finalVecs[1].x, finalVecs[1].y, finalVecs[1].z);
p.vertex(finalVecs[2].x, finalVecs[2].y, finalVecs[2].z);
p.vertex(finalVecs[3].x, finalVecs[3].y, finalVecs[3].z);

// back
p.vertex(finalVecs[5].x, finalVecs[5].y, finalVecs[5].z);
p.vertex(finalVecs[4].x, finalVecs[4].y, finalVecs[4].z);
p.vertex(finalVecs[7].x, finalVecs[7].y, finalVecs[7].z);
p.vertex(finalVecs[6].x, finalVecs[6].y, finalVecs[6].z);

// left
p.vertex(finalVecs[4].x, finalVecs[4].y, finalVecs[4].z);
p.vertex(finalVecs[0].x, finalVecs[0].y, finalVecs[0].z);
p.vertex(finalVecs[3].x, finalVecs[3].y, finalVecs[3].z);
p.vertex(finalVecs[7].x, finalVecs[7].y, finalVecs[7].z);

// right
p.vertex(finalVecs[1].x, finalVecs[1].y, finalVecs[1].z);
p.vertex(finalVecs[5].x, finalVecs[5].y, finalVecs[5].z);
p.vertex(finalVecs[6].x, finalVecs[6].y, finalVecs[6].z);
p.vertex(finalVecs[2].x, finalVecs[2].y, finalVecs[2].z);

// top
p.vertex(finalVecs[0].x, finalVecs[0].y, finalVecs[0].z);
p.vertex(finalVecs[4].x, finalVecs[4].y, finalVecs[4].z);
p.vertex(finalVecs[5].x, finalVecs[5].y, finalVecs[5].z);
p.vertex(finalVecs[1].x, finalVecs[1].y, finalVecs[1].z);

// bottem
p.vertex(finalVecs[3].x, finalVecs[3].y, finalVecs[3].z);
p.vertex(finalVecs[2].x, finalVecs[2].y, finalVecs[2].z);
```

```
  p.vertex(finalVecs[6].x, finalVecs[6].y, finalVecs[6].z);
  p.vertex(finalVecs[7].x, finalVecs[7].y, finalVecs[7].z);
  p.endShape();
}


// For use outside Interactor.java class
public void create(){
  p.beginShape(p.QUADS);
  // front
  p.vertex(vecs[0].x, vecs[0].y, vecs[0].z);
  p.vertex(vecs[1].x, vecs[1].y, vecs[1].z);
  p.vertex(vecs[2].x, vecs[2].y, vecs[2].z);
  p.vertex(vecs[3].x, vecs[3].y, vecs[3].z);

  // back
  p.vertex(vecs[5].x, vecs[5].y, vecs[5].z);
  p.vertex(vecs[4].x, vecs[4].y, vecs[4].z);
  p.vertex(vecs[7].x, vecs[7].y, vecs[7].z);
  p.vertex(vecs[6].x, vecs[6].y, vecs[6].z);

  // left
  p.vertex(vecs[4].x, vecs[4].y, vecs[4].z);
  p.vertex(vecs[0].x, vecs[0].y, vecs[0].z);
  p.vertex(vecs[3].x, vecs[3].y, vecs[3].z);
  p.vertex(vecs[7].x, vecs[7].y, vecs[7].z);

  // right
  p.vertex(vecs[1].x, vecs[1].y, vecs[1].z);
  p.vertex(vecs[5].x, vecs[5].y, vecs[5].z);
  p.vertex(vecs[6].x, vecs[6].y, vecs[6].z);
  p.vertex(vecs[2].x, vecs[2].y, vecs[2].z);

  // top
  p.vertex(vecs[0].x, vecs[0].y, vecs[0].z);
  p.vertex(vecs[4].x, vecs[4].y, vecs[4].z);
  p.vertex(vecs[5].x, vecs[5].y, vecs[5].z);
```

```
      p.vertex(vecs[1].x, vecs[1].y, vecs[1].z);

      // bottom
      p.vertex(vecs[3].x, vecs[3].y, vecs[3].z);
      p.vertex(vecs[2].x, vecs[2].y, vecs[2].z);
      p.vertex(vecs[6].x, vecs[6].y, vecs[6].z);
      p.vertex(vecs[7].x, vecs[7].y, vecs[7].z);
      p.endShape();
  }
}
```

The block construction algorithm is very straightforward; it uses eight vertices to form six quads around the faces of the block. Notice that the initial eight vertices are calculated using the vecs array, but in the overloaded create(PVector[] finalVecs) method the actual drawing occurs using the finalVecs array. This is done because the vecs array is processed internally by the Interactor.java class—which we'll look at next—and then drawing/rendering occurs using the transformed finalVecs array, which is passed back from the Interactor object. The other create() method was added for testing (or using) the Block class on its own. For example, enter the following code into the current sketch main tab and run the sketch. You should get an image resembling Figure 8-1.

```
/**
 * Data Visualizer-Stage 1
 * Main Processing Tab
 * By Ira Greenberg <br />
 * The Essential Guide to Processing for Flash Developers,
 * Friends of ED, 2009
 */


import processing.opengl.*;

Block cube;

void setup(){
  size(600, 600, OPENGL);
  cube = new Block(this, 225);
  fill(45, 100, 127);
  noStroke();
```

```
}

void draw() {
  background(75);
  translate(width/2, height/2, -100);
  rotateY(PI/8);
  rotateX(PI/8);
  lights();
  cube.create();
}
```

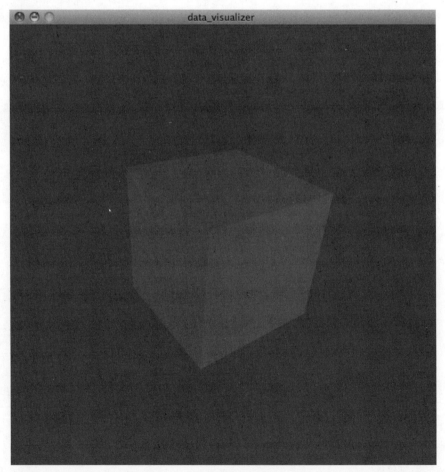

Figure 8-1. Data visualization test render 1

Without the `Interactor` class, you can still add event behavior and transformations, but you'd add that behavior into the main tab. I chose to encapsulate this behavior to make it simpler to use and build upon the overall sketch. I also chose to manually handle some transformations rather than use Processing's built-in capabilities. To help understand why I did this, I've created a short sketch we'll look at next. Replace the entire `draw()` function in the main tab of the current sketch with the following:

```
void draw() {
  background(75);
  lights();
  translate(width/2, height/2, -100);
  rotateX(frameCount*PI/360);
  rotateY(radians(mouseX));
  cube.create();
}
```

As you run the example, move your mouse back and forth along the *x* axis. You'll notice that as the block rotates around the *x* axis, it affects how it rotates along the *y* axis, sometimes rotating in the direction your mouse is moving and sometimes in the opposite direction. What's happening is the overall transformation along all three axes (technically its orientation relative to a virtual camera) of the block is considered in Processing's internal transformation calculations, not just the localized rotation along any individual axis. You might initially think this is just an annoying academic point (by an annoying academic even!) but as you manipulate an object in 3D space, it truly is annoying—and even confusing—when the object doesn't seem to respond as expected. By coding our own rotations in the `Interactor` class, we can avoid this problem.

Interactor.java

As a child I always preferred that a nurse or doctor tell me the truth: "Yes, this really will hurt..." So I'll provide the same courtesy and admit that this class may hurt a little (but I promise no blood). Create a new tab named "`Interactor.java`" and enter the following code:

```
/**
 * Data Visualizer
 * Interactor.java class
 * By Ira Greenberg <br />
 * The Essential Guide to Processing for Flash Developers,
 * Friends of ED, 2009
 */


import processing.core.*;
```

```
import java.awt.event.*;
import java.util.*;

public class Interactor extends PApplet{

  private VizObj vo;
  private PApplet p;

  private PVector[][] vecs;
  private PVector[][] vecs_rotY;
  private PVector[][] vecs_rotX;
  private PVector[][] finalVecs;

  private float mx, my;
  private float dx, dy;
  private boolean isSpunOn;
  private float damping = .985f;
  private float spdY, spdX;
  private float mouseXIn, mouseYIn;
  private float timeIn;
  private float rotSpd = 10.0f;

  // ArrayList used to dynamically reference VizObj objects
  private ArrayList objBin;

  // default constructor
  public Interactor(){
    objBin = new ArrayList();
  }

  // constructor with VizObj obj array
  public Interactor(VizObj[] vos){
    objBin = new ArrayList();
    for (int i=0; i<vos.length; i++){
```

```
      objBin.add(vos[i]);
    }
    init();
  }


  // constructor with single VizObj obj
  public Interactor(VizObj vo){
    objBin = new ArrayList();
    objBin.add(vo);
    init();
  }


  // update dynamics values
  public void setDynamics(float rotSpd, float damping){
    this.rotSpd = rotSpd;
    this.damping = damping;
  }


  // initialize stuff
  public void init(){
    this.p = ((VizObj)objBin.get(0)).p;
    vecs = new PVector[objBin.size()][0];
    vecs_rotY = new PVector[objBin.size()][0];
    vecs_rotX = new PVector[objBin.size()][0];
    finalVecs = new PVector[objBin.size()][0];

    for (int i=0; i<objBin.size(); i++){
      for (int j=0; j<((VizObj)objBin.get(i)).vecs.length; j++){
        vecs[i] = (PVector[])append(vecs[i], ((VizObj)objBin.get(i)).vecs[j]);
        vecs_rotY[i] = (PVector[])append(vecs_rotY[i], new PVector());
        vecs_rotX[i] = (PVector[])append(vecs_rotX[i], new PVector());
        finalVecs[i] = (PVector[])append(finalVecs[i], new PVector());
      }
      arrayCopy(vecs[i], finalVecs[i]);
```

```
  }

  // start visualization spinning
  isSpunOn = true;
  spdX = 4;
  spdY = 4;

  // allows Mouse events to be handled in this class
  p.registerMouseEvent(this);
}

// add individual VizObj object
public void addTo(VizObj vo){
  objBin.add(vo);
  init();
}

// add array of VizObj objects
public void addTo(VizObj[] vos){
  for (int i=0; i<vos.length; i++){
    objBin.add(vos[i]);
  }
  init();
}

// add 2D array of VizObj objects
public void addTo(VizObj[][] vos){
  for (int i=0; i<vos.length; i++){
    for (int j=0; j<vos[i].length; j++){
      objBin.add(vos[i][j]);
    }
  }
  init();
}
```

```
/* Access Processing Mouse events
 enabling event encapsulation */
public void mouseEvent(MouseEvent event) {
  switch (event.getID()) {
  case MouseEvent.MOUSE_PRESSED:
    isSpunOn = false;
    mx = p.mouseX;
    my = p.mouseY;

    mouseXIn = p.mouseX;
    mouseYIn = p.mouseY;
    timeIn = millis();
    break;
  case MouseEvent.MOUSE_RELEASED:
    isSpunOn = true;
    update();
    // conditional used to avoid /0 calculation
    float tm = millis() - timeIn;
    if (tm==0) {
      tm =100;
    }
    spdX = ((p.mouseX - mouseXIn)/tm)*rotSpd;
    spdY = ((p.mouseY - mouseYIn)/tm)*rotSpd;
    break;
  case MouseEvent.MOUSE_CLICKED:
    // do something for mouse clicked
    break;
  case MouseEvent.MOUSE_DRAGGED:
    rot(radians((p.mouseX-mx)), -radians((p.mouseY-my)));
    break;
  case MouseEvent.MOUSE_MOVED:
    // do something for mouse moved
    break;
  }
```

```
}

// allows VizObj objects to be rotated
public void runMouseEvents(){
  if (isSpunOn){
    rot(radians((spdX)), -radians((spdY)));
    update();
    spdX*=damping;
    spdY*=damping;
  }


  for (int i=0; i<objBin.size(); i++){
    VizObj vo = (VizObj)objBin.get(i);
    if(vo.isMouseEnabled && vo.isOver()){
      vo.updateRGB(vo.hoverR, vo.hoverG, vo.hoverB);
    }
    else {
      vo.updateRGB(vo.upR, vo.upG, vo.upB);
    }
  }
}


// returns VizObj object info property value
public String getVizObjInfo(){
  for (int i=0; i<objBin.size(); i++){
    VizObj vo = (VizObj)objBin.get(i);
    if(vo.isMouseEnabled && vo.isOver()){
      return(vo.info);
    }
  }
  return "";
}


// rotate VizObj objects' vertices
```

```
public void rot(float tx, float ty) {
  // pre calc trig vals
  float sx = sin(tx);
  float sy = sin(ty);
  float cx = cos(tx);
  float cy = cos(ty);

  // mouse drag along x-axis = y-axis rotation
  for ( int i=0; i<vecs.length; i++){
    for (int j=0; j<vecs[i].length; j++){
      vecs_rotY[i][j] = new PVector(sx*vecs[i][j].z + cx*vecs[i][j].x, ⏎
          vecs[i][j].y, cx*vecs[i][j].z - sx*vecs[i][j].x);
    }
    // mouse drag along y-axis = x-axis rotation
    for (int j=0; j<vecs[i].length; j++){
      vecs_rotX[i][j] = new PVector(vecs_rotY[i][j].x, cy*vecs_rotY[i][j].y - ⏎
          sy*vecs_rotY[i][j].z, sy*vecs_rotY[i][j].y + cy*vecs_rotY[i][j].z);
    }
    arrayCopy(vecs_rotX[i], finalVecs[i]);
  }
}

/* copy finalVecs array values to vecs array
 - updates transformations */
public void update(){
  for ( int i=0; i<vecs.length; i++){
    arrayCopy(finalVecs[i], vecs[i]);
  }
}

/* call create() method for each VizObj object
and do mouse events */
 public void run(){
```

433

```
    for (int i=0; i<objBin.size(); i++){
      ((VizObj)objBin.get(i)).create(finalVecs[i]);
    }
    runMouseEvents();
  }
}
```

The reason the `Interactor` class is complicated is that its main role is to encapsulate behavior, handling most of the heavy lifting so users of the overall sketch don't have to. Before looking at the code, let's first see it in action. If you've been following along, you should have a tab with the `VizObj.java` class, another with the `Block.java` class, and one with `Interactor.java`. Replace whatever code is currently in your main tab with the following and then run the sketch.

```
import processing.opengl.*;

Interactor ia;

void setup(){
  size(600, 600, OPENGL);
  ia = new Interactor();
  Block cube = new Block(this, 225);
  cube.initRGB(45, 127, 100);
  cube.setMouseEnabled(true);
  ia.addTo(cube);
  noStroke();
}


void draw() {
  background(75);
  translate(width/2, height/2, -100);
  lights();
  ia.create();
  ia.setMouseEvents();
}
```

Try rotating and hovering over the block. Notice if you move around one axis and then try rotating on another, the block will still always rotate as expected. Both the hover highlighting and the mouse drag behavior are encapsulated in the Interactor class. The drag also includes some simple simulated physics, allowing you to spin the block faster by dragging faster. There is also a damping effect that slowly brings the block to rest. Best of all, this behavior will work no matter how many blocks (or other types of VisObj shapes) you create. Also included in the class is a reporting system, for connecting data with the hover operation. For an example of all this, replace the current code in the main tab with the following and try running the sketch again, shown in Figure 8-2.

```
/**
 * Data Visualizer-Stage 4
 * Main Processing Tab
 * By Ira Greenberg <br />
 * The Essential Guide to Processing for Flash Developers,
 * Friends of ED, 2009
 */


import processing.opengl.*;


Interactor ia;


void setup(){
  size(600, 600, OPENGL);
  ia = new Interactor();
  int rows = 8;
  float totalHt = 375;
  float gap = totalHt/rows;
  int cubeCount = 20;
  int counter = 0;
  float ringRadius = 240;
  float theta;
  float y = -totalHt/2;
  Block[][] cubes = new Block[rows][cubeCount];
  for(int i=0; i<cubes.length; i++){
    theta = 0.0;
    for(int j=0; j<cubes[i].length; j++){
```

435

```
        cubes[i][j] = new Block(this, 20);
        cubes[i][j].setRot(new PVector(0, theta, 0));
        cubes[i][j].setLoc(new PVector(sin(theta)*ringRadius, y, cos(theta)*ringRadius));
        theta += TWO_PI/cubeCount;

        cubes[i][j].initRGB(int(random(200)), int(random(200)), int(random(200)));
        cubes[i][j].setMouseEnabled(true);
        cubes[i][j].setInfo("hovering over block " + counter++);
        ia.addTo(cubes[i][j]);
      }
      y+=gap;
    }
  noStroke();
}


void draw() {
  background(75);
  translate(width/2, height/2, -100);
  lights();
  ia.create();
  ia.setMouseEvents();
  println(ia.getVizObjInfo());
}
```

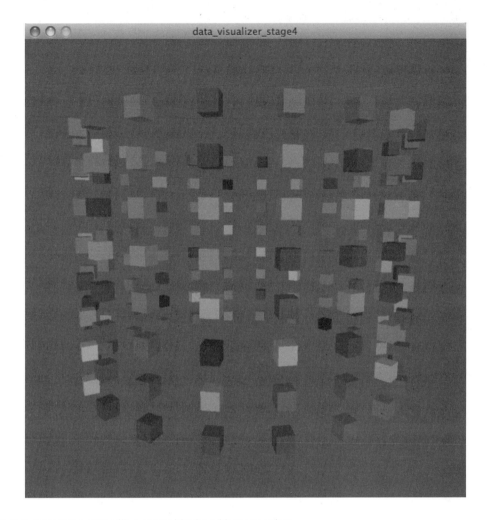

Figure 8-2. Interactor controlling many blocks with messaging

As you hover over the blocks notice the output in the text area. We'll use this reporting feature eventually to output information stored within the XML document to the screen.

Returning to the `Interactor.java` code, the first new elements to discuss are the two import statements:

```
import java.awt.event.*;
import java.util.*;
```

As you might guess from the directory names, these are Java packages we're importing. The first statement is for the encapsulated mouse event behavior, and the second is for the ArrayList data type.

437

You can see a reference to ArrayList at the bottom of the instance property declarations in the Interactor class, the statement

private ArrayList objBin;

The ArrayList type is a Java type that lives in the Java.util package. It is listed in the Processing reference, but the class is not within the Processing core, which is why I needed to explicitly import its package. When you are working within Processing, (not in a .java file) import statements are automatically written when the pde is converted to Java. To test this, open a new Processing sketch and select **Export** under the File menu (you can leave the sketch blank). The Java file created will look something like this:

```
import processing.core.*;
import processing.xml.*;

import java.applet.*;
import java.awt.*;
import java.awt.image.*;
import java.awt.event.*;
import java.io.*;
import java.net.*;
import java.text.*;
import java.util.*;
import java.util.zip.*;
import java.util.regex.*;

public class sketch_nov03d extends PApplet {
  public void setup() {


  noLoop();
}
  static public void main(String args[]) {
    PApplet.main(new String[] { "--bgcolor=#FFFFFF", "sketch_nov03d" });
  }
}
```

The ArrayList is a dynamic composite structure that can be assigned any data type. It includes methods for easily adding and removing objects dynamically. I used it to collect all the VizObj objects passed into the Interactor object. In addition to the ArrayList, I declared a bunch of 2D arrays:

```
private PVector[][] vecs;
private PVector[][] vecs_rotY;
private PVector[][] vecs_rotX;
private PVector[][] finalVecs;
```

Honestly, I could have coded the class with a few less arrays, reusing a couple. However, since the arrays are used primarily during initialization (and not during memory-sucking draw() cycles) I found it semantically simpler to use all of them. Also, since I don't know in advance how many vertices per VizObj there will be, I initialized the 2D arrays with 0 vertices and then used Processing's append() function to increase the array sizes dynamically. Again, there is a bit of extra vertex book keeping going on here, but I still found this approach simplest for keeping track of what was happening in the class; in programming there often needs to be a trade-off between economy and clarity.

The line arrayCopy(vecs[i], finalVecs[i]); copies all the vertex data in the vecs array to the finalVecs array for transformations. Remember that copying is different than assigning in Processing/Java. When you assign an object to another reference variable, you're not really assigning the object data, but rather assigning the memory address of the object, making the variable point only to the address. When you need to actually copy the data, you can use arrayCopy(); the following example illustrates the difference.

```
/**
 * Data Visualizer-Stage 4
 * arraycopy() example
 * By Ira Greenberg <br />
 * The Essential Guide to Processing for Flash Developers,
 * Friends of ED, 2009
 */


int[] f = {1, 2, 3, 4, 5};


/* make g point to the memory address of f,
 referencing the same data */
int[] g = f;


/* copy the actual data in f to h,
 and assign h a unique memory address */
```

```
int[] h = new int[f.length];
arrayCopy(f, h);

// print memory addresses
print("the memory address f points to is " + f +"\n");
print("the memory address g points to is " + g +"\n");
print("the memory address h points to is " + h +"\n");

// change data in g array and print data in f & h arrays
g[0] = 23;
print("\nf array:\n");
println(f);
print("\nh array:\n");
println(h);
```

Returning to the Interactor class, the line p.registerMouseEvent(this); near the bottom of the init() method allows Processing mouse events to be handled within this class. It might also seem possible, to more experienced coders, to use Java classes for event handling, which theoretically may work. However, there are some potential issues when trying to do this, which you can read about here: http://dev.processing.org/libraries/basics.html.

The overloaded addTo() methods let VizObj objects be added dynamically to the objBin ArrayList, mentioned earlier. The method mouseEvent(MouseEvent event) needs to be included in the class to receive Processing mouse events. I included all the different mouse events in the switch statement, though I only use MouseEvent.MOUSE_PRESSED, MouseEvent.MOUSE_RELEASED, and MouseEvent.MOUSE_DRAGGED. When a user presses down with the mouse over a VizObj object, a time stamp and location are recorded. The user can then drag the mouse, and the VizObj object will rotate accordingly based on the distance dragged. When the user releases the mouse both the distance dragged and time (between press and release) are used to calculate the speed to rotate the object(s). I also use a damping variable to slowly bring the object to rest. The class includes default dynamics values, as well as a setDynamics(float rotSpd, float damping) method that allows you to change these values.

The rest of the class should be self-explanatory, with methods that handle rotation, mouse hover effects, message retrieval, and updating the vertex arrays. Notice that the rotation calculations in the rot(float tx, float ty) method are essentially the same ones we looked at in the VizObj.java class. Next, we'll add the rest of the VizObj subclasses to the sketch.

Icosahedron.java

You surely know the routine by now—create a new tab named "`Icosahedron.java`" in the current sketch and add the following code:

```java
/**
 * Data Visualizer
 * Icosahedron.java class
 * By Ira Greenberg <br />
 * The Essential Guide to Processing for Flash Developers,
 * Friends of ED, 2009
 */

import processing.core.*;

public class Icosahedron extends VizObj{

  private PVector[] terminals = new PVector[2];
  private PVector[] topPent = new PVector[5];
  private PVector[] bottomPent = new PVector[5];

  // default constructor
  public Icosahedron(){
  }

  // constructor
  public Icosahedron(PApplet p, float radius){
    super(p, radius);
    init();
  }

  // required implementation - calculates geometry
  public void init(){

    float theta = 0.0f;
```

```
float dist1 = 0.0f;
float dist2 = 0.0f;
float triHt = 0.0f;
float phi = p.TWO_PI/5.0f;

// treat vecs as a stacked 1D array.
vecs = new PVector[terminals.length + topPent.length + bottomPent.length];
dist2 = p.dist(p.cos(0)*radius, p.sin(0)*radius, p.cos(phi)*radius,  p.sin(phi)*radius);
dist1 = (float)(Math.sqrt(((dist2*dist2)-(radius*radius))));
triHt = (float)(Math.sqrt((dist2*dist2)-((dist2/2)*(dist2/2))));

terminals[0] = new PVector(loc.x, loc.y, loc.z + triHt/2.0f+dist1);
terminals[1] = new PVector(loc.x, loc.y, loc.z -(triHt/2.0f+dist1));
vecs[0] = terminals[0];
vecs[1] = terminals[1];

for (int i=0; i<topPent.length; i++){
  topPent[i] = new PVector(loc.x + p.cos(theta)*radius, loc.y + p.sin(theta)*↵
     radius, loc.z + triHt/2.0f);
  vecs[terminals.length+i] = topPent[i];
  theta+=phi;
}

theta = p.PI + phi;
for (int i=0; i<topPent.length; i++){
  bottomPent[i] = new PVector(loc.x + p.cos(theta)*radius, loc.y + ↵
     p.sin(theta)*radius, loc.z -triHt/2.0f);
  vecs[terminals.length+topPent.length + i] = bottomPent[i];
  theta+=phi;
}
}

// required implementation - draws geometry
```

```
public void create(PVector[] finalVecs){
  this.finalVecs = finalVecs;
  p.fill(r, g, b);
  int pos1 = terminals.length;
  int pos2 = terminals.length + topPent.length;
  p.beginShape(p.TRIANGLES);
  for (int i=0; i<topPent.length; i++){
    // icosahedron top
    if (i<topPent.length-1){
      p.vertex(finalVecs[pos1 + i].x, finalVecs[pos1 + i].y, finalVecs[pos1 + i].z);
      p.vertex(finalVecs[0].x, finalVecs[0].y, finalVecs[0].z);
      p.vertex(finalVecs[pos1 + i+1].x, finalVecs[pos1 + i+1].y, finalVecs[pos1 + i+1].z);
    }
    else {
      p.vertex(finalVecs[pos1 + i].x, finalVecs[pos1 + i].y, finalVecs[pos1 + i].z);
      p.vertex(finalVecs[0].x, finalVecs[0].y, finalVecs[0].z);
      p.vertex(finalVecs[pos1].x, finalVecs[pos1].y, finalVecs[pos1].z);
    }

    // icosahedron bottom
    if (i<bottomPent.length-1){
      p.vertex(finalVecs[pos2 + i].x, finalVecs[pos2 + i].y, finalVecs[pos2 + i].z);
      p.vertex(finalVecs[1].x, finalVecs[1].y, finalVecs[1].z);
      p.vertex(finalVecs[pos2 + i + 1].x, finalVecs[pos2 + i + 1].y, ↵
          finalVecs[pos2 + i + 1].z);
    }
    else {
      p.vertex(finalVecs[pos2 + i].x, finalVecs[pos2 + i].y, finalVecs[pos2 + i].z);
      p.vertex(finalVecs[1].x, finalVecs[1].y, finalVecs[1].z);
      p.vertex(finalVecs[pos2].x, finalVecs[pos2].y, finalVecs[pos2].z);
    }
  }
```

```
// icosahedron body
for (int i=0; i<topPent.length; i++){
  if (i<topPent.length-2){
    p.vertex(finalVecs[pos1 + i].x, finalVecs[pos1 + i].y, finalVecs[pos1 + i].z);
    p.vertex(finalVecs[pos2 + i + 1].x, finalVecs[pos2 + i + 1].y, finalVecs[pos2 + ↩
        i + 1].z);
    p.vertex(finalVecs[pos2 + i + 2].x, finalVecs[pos2 + i + 2].y, finalVecs[pos2 + ↩
        i + 2].z);


    p.vertex(finalVecs[pos2 + i + 2].x, finalVecs[pos2 + i + 2].y, finalVecs[pos2 + ↩
        i + 2].z);
    p.vertex(finalVecs[pos1 + i].x, finalVecs[pos1 + i].y, finalVecs[pos1 + i].z);
    p.vertex(finalVecs[pos1 + i+1].x, finalVecs[pos1 + i+1].y, finalVecs[pos1 + i+1].z);
  }
  else if (i==topPent.length-2){
    p.vertex(finalVecs[pos1 + i].x, finalVecs[pos1 + i].y, finalVecs[pos1 + i].z);
    p.vertex(finalVecs[pos2 + i + 1].x, finalVecs[pos2 + i + 1].y, finalVecs[pos2 + ↩
        i + 1].z);
    p.vertex(finalVecs[pos2].x, finalVecs[pos2].y, finalVecs[pos2].z);


    p.vertex(finalVecs[pos2].x, finalVecs[pos2].y, finalVecs[pos2].z);
    p.vertex(finalVecs[pos1 + i].x, finalVecs[pos1 + i].y, finalVecs[pos1 + i].z);
    p.vertex(finalVecs[pos1 + i+1].x, finalVecs[pos1 + i+1].y, finalVecs[pos1 + i+1].z);
  }
  else if (i==topPent.length-1){
    p.vertex(finalVecs[pos1 + i].x, finalVecs[pos1 + i].y, finalVecs[pos1 + i].z);
    p.vertex(finalVecs[pos2].x, finalVecs[pos2].y, finalVecs[pos2].z);
    p.vertex(finalVecs[pos2 + 1].x, finalVecs[pos2 + 1].y, finalVecs[pos2 + 1].z);


    p.vertex(finalVecs[pos2 + 1].x, finalVecs[pos2 + 1].y, finalVecs[pos2 + 1].z);
    p.vertex(finalVecs[pos1 + i].x, finalVecs[pos1 + i].y, finalVecs[pos1 + i].z);
    p.vertex(finalVecs[pos1].x, finalVecs[pos1].y, finalVecs[pos1].z);
```

```
    }
  }
  p.endShape();
}


// For use outside Interactor.java class
public void create(){
  int pos1 = terminals.length;
  int pos2 = terminals.length + topPent.length;
  p.beginShape(p.TRIANGLES);
  for (int i=0; i<topPent.length; i++){
    // icosahedron top
    if (i<topPent.length-1){
      p.vertex(vecs[pos1 + i].x, vecs[pos1 + i].y, vecs[pos1 + i].z);
      p.vertex(vecs[0].x, vecs[0].y, vecs[0].z);
      p.vertex(vecs[pos1 + i+1].x, vecs[pos1 + i+1].y, vecs[pos1 + i+1].z);
    }
    else {
      p.vertex(vecs[pos1 + i].x, vecs[pos1 + i].y, vecs[pos1 + i].z);
      p.vertex(vecs[0].x, vecs[0].y, vecs[0].z);
      p.vertex(vecs[pos1].x, vecs[pos1].y, vecs[pos1].z);
    }


    // icosahedron bottom
    if (i<bottomPent.length-1){
      p.vertex(vecs[pos2 + i].x, vecs[pos2 + i].y, vecs[pos2 + i].z);
      p.vertex(vecs[1].x, vecs[1].y, vecs[1].z);
      p.vertex(vecs[pos2 + i + 1].x, vecs[pos2 + i + 1].y, vecs[pos2 + i + 1].z);
    }
    else {
      p.vertex(vecs[pos2 + i].x, vecs[pos2 + i].y, vecs[pos2 + i].z);
      p.vertex(vecs[1].x, vecs[1].y, vecs[1].z);
      p.vertex(vecs[pos2].x, vecs[pos2].y, vecs[pos2].z);
    }
  }
```

```
    // icosahedron body
    for (int i=0; i<topPent.length; i++){
      if (i<topPent.length-2){
        p.vertex(vecs[pos1 + i].x, vecs[pos1 + i].y, vecs[pos1 + i].z);
        p.vertex(vecs[pos2 + i + 1].x, vecs[pos2 + i + 1].y, vecs[pos2 + i + 1].z);
        p.vertex(vecs[pos2 + i + 2].x, vecs[pos2 + i + 2].y, vecs[pos2 + i + 2].z);

        p.vertex(vecs[pos2 + i + 2].x, vecs[pos2 + i + 2].y, vecs[pos2 + i + 2].z);
        p.vertex(vecs[pos1 + i].x, vecs[pos1 + i].y, vecs[pos1 + i].z);
        p.vertex(vecs[pos1 + i+1].x, vecs[pos1 + i+1].y, vecs[pos1 + i+1].z);
      }
      else if (i==topPent.length-2){
        p.vertex(vecs[pos1 + i].x, vecs[pos1 + i].y, vecs[pos1 + i].z);
        p.vertex(vecs[pos2 + i + 1].x, vecs[pos2 + i + 1].y, vecs[pos2 + i + 1].z);
        p.vertex(vecs[pos2].x, vecs[pos2].y, vecs[pos2].z);

        p.vertex(vecs[pos2].x, vecs[pos2].y, vecs[pos2].z);
        p.vertex(vecs[pos1 + i].x, vecs[pos1 + i].y, vecs[pos1 + i].z);
        p.vertex(vecs[pos1 + i+1].x, vecs[pos1 + i+1].y, vecs[pos1 + i+1].z);
      }
      else if (i==topPent.length-1){
        p.vertex(vecs[pos1 + i].x, vecs[pos1 + i].y, vecs[pos1 + i].z);
        p.vertex(vecs[pos2].x, vecs[pos2].y, vecs[pos2].z);
        p.vertex(vecs[pos2 + 1].x, vecs[pos2 + 1].y, vecs[pos2 + 1].z);

        p.vertex(vecs[pos2 + 1].x, vecs[pos2 + 1].y, vecs[pos2 + 1].z);
        p.vertex(vecs[pos1 + i].x, vecs[pos1 + i].y, vecs[pos1 + i].z);
        p.vertex(vecs[pos1].x, vecs[pos1].y, vecs[pos1].z);
      }
    }
    p.endShape();
  }
}
```

Alright, I admit it, I like icosahedra. The icosahedron is the top dog of the platonic solids, with 20 symmetrical faces (all equilateral triangles). Interestingly, according to Wikipedia many viruses have the shape of the icosahedron (http://en.wikipedia.org/wiki/Icosahedron, October 4, 2009, 14:15). Coding an icosahedron is not as complex as you might think. The trick to constructing one, according to my self-discovered approach, is to notice what you get if you divide the form into a top, bottom, and middle and then throw away the middle (shown in Figure 8-3).

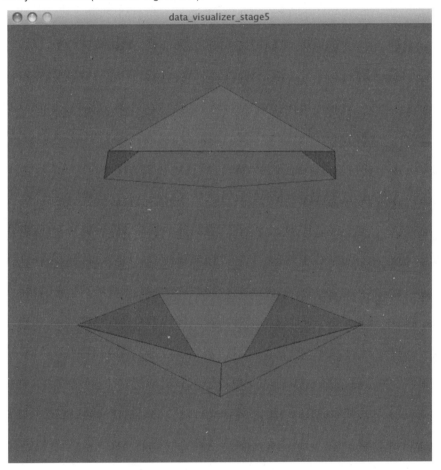

Figure 8-3. Anatomy of an icosahedron

If it's not obvious, you have two pentagonal domes, one rotated relative to the other by half the rotation angle of a pentagon, which we know is 360/5 (or technically TWO_PI/5). So the offset rotation of one of the domes to the other is 36 degrees. Once you have this part solved, you simply patch the middle with triangles. To create the domes by hand, you could begin with a pentagon and then take each side and make an equilateral triangle based on that length. Place the five triangles on the pentagon, so the bottom of each triangle is aligned to a side of the pentagon; then angle the triangles up so they meet at a point, which is the top of the dome. To code this, I found it easier to use a little trig to figure out the location of the terminal point at the height of the dome, based on the radius of the pentagon. The right triangle I formed to solve for the height is shown in Figure 8-4. Once I had the height I programmatically moved around the pentagon creating triangles with contiguous vertices and the terminal vertex. The other dome was then done the same way, only inverting the height, and the middle was then surfaced using the vertices of the top and bottom dome, as mentioned earlier.

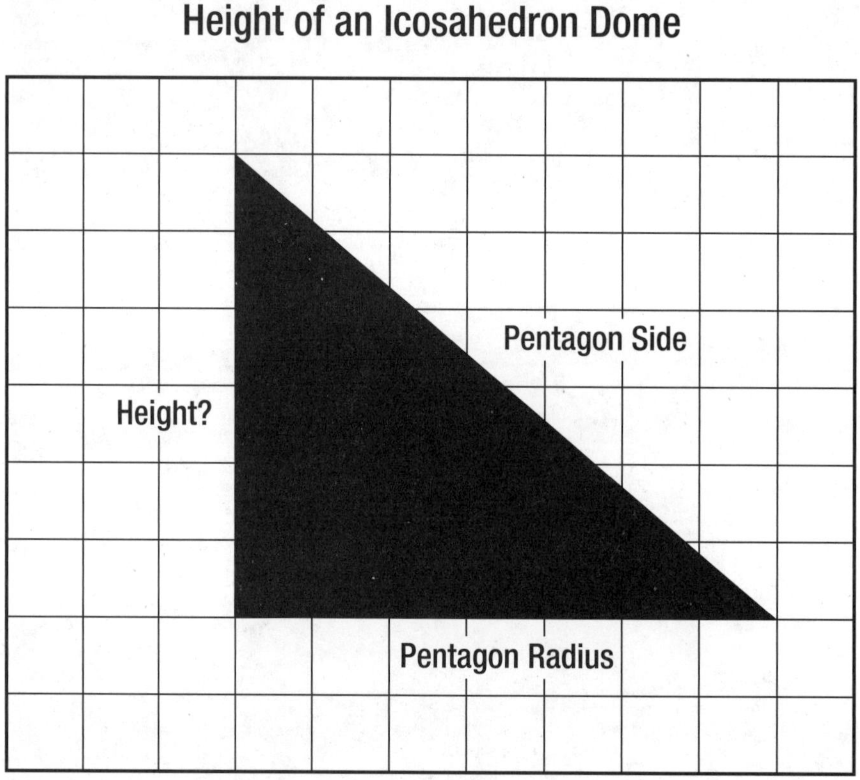

Height of an Icosahedron Dome

Figure 8-4. Calculating the height of an icosahedron dome

To render the icosahedron, shown in Figure 8-5, replace the code in the main tab of the current sketch with the following:

```
/**
 * Data Visualizer-Stage 5
 * Main Processing Tab
 * By Ira Greenberg <br />
```

```
 * The Essential Guide to Processing for Flash Developers,
 * Friends of ED, 2009
 */

import processing.opengl.*;

Interactor ia;

void setup(){
  size(600, 600, OPENGL);
  ia = new Interactor();
  Icosahedron icos = new Icosahedron(this, 225);
  icos.initRGB(45, 117, 130);
  icos.setMouseEnabled(true);
  ia.addTo(icos);
  noStroke();
}

void draw() {
  background(75);
  translate(width/2, height/2, -100);
  lights();
  ia.run();
}
```

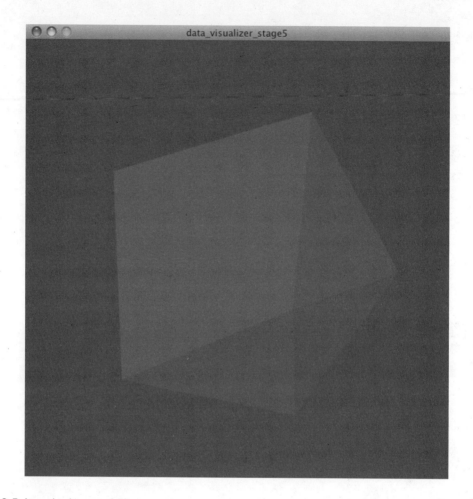

Figure 8-5. Icosahedron rendering

Cylinder.java

I'll use small cylinders to join blocks to the icosahedra. Cylinders are simply extruded circles. The easiest way to code one is to create two parallel circles the height of the cylinder apart and then connect the vertices. I connected the vertices with quads, but of course you could also use triangles. Here's the code, which should be put in a new tab named "`Cylinder.java`".

```
/**
 * Data Visualizer
 * Cylinder.java class
 * By Ira Greenberg <br />
```

```
 * The Essential Guide to Processing for Flash Developers,
 * Friends of ED, 2009
 */

import processing.core.*;

public class Cylinder extends VizObj{

  private int detail = 12;

  // default constructor
  public Cylinder(){
  }

  // constructor
  public Cylinder(PApplet p){
    super(p);
    init();
  }

  // constructor
  public Cylinder(PApplet p, float w, float h){
    super(p, w, h);
    init();
  }

  // constructor
  public Cylinder(PApplet p, float w, float h, int detail){
    super(p, w, h);
    this.detail = detail;
    init();
  }

  // required implementation - calculates geometry
```

```
protected void init(){
  float theta = 0.0f;
  float y = -h/2;
  vecs = new PVector[detail*2];
  for (int i=0; i<vecs.length; i++){
    vecs[i] = new PVector(loc.x + p.sin(theta)*w, loc.y + y, loc.z + p.cos(theta)*w);
    theta += p.TWO_PI/(vecs.length/2);
    if (i == vecs.length/2-1){
      y += h;
      theta = 0.0f;
    }
  }
}


// required implementation - draws geometry
public void create(PVector[] finalVecs){
  this.finalVecs = finalVecs;
  p.fill(r, g, b);
  int id = finalVecs.length/2;
  p.beginShape(p.QUADS);
  for (int i=1; i<finalVecs.length/2; i++){

    p.vertex(finalVecs[i-1].x, finalVecs[i-1].y, finalVecs[i-1].z);
    p.vertex(finalVecs[i].x, finalVecs[i].y, finalVecs[i].z);
    p.vertex(finalVecs[id + i].x, finalVecs[id + i].y, finalVecs[id + i].z);
    p.vertex(finalVecs[id + i-1].x, finalVecs[id +i-1].y, finalVecs[id +i-1].z);

    if (i == finalVecs.length/2-1){
      p.vertex(finalVecs[i].x, finalVecs[i].y, finalVecs[i].z);
      p.vertex(finalVecs[0].x, finalVecs[0].y, finalVecs[0].z);
      p.vertex(finalVecs[id].x, finalVecs[id].y, finalVecs[id].z);
      p.vertex(finalVecs[id + i].x, finalVecs[id +i].y, finalVecs[id +i].z);
    }
  }
```

```
  p.endShape();

  // seal cap
  p.beginShape();
  for (int i=0; i<finalVecs.length/2; i++){
    p.vertex(finalVecs[i].x, finalVecs[i].y, finalVecs[i].z);
  }
  p.endShape(p.CLOSE);

  // seal cap
  p.beginShape();
  for (int i=finalVecs.length/2; i<finalVecs.length; i++){
    p.vertex(finalVecs[i].x, finalVecs[i].y, finalVecs[i].z);
  }
  p.endShape(p.CLOSE);
}

// For use outside Interactor.java class
public void create(){
  int id = vecs.length/2;
  p.beginShape(p.QUADS);
  for (int i=1; i<vecs.length/2; i++){

    p.vertex(vecs[i-1].x, vecs[i-1].y, vecs[i-1].z);
    p.vertex(vecs[i].x, vecs[i].y, vecs[i].z);
    p.vertex(vecs[id + i].x, vecs[id + i].y, vecs[id + i].z);
    p.vertex(vecs[id + i-1].x, vecs[id +i-1].y, vecs[id +i-1].z);

    if (i == vecs.length/2-1){
      p.vertex(vecs[i].x, vecs[i].y, vecs[i].z);
      p.vertex(vecs[0].x, vecs[0].y, vecs[0].z);
      p.vertex(vecs[id].x, vecs[id].y, vecs[id].z);
      p.vertex(vecs[id + i].x, vecs[id +i].y, vecs[id +i].z);
    }
```

```
    }
    p.endShape();

    // seal cap
    p.beginShape();
    for (int i=0; i<vecs.length/2; i++){
      p.vertex(vecs[i].x, vecs[i].y, vecs[i].z);
    }
    p.endShape(p.CLOSE);

    // seal cap
    p.beginShape();
    for (int i=vecs.length/2; i<vecs.length; i++){
      p.vertex(vecs[i].x, vecs[i].y, vecs[i].z);
    }
    p.endShape(p.CLOSE);
  }


  // updates vertices and calculates joint position to add blocks
  protected void update(){
    joint = new PVector();
    for (int i=vecs.length/2-1; i<vecs.length; i++){
      joint.add(vecs[i]);
    }
    joint.div(vecs.length/2);
    joint.add(loc);

    // add location to vertices
    for (int i=0; i<vecs.length; i++){
      vecs[i].add(loc);
    }
  }
}
```

Again, the Interactor class is smart and can render and control any VizObj subclass. For example, replace the code in the main tab of the current sketch with the following and run the sketch; you should see something similar to Figure 8-6.

```
/**
 * Data Visualizer-Stage 6
 * Main Processing Tab
 * By Ira Greenberg <br />
 * The Essential Guide to Processing for Flash Developers,
 * Friends of ED, 2009
 */


import processing.opengl.*;


Interactor ia;


void setup(){
  size(600, 600, OPENGL);
  ia = new Interactor();
  VizObj[] nodes = new Icosahedron[6];
  VizObj[] bonds = new Cylinder[nodes.length];


  // Main central block
  VizObj hub = new Block(this, 80);
  hub.initRGB(160, 80, 30);
  ia.addTo(hub);
  hub.setMouseEnabled(true);


  float theta = 0.0;
  float rotVal = PI/2;
  for (int i=0; i<nodes.length; i++){
    // connecting bonds between block and icosahedron nodes
    bonds[i] = new Cylinder(this, 14, 210, 18);
    // icosahedra
```

```
    nodes[i] = new Icosahedron(this, 68);
    bonds[i].initRGB(120, 120, 120);
    nodes[i].initRGB(int(random(255)), int(random(255)), int(random(255)));
    // shift bonds to edge of block
    PVector bondShift = new PVector(0, bonds[i].h/2+hub.radius, 0);
    bonds[i].setLoc(bondShift);
    // move node to end of each bond
    nodes[i].setLoc(bonds[i].getJoint());
    // rotate bonds and nodes around block
    if (i<4){
      bonds[i].setRot(new PVector(theta, 0, 0));
      nodes[i].setRot(new PVector(theta, 0, 0));
      theta += rotVal;
    }
    else {
      theta = 0;
      theta += rotVal;
      bonds[i].setRot(new PVector(0, 0, theta));
      nodes[i].setRot(new PVector(0, 0, theta));
      rotVal *= 3;
    }
    nodes[i].setMouseEnabled(true);

    ia.addTo(bonds[i]);
    ia.addTo(nodes[i]);
  }
  noStroke();
}

void draw() {
  background(75);
  translate(width/2, height/2, -100);
  lights();
  ia.run();
}
```

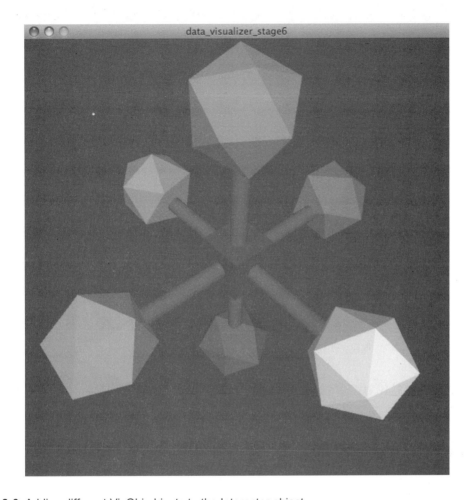

Figure 8-6. Adding different VizObj objects to the Interactor object

Eventually, we'll create a `Visualizer` class to encapsulate what we did in the main tab. Notice that I declared all the VizObj subclass references as type `VizObj` (e.g., `VizObj hub`) not their individually declared types (e.g., `Block hub`). I can do this because of the magic of inheritance and polymorphism, where a subclass object can be assigned to a reference of its superclass type (e.g. superclass obj = new subclass()). After instantiating the objects, I set their color and mouse detection capabilities; the latter is handled by the method `setMouseEnbaled(true)`—it's disabled by default—which I did with the hub and nodes but not the bonds. I also needed to do a little math to rotate the bonds to attach properly to each face of the block. Since the angles are orthogonal to each other (at 90 degrees), it just required a bunch of `PI/2` rotations. I also specified the objects' locations using the `setLoc()` methods and the attachment point for each bond using the `getJoint()` property, which returns the center point location on one of the cylinder ends. (This method is only implemented in the `Cylinder` class). The last step is adding the individual VizObj objects to the `Interactor` object, with its `addTo()` method. Again, you can add as many objects as you want, and the Interactor class will very hospitably manage them all. Next, we'll add our last VizObj subclass, Helix.java.

Helix.java

Create a new tab named "**Helix.java**" and enter the following code:

```java
/**
 * Data Visualizer
 * Helix.java class
 * By Ira Greenberg <br />
 * The Essential Guide to Processing for Flash Developers,
 * Friends of ED, 2009
 */

import processing.core.*;

public class Helix extends VizObj{

  //instance properties with default values
  private int rots = 1, helixDetail = 24;
  protected PVector[] path;
  protected float tubeRadius = 4.0f;
  private int tubeDetail = 12;

  // default constructor
  public Helix(){
  }

  // constructor
  public Helix(PApplet p){
    super(p);
    init();
  }
```

```
// constructor
public Helix(PApplet p, float w, float h, int rots){
  super(p, w, h);
  this.rots = rots;
  init();
}


// constructor
public Helix(PApplet p, float w, float h, int rots, int helixDetail){
  super(p, w, h);
  this.rots = rots;
  this.helixDetail = helixDetail;
  init();
}


// constructor
public Helix(PApplet p, float w, float h, int rots, int helixDetail, ↵
    float tubeRadius, int tubeDetail){
  super(p, w, h);
  this.rots = rots;
  this.helixDetail = helixDetail;
  this.tubeRadius = tubeRadius;
  this.tubeDetail = tubeDetail;
  init();
}


// required implementation - calculates geometry
protected void init(){
  // generate spiral path for helix
  path = new PVector[helixDetail];
  vecs = new PVector[path.length*tubeDetail];
  float helixTheta = 0.0f;
  float offset = h/helixDetail;
```

```
    for (int i=0; i<path.length; i++){
      path[i] = new PVector(p.sin(helixTheta)*w/2.0f, -h/2.0f+offset*i, ↵
        p.cos(helixTheta)*w/2.0f);
      float tubeTheta = 0.0f;
      for (int j=0; j<tubeDetail; j++){
        // create cross-sections around helix, with uncorrected y-rotation
        PVector temp = new PVector(0, p.cos(tubeTheta)*tubeRadius, ↵
          p.sin(tubeTheta)*tubeRadius);
        // correct for y rotation of cross-section.
        PVector fixed = new PVector(p.sin(helixTheta)*temp.z - p.cos(helixTheta)* ↵
          temp.x, temp.y, p.cos(helixTheta)*temp.z + p.sin(helixTheta)*temp.x);
        // populate vecs array with cross-section vertices, at Path vertex positions.
        vecs[tubeDetail*i + j] = new PVector(path[i].x + fixed.x, path[i].y + ↵
          fixed.y, path[i].z + fixed.z);
        tubeTheta += p.TWO_PI/tubeDetail;
      }
      helixTheta += p.TWO_PI/helixDetail*rots;
    }
  }


  /* required implementation - draws geometry
   patch helix body with quads, includes
   solid and gradient rendering options */
  public void create(PVector[] finalVecs){
    this.finalVecs = finalVecs;
    // gradient rendering option
    if (arrR != null && arrG != null && arrB != null ){
      // gradient start cap
      p.fill(arrR[0], arrG[0], arrB[0]);
      p.beginShape();
      for (int i=0; i<tubeDetail; i++){
        p.vertex(finalVecs[i].x, finalVecs[i].y, finalVecs[i].z);
```

```
    }
    p.endShape(p.CLOSE);
    // body
    p.beginShape(p.QUADS);
    for (int i=1; i<path.length; i++){
      for (int j=1; j<tubeDetail; j++){
        if (j == tubeDetail-1){
          p.fill(arrR[i-1], arrG[i-1], arrB[i-1]);
          p.vertex(finalVecs[tubeDetail*(i-1)+(j-1)].x, finalVecs[tubeDetail*(i-1)+↩
              (j-1)].y, finalVecs[tubeDetail*(i-1)+(j-1)].z);
          p.fill(arrR[i], arrG[i], arrB[i]);
          p.vertex(finalVecs[tubeDetail*(i)+(j-1)].x, finalVecs[tubeDetail*(i)+↩
              (j-1)].y, finalVecs[tubeDetail*(i)+(j-1)].z);
          p.fill(arrR[i], arrG[i], arrB[i]);
          p.vertex(finalVecs[tubeDetail*(i)+(0)].x, finalVecs[tubeDetail*(i)+(0)].y,↩
              finalVecs[tubeDetail*(i)+(0)].z);
          p.fill(arrR[i-1], arrG[i-1], arrB[i-1]);
          p.vertex(finalVecs[tubeDetail*(i-1)+(0)].x, finalVecs[tubeDetail*(i-1)+↩
              (0)].y, finalVecs[tubeDetail*(i-1)+(0)].z);
        }
        p.fill(arrR[i-1], arrG[i-1], arrB[i-1]);
        p.vertex(finalVecs[tubeDetail*(i-1)+(j-1)].x, finalVecs[tubeDetail*(i-1)+↩
            (j-1)].y, finalVecs[tubeDetail*(i-1)+(j-1)].z);
        p.fill(arrR[i], arrG[i], arrB[i]);
        p.vertex(finalVecs[tubeDetail*(i)+(j-1)].x, finalVecs[tubeDetail*(i)+(j-1)].y, ↩
            finalVecs[tubeDetail*(i)+(j-1)].z);
        p.fill(arrR[i], arrG[i], arrB[i]);
        p.vertex(finalVecs[tubeDetail*(i)+(j)].x, finalVecs[tubeDetail*(i)+(j)].y, ↩
            finalVecs[tubeDetail*(i)+(j)].z);
        p.fill(arrR[i-1], arrG[i-1], arrB[i-1]);
        p.vertex(finalVecs[tubeDetail*(i-1)+(j)].x, finalVecs[tubeDetail*(i-1)+(j)].y, ↩
            finalVecs[tubeDetail*(i-1)+(j)].z);
```

461

```
    }
  }
  p.endShape();
  // gradient end cap
  p.beginShape();
  p.fill(arrR[arrR.length-1], arrG[arrG.length-1], arrB[arrB.length-1]);
  for (int i=0; i<tubeDetail; i++){
    int j = tubeDetail*(path.length-1) + i;
    p.vertex(finalVecs[j].x, finalVecs[j].y, finalVecs[j].z);
  }
  p.endShape(p.CLOSE);
}
else {
  // BEGIN solid color rendering
  // solid start cap
  p.fill(r, g, b);
  p.beginShape();
  for (int i=0; i<tubeDetail; i++){
    p.vertex(finalVecs[i].x, finalVecs[i].y, finalVecs[i].z);
  }
  p.endShape(p.CLOSE);
  // body
  p.beginShape(p.QUADS);
  for (int i=1; i<path.length; i++){
    for (int j=1; j<tubeDetail; j++){
      if (j == tubeDetail-1){
        p.vertex(finalVecs[tubeDetail*(i-1)+(j-1)].x, finalVecs[tubeDetail*(i-1)+↩
            (j-1)].y, finalVecs[tubeDetail*(i-1)+(j-1)].z);
        p.vertex(finalVecs[tubeDetail*(i)+(j-1)].x, finalVecs[tubeDetail*(i)+↩
            (j-1)].y, finalVecs[tubeDetail*(i)+(j-1)].z);
        p.vertex(finalVecs[tubeDetail*(i)+(0)].x, finalVecs[tubeDetail*(i)+(0)].y, ↩
            finalVecs[tubeDetail*(i)+(0)].z);
```

```
            p.vertex(finalVecs[tubeDetail*(i-1)+(0)].x, finalVecs[tubeDetail*(i-1)+↩
                (0)].y, finalVecs[tubeDetail*(i-1)+(0)].z);
        }
        p.vertex(finalVecs[tubeDetail*(i-1)+(j-1)].x, finalVecs[tubeDetail*(i-1)+↩
            (j-1)].y, finalVecs[tubeDetail*(i-1)+(j-1)].z);
        p.vertex(finalVecs[tubeDetail*(i)+(j-1)].x, finalVecs[tubeDetail*(i)+(j-1)].y, ↩
            finalVecs[tubeDetail*(i)+(j-1)].z);
        p.vertex(finalVecs[tubeDetail*(i)+(j)].x, finalVecs[tubeDetail*(i)+(j)].y, ↩
            finalVecs[tubeDetail*(i)+(j)].z);
p.vertex(finalVecs[tubeDetail*(i-1)+(j)].x, finalVecs[tubeDetail*(i-1)+(j)].y, ↩
    finalVecs[tubeDetail*(i-1)+(j)].z);
        }
    }
    p.endShape();
    // solid end cap
    p.beginShape();
    p.fill(r, g, b);
    for (int i=0; i<tubeDetail; i++){
      int j = tubeDetail*(path.length-1) + i;
      p.vertex(finalVecs[j].x, finalVecs[j].y, finalVecs[j].z);
    }
    p.endShape(p.CLOSE);
  }
}


// For use outside Interactor.java class
public void create(){
  // patch helix body with quads
  p.beginShape(p.QUADS);
  for (int i=1; i<path.length; i++){
    for (int j=1; j<tubeDetail; j++){
      if (j == tubeDetail-1){
```

```
      p.vertex(vecs[tubeDetail*(i-1)+(j-1)].x, vecs[tubeDetail*(i-1)+(j-1)].y, ⏎
          vecs[tubeDetail*(i-1)+(j-1)].z);
      p.vertex(vecs[tubeDetail*(i)+(j-1)].x, vecs[tubeDetail*(i)+(j-1)].y, ⏎
          vecs[tubeDetail*(i)+(j-1)].z);
      p.vertex(vecs[tubeDetail*(i)+(0)].x, vecs[tubeDetail*(i)+(0)].y, ⏎
          vecs[tubeDetail*(i)+(0)].z);
      p.vertex(vecs[tubeDetail*(i-1)+(0)].x, vecs[tubeDetail*(i-1)+(0)].y, ⏎
          vecs[tubeDetail*(i-1)+(0)].z);
    }
    p.vertex(vecs[tubeDetail*(i-1)+(j-1)].x, vecs[tubeDetail*(i-1)+(j-1)].y, ⏎
        vecs[tubeDetail*(i-1)+(j-1)].z);
    p.vertex(vecs[tubeDetail*(i)+(j-1)].x, vecs[tubeDetail*(i)+(j-1)].y, ⏎
        vecs[tubeDetail*(i)+(j-1)].z);
    p.vertex(vecs[tubeDetail*(i)+(j)].x, vecs[tubeDetail*(i)+(j)].y, ⏎
        vecs[tubeDetail*(i)+(j)].z);
    p.vertex(vecs[tubeDetail*(i-1)+(j)].x, vecs[tubeDetail*(i-1)+(j)].y, ⏎
        vecs[tubeDetail*(i-1)+(j)].z);
  }
}
p.endShape();

// add end caps
p.beginShape();
for (int i=0; i<tubeDetail; i++){
  p.vertex(vecs[i].x, vecs[i].y, vecs[i].z);
}
p.endShape(p.CLOSE);

p.beginShape();
for (int i=0; i<tubeDetail; i++){
  int j = tubeDetail*(path.length-1) + i;
```

```
      p.vertex(vecs[j].x, vecs[j].y, vecs[j].z);
    }
    p.endShape(p.CLOSE);
  }


  // returns number of vertices in path (spine of helix)
  public int getHelixDetail() {
    return helixDetail;
  }
}
```

The helix will function as the spine of the visualization. The class includes properties to control the helix's overall width and height, angle of rotation and the radius (thickness of the actual strand). The construction algorithm creates a path on which vertices forming elliptical cross-sections at each path vertex are calculated. Quads are then drawn between the cross-sectional vertices. Figure 8-7 illustrates the structure, showing front and top perspective views.

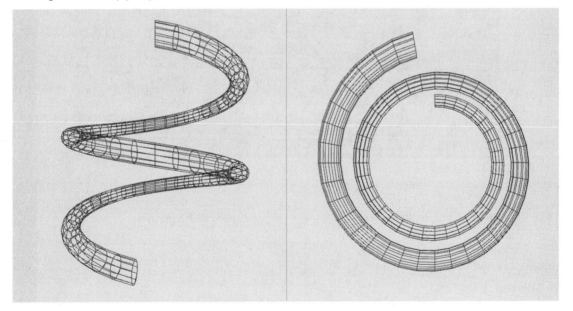

Figure 8-7. Helix wireframe showing front and top views

Figure 8-8 shows a rendering of a filled helix.

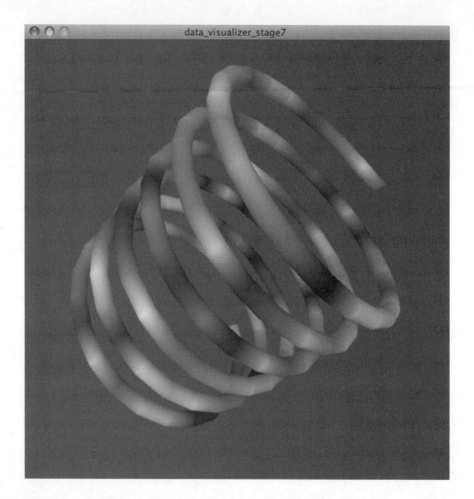

Figure 8-8. Helix solid rendering

To generate this yourself, replace the current code in the main tab with the following:

```
/**
 * Data Visualizer-Stage 7
 * Main Processing Tab
 * By Ira Greenberg <br />
 * The Essential Guide to Processing for Flash Developers,
 * Friends of ED, 2009
 */
```

```
import processing.opengl.*;

Interactor ia;

void setup(){
  size(600, 600, OPENGL);
  ia = new Interactor();

  Helix helix = new Helix(this, 380, 430, 6, 144, 13, 24);
  int[] r = new int[helix.getHelixDetail()];
  int[] g = new int[helix.getHelixDetail()];
  int[] b = new int[helix.getHelixDetail()];
  for (int i=0; i<helix.getHelixDetail(); i++){
    r[i] = int(random(255));
    g[i] = int(random(255));
    b[i] = int(random(255));
  }
  helix.initRGB(r, g, b);
  ia.addTo(helix);
  noStroke();
}


void draw() {
  background(75);
  translate(width/2, height/2, -100);
  lights();
  ia.run();
}
```

Perhaps seeing the rainbow gradient painted across the surface of the helix was surprising. In the final visualization we'll use this feature to show how the color data changes between the different widgets.

Looking back at the Helix.java code, the init() method is where the path and cross-section geometry is calculated. The trig rotations used are similar to what we looked at in the earlier rotation methods in both the VizObj and Interactor classes. Like the other VizObj subclasses, Helix has two create() methods, one for using a helix as a stand-alone object and one called from within the Interactor object. In addition,

I added a gradient option in the Helix class. Within the create(PVector[] finalVecs) method, notice the alternating p.fill() and vertex() calls. Working in 3D in Processing, you're able to specify color per vertex, and Processing then creates appropriate gradients between the vertices. The gradient feature in the Helix class is automatically implemented by passing in int arrays to the initRGB() call, rather than single int values (the latter produces a single fill color). However, be aware that when using the gradient option, the setMouseEnabled(true) method won't work. (It will work using the single fill color option.) Before we look at the final class, I recommend creating a couple helixes first and experimenting with different argument values.

Visualizer.java

The Visualizer class encapsulates a visualization concept. Ideally, if this were a more comprehensive library, in addition to more VizObj subclasses, there would be other Visualizer-type classes. It might also be a good idea to create a base Visualizer class and extend it, as I did with VizObj. However, as this is the final chapter and a long one at that, I'll leave these challenges to a motivated reader. In fact, I look forward to seeing such a library appear in the user-submitted section of processing.org.

You know the routine by now—create a new tab named "**Visualizer.java**" and enter the following code:

```
/**
 * Data Visualizer
 * Vizualizer.java class
 * By Ira Greenberg <br />
 * The Essential Guide to Processing for Flash Developers,
 * Friends of ED, 2009
 */


import processing.core.*;
import processing.xml.*;
import java.util.*;


public class Visualizer{

    private Interactor ia;
    private Helix helix;
    private Icosahedron[] icos;
    private Cylinder[][] bonds;
    private Block[][] cubes;
```

```
private PApplet p;
// for data
private int count;
private XMLElement[][] childNodes;
private XMLElement xml;
//text output
private PFont font;

// default constructor
public Visualizer(){
}

// constructor
public  Visualizer(PApplet p){
  this.p = p;
  ia = new Interactor();
  init();
}

// constructor
public Visualizer(PApplet p, XMLElement xml){
  this.p = p;
  this.xml = xml;
  ia = new Interactor();
  init();
}

// constructor
public  Visualizer(PApplet p, Interactor ia){
  this.p = p;
  this.ia = ia;
  init();
}
```

```
// update XML
public void setXML(XMLElement xml){
  this.xml = xml;
  init();
}


// initialize stuff
protected void init(){
  font = p.loadFont("Verdana-16.vlw");

  // get xml child count
  count = xml.getChildCount();
  //initialize and parse xml region data into arrays
  childNodes = new XMLElement[count][0];
  for (int i=0; i<count; i++){
    childNodes[i] = xml.getChild(i).getChildren();
  }

  // populate colors calculating weighted averages
  int avgR, avgG, avgB;
  int[]arrR = new int[count];
  int[]arrG = new int[count];
  int[]arrB = new int[count];
  int[][]cubeR = new int[count][0];
  int[][]cubeG = new int[count][0];
  int[][]cubeB = new int[count][0];
  int weightTotal = 0;
  for (int i=0; i<count; i++){
    // reset avgs.
    avgR = avgG = avgB = 0;
    weightTotal = 0;
    int len = childNodes[i].length;
    for (int j=0; j<len; j++){
      // color component values
```

```
    int r = childNodes[i][j].getIntAttribute("r");
    int g = childNodes[i][j].getIntAttribute("g");
    int b = childNodes[i][j].getIntAttribute("b");
    int weight = Integer.parseInt(childNodes[i][j].getContent());

    // create weighted avgs
    avgR += r*weight;
    avgG += g*weight;
    avgB += b*weight;
    weightTotal += weight;

    cubeR[i] = (int[])p.append(cubeR[i], r);
    cubeG[i] = (int[])p.append(cubeG[i], g);
    cubeB[i] = (int[])p.append(cubeB[i], b);

  }
  arrR[i] = avgR/weightTotal;
  arrG[i] = avgG/weightTotal;
  arrB[i] = avgB/weightTotal;
}

helix = new Helix(p, 325, 375, 2, count, 8, 36);
helix.initRGB(arrR,  arrG,  arrB);
icos = new Icosahedron[helix.path.length];
for (int i=0; i<helix.path.length; i++){
  icos[i] = new Icosahedron(p, 20);
  icos[i].initRGB(helix.arrR[i], helix.arrG[i], helix.arrB[i]);
  icos[i].setLoc(helix.path[i]);
  icos[i].setMouseEnabled(true);
  icos[i].setInfo(xml.getChild(i).getStringAttribute("name"));
}

bonds = new Cylinder[count][0];
cubes = new Block[count][0];
```

471

```
for (int i=0; i<count; i++){
  int len = childNodes[i].length;
  for (int j=0; j<len; j++){
    int sz = p.round(p.random(helix.tubeRadius-5, helix.tubeRadius+5));
    bonds[i] = (Cylinder[])p.append(bonds[i], new Cylinder(p, 2, 40));
    bonds[i][j].initRGB(120, 120, 120);
    /* Please note: order of operations of transformations is meaningful */
    // move to edge of icosahedron
    PVector bondShift = new PVector(0, bonds[i][j].h/2+icos[i].radius*.75f, 0);
    bonds[i][j].setLoc(bondShift);
    // angles to rotate bonds
    float theta = p.TWO_PI/len*j;  // around x-axis
    float phi = p.atan2(icos[i].loc.x, icos[i].loc.z); // around y-axis
    /* rotate bonds evenly around individual icosahedron
     and then again to align with vector to helix center */
    bonds[i][j].setRot(new PVector(theta, phi, 0));
    // move to each icosahedron
    bonds[i][j].setLoc(icos[i].loc);

    // add blocks
    int val = Integer.parseInt(childNodes[i][j].getContent());
    cubes[i] = (Block[])p.append(cubes[i], new Block(p, p.min(val, 25)));
    cubes[i][j].initRGB(cubeR[i][j], cubeG[i][j], cubeB[i][j]);
    cubes[i][j].setRot(new PVector(theta, phi, 0));

    // move to end of each bond
    cubes[i][j].setLoc(bonds[i][j].joint);
    cubes[i][j].setMouseEnabled(true);

    // set information that shows when mouse hover
    cubes[i][j].setInfo("color: "+ childNodes[i][j].getStringAttribute("name") + ↩
      "\n["+childNodes[i][j].getStringAttribute("r")+", " + ↩
      childNodes[i][j].getStringAttribute("g")+", "+ ↩
```

```
        childNodes[i][j].getStringAttribute("b")+ ⏎
        "]\n"+ childNodes[i][j].getContent()+ " units");
    }
  }


  /* add geometry to Interactor object
   to get transformed and rendered */
  ia.addTo(helix);
  ia.addTo(icos);
  ia.addTo(bonds);
  ia.addTo(cubes);
}


// starts visualizer
public void start(){
  ia.run();
  p.fill(0);
  p.textFont(font);
  p.textMode(p.SCREEN);
  p.text(ia.getVizObjInfo(), p.width-160, p.height-75);
  }
}
```

The main job of the Visualizer class is to assemble the visualization. In addition, it also handles data loading using Processing's very simple XML capabilities. Compared to ActionScript, Processing's XML approach is very barebones, which makes it also very simple to use. For example, to grab all the children in an XML doc, you would do something like this:

```
XMLElement xml  = new XMLElement(this, "path to XML doc here");
xml.getChildren();
```

The latest Processing XML API is here: http://processing.org/reference/XMLElement.html (November 7, 2009, 14:13). For an expanded developer's API, see http://dev.processing.org/reference/everything/javadoc/processing/xml/package-summary.html. (November 7, 2009, 14:22). If you still yearn for additional XML features, Java delivers all that and more, which you can read about here: http://www.vogella.de/articles/JavaXML/article.html (November 5, 2009, 17:00).

The XML data we'll use for the visualization is in the form

```
<Widget_color_popularity_2008>
        <product name="Widget A">
                <color name="silver" r="170" g="179" b="183">20</color>
                <color name="black" r="20" g="20" b="20">15</color>
                <color name="red" r="190" g="10" b="10">8</color>
                <color name="brown" r="108" g="60" b="30">11</color>
                <color name="blue" r="10" g="10" b="190">19</color>
                <color name="gold" r="190" g="140" b="10">10</color>
        </product>
        ( ------ data for 17 additional widgets go here ------)
</Widget_color_popularity_2008>
```

There are 18 widgets in all, and each widget is represented by an icosahedron attached to a helix. Off of each icosahedra are cubes attached by cylinders. The number of cubes is based on the number of widget colors as shown in the previous XML code for widget A. The size of each cube is based on the number of widgets in that cube color, listed within the XML as the value between the color tags (e.g., 20 for silver). The color of each icosahedron is determined by a weighted average of the surrounding cube colors. For example, based on the XML snippet, the red color component value for widget A is calculated with the weighted average expression

$$\frac{170(20)+20(15)+190(8)+108(11)+10(19)+190(10)}{20+15+8+11+19+10}$$

The color of the helix reflects the overall weighted averages, with a continuous gradient generated between the contiguous icosahedra. Finally, as users roll over the icosahedra and cubes, associated data from the XML doc. is output to the window.

I did also use a few new commands in the example

```
int weight = Integer.parseInt(childNodes[i][j].getContent());
```

and

```
textMode(SCREEN);
```

The former borrows some Java to force the returned String data into an integer, and the latter uses Processing's SCREEN constant to force the text output to be in front of everything else in the window, preventing the rotating nodes from obscuring the text.

To run the final example, you'll need to add the file "**widget_color_popularity.xml**" and the bitmap font "**Verdana-16.vlw**" into the current sketch's data directory. You can download these from the book's download area on the friends of ED site. You can also use a different font, by selecting "**Create Font**..." from the Tools menu; just be sure to change the line font = p.loadFont("Verdana-16.vlw"); to the new font you created. You can also create your own XML file by adhering to the structure in the XML snippet shown earlier and inventing your own widget data. The visualization is dynamically generated from the data, so the content can change as long as the overall nesting structure remains the same. (And, of course, you can also change the XML structure and edit the parsing methods in the Visualizer.java class.) Once you have the XML file and font loaded in the data directory, replace the code in the main tab with the following:

```
/**
 * Final Data Visualizer
 * Main Processing Tab
 * By Ira Greenberg <br />
 * The Essential Guide to Processing for Flash Developers,
 * Friends of ED, 2009
 */


import processing.opengl.*;


Visualizer vo;


void setup(){
  size(600, 600, OPENGL);
  // get data
  XMLElement xml = new XMLElement(this, "widget_color_popularity.xml");

  // instantiate Visualizer object
  vo = new Visualizer(this, xml);
  noStroke();
}


void draw(){
  background(75);
  translate(width/2, height/2, -100);
```

```
ambientLight(105, 105, 105);
lightSpecular(200, 200, 200);
directionalLight(250, 250, 250, 0, 1, -1);
specular(190, 190, 230);
shininess(25.0);

// start visualization
vo.start();
}
```

If the sketch ran successfully, you should have seen something similar to Figure 8-9. I added 3D lighting to create a more metallic and slick-looking object. When you roll over the cubes and icosahedron you should also see the data output as text at the bottom right corner of the screen. Finally, notice that by encapsulating the visualization concept in the Visualizer class (and event handling in the Interactor class), only a minimal amount of code is needed, in the main tab, to run the visualization.

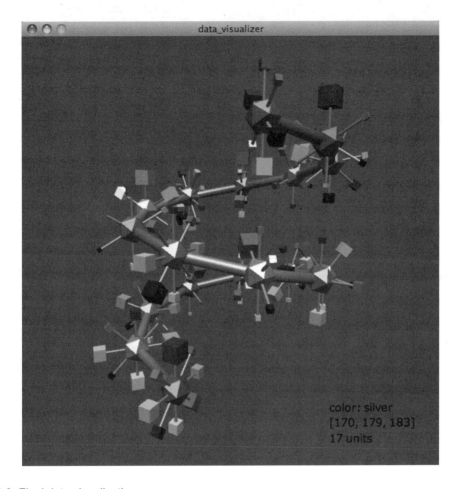

Figure 8-9. Final data visualization

Summary

Information visualization is an exciting area of research, with ample room for both serious data analysis and aesthetic experimentation. The chapter example probably emphasized the latter over the former–I am an artist remember–though the data was also accurately visualized. This continuum is part of what makes this research area so intriguing, to such a wide range of people. Processing is an excellent environment for visualizing data, well suited for handling large and dynamic data sources, and, as illustrated in the example, 3D, interactive treatments of the data. Processing's special relationship to Java also gives it expansive capabilities, including seamlessly integrating the two languages. As you progress with Processing, I encourage you to delve deeper into Java, as well as Processing's hardware 3D renderer OpenGL. In addition, I recommend exploring Processing's libraries, which open up many exciting areas of creative coding. I also hope you enjoyed the book.

Index

You Need the Companion eBook

Your purchase of this book entitles you to buy the °companion PDF-version eBook for only $10. Take the weightless companion with you anywhere.

We believe this Apress title will prove so indispensable that you'll want to carry it with you everywhere, which is why we are offering the companion eBook (in PDF format) for $10 to customers who purchase this book now. Convenient and fully searchable, the PDF version of any content-rich, page-heavy Apress book makes a valuable addition to your programming library. You can easily find and copy code—or perform examples by quickly toggling between instructions and the application. Even simultaneously tackling a donut, diet soda, and complex code becomes simplified with hands-free eBooks!

Once you purchase your book, getting the $10 companion eBook is simple:

❶ Visit **www.apress.com/promo/tendollars/**.

❷ Complete a basic registration form to receive a randomly generated question about this title.

❸ Answer the question correctly in 60 seconds, and you will receive a promotional code to redeem for the $10.00 eBook.

233 Spring Street, New York, NY 10013

Offer valid through 4/10.